Life in a Business-Oriented Society

A Sociological Perspective

Richard J. Caston
East Carolina University

Allyn and Bacon
Boston • London • Toronto • Sydney • Tokyo • Singapore

This book is dedicated in memory of my father,
Ralph L. Caston, Jr.,
a gentle, determined man and successful entrepreneur.

Series Editor: Sarah L. Kelbaugh
Editor-in-Chief, Social Science: Karen Hanson
Editorial Assistant: Jennifer Muroff
Production Coordinator: Christopher H. Rawlings
Editorial-Production Service: Omegatype Typography, Inc.
Composition and Prepress Buyer: Linda Cox
Manufacturing Buyer: Suzanne Lareau
Cover Administrator: Suzanne Harbison

Copyright © 1998 by Allyn & Bacon
A Pearson Education Company
160 Gould Street
Needham Heights, MA 02194

Internet: www.abacon.com
America Online: keyword: College Online

Library of Congress Cataloging-in-Publication Data

Caston, Richard J., 1950–
    Life in a business-oriented society : a sociological perspective /
by Richard J. Caston.
      p. cm.
    Includes bibliographical references and index.
    ISBN 0-205-15975-3
    1. Industries—Social aspects. 2. Business ethics. 3. Industrial
sociology. 4. Industries—Social aspects—United States.
I. Title.
HM35.C37   1998
306.3′6—dc21   97-25014
                                  CIP

Printed in the United States of America

10 9 8 7 6 5 4 3 2 1   02 01 00 99 98 97

Contents

Preface

This book is unique in its use of a sociological perspective to examine the full range of issues that are traditionally considered under the rubric of "business and society." The great bodies of literature in sociology and in "business and society" are synthesized here for the first time.

As this book documents, businesses directly and profoundly influence virtually all aspects of our personal lives and the structure of society itself. As social phenomena, businesses have provided us with a set of guidelines for organizing our relations with each other into recurring social patterns. These patterns simultaneously give meaning and stability to our personal lives and give structure and coherence to the larger social order. For this reason, an understanding of how businesses operate in society is essential if we are to understand ourselves, our families, our communities, our religions, our governments, or any other facet of our society or the major public issues confronting society at large.

Businesses are now so central to the organization of our society and to our personal lives that it is fair to say we today live in a "business-oriented society" and lead "business-oriented lives." The intent of this book is to explore the nature of life in a business-oriented society by surveying the interconnections between businesses and other sectors of society. No matter where we look in social life, we find businesses. From our birth—aided by business enterprises related to obstetrics—to our death—handled by business enterprises related to interment—and every step along the way in our lives, we are business-oriented people leading business-oriented lives. The meaning of our lives is business oriented as we are processed through one business-structured event after another. The presence and needs of businesses have shaped and given organization to our families, communities, educational institutions, religions, governments, health care systems, and our media of communication and transportation. Everywhere we look today, we see ourselves surrounded by a society that is business oriented. We cannot understand ourselves or the social world around us without starting with this elemental fact.

This book has been written for readers who are just beginning to consider the many issues related to the role of businesses in society. The intent is that the book will be highly readable, provocative, and helpful as readers grapple with issues confronting them in their lives and as they ponder possible solutions to larger public problems.

This book is well suited for several different college courses. It could serve as a stand-alone text in courses on the sociology of business because it is the only comprehensive book on this topic from a sociological perspective. It also could serve as an important supplementary text in courses on economic sociology (where most existing literature focuses on markets and market dynamics rather than on businesses and on the interrelations between businesses and other parts of society).

Because this book emphasizes the use of the sociological imagination in conceptualizing how businesses affect all facets of society, it also would be ideal as a supplementary text in courses on an introduction to sociology. In its survey of life in a business-oriented society, this book covers most of the issues traditionally found in an introduction to sociology, including social theory, social methodology, social institutions (family, education, religion, economy, polity, health care, military), social inequality (by class, race, gender, age), social movements, social change, population trends, communities, socialization, deviance, values, and normative order. All these issues are presented in this book in the context of analyses that reveal how businesses shape our personal lives and our social order.

This book possesses several features that also make it well suited to serve as a supplementary text in the courses on business and society that are traditionally found in business schools. First, it brings a completely new perspective (sociology) to bear on the issues traditionally found in business and society courses. Second, the organization of the chapters of the book (especially in Part III) is designed to parallel the topical chapters traditionally found in business and society texts (including topical chapters related to governments, corporate governance, employees, consumers, our environment, and international relations). Third, a central theme that ties the book together is the concept of the social responsibilities of businesses, which is a popular concept in traditional business and society literature. In this book the concept is defined from a sociological point of view and is used to derive concrete recommendations for business reform and social policy. Fourth, this book also contains a unique historical presentation of the evolution of business-oriented societies that is not found in other business and society texts. This presentation provides an essential background for helping readers to understand the significance of the major business-society issues of our time.

Beyond the classroom I also hope that this book will reach a general readership. It is my desire that the general reader will come away from the book with a better understanding of the social order and of their personal lives. With this understanding, readers should be better equipped to deal successfully with problems in their lives and to contribute to the resolution of problems that are society-wide.

The book is organized into three parts. Part I (Chapters 1 through 3) sets out sociological definitions for businesses, the social environment of businesses, business-oriented societies, and the social responsibilities of businesses. Part II (Chapters 4 through 6) describes in some detail the historical rise of business-oriented societies. All parts of society and of our personal lives have been shaped by this historical process. Part III consists of seven chapters that explore topics of traditional concern in business and society texts, including governmental regulation of businesses and the influences of businesses on governments, especially through PACs (Chapter 7); corporate management and improving the moral performance of businesses (Chapter 8); employee safety, employee welfare, and human diversity in the work place (Chapters 9 and 10); environmental pollution and resource depletion (Chapter 11); and international business issues (Chapter 12). Chapter 13 considers the future of business-oriented societies such as our own.

I am indebted to the editorial staff of Allyn and Bacon for their encouragement and assistance. In addition I want to acknowledge the early encouragement of Vivian Strand, Niki Benokraitis, Rita Braito, and Wayne Markert. I also wish to acknowledge the comments and suggestions of the reviewers of my manuscript, in particular: Robert Faulkner, University of Massachusetts Amherst; Thomas W. Norton, Lafayette College; David R. Simon, University of California at Berkeley; and David Swanson, Portland State University.

I also wish to acknowledge the unfailing support of my wife, Jan. This book could not have been written without Jan's belief in me and her extraordinary accommodation to the burden that producing this book has required. Thank you, Jan, for your tolerance and love.

If you are ready for a voyage of intellectual discovery on which the chief discoveries will be yourself, the meaning of your life, and the nature of social order itself, then you are ready to begin Chapter 1 of this book. Please share your thoughts with me about this book. I can be reached at CASTONR@MAIL.ECU.EDU or at the Department of Sociology, East Carolina University, Greenville, N.C. 27858.

R. J. C.

Part I

A Framework for Conceptualizing Businesses, Their Social Environments, and Their Social Responsibilities

C h a p t e r *1*

Businesses as
Social Phenomena

Why Read This Book?

Why should you read a book about businesses in our society? There is a very good reason for doing so. An understanding of the role of businesses in society can make you into a more effective participant in society and can liberate you from constraints on your life that you may not have previously recognized. From this book you will see that businesses exert extraordinary influences over our society and over the lives of each of us as everyday people. Unless we recognize and understand these influences, we cannot hope to find success in confronting, managing, and resolving the types of problems and issues we collectively face as a society or those we encounter in our personal lives. This book, then, is important to you.

From this book you will learn that businesses in our society have shaped most facets of our lives: such as the relations we have with our families, friends, and neighbors; the education we have received; the religious beliefs we espouse; the legal system that defines and protects our rights and privacy as citizens; the political processes that guide national and local public affairs; the military orientation and capacity of our society; the standard of living and quality of life we experience; our opportunities for employment and to "get ahead" in life; our sense of "self-esteem" and social prestige; the satisfaction we find with our lives; and the philosophy of life that we hold. Because businesses influence so much of what goes on in our society and in our personal lives, I describe our society as being business oriented. It is the intent of this book to explore the nature of life in the business-oriented society and to propose solutions to a number of social problems that confront us.

Many books examine how businesses relate to society. Those that are available draw primarily on perspectives from business management, political science/public policy, or philosophy/ethics.[1] The uniqueness of this book, however, lies in the fact that its perspective is that of sociology.[2]

TABLE 1.1   Examples of Questions to Be Addressed in This Book

Chapter	Example Questions
1	What is society, and what distinguishes businesses as a part of society?
2	How do businesses relate to other parts of society?
3	Do businesses have social responsibilities.
4	Why were businesses viewed as evil by most of our ancestors? Are businesses inherently evil?
5	Do the improvements brought to our lives by businesses outweigh the adverse influences they also have on us?
6	How have businesses played a role during this century in fostering dramatic growth in our governments and in our welfare systems?
7	Which view is more true: that government regulations intrude too much into business affairs today, or that business interests exert too much control over our government?
8	Why do we find so much business corruption, and what can be done about it?
9	What rights and provisions for welfare should employees of businesses have?
10	Should businesses have affirmative action programs, or are such programs intrinsically unfair?
11	What protection should consumers have in our society?
12	What actions should businesses take to protect our environment?
13	What role do businesses play in world modernization?
14	What are the future prospects for our business-oriented society?

Do you need prior training in sociology to follow the discussions and arguments in this book? No. It is my intention to present the ideas and issues in this book in a nontechnical and interesting way. As a preview of the book, Table 1.1 illustrates the types of questions that will be addressed. The questions in Table 1.1 are only a selection of those to be considered in this book. In the next section I describe the sociological perspective that I use in the search for answers to these questions.

Sociology and Social Reality

Sociology is a science that undertakes systematic investigations in order to obtain empirical knowledge about society. The expectation is that sociology will be able to provide a body of knowledge to help us understand and improve our lives. Sociology, however, is still a very young science. It dates back only about 100 years, and almost all sociological research that has been conducted to date has occurred only within the last thirty years. Nonetheless, some significant progress has been made in studies of the components, structures, and dynamics of society.

The Sociological Imagination

It is usually helpful to begin a discussion of sociology by considering the sociological imagination.[3] All sciences involve an imaginative activity, and sociology is no exception. What we find through the imagination of science frequently is very different from what common sense leads us to believe about the world.

For example, physics and chemistry tell us that the book in front of you is actually a swirling array of atoms held together by subatomic forces. Do you see a swirling array of atoms in front of you, or do you see a book? Which is the reality: the atoms or the book? It is only by imagination that physical sciences can claim to see a world full of atoms instead of the common-sense world of objects that you and I see.

Biologists tell us that the hands holding the book in front of you are actually highly co-ordinated systems of specialized cells, each of which contains its own intelligence and all of which are coordinated together through a system of intercellular communication. Do you see hands in front of you, or a complex network of intelligent cells? Again, scientific imagination leads us to see a reality that common sense does not see.

Astronomers tell us that the book and hands in front of you are moving at incredibly high speed at this very moment so as to simultaneously circle the earth's axis, our sun, and the center of our galaxy. Is this true? Are your hands and the book in front of you stationary, or are they moving at phenomenal speed? Which is true: the reality that you see or that science imagines?

Scientific imagination often leads us to perspectives that challenge our common sense view of the world around us. As you will see throughout this book, sociology is no different in this regard. Again and again sociology finds a reality that is quite different from what common sense leads us to believe. It accomplishes this with a sociological imagination.

Through the exercise of your sociological imagination, you will see how businesses are related to other parts of society, and how these relations affect each of us as persons. You will find that businesses serve as a central source of power in organizing and holding society together. You will also see that many contemporary public problems and personal troubles derive from the presence of businesses in society.

Theoretical Frameworks

Sociology provides us with exciting and frequently surprising perspectives on the conditions of our lives. However, because it is so young as a science, sociology has not yet developed a unified theoretical framework to which most sociologists subscribe. Several theoretical frameworks have been developed, with each having some advantages and disadvantages in comparison to the others.

The approach in this book is eclectic: I draw on a number of different theoretical frameworks in sociology. One closely related set of frameworks that I use in this book might be called the "interpretive" tradition in sociology. A central interest of interpretive sociology is trying to understand how people experience their social environments. This is a very useful perspective for focusing our attention on how individuals are influenced by their environments and how they in turn respond to or work to alter those environments.

However, were we to focus only on the experiences of individuals we would miss the larger relations between major sectors of society that individuals may not easily be able to see. Therefore, I also draw on theoretical frameworks that consider how large social structures are held together and change over time. I use frameworks that fall into the general traditions of structural functionalism and conflict theory for these purposes.[4]

The Murky, Tenuous Nature of Social Reality

Before considering how businesses relate to other parts of society, we first need a basic understanding of the nature of society and its components. One fact that quickly becomes clear to anyone who studies society is its complexity; we cannot describe either society as a whole or its internal parts without relying on considerable simplification. Much of the problem lies in the murky, tenuous character of society. As a social reality, *society* possesses no well-defined boundaries, either as a whole or of its internal parts. Rather, it appears to the careful observer to be constantly changing—never quite the same as before.[5]

Society as a Stage Play

A useful analogy for trying to conceptualize society is that of the stage play.[6] Suppose all of society were a stage play, and we were mere actors in that play. The stage obviously is gigantic, including family settings, school settings, government settings, business settings, and so on. Subplots related to each of these settings are performed by us as actors to create the social reality of families, schools, governments, businesses, and so forth. We have no written scripts to guide our performance. Rather, we as actors appear to learn or compose these scripts as we carry them out in our performances on the multiple stage settings of society. Socialization, peer pressures, schooling, and on-the-job training all serve to help us to grasp the plots of the scripts we are to perform. If we don't perform these plots properly, we may be called to task by our fellow actors.

The contrived nature of social reality is most evident to us actors in situations that are new to us, in which we have not already established a prior routine for our behaviors. Examples include newlyweds who must figure out how to construct a marriage together but don't know how to, or new parents who must figure out how to parent without ever having done so before. It is common for us as actors to ad-lib a lot in these and in other circumstances. By ad-libbing, we guess at and create, through our actions, the social reality that we live in.

Because of our extensive ad-libbing, the stage plays that constitute social reality are never performed exactly the same way by different actors, nor necessarily the same way consecutively by the same actor. Thus there is the problem of a lack of continuity and coherence to social reality. Social reality has this tentative, changing, ad-libbed character, but its complexity is compounded many times over because of the many overlapping subplots it includes and that we actors frequently must perform simultaneously. These subplots typically have no precise boundaries between them and shade into each other in complex ways.

Multiple Subplots

For example, the social reality of your current life probably includes several partially overlapping subplots that tie you together with other people in at least some of the following contexts: a family, a clique of friends, a love relationship, a neighborhood, an employment or school setting, a church, a political process, a marketplace, and others. For each subplot that you are involved in, there are recurring actors, scenes, and props; not infrequently the actors, scenes, and props are shared between subplots.

Let's see how these considerations look in the context of the concrete social phenomenon that you call your family. When you begin to appreciate the tenuous, murky nature of your family, you will better understand the problems facing us as we set out to explore how businesses relate to society at large.

The Family as an Example

You know that you have a family and that it is a real social phenomenon, don't you? Why else would you feel compelled to devote so much attention to your family and feel such an attachment to it if it did not exist? A researcher, however, would have a great deal of difficulty in finding your family or in defining families in general as a social phenomenon. What sociology reveals about families is quite surprising.

Consider this: if your family is a concrete reality, it should have boundaries in time and space, shouldn't it? How else could you tell researchers where to look to find your family? Indeed, if you did not know where its boundaries were in time and space, how could you find your family again and know that you have found all of it? But try to specify precisely where the boundaries of your family are. If you try to do so, you will find that you cannot.

For example, surely you must know who all of the people are in your family. Try to list the names of all those people right now. Who should be on the list? Should you include parents, siblings, spouse, children? Should you include aunts, cousins, grandparents, in-laws, ex-spouses, stepchildren/parents, stepcousins, second cousins, godparents, God, your favorite deceased relative who you regard still to be a strong presence in your life, your family pet, and so forth?

Having constructed your list, now ask people on your list to write their own lists. When you compare all lists, you will find that they do not match. Furthermore, if you repeat this exercise several times, you will find that the lists change over both long and short periods of time. Where, then, are the boundaries in space and time on your family? How can you say that you have a family when there is no consensus on who the members are?

Which is true: that you have a family or you only suppose that you do? The murky, tenuous character of your family is further compounded by other factors that researchers must consider. Any social phenomenon (such as a family, business, or "what have you") is not just a list of people but involves both relationships among people and the meanings that these people share together. We cannot see these relationships and meanings simply by looking at the people, but we must guess at them based on how the people behave toward each other or based on what they say. Again, however, if you ask your family members to describe these relationships and meanings, you will no doubt find considerable disagreement among them.

If all family members are to coordinate their behaviors together to create (as a stage performance) a single, cohesive, functioning family, how can they do so without agreeing on who all the family members are and what all the relationships and meanings are that hold the members together? This situation points to a lack of precise, enduring boundaries on the family as a social phenomenon.

Overlapping Boundaries

Now we add one more bit of complexity, that of overlapping boundaries. As social phenomena, families overlap considerably with each other so it is hard to say where one family begins and another ends. We see this, for example, in the incredibly complex interweaving of families through intermarriages. If we could trace back through history far enough, we would probably find that all families in our society are related to each other in at least some distant way. If so, we could say that the social reality of families is that we are all part of one giant family.

Not only do the social boundaries between families overlap in our society through intermarriage, but they also overlap with great frequency with many other social phenomena, making it harder still to tell where each phenomenon begins and ends. For example, in the small-business family, where does the business end and the family begin? Or, as parents teach religious beliefs to their children, where does the family end and religion as a social phenomenon begin? Or where do families end and communities or schools or health care systems begin? The overlapping boundaries of social phenomena that we see in these examples lend an incoherence, fuzziness, or murkiness to the social reality of society and to its subcomponent phenomena. It is through overlapping boundaries that social phenomena shade into and affect each other. This shading process of overlapping boundaries creates a pattern of interdependence among social phenomena (and their stage plots). Within this pattern of interdependence, some social phenomena may become more central and dominant. And as I show later, businesses now play the dominant role in the interdependent social phenomena of our society, so that the stage plot of business strongly influences the plots of other social phenomena of society.

The Show Must Go On

With the boundaries on the social reality of our families so much at question, why then do we as everyday actors feel so confident that our families do in fact exist? It is abundantly evident that we as actors have remarkable propensities for guessing at the nature of the scripts we are to perform and then ad-libbing thoughts, feelings, and behaviors based on our guesses. But more to the point here, it is also abundantly evident that we possess equally remarkable abilities to gloss over most ambiguities and uncertainties that we encounter in social life. It appears that the "rule," "The show must go on," holds for us even when we don't know who all the relevant actors are, what all the relationships and meanings are, or whether our fellow actors concur in our conception of the script. Therefore, in everyday life we simply gloss over ambiguities, uncertainties, and inconsistencies by assuming that our family exists, that it is the same and equally real for all family members, and that we all mean the same thing when we talk about families as social phenomena in our society.

This ability to gloss over ambiguities and uncertainties, coupled with our ability to ad-lib as actors, makes it possible for each one of us to carry out our daily family affairs as though our family has a well-bounded, cohesive, continuous existence. And the most remarkable thing is that, as family members organize their behaviors, feelings, and thoughts to conform to the assumption that their family exists, they in fact construct their family as a concrete social reality.[7] In short, we create social reality by believing in it, by guessing at its nature, by ad-libbing, and by glossing over discrepancies and uncertainties where they occur. Though the resulting creation would be seen as tenuous and with uncertain boundaries from the perspective of an outside observer, we as everyday actors usually do not see such problems and instead regard our creation as being a cohesive, continuous reality.

Although everyday actors may not be perturbed by the murky, tenuous nature of social reality, it should be obvious that the issues described here pose special problems when one wishes to engage in rigorous analyses of these phenomena, which is the intent of sociologists. Had I wished to write a book on how families as social phenomena influenced the rest of society, I would need a reasonably rigorous definition of families that would allow me to identify all examples of families, to say where families are in space and time, and to say where the boundaries are between different families and between families and other parts of society. I would want families to exhibit sufficient continuity and coherence so as to be able to say that there is something real and enduring about them that could in fact influence other parts of society. The analytic needs of such an undertaking would be challenging indeed. But it is not to this challenge that I must rise. Rather I must develop a reasonably rigorous framework for understanding businesses.

I have described the difficulties in conceptualizing social reality and social phenomena by using your family as an example. I did this because families are likely to be phenomena that you feel more knowledgeable about than businesses. I turn now to apply the same insights developed here to businesses as social phenomena.

Business as an Example

For many people, businesses are rather remote, mysterious, and incoherent. This is especially true when we consider the colossally large businesses that dominate the economy today. Even the senior managers of such large businesses find that much of their business lies beyond the round of their personal experience; they must rely on subordinates to deal with areas of the business they don't know.

As an illustration of a very large business in our society, consider the International Business Machines Corporation (IBM). In 1990, IBM had over 350,000 employees and annual revenues exceeding 69 billion dollars. Again, let's ask the questions I asked before, questions that must be answered precisely in order to conduct careful social analyses. Where does IBM sit in space and time? What are its boundaries? Where would you go to position yourself so that you could "see" IBM? How can we know that we all see the same "IBM", or even that it is an enduring phenomenon we could recognize again as being the same IBM if we saw it twice?

If all the buildings that IBM owns or leases were measured and considered together, could we then say that we have seen or have a definition of IBM as a business? Of course not; IBM is more than mere buildings. It is more than its merchandise, employees, production processes, sales systems, financial operations, shareholders, managers, research divisions, or global presence in political affairs.

Each person who is in contact with IBM as an employee, stock owner, consumer, supplier, accountant, regulator, and so forth has a different experience of IBM. And no one of these people could possibly know who all of the other people are who are involved in IBM or what all the meanings and relationships are among these people. Thus no one person knows where the boundaries of IBM are, and hence no one knows IBM as a single, unified social entity. Indeed, as is true for all businesses, the boundaries of IBM overlap extensively with other businesses (such as suppliers and buyers, purveyors of transportation and communication services, and so forth) and with other social phenomena (such as families, governments, local communities, and so on).

Yet the remarkable thing is that all of the people involved in IBM are able to figure out (ad-lib) ways to negotiate their experiences together to create a common-sense feeling that they are all oriented to the same IBM as a real, unified, continuous social phenomenon. Isn't this amazing? Any uncertainties these people may feel are simply glossed over along the way. We see in IBM, then, both the same problems concerning boundaries and the same everyday ways of circumventing these problems that we observed when considering the family as a social phenomenon.

As social phenomena, businesses are not fixed, independent, and well-bounded physical things. Rather, as is typical for social reality, they exist much as stage plays exist. They exist to the degree that we, in ad-lib fashion, follow unwritten scripts in coordinating our behaviors, thoughts, and feelings with others to create together a socially constructed performance that we call IBM (or any other business). To say that a business exists as a social construction or performance rather than as a physical thing is not to denigrate its reality. Businesses are indeed real; they are as real as your family, even if they are by the nature of social reality murky, tenuous, and with overlapping boundaries. As this book amply documents, the overlapping boundaries that businesses have with other social phenomena create patterns of interdependence and dominance among social phenomena that have very real and occasionally adverse consequences for society and for you.

Restrictions on Social Reality and Social Phenomena

Because unwritten social scripts appear to play such a central role in the construction of social reality, two questions about them are particularly important to sociologists. One question concerns where these social scripts come from; the other concerns whether there are any restrictions on the form that these scripts may take. The answers to these questions provide an important backdrop to the analyses to be presented throughout this book.

The Sources of Social Scripts

The first question regarding the source of the social scripts of society is a fundamental one for sociological inquiry. It is important at the start to recognize that these scripts are not psychological phenomena. We do not individually create the social scripts of society, even if we each have our own unique individual perspective on these scripts and we ad-lib extensively in performing these scripts.

The scripts that you and I follow (as, for example, for schooling, for our federal government, for IBM, etc.) typically give the appearance of having an existence separate from us. Each such script, and we can take the one for our federal government as an example here, appears to us to have existed before we were born and to be likely to continue to exist after we die. Scripts seem to operate independent of us when we are not directly participating in them, and they appear to change in ways that are independent of our personal desires, consistent instead with larger historical forces. Thus, so far as we can see, these scripts rest in an order of reality apart from psychological phenomena; they exist, rather, in an order of *social* reality. The study of where the scripts come from is therefore not the study of the psychology of the individual, but involves a sociological investigation into social history. In this book I trace the social history of the changing scripts that underlie businesses and other parts of society. By doing so I reveal the influences of businesses on these other parts of society and, ultimately, on you.

Limits on Social Scripts

The other question we would want to ask concerning these scripts is what limits may exist on how they may be formulated. There are several relevant restrictions.

Need for Consistency.   One restriction is that there must be some consistency among the several scripts or subscripts that comprise society, because they overlap and are interdependent to such a considerable degree. Thus the scripts for religions, families, political processes, commercial processes, and other parts of society must be sufficiently consistent with each other to permit all scripts to be performed together (and perhaps simultaneously) by the same actors. For example, there would be great conflict in a society that had a family script calling for lifelong obedience to one's elders, and a simultaneous script for an industrial system requiring a large, ready supply of young laborers willing to leave home and move to wherever industry needs them. Whenever scripts conflict, ad-libbed revisions that bring them into conformity must occur. Thus, throughout this book I emphasize how historical changes in one social phenomenon, such as businesses, created conflict and eventual changes in the other social phenomena of society.

Role of Power.   Another limitation on the types of scripts that can be created lies in the way power is distributed in society. Because powerful people command the attention of others, the scripts that reflect their central concerns are those most likely to be emphasized and developed, often at the expense of other possible scripts. For example, throughout much of written history the concerns of kings for conquest and for protection of their kingdoms have led to an emphasis on military scripts. The resources required to support military undertakings were great and had to come from somewhere. Typically the scripts for community welfare and peasant family life suffered as a result.

I previously noted above that ad-libbed script changes tend to occur whenever scripts are in conflict. In this connection, ad-libbed script changes that are favored by the powerful are the ones most likely to become recurring parts of our common understanding of social reality. For example, the growing affluence of merchants played an important role in the Protestant Reformation; their wealth provided a source of power that helped make this new change in the religious script an enduring one for a large portion of the European population. This script change resulted in a major new perspective on God and on the purpose of life for hundreds of millions of people.

To summarize, the sources of power in a society are critical factors to consider in any analysis of social phenomena. In contemporary society, the control of economic processes by business is a major source of power and results in substantial influences over the rest of society by businesses. These influences are highlighted throughout this book.

Physical Reality As a Restriction.   A final restriction on the types of scripts that can occur in society is physical reality itself. At least at this moment, for example, no amount of collective ad-libbing will permit businesses to set up sales offices in outer space. Likewise, the Sahara Desert is unlikely to sustain an advanced industrial society at any time soon. Physical reality sets obstacles to the scripts and ad-libs that can be performed; these obstacles also must be considered in any social analysis.

With the background of this conceptual framework to help explain the tenuous and murky nature of social reality in general, and of businesses as social phenomena in particular, you should now be ready to consider the definition of business that guides the analyses and discussions of this book.

A Definition of Business

Any definition of business necessarily must involve substantial simplification. Furthermore, any definition must be regarded only as an heuristic guide that helps to initiate analyses, but that may need further refinement as analyses proceed. In forming an initial definition of businesses as social phenomena I attempt to identify critical features that are most central to the script for businesses and that are much less so for scripts for other types of social phenomena. The definition to be developed should be adequate to lead us to conclude, for example, that IBM is a business and that Ed's Barber Shop also is a business.

The most distinguishing feature of the script for businesses (in contrast to those for other types of social phenomena) is the special motive that the script contains for organizing the behaviors, thoughts, and feelings of business actors. This special motive is the profit motive.

The Role of Profit Motive

Profit-motivated behaviors involve efforts to add something desirable to one's experiences.[8] Such behaviors, however, may be found in many settings in social life, such as in winning the friendship of another person, in being lucky in love, in learning from our mistakes, in finding spiritual salvation, or in intellectual or artistic fulfillment, to give but a few examples. These are all examples of nontangible profit seeking. An orientation toward obtaining nontangible profits, however, is not what characterizes the script of businesses such as IBM or Ed's Barber Shop. More at issue for these businesses is the search for tangible profits, or the increase in the supply of material goods that one experiences.

Profit motives oriented toward increasing material goods, however, also can be seen in a great many types of social phenomena in society. Consider the following examples. Kings may seek to expand their material holdings through conquest, and this is a tangible, profit-motivated endeavor. Parents may seek to add more children to their household, and this too may be, at least in part, a tangible, profit-motivated endeavor. Religious leaders may work to expand the property and other material holdings of the church, and in this way they take on an orientation of tangible profit seeking. Other nonprofit organizations also may use their revenues to expand the physical size and comfort of their working conditions or the amount of their administrative salaries and benefits, and herein we see yet another example of a tangible, profit-seeking orientation in a social script. Even the average homeowner acts in a tangible, profit-seeking fashion insofar as he or she views a house as an investment with future appreciation prospects. Likewise, the teenager who babysits for pocket money is seeking tangible profits.

These forms of tangible profit seeking do not directly interest us in this book. Therefore, we need to add yet another distinguishing feature to the definition to limit the focus further. The tangible profit seeking of interest in identifying a social phenomenon as being a business occurs within a special setting or stage called a market.

Role of the Market

A market may be conceived of as any part of social life in which a recurring process of exchange occurs for the purpose of seeking tangible profit.[9] Certainly the supermarkets where you and I buy groceries provide markets of this sort. The stock market is another market. So are farmers' markets, shopping malls, movie theaters, and many other places where goods or services are regularly exchanged for tangible profits. We might even speak meaningfully about all of the consumer product and service markets in the United States taken together as constituting "the U.S. market."

Adding markets as a distinguishing feature to the scripts for identifying a business gives a definition that fits IBM and Ed's Barber Shop as well as other commercial operations traditionally considered to be businesses. Under this new definition, a babysitter qualifies as conducting a business only if he or she establishes a market of regular exchanges of service for profits. The average homeowner does not qualify as operating a business because he or she does not engage in a regular pattern of buying and selling homes for profit. A religious institution, however, may be a business if it establishes a regular market for the exchange of its services for tangible profit. This would have to be established for any particular religion by empirical study. Likewise, an officially designated nonprofit organization would in fact be a business if it managed to find or create a market from which it obtained regular increases to its material holdings. Again, an empirical study would have to establish whether this was happening for any given nonprofit organization.

Role of Money

Money, as you know, plays an important role in the markets and profits of our society. It would be useful at this point to comment on the role of money as a facilitator of market transactions and as a measure of tangible profits. Certainly businesses can operate without money because only the seeking of an addition to one's material holdings in a market context is necessary to define a social phenomenon as a business. Indeed, the desired tangible goods could be anything: sheep, land, ornaments, or "what have you." Money, however, is a "stage prop" that greatly facilitates the conduct of businesses as a stage play. It does this by our common, implicit agreement to regard money as a symbol that represents to all participating actors the concept of desired physical things. The strength of our collective belief in this symbol makes us willing to exchange actual, desired physical objects for paper money, and to seek paper money itself as a desired physical item. In a market context, setting prices for all goods and services based on a common monetary unit greatly facilitates market exchange operations. Furthermore because money lends itself to easy mathematical applications, it greatly facilitates bookkeeping, the counting of profits, and the use of the various forms of rational management and profit-making strategies that are evident in businesses in today's society.

Businesses Defined

To summarize, businesses are defined here as social phenomena in which actors are motivated to organize their behaviors, thoughts, and feelings into a pattern that seeks tangible profits in a market context. Money may or may not be involved in this context, though it is the typical measure of profits for today's businesses and it greatly simplifies market transactions. When this definition is applied to the world around us, all the companies listed on the major U.S. stock exchanges qualify as businesses, provided that they have, in fact, created markets for their products or services. Likewise, the shoe shop that my father owned was a business, as are other small or privately owned commercial operations, provided that they too have created markets for their products or services.

With some exceptions, the distinguishing characteristics described here lead us to identify as businesses those social phenomena that typically are also identified as businesses by the popular mass media and by governments—at federal, state, or local levels.

Importance of Perspective

Two considerations are important to note at this point. First, we should not rely solely on existing sources of social power, such as mass media and governments, to determine what constitute businesses in our society; such a strategy may make it harder to see how businesses shade into and influence other sectors of society. If current sources of power serve as judges of what are real businesses, the biases and interests of these sources of power may seep into the analyses, glossing over important distinctions, ambiguities, or factors that otherwise should be considered. Furthermore, it would be unwise for a social analyst to rely solely on existing power sources for definitions of social reality because, as we have seen in the past, political forces may change—sometimes by revolution; consequently, the definitions of social reality favored by the newly powerful may also change.

To arrive at an understanding of the influences of businesses on society that is more timeless and independent of momentary political perspectives, I make repeated efforts throughout this book to step back from prevailing political perspectives and to search out contrary perspectives. It is not difficult to do this for societies of the past, as we are not now influenced by the power sources that were in operation then. It is much more difficult, however, to be likewise disassociated from the perspectives of currently operating power sources. Nonetheless, I do my best to do so. It is my strategy to use politically derived designations of businesses whenever consistent with the definition of business given above, but to seek ways to think beyond these designations whenever it is useful to do so.

A second consideration to be noted here concerns the relative importance of different businesses for the analyses in this book. Most important for consideration in this book are the large for-profit corporations because they constitute the most significant business presence in contemporary society. However, I also discuss middle-sized and small businesses wherever appropriate to an extent proportionate to their relative role in society.

Chapter 2

The Social Environment
of Businesses

In Chapter 1 a framework was developed to aid us in thinking about businesses as social phenomena. That framework is further refined and expanded in this chapter to include the social environment that surrounds business. After the key components of this environment are identified, three models are presented for conceptualizing how businesses are related to their social environment.

In the second half of this chapter an exercise in sociological imagination is presented as a preview to the many issues to be considered in this book. This exercise serves to highlight the pervasive and profound influences that businesses have on both the organization of our society and the daily round of our personal lives. The exercise describes a widespread secular religious movement in our society that centers our attention on business needs; that demands ritualistic sacrifice, obedience, and devotion from all of us; and that is reflected in a set of social processes that have transformed much of our society. I call this religious movement the "cult of the business-oriented society," and I intentionally illustrate it in a way that is designed to shake loose your thinking, at least momentarily, from the powerful hold that this cult may have upon how you see yourself and the world around you. This illustration is designed to help us to see businesses, society, and ourselves from a fresh and thought-provoking perspective and not simply through the filter of powerful interests in our business-oriented culture.

The Social Environment of Businesses

The social environment of businesses includes many social phenomena that both affect businesses and are affected by them. As noted in Chapter 1, these social phenomena are themselves tenuous and murky, in the sense that they lack clear boundaries on their participating actors, relationships, and meanings. Indeed, they typically shade into businesses and into each other, so that there are no precise boundaries between businesses and other social phenomena. I use the term "sectors" to refer to the major social phenomena of the social environment.

The Key Sectors

Figure 2.1 presents a list of the most important sectors of the social environment of businesses. I wish I could say that this list is exhaustive and mutually exclusive. But in view of the problems described in Chapter 1 concerning the lack of precise boundaries around social phenomena, I make no such claims. Instead, many alternative listings could be devised depending on how one wishes to slice up social reality into sectors. Furthermore, the sectors that are presented on the list overlap greatly with each other.

For example, the federal government plays a key role in the financial institutions of U.S. society through the federal reserve system. The boundaries between these two sectors of society, therefore, do not neatly divide one from the other. Likewise, many other overlaps are evident: some business owners are also managers; managers are also employees; governments play key roles in community affairs, in education, and in mass transportation; religions intertwine with many other facets of society (as will be highlighted later in this chapter); activist groups may represent communities; unions may be classified as activist groups; and families cut across a good many of the other sectors and may intertwine considerably with businesses, especially in the case of family-owned or family-operated businesses.

The intent of the list in Figure 2.1 is only to identify for you the sectors of society that will be considered in this book. Although the list is not definitive and cannot be made so, it includes the sectors of society commonly highlighted by sources of power in our society,

---

FIGURE 2.1   Important Sectors of the Social Environment of Businesses

Immediate Sectors:

Management
Financial institutions
Suppliers/wholesalers/retailers
Competitors
Consumers
Production processes (including technology, physical plant operations and research and development)

Intermediate Sectors:

Owners/stockholders
Employees (including unions)

Other Sectors:

Governments (including regulatory agencies, legislative bodies and written law, courts, police and military, and foreign governments)
Mass media
Mass transportation/communication
Education (including primary and secondary schools, universities and university research, and "think tanks")
Communities (including environmental issues)
Activist groups (e.g., civil rights, environment)
Religions/ethical codes
Families/kinship
Trade associations, chambers of commerce, and political action committees

including mass media and governments. (Note again that these sources of power play important roles in shaping our understanding of social reality.)

Different Market Roles

The list separates immediate market participants who play the most salient role in business decision making from participants who play intermediate roles and, in turn, from those who may play other, less direct roles. There are overlapping boundaries here as well, however. In some cases owners play immediate roles in decision making and belong in the classification of immediate market participants. But in the more typical case for large businesses, owners are remote shareholders whose influence is so slight as to warrant their placement in the "other sectors" list.

Immediate Market Participants. Much attention necessarily is devoted by business managers to immediate market participants. Management, consumers, competitors, suppliers, production processes, and financial institutions are the sectors that immediately influence the profitability of a business. Immediate market participants, however, do not operate in a social vacuum; they require a society structured in ways that support market operations.

Intermediate and "Other" Participants. To give just a few examples, businesses depend on a legal system to define and enforce contracts, patents, and property rights; on police and military forces for protection of property; on schools to provide the literacy and advanced skills (e.g., engineering, accounting, computer technology, law) required of employees in a technologically advanced market system; on religions to promote ethical codes that help to persuade people to be honest and willing participants in market transactions; on communities to provide labor pools and mass markets; on transportation and communication systems for the delivery of goods, the movement of labor, and to facilitate the expansion of mass markets; on governments to serve as major consumers of business goods and services and to work as agents to ensure both monetary stability and fair marketplace practices; and on mass media to provide an advertising avenue for expanding mass markets. Though activist groups and unions may be more troublesome than helpful to businesses, in some cases unions may become quasi-extensions of management in the control of workers. Lastly, trade associations, chambers of commerce, and business political action committees aid businesses in lobbying for legislation and in influencing public policies that are helpful to business.

To summarize, businesses do not stand alone and independent of other sectors of society; instead they are greatly dependent on these other sectors to be organized and to operate in ways that facilitate business activities. Throughout this book I examine the many relations between businesses and their social environments with the goal of providing greater insight into what businesses are, how they influence other sectors of society, and their resulting moral and social obligations.

The Concept of Stakeholders

A useful term to introduce at this point is that of "stakeholders." This is a popular term in current literature on business and society,[1] and it is intended to signify the great importance that business decisions have for many other sectors of society. To the degree that other sectors of society are affected by business decisions and in turn can take some action to influence these decisions, we can say that these other sectors have a stake in how business decisions are made.

Stakeholder as a Political Designation

Three considerations concerning the concept of stakeholders warrant attention. First, it is a political designation. This is seen in the fact that, in contrast to the more neutral term of sector, *stakeholder* implies that a sector has a legitimate right to influence business decisions. To keep the analyses in this book as impartial as possible, I have chosen to use the more neutral term of sectors in describing the social environment of businesses. However, when political implications in fact warrant the use of the term stakeholder, I'll switch to this latter term.

Stakeholder Analysis Is Important

Second, the list of sectors (or stakeholders) provided in Figure 2.1 is a generic one. Because each business is unique, the actual list of sectors or stakeholders of relevance to a particular business would have to be determined empirically. A body of literature exists on stakeholder analysis that suggests techniques for constructing a list of stakeholders; interested readers may wish to refer to this literature.[2]

Stakeholders, the Focus Later in This Book

Third, though each of the various sectors (or stakeholders) listed in Figure 2.1 will be considered at several points throughout this book, some of them will be the focus of selected chapters. In particular, consumer issues will be highlighted in Chapter 11; owners will be considered in Chapter 8; employees will be considered in Chapters 9 and 10; government, legal systems, police, and military will be given primary attention in Chapters 6 and 7; and communities and the physical environment will be discussed in Chapter 12. In addition, the various social sectors identified in Figure 2.1 will be considered in the context of international affairs in Chapter 13.

Three Models of the Social Environment of Businesses

The many discussions throughout this book of the relations between businesses and the other sectors of their social environment are guided by three different models of how those relations are organized. These three models are illustrated in Figure 2.2.[3]

The Market Model

The market model is the first model of the social environment of businesses that is presented in Figure 2.2. This model shows businesses to be surrounded by two concentric circles of social sectors. The inner circle includes all market-related sectors with which businesses must contend, such as financial institutions, customers, suppliers, and so forth. The outer circle includes all other sectors in the social environment, such as governments, churches, communities, and families.

1. The Market Model

2. The Dominance Model

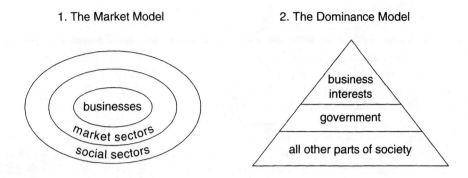

3. The Pluralist Model

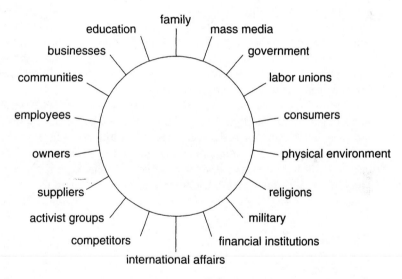

FIGURE 2.2   Three Models of the Social Environment of Businesses

The market model regards the immediate market conditions of the inner circle as buffers between businesses and all the other sectors of society that are to be found in the outer circle. Thus businesses are believed to be influenced directly by conditions in the immediate market in the inner circle (such as patterns of finance, supply, production, consumption, and competition). But they are believed to be only indirectly affected by other nonmarket sectors of the social environment present in the outer circle. Nonmarket sectors of the social environment are viewed in this model either as influencing businesses not at all or only minimally and indirectly through their influence on the marketplace. Reciprocally, businesses are viewed either as having no direct influence on other sectors of society or only minimal influences that are mediated indirectly through forces in the marketplace.

This is a standard model used by economists when studying businesses. The assumption is that businesses and their immediate market conditions can be meaningfully understood by themselves and apart from other surrounding social forces. In other words, it is assumed that there are law-like economic forces operating within the market that form a reality that is largely independent from other forces in society.

Unfortunately for subscribers to this model, history shows that, whenever businesses have appeared, they have been subjected to substantial and direct influences by nonmarket forces in society. This fact is quite annoying to those who prefer this model. Consequently, a modified version of the market model is more frequently espoused—one that says that social reality should conform to this model even though it does not now. In other words, businesses and the marketplace should be left to operate in a fashion that is largely independent of the influences of other forces of society. The modified market model commonly interprets governments as behaving improperly by "intruding" into business or market affairs.

The leap from focusing on what actually exists in social reality to what *should* exist catapults the "leapers" from the hoary halls of the sciences (which allege as their goal the study of what exists) into the cloisters of a secular religion (or a secular ethical system), in which the current conditions of reality are held to be unimportant in comparison to the pursuit of a desired future reality. This leap into a form of secular religious fervor concerning how economic life *should* operate is at the heart of the complex belief system of orthodox capitalism. This leap was taken by Adam Smith, who is simultaneously the "father" of orthodox capitalism and of modern economics.

The first model comes closest to describing social reality when we look at the situation of small businesses in the early years after the founding of the United States and, to a far more limited degree, to small businesses today. In these instances, the market factors of competition, customers, suppliers, production processes, and finance are far more significant to daily business operations than are other nonmarket social factors. However, for larger businesses, nonmarket factors, such as are represented by the "long noses" of governments, have played a considerably greater role in determining day-to-day operations.

The Dominance Model

The second model, the dominance model, presents a very different picture of how businesses relate to their environment. In this model, businesspeople (owners and top managers) hold fundamental power in our society. Together they are able to dominate and control governments. Then, through their control of governments, they are able to exert substantial control over all other sectors of society.

Because this second model doesn't quite fit current social reality, it too has been modified to take on a religious character among many of its adherents. But unlike the zealous devotees of the first model, who regard the first model as representing a good state of affairs toward which social reality should aspire, the equally zealous devotees of the second model regard the second model as presenting an existing *evil* state of affairs away from which social reality should flee. Followers of Karl Marx and of the complex belief system of communism hold this second view.

The second model best represents what we see in social reality when we consider the remarkable concentration of business operations in the hands of a relatively few people. The second model also fits some of the relations we see between businesses and government. It departs from reality, however, by downplaying the influences on businesses exerted by forces that derive from independent sources in governments and from other sectors of society. I discuss these forces in detail in Chapters 6 and 7.

The Pluralist Model

I call the third model the *pluralist* model because it regards all sectors of society as influencing each other. Thus, not only are activities in the business world influenced by all other sectors, but businesses influence the other sectors in turn. As is true for the previous two models, it is easy to approach this model with a sort of religious fervor, seeing it as representing a good state of affairs toward which social reality should strive. Indeed, this model might be called the "democratic model," with all the flag-waving connotations this term carries. We could then proclaim that in the good society all sectors of society should have their say in what any one sector does, so that no one sector of society could damage any other (as, say, business practices may damage our communities, our family relations, our national interests, or our physical environment).

The pluralistic model has come increasingly closer to representing the social reality that has existed in U.S. society since about the turn of this century as governments, unions, and special interest groups have grown in the influence they exert over decisions in the business sector. However, it falls short of being a fair representation of reality by failing to emphasize the disproportionately greater power that the business sector wields in our society, which translates into a great imbalance in the capacities for mutual influence among the sectors of society. The pluralistic model also fails to take note of the fact that immediate market conditions frequently bear an importance on business decisions that overrides pressures from other sectors of society; that is, businesses do have to continue to be profitable in order to be businesses.

The Three Models Summarized

To summarize, each of the three models accurately portrays some part of the complex relations between businesses and other sectors of society. Hence all three models are useful to some degree, though no single model is entirely accurate by itself. Throughout this book these three models serve as a backdrop for discussions of businesses' relations with their social environment. As much as possible I shall attempt to avoid religious fervor in applying these models, though my personal inclinations tend toward the pluralist model. (I trust, however, that you will forgive me when I occasionally climb on a soapbox for a bit of moralizing here and there. Permitting myself an intermittent moral excess increased my own interest in writing this book, and I believe it will add to the interest you will find in the book.)

An Exercise in Sociological Imagination: The Cult of the Business-Oriented Society

Thus far this chapter has listed the important sectors of the social environment of businesses and presented the three models that serve as a backdrop for my descriptions of how businesses relate to their social environment. Because this initial portrayal of the relations between businesses and other sectors of society has been rather abstract, I would now like to make it much less so by describing how some of these relations have immediate, personal significance to you in your life.

My intent in the remainder of this chapter is to provide an exercise that will help you to develop a sociological imagination. This exercise will stretch and expand your perceptivity so that you can see yourself and the world around you afresh, and not through the filters of common sense or prevailing ideology. From this exercise you will begin to appreciate just how extraordinarily pervasive the influences of businesses are, both on society and on you, and how strong their power is to motivate, indeed to dominate, your thoughts, feelings, and behaviors.

Businesses and Religion

There are several perspectives that I could use in this exercise; the perspective I have chosen is based on a modified version of the dominance model, in which the influences of businesses in changing and controlling other sectors of society to suit business needs are seen as flowing primarily through the overlapping boundaries between businesses and religion, rather than between businesses and governments.

By focusing on only this one pattern of influence in society—that is, the pattern of influence tying businesses and religion together with other sectors of society—I am, of course, presenting a rather narrow, simplified, and occasionally overstated perspective on the otherwise complex relations that hold society together. Nonetheless, it is an interesting and thought-provoking pattern to examine. Furthermore, despite its drawbacks, it serves very well as an exercise in sociological imagination to help you to begin to appreciate the many subtle yet powerful ways in which your life has been shaped by the presence of businesses in our society. Throughout the rest of the book I shall make use of many other contrasting, qualifying, or supplemental perspectives to round out your understanding of the very complex dynamics that relate businesses to their social environments.

Because the approach I have selected here examines a secular religious movement in tracing the influences that businesses have on society and on you, first you must understand the nature of religion as a social phenomenon.

The Nature of Religion

Religions, of course, are themselves complex social phenomena.[4] One distinguishing feature in the typical script for religious experiences is that the script presents us with a sense of the ultimate goals for our lives. These are goals that we are expected to devote ourselves to, that give meaning to our lives. For example, among Christians in the Middle Ages, "heaven" took on the character of being an ultimate goal toward which believers were to strive; it gave their lives meaning. The concept of heaven still holds this significance for many Christians today.

In addition to an ultimate goal, we see two other features in the typical script for religious experiences. One is that some objects or concepts take on the reverential character of being "sacred" and give believers a sense of awe when they are in their presence. The other is that believers feel compelled to engage in ritualized patterns of behavior, thought, and emotion. These rituals bind together the community of believers, orient them toward the ultimate desired goals, provide a means for displaying their reverence for sacred things, and aid in eliciting from them a sense of awe. Christians, for example, are brought together as a community of believers in the ritual of the sacrament of communion, which represents a sacred bond with the deity and a promise of salvation. To the degree that Christians are devout in their beliefs, their engagement in this ritual engenders in them a sense of awe and reverence.

Religious experiences do not begin and end at the doorway of a church; they pervade many facets of the typical round of everyday life. Our diverse religious experiences can be classified into two basic sorts by the goals they set: some orient us toward otherworldly goals, and some toward secular, or worldly, goals.

The ultimate goals of life in otherworldly religious experiences may focus, for example, on the attainment of salvation of the soul and on its eternal future domicile in a heavenly state hereafter. Or the goals may focus on becoming at one with a supreme being or with the source of being. By contrast, the ultimate goals of secular religious experiences typically focus on attaining a material abundance that enriches life here on earth.

Of course, both secular and otherworldly religious experiences may be present simultaneously in a society, influencing different aspects of the everyday round of life. Here I argue that as businesses increasingly have become the dominant social phenomena in society, they have brought into being a pattern of goals, sacred objects, rituals, and a sense of reverential awe that together constitute a secular religious movement and that have had profound influences on the rest of society and on you and me. I call this secular religious movement the cult of the business-oriented society.[5]

Are you and I devotees of a secular religious cult that reveres the role of businesses in our society? If we were, we would know it, wouldn't we? Actually, we probably would not know it, because it is typically difficult for followers of a cult to see how much they are controlled by its influence. Rather than seeing themselves as cult members, they regard their beliefs and ritualistic practices as representing the "true path" in life, the only way that life is supposed to be lived, and representing reality as it actually is. In order to see the powerful, controlling character of the cultish beliefs and rituals that occupy our contemporary lives, it would be helpful to consider in some detail an example of another secular cult, the so-called "cargo cult," and then to draw analogies from this example to our own lives.

An Example of a Cargo Cult

Here, in composite form, I have prepared a generic description of a secular religious movement that anthropologists know as a cargo cult. This cult has arisen in Melanesia and in other places around the world.

Imagine a society of people who live on an island in the Pacific. Each day these people fish, hunt small game, gather wild fruits and roots, and tend to small gardens. Their agricultural techniques and their tools, dwellings, garments, and other material possessions are very limited and primitive by our standards. Indeed, these people live largely a stone-age type of existence. Furthermore, the lifestyle and standard of living of each successive generation are virtually identical to those of the preceding generations as far back as these people can tell by oral history.

Now imagine that one day these people are fishing, hunting, gathering fruits, weeding their gardens, and so forth, just as they have done every day throughout their lives. Suddenly, shouts are heard from some fishermen and all the people run down to the shore of their island to see what the ruckus is about. There on the horizon of the great sea is a small dark patch unlike any the people have previously seen. They are alarmed, uncertain, and awed by the sight. They call out to the spirits they believe in to help them understand what is happening and to protect them from any evil that this patch may represent.

Hour by hour they watch as the dark patch grows larger and larger; indeed it is approaching their island. As they watch this unknown thing come closer into view, they are able to see that it rests upon the waters like one of their boats, but it is far larger than any boat they have ever seen. On this boat swarm small white creatures who appear to be wearing colorful garments unlike any the people have seen before. Eventually several small boats drop from the larger boat and come to the island bringing many of these white creatures. In addition to the amazing garb of these creatures, they speak a language never before heard, and they display many tools, ornaments, and weapons the people have never before seen and that sparkle in the sun.

These white creatures, the first Europeans to come to the island, eventually conquer the native people, bringing bloodshed and European diseases in their wake. The Europeans establish political control over the island and operate it as a colonial business, putting the people to work as forced labor to produce goods that can be sold in markets elsewhere in the world.

As a result of the arrival of these Europeans, the conquered people gain access to all sorts of remarkable goods they have never seen before. At first these goods are given to them as gifts, but later they must purchase them with their labor. They become much impressed by, and come greatly to desire, such items as cloth, flour, sugar, rice, knives, metal fish hooks, and jewelry. Each boat that arrives from over the horizon brings another cargo of these wonderful goods. The people are unable to make these highly desirable goods themselves. Rather they are totally dependent on the great boats to bring yet more loads of these goods. Indeed, they have no conception of the plantation and industrial processes that produce the goods or of the world market that moves the goods for profit. How then do they make sense of the arrival of these remarkable goods?

In a cargo cult, a phenomenon which has been studied extensively among the Pacific Islanders of Melanesia, but which also has occurred elsewhere around the world,[6] people living a lifestyle significantly less advanced than the persons who arrive to colonize them experience a culture shock of great proportions. The cargo cult develops as a means for them to make sense of their new situation, as a means to ensure the continuing flow of desired cargos of highly valued goods, and, in part, as a means to overthrow the yoke of oppression that the cargo carriers bring with them.

The cargo cult is developed out of the cultural elements already available to these people. In particular, their religious tradition of ancestor worship holds that the bounty of their harvest is either a gift of, or is strongly influenced by, the continuing spiritual presence of their ancestors. Consistent with this traditional belief, they come to believe that the cargo brought by the ships must likewise be a gift from their ancestors, which apparently is being momentarily intercepted and controlled by the white colonists.

Their traditional religious practices also include efforts to increase their harvests by engaging in special sacrifices and in ritualistically controlled patterns of behavior, thought, and emotion, which are designed to show honor toward, and to appease, their ancestors' spirits. They now try similar techniques in an effort to facilitate the arrival and overall supply of cargo goods. Indeed, in some cases they may go so far as to give up food gathering, hunting, and gardening altogether in order to devote themselves full-time to building loading docks, to sacrificial practices of self-denial, and to other rituals dedicated to honoring their ancestors in the belief that this will speed up the arrival and expand the supply of cargo. In some cases the strategy actually produces the desired end, as the colonists are forced to ship in more food to keep the people from starving.

Are We Modern-Day Cargo Cultists?

From the vantage point of our culture, the response of these island people to cargo goods looks a bit bizarre, to say the least. Surely, as culturally advanced as we are, we would respond differently to the arrival of new and marvelous material goods. Or would we?

Try to see the history of our own culture from a fresh point of view. First note that, for the past three thousand years, virtually all of our ancestors toiled daily over the earth as farmers. For generation after generation the bounty of the good earth was a forefront concern of our ancestors, and efforts to obtain this bounty dominated the daily round of their activities. Food selections were severely limited, as were clothing, furniture, ornaments, cosmetics, health products, and most other forms of luxury that today we take for granted as necessities.

But in the last few centuries after all these many generations of farming, there began to appear over the social horizon some ill-understood forces that loomed larger and larger in the social landscape. These were the forces of business, including mercantilism, colonialism, and, later, industrialization. These forces made available goods that our ancestors either never had seen before or had previously found to be out of their financial reach, including sugar, tea, coffee, tobacco, chocolate, and many other things. Particularly with the rise of industrialization, many goods could be mass produced cheaply enough to become affordable for the first time for larger and larger portions of the population. These goods included garments of all kinds, eating and cooking utensils, tools of all sorts, and many items for amusement.

Colonial empires spanning half a globe could have had little concrete meaning for our typical ancestor. No more comprehensible to them would have been the industrial factories, with their awesome machinery, their great clamor, foul smell, and belching smoke. Yet the goods that arrived from these sources were highly desirable, and their continued delivery was something to be facilitated if at all possible. How could our ancestors make sense of the appearance of this new flood of desirable goods, and how could they act to ensure its continued bounty?

There are ample clues that can be found in our secular culture today and in our current everyday round of life that indicate how we have in fact come to adjust ourselves and all sectors of our society to facilitate the arrival of these new goods that the businesses of mercantilism, colonialism, and industrialization brought. Furthermore, these clues give evidence at several points of a distinctly religious character, including rituals carried out on an extraordinarily large scale, great personal sacrifices, and sacred objects that elicit in us a sense of reverential awe. These clues all point toward a secular goal of obtaining a material bounty on earth. Let's look at some of these clues.

The Sacred Character of Money

Money, you will recall from Chapter 1, is a symbol that represents at an abstract level all desired material goods; it has become the common measure of profits for businesses. Indeed, it is the oil that lubricates the social machinery of business by facilitating market transactions in our society. I want to consider here some interesting religious connotations that money holds in our society; they suggest an underlying reverential attitude we hold toward the forces of business and toward the related goods businesses make available to us.

No doubt because such people are interesting to us, written and oral histories tend to focus on the rich and powerful. By contrast, the poor groveling masses tend to be slighted. But such a focus misrepresents the life of our typical ancestor, who was a part of the poor groveling masses. In the life of our typical farming ancestor, money and commercial establishments would have played little role until relatively recently in human history. Indeed, it would have been rare until recently for our farming ancestors to have carried any money at all on their person. Why should they? Opportunities to earn or spend money were exceedingly infrequent and largely unnecessary in the context of their social position (frequently that of slave or serf).

But this is quite in contrast with the situation confronting us today. Businesses have become increasingly central to our society, and our orientation to money has changed dramatically. Today for you or me to be found with no money, credit cards, or checkbook on our person or very near at hand would be cause for great anxiety indeed! More important to most Americans than carrying a talisman or an otherworldly religious symbol such as a crucifix, is the carrying of money. Its presence reassures us of our social potency in dealing with life's contingencies. For us, money has become our admission ticket to the goods that businesses make available and that, unlike our ancestors, we cannot live without. Indeed, we often stand in awe of money as if it were something sacred. We see this attitude of awe most plainly when we are confronted by large quantities of money or by a person who is known to possess great amounts of money.

Consider too the time of year when we are most likely to spend our money. During what time of the year do we hear the most "jing-jingling" of money being spent and the most "ring-ringing" of business cash registers being rung? Of course it is the Christmas season, one of the two most important religious observances in our predominantly Christian culture. What message do we see in the fact that a time of our year set aside for sacred religious observance has become a principal time of money changing and business profit taking, or that an observance intended for spiritual reawakening has become our biggest celebration of the secular, materialistic plenty afforded by money?

Well, let's also take a closer look at money itself; I mean *very* close. Take out all the coins and paper currency you are carrying on your person at this moment. What motto is inscribed on each? Why, it is: "In God we trust." Imagine: in God we trust! If you and I were to recite this motto together while holding our money heavenward, we would feel a bit foolish in doing so, wouldn't we? Yet we don't feel foolish walking around with a pocketful of metallic and paper symbols that proclaim our trust in God. We don't feel foolish that these symbols proclaiming our trust in God are intended not to serve the ends of otherworldly goals, but rather to serve as our personal claim on the material bounty on earth and to simultaneously facilitate market transactions and the profit counting of businesses in our society. Far from feeling foolish about it, we slavishly throw ourselves into ritualistic patterns of extraordinary sacrifice in the hope of increasing our supply of these symbols and thereby currying the favor of the mysterious forces of plenty that reside in our marketplaces.

I'll describe these rituals a little later on. Next I want to consider some other sacred, awe-inspiring things in our society.

Majestic Monuments, to What?
Throughout the most recent two thousand years of the lives of our ancestors, we see that again and again the religious sector of society pulled together considerable resources to erect temples, cathedrals, and other monuments as testimonies of spiritual faith and of the position of honor that the deity held in the community. These monuments were typically the largest and most ornate constructions of the time. A traveler would no doubt be struck with a profound sense of awe by the majestic size and beauty of many of the religious constructions that dominated the landscape of a community. The church held for our ancestors the central revered place in the community. Indeed, these monuments were typically regarded as homes of the deity and as places where believers could go to commune with the deity. It was the place where everyone looked to find spiritual fulfillment, and it was a center of social life, bringing people together regularly for ceremonies, rituals, and other social activities and community affairs.

If our ancestors could cross the gulf of time to visit our metropolises today, what towering constructions would they see dominating our landscapes and serving as modern-day "Meccas" to orient our prayers and to provide a central place for ritual and social contact? Well, in addition to our towering, glittering office buildings, which are themselves monuments to business, such a visitor would have to be awed by the magnificent size and extravagant appearance of our other monuments to business: our gigantic shopping malls that provide marketplaces for business goods and services. They are places in which the mysterious forces of business reside and to which we can go, sacred money clutched in hand, to commune with these forces in the hope of being delivered an earthly abundance of goods. Shopping malls orient our thoughts, rivet our attention, and provide places to bring us together in social interaction as a community of believers.

We can see in this discussion that a number of religious elements are tying us to the business world, both through our approach to money, and through the monuments we have constructed to house the most significant, beneficial forces of our time. But a religion involves more than awe-inspiring sacred things. It also involves rituals that orient us to ultimate goals and that tie us together as a community of believers.

Are we ritualistically controlled by our secular desires for the good life here on earth? Are we, as is true of the cargo cultists, confronted with a material abundance that has appeared before us from sources we do not understand, but wish desperately to control so as to ensure its continued delivery? Are we so awed by this worldly plenty that we are willing to submit ourselves to great sacrifice through ritualistically controlled behaviors, thoughts, and emotions in the hope of gaining favor with the unknown source of this bounty and thereby increasing our share of it?

Well, not you and me! We are too rational and our culture is too advanced for us to become modern-day cargo cultists, caught up in outrageous programmed rituals and mind-dulling mumbo jumbo belief systems. Or are we? Let's look at some of the significant rituals that play major roles today in organizing the round of our everyday lives and ask how they may tie in to the presence of businesses in our society.

Ritualistic Sacrifices in Schooling

Start with our ritualistic devotion to schooling. Hardly any of our ancestors went to schools of any sort; it is only in the last three generations or so that we have become so obsessed with schooling. This obsession is so great that an outside observer of our society would be forced to conclude that there must be some absolutely critical skills or information that only the schools of our society can impart to us, and that we would find life-threatening to be without. Why else would people in our society exhibit such slavish devotion to schooling? But looking closely at schooling, it is not easy to discern any critical skills or information that is imparted.[7]

For more than three thousand years, our ancestors learned whatever skills and information they needed for their everyday lives through their families and church. In contrast to the orientations toward family and otherworldliness that this learning process entailed, schooling in our society pulls us away from the authority and tradition of both the family and otherworldly religions by emphasizing instead individual achievement and secular, worldly goals.

The slavish obsession we exhibit for schooling would certainly startle our ancestors and make them question our piety and quite possibly our sanity. For example, think about this: you and I have spent thirteen years (including kindergarten) of our preciously limited lives caught up in the daily grind of primary and secondary schooling. *Thirteen years!* This is more than one-sixth of our lifetime if we are lucky enough to live to an age of 75! We have sacrificed our youth to schooling, allowing our thoughts, emotions, and behaviors to conform to the ritualistic schedules imposed on us by authoritarian and bureaucratic schools. Why have we done this?

The system of schooling created during this century would have to look bizarre and uninviting to our ancestors. In some respects, our schools bear institutional resemblances to the prisons we have also created, though schools differ from prisons in the liberal evening, weekend, and summer leave privileges provided for their inmates. We are so obsessed with schooling and so rigorously controlled by it, that we have enacted legislation to require our attendance in schools for at least seven or eight years. During this period, we would be hunted down and forced to return to the school if we failed to appear daily. It is as though we have sentenced all persons between the ages of 6 and 14 to institutional confinement; there they participate in habilitation programs to replace undesirable traits with whatever desirable traits schooling is supposed to instill.

And how is it that we are habilitated? The habilitation program of schooling includes a round of institutionalized life that is highly regimented and restrictive. It is a round of life spent largely doing whatever we are told, being "creative" on command (but always within the bounds set by schooling officials for acceptable creativity), sitting still for long periods of time while simultaneously denying our physical, psychological, and social impulses that do not suit school authorities or school schedules, and being continually threatened or actually punished for infractions of innumerable, and frequently, petty rules. As in any confinement process, we are effectively isolated from other social contexts. In particular, from the tender age of five or six onward we are removed from the family for much of each weekday. This isolation process works to break both the authority and the traditions of the family. These are replaced by a common set of communal values oriented around obedience to bureaucratic authority, which is the form of authority typified in modern corporate businesses and governments.

Why do we subject ourselves to and endure such a system? Well, in our younger years we do not have enough sense to ask such a question, or if we do our parents insist that it "is the law" and that it is necessary for us to go to school in order to "get ahead in life." (If this reasoning fails, they usually resort to threatening us.) But in later years of our schooling, many of us continue to attend because we accept the belief that an education or, perhaps more particularly, "educational credentials," will indeed be our ticket to good-paying jobs and to the good life that our business-oriented world makes available and conditions us to expect. In short, we buy into the belief that schooling is a ladder to be climbed to reach for ever-better jobs and paychecks. Schooling is a means to appease and curry favor with some great unknown forces "out there" that control the bounty on earth we are expected to desire.[8]

We come to believe that, if we just do as we are told, scrape the floors repeatedly and ritualistically with our bows to secular authority, deny our juvenile urges, sacrifice our youth, endure seemingly unending periods of boredom with at least a faint look of interest painted on our face, and generally "gut it out," serving our institutional habilitation time as best we can while maintaining the appearance of "model students," then it will all be made worthwhile by a material abundance that will come into our lives later. We don't do it to get into heaven or to "save" our souls. We don't do it because it makes us pious or is pleasing to an otherworldly god. We do it because we come to believe that our business-oriented world demands it of us as a prerequisite for "good jobs" and a good life on earth.[9]

Many of us become so addicted to the ritual and routine of schooling, or so enamored with the prospects of gaining even greater material rewards in return for higher educational degrees, that we go on beyond high school for four or more years of college and perhaps four or more additional years for a postgraduate degree. I, for example, spent 23 years or almost one-third of my expected life, as a student in educational institutions. Has all the bowing and conforming, the sacrifice of my youth, and the self-denial of my many other desires been worth it? Well, I have a pretty good job, the income from which supports a modest middle-class lifestyle. I have a "nice" home, two cars, two televisions and a microwave oven in which I can "zap" my frozen dinners when I arrive home from work at 7 in the evening. Yes, I guess it was all worthwhile. Or was it?

Ritualistic Sacrifices in the Workworld

The ritualistic sacrifice of our youth on the altars of school appears not to be enough to appease the great mysterious forces that control the bounty of material goods in our society. No, the expectation that we spend one-sixth to one-third of our lives in ritualized supplication in schooling is not enough. Rather we also are expected to spend much of the rest of our lives ritualistically sacrificing ourselves to the demands of the workworld.[10]

Our ancestors worked very hard, and their lives were shorter than ours (largely because of the lack of adequate public health measures). But their work schedules followed the needs of agriculture, so there were periods or seasons of very hard work and other periods or seasons with little to do.

The typical workday for us, however, follows a ritualistic year-long pattern that suits modern business needs. Modern business practices require rigid temporal coordination of work efforts, so we have all become a society of clock watchers. Indeed many of us, myself included, would not dare to go anywhere without a wristwatch to track the scheduling and efficiency of our day. How odd we would look to our ancestors. We retire with confidence at night only after reassuring ourselves that our alarm clock has been set to alert us to the appropriate time to arise the next morning to get to work punctually. Years of clock-watching and clock-scheduled learning in school have helped to inculcate these habits so helpful to business.

We engage in rituals of showering, grooming, and dressing, all to suit the needs of our employer. We fight traffic, scramble for parking places, and frequently leave our children alone to fend for themselves, all for the benefit of business needs. We do this day after day, lapsing into a more natural, slovenly appearance and family orientation only on weekends. After an eight-hour day controlling our behavior, thoughts, and emotions to serve the needs of our employers, we retire back to our home to recuperate for another day. We do this day after day, year after year, for perhaps as many as 45 years to appease the forces that make the material comforts of our lifestyles possible. We may enjoy some or many aspects of our jobs, or we may not. It is of little matter in view of the extraordinary toll this process of sacrifice takes on us.

In our obsession, we deny and sacrifice family needs, the needs of our spouses, children and parents, our own youth and personal needs, and possibly even our health. We make these sacrifices because we believe them to be "right and proper" and because we believe that these sacrifices are necessary for us to "get ahead" and to "stay ahead" in life. But do all these sacrifices in fact get us ahead materially? Are they worthwhile? For most, though not all, a materially better life *does* result, so the ritualistic behaviors, sacrifices, and self-denial appear to produce at least some of the desired results, though these appearances may themselves be illusions as I discuss in Chapter 6.

How very odd our culture must look to an outsider. We willingly endure many years of highly restricted existence in educational institutions so we can submit ourselves to a staggeringly greater number of years of equally severe restrictions in a work setting, all in the hope of finding material abundance. Interspersed in this round of life (consisting of work, work, work, restrictions, restrictions, restrictions, sacrifices, sacrifices, sacrifices), we frequently are observed engaging in cathartic binges of self-indulgent shopping behavior and consumption. What very strange behavior this is.

Changes in Other Sectors of Society

Other changes can be seen in several sectors of our society that reflect our slavish devotion to the needs of business. For example, in response to the increasing growth and material plenty made available by businesses, we, as was true for some of the cargo cultists, have thrown down our hoes and given up farming in order to devote ourselves full time to the new round of ritualized work life which we believe, rightly or wrongly, will facilitate the arrival and continuing flow of a bounty of goods to us from the business world. This loss of self-sufficiency in food production places us in a precarious state. If the business world were to collapse today and cease delivering its wonderful cargo of foods, most of us would likely starve. The fact is that you and I no longer personally possess the knowledge, skills, tools, material, or access to land to produce our own foods. We are now wholly dependent on businesses to provide our "daily bread."

We have left our rural past, in large part, as a response to the needs that the business world has for large local labor pools and for easily reached mass markets.[11] This mass migration has resulted in us crowding ourselves together around emerging business centers. In this process we created the gigantic metropolitan areas of today, with all their attendant problems of urban stress, pollution, disease, vermin, depersonalization, crime, and slums. We also have left behind our extended family and the neighbor and community relations that for thousands of years were so central to the lives of our ancestors.[12] In their place we have substituted a new focus on our individual freedom, individual mobility, and individual goal attainment. Thus in the search for the material abundance promised by the business world, the pace and congestion of our living environment have increased at the same time that the potential buffers of family and community relations have decreased.

Our business-oriented world is supported not only by the rapid growth of metropolitan areas but also by the rise of secular, individual-focused education; by the quickened pace and clock-oriented round of work life; and by the declining significance of the family and community. Changes favorable to businesses also have occurred in our otherworldly religions. The Protestant Reformation, for example, decreased the control exercised over the individual by the church, while emphasizing new virtues more favorable to the business culture, such as the value of individual effort, of hard work, and of thrift as signs in this world of salvation in the next. Also, changes have occurred in governments (such as in the rise of democratic republics) that emphasize the individual and that free the businessperson from control by nobility or clergy. Furthermore, changes in the family have decreased patriarchal control over individuals, decreased the size of the family unit, and generally increased the fluidity of family structures in ways that permit more rapid response to business-driven labor pool needs. All of these changes are described in greater detail in Chapters 5 and 6.

The many social changes alluded to here, as well as the ritualistic round of our everyday life and the religious connotations that tie us to these rituals and to the business world, all describe a pattern of extraordinary influences that businesses exert over the major sectors of our society and ultimately on you and me. The fact that we not only willingly submit to these changes, but also quite often engage in them with fervor, suggests that we, as is true of the cargo cultists, are caught up in a secular religious movement. After all, don't we, as is true of the followers of a cargo cult, seek goods more marvelous than our ancestors ever dreamed of, that derive from a set of forces we do not understand? Don't we believe that the forces that are the source of these goods can be appeased through ritual, sacrifice, and self-denial? Haven't you sacrificed yourself and your family to appease these forces? And indeed, haven't your past and your present circumstances been shaped by the promise of the material abundance that these forces may bring?

The cargo cultists believed that the spirits of their own ancestors were the source of the goods they desired. This made sense in their view of reality. But we know the sources of the goods we desire by a different name, though of only slightly less ethereal nature. We know them as businesses. In the reality of the cargo cultists, the spirits of their ancestors may have walked among them, just as the gods did among the ancient Greeks or as Jesus does in the life of the reborn Christian. But just as real and awesome as a living presence to us today are businesses. As the cargo cultists looked to the spirits of their ancestors for earthly plenty, and as Christians, Jews, Muslims, Hindus, and Buddhists looked to the deity for spiritual fulfillment, so in our secular preoccupations today we look to businesses for the only piece of heaven we believe we can enjoy on earth.

In summary, the profound influences that businesses have on you and me have changed our behaviors, thoughts, and emotions in extraordinary ways and have resulted in widespread transformations in all major sectors of our society. As a result we are currently confronted with what I call the business-oriented society. In a sense, you and I are like modern day cargo cultists who are caught up in a secular fervor for the good life that we believe the business-oriented society can give us. And, as is true of the cargo cultists, aren't you and I sacrificing and fervently praying for that day of material plenty when at long last our "ship comes in?"

Sociological Imagination: Concluding Remarks

I have just taken you through an exercise in sociological imagination. The purpose was to shake up your perceptivity so that you can begin to see, perhaps for the first time, the larger social forces that shape our social world and personal lives. Without sociological imagination, we may not see these forces and may have our thinking misled by the ideologies and common sense conventions of our time. It is only by a close examination of the social world that we may hope to succeed in developing solutions for the problems that confront us collectively or that arise in our lives.

I initiated this exercise with the caution that I would be using only one, highly simplified perspective on the otherwise rich complexity of our society. I could not do otherwise within the confines of the few pages of this brief exercise. The perspective I chose for the exercise focused on the religious character of the influence of businesses on society. Other perspectives, however, are also useful and equally insightful in examining business influences on us. Throughout the remainder of this book, I shall not limit myself to the use of one perspective. Rather I shall use several different perspectives as seem most fitting for exploring the issues at hand.

C h a p t e r *3*

Do Businesses Have Social Responsibilities?

In Chapter 2, I listed the key sectors of the social environment of businesses. In this chapter I consider the question of whether businesses are responsible for any part of their social environment. To start us thinking about this question, consider the following issues that were being written about in the mass media during the time I composed this chapter:

- When several key contracts were terminated in the defense industry, many employees lost their jobs. Should businesses be responsible for helping the employees they lay off to find new jobs and to avoid losing their homes and health care insurance while they are unemployed?
- Carpal tunnel syndrome is a debilitating neural disorder that may afflict employees as a result of the structure and pace of their work setting. Should businesses be responsible for ensuring that their workplaces and work schedules will not contribute to the development of such disorders among their employees?
- Lawn darts (no longer sold, by law) are heavy metal darts that were sold in toy sections of many department stores. They were intended to be thrown at targets on lawns for fun and as a test of skill. Unfortunately, they can and did pierce peoples' heads, causing brain damage and death. Should the businesses that made or sold these products be responsible for injuries to consumers who used them?
- The noise of jet aircraft around airports is a source of serious noise pollution for surrounding residents. Should airlines be responsible for the noise pollution their aircraft create in the communities where they operate?
- Freon is believed to damage the earth's ozone layer, which protects us from the harmful effects of ultraviolet light. Should businesses that sell freon or that sell products that use freon (such as air-conditioners or refrigerators) be responsible for the damages that the use of their products cause to our environment?

- When land developers strip land of trees and level the ground for landscaping, the resulting silt runoff during storms pollutes nearby streams, rivers, and other bodies of water. Should land developers be responsible for the damage they cause to our environment?
- When land developers are finished setting up a new housing community, should they be responsible for the costs of construction and maintenance of roads, water and sewer treatment plants, and schools that consumers will need in order to make use of the developers' housing products?
- The interstate highway system is an infrastructural feature of our economic system—that is, it is critical to businesses for the mass transportation of goods from production locations to consumer markets. Should businesses be responsible for building and maintaining this highway system?
- Years of systematic hiring and wage discrimination practices by businesses have left African Americans and single women disproportionately poor. Do businesses have a responsibility to work to remedy poverty among African Americans and single women?
- As "real" wages (that is, wages controlling for inflation) have fallen in the United States, there has been a substantial increase in the number of dually employed parents. This in turn has placed great strain on families and has contributed to the burgeoning number of "latchkey" children. Should businesses be responsible for promoting the welfare of the families of their employees by providing after school and on-site child care services, by instituting flex-time schedules for working parents, or by providing family leave benefits?
- The business community has been complaining that new employees often are inadequately educated by our schools. Should businesses be responsible for providing the skills and training they believe their employees need to be competent workers?
- Through the power they typically hold over their own board of directors, CEOs of U.S. corporations are in a position to exert considerable influence over the total compensation that their jobs provide to them and to their senior management team, regardless of their actual job performance in managing their corporations. This mechanism for enhancing the salaries and benefits for senior management employees has been far more effective than unions have been in achieving similar income goals for rank and file workers. And, of course, these increased forms of compensation reduce the profits available, if any, for distribution to shareholding owners or for use in business expansion. To what degree, if at all, should corporate businesses be responsible for maximizing the profits of shareholding owners by holding down management costs?
- The collapse in the 1980s of many banking and savings and loan institutions nationwide, which may cost U.S. taxpayers more than half a trillion dollars, was the result of poor management of business assets by senior management and poor regulatory oversight by governments. Unless action was taken to protect depositors, the entire financial structure of our economy was threatened by this crisis. To what degree, if at all, should businesses in the banking and saving and loan industries be responsible for setting up their own management control mechanisms to ensure that such a crisis will not happen again or for forcing governments to devise and carry out more effective regulatory processes in the future?
- Through political action committees, businesses contribute large sums of money and other forms of assistance to candidates for political office and to current lawmakers. To

what degree, if at all, should businesses be responsible for deciding who should be elected to government offices and for deciding what legislation should be enacted and what policies should be devised and enforced?

- To protect business interests, the United States maintains a worldwide military presence. The recent war in Iraq, for example, was fought not to promote democracy but to protect oil interests that figure so greatly in U.S. industries. To what degree, if at all, should U.S. businesses pay for the military costs connected with protecting U.S. business interests worldwide?

- Multinational corporations maintain production processes in more than one nation. Should a multinational corporation be responsible for promoting the national interests of each country in which it operates, or should it be responsible only for the interests of the home country in which its headquarters is located—or should it promote any national interests at all?

These issues illustrate only a few of those of current concern regarding the social responsibilities of businesses. In order to address these issues, we need to consider closely what is meant by being responsible or by businesses having social responsibilities.

The Nature of Social Responsibility

The term social responsibility refers simultaneously to an ethical or moral stance and to a social relationship. The moral stance is that of responding to another party in a social relationship in a way that promotes the welfare of the other party. In Chapter 2 I listed the major sectors of society with which businesses have social relationships. To ask, then, whether businesses have social responsibilities is to ask whether they should behave deliberately in ways that promote the welfare of these other sectors of society.

The important moral imperative embodied in the term social responsibility goes beyond merely asserting that businesses should recognize and respond to the presence of other sectors of society. A business could respond in any number of ways to other sectors of society and yet not do so in ways that reflect the moral imperative of being responsible for the welfare of these other sectors. As I explore the relationships between businesses and other sectors of society throughout this book, I will also examine the moral issues surrounding business social responsibilities.

Should Businesses Have Social Responsibilities?

Over the past few decades much discussion has occurred on the topic of whether businesses should have social responsibilities. Using the definition just given, these discussions can be seen as asking whether businesses should act in a fashion that indicates a willful concern for the well-being of other sectors of society. At issue is not just that businesses provide jobs, incomes, and desired goods and services, all of which benefit society at large. Rather, it is asked, for example, whether it is the responsibility of the business sector to overcome racial and sexual discrimination in our society, to alleviate the problems of urban blight, to improve the functioning of governments and schools, to serve the political interests of our nation in international affairs, to ensure that their products and services are safe for consumers and for our environment, to provide a safe working environment for employees, and to provide for the health and welfare of employees and their families. These questions reflect only a sampling of the sectors of society and of issues related to these sectors for which businesses are asked to become responsible.

Friedman's Arguments

If we look at this issue from a sociological perspective, we can see that most people who oppose each other on either side of the question of whether businesses should have social responsibilities typically conceptualize the social environment of businesses in terms of the market model described in Chapter 2. That is, most opponents and proponents share the assumption that businesses are largely independent of other sectors of society. From this assumption one camp argues that businesses should *remain* independent from other sectors of society and be responsible only for satisfying the alleged singular desire of their owners to maximize profits. By contrast, operating from the same assumption, the opposing camp argues that, for a variety of reasons, businesses should cease being independent and instead become more active in helping other sectors of society.

The best-known spokesperson who opposes the idea of businesses having social responsibilities is Milton Friedman, a Nobel Prize–winning economist and a fervent adherent of the market model. In a frequently cited article,[1] Friedman claims that the only responsibility businesses have is to maximize profits for their owners. According to Friedman, businesses cannot take any legitimate action toward resolving social problems, because only democratically elected governments hold the legitimate authority to deal with such problems. Therefore, if businesses were to do anything about these problems, they would be taking on government functions. The result would be political processes that are controlled by businesses, and these would operate on an inherently unfair, nondemocratic basis of taxation without representation. That is, all of us consumers would have to pay through higher prices on goods and services for the political actions that businesses decide to undertake to resolve social problems in the name of social responsibility. At the same time, however, we would have no effective means for voicing our desires for the nature of the business actions for which we are otherwise paying. Rather, the power to make these decisions in the typical corporate business would rest in the hands of senior management and a board of directors, who in turn, according to Friedman, represent the narrow interests of shareholding owners in our society.

Friedman's arguments create a difficult antinomy for followers of the market model. If governments are the only proper authority to work toward remedying social problems, but we find that many of the major social problems of our time concern business practices (e.g., environmental pollution, discrimination in employment, political bribery, unsafe products), then it follows that governments must increase their regulation of businesses. Being a zealous proponent of the market model, however, Friedman clearly sees such intervention in business affairs as undesirable and to be avoided as much as possible. Yet if businesses are not themselves to initiate socially responsible behavior with regard to the social problems to which they contribute and are instead to be made to behave responsibly only under duress by government, how then are businesses to avoid extensive intrusions of governments into their affairs? The contradiction in Friedman's arguments is that he would remove from businesses the only protective strategy that they can implement to ward off the kind of encroachment of governments into business affairs that he and other zealous market model followers see as so undesirable.

But let's approach this issue from a different point of view. If we deny the accuracy of the market model as a portrayal of the reality of the social environment of businesses, as I did in Chapter 2, and if we do not follow Friedman in allegiance to this model as a portrayal of what reality should be like, then all of his arguments fall apart. As I noted in Chapter 1 and illustrated in Chapter 2 with a description of the cult of the business-oriented society, businesses are not distinctly bounded phenomena separate and independent from governments or from any other social phenomena in their environment. Rather, the boundaries of businesses as social phenomena shade extensively into other social phenomena, so that businesses are supported in very fundamental ways by these other phenomena and in turn exert considerable influences in shaping them. Therefore, many problems in the social environment of businesses either may have been caused by businesses or may have been deeply influenced by business operations; these problems are not independent of business.

Businesses are a central source of power in our society and a major contributor to the social problems of our times; therefore, it would seem very unwise for us not to expect them to make a moral commitment to control their own behavior for the welfare of other sectors of society. Furthermore, it would be unwise for businesses not to make such a commitment, because their existence depends on the vitality of the many sectors of society their behaviors may threaten. Drawing on these considerations, the position I take in this book is that businesses necessarily must seek to act in a socially responsible fashion. Businesses are not independent of other sectors of society, and the vitality of these other sectors is essential to the viability of business.

Socially responsible actions, however, may be badly conceived and poorly enacted by businesses. This is especially true if businesspersons lack a sound understanding of the social environment of businesses and of how businesses contribute to larger social problems. My intention in preparing this book was to develop a conceptual framework that will facilitate such an understanding.

Restrictions on the Social Responsibilities of Businesses

As a backdrop for exploring the social responsibilities of businesses throughout the remainder of this book, it is important to note three basic principles that serve to restrict how businesses engage in socially responsible action. The first concerns the role of profits in businesses. The second concerns how businesses influence their social environments. And the third concerns how social environments influence businesses. These three principles are described in this section.

The Rule of Profits

The first principle that serves as a limit on socially responsible business behavior concerns available resources. It is a fairly standard rule that one's actions must be restricted in scope by one's available resources, and this rule holds equally for socially responsible actions by businesses.

However, to understand a unique implication of how this rule works in businesses, we must recall that businesses were defined in Chapter 1 as social phenomena that operate to make a profit. Thus the very viability of businesses as social phenomena rests on their ability to create a regular flow of profits. We cannot expect, therefore, that socially responsible actions will be undertaken by businesses when these actions threaten their profitability and hence their very existence as businesses.

This restriction certainly does not mean that businesses cannot (or should not) engage in socially responsible behavior. Rather (as will become evident throughout this book), socially responsible actions often are not in conflict with standard profit making-strategies.

As corollaries of this first restriction on business' social responsibilities, one could expect businesses that are making little or no profits to be those that are least likely to be able to pursue socially responsible behavior. In contrast, businesses that are flush with profits are those most likely to be able to commit resources to socially responsible behavior. Furthermore, hard economic times should make businesses less able to engage in socially responsible behavior, and prosperous times should increase their ability to do so. And, in deciding which of several socially responsible courses of action to take, a business would likely choose those that are consistent with, or do not differ from, their profit goals.

Operationally Based Social Problems

A second principle that should serve to restrict the extent of socially responsible business behavior concerns the fact that not all social problems in society derive from business practices. A more compelling case can be made for why businesses should work toward avoiding or alleviating those social problems that derive in part from their own business operations, than can be made for problems that derive from societal dynamics independent of businesses. The former type of problems I call operationally based social problems, and the latter I call nonoperationally based social problems.

Consider employment discrimination as an example. In hiring people as employees, businesses may either follow racist, sexist, and ageist practices in making these hires, or they may seek to make their decisions based directly on worker qualifications. When considered in the context of business decisions that involve hiring, promotion, compensation, and termination of employees, the processes of racism, sexism, and ageism are operationally based social problems for which we may expect businesses to behave in a socially responsible fashion. However, when racism, sexism, and ageism appear in other sectors of social life, such as in religions, in public places, in neighborhoods, or in governments, they are nonoperationally based social problems. In these latter settings, we can reasonably expect businesses to feel less moral compulsion to address these problems.

We can imagine, therefore, a moral continuum for the social responsibilities of businesses. Businesses should be expected foremost to address problems that derive directly from their own operations. They should be expected to exhibit proportionately less commitment to resolving problems that derive less directly from their operations. And they should be expected to exhibit no commitment to address problems deriving independently from their operations.

The ability to make these distinctions would have to rest on an empirical study of the influences that the operations of any particular business have on the social environment of the business. Without such a study, a business is not in a good position to determine how they should become socially responsible.

The fact that the typical corporation is not likely to have a detailed study of how its operations contribute to problems in its social environment probably accounts for why in recent years philanthropic contributions have become such an overused strategy for discharging a corporation's social responsibilities. Such contributions often reflect great ignorance and cynicism. Corporations know they are being pressured to behave in a more socially responsible fashion, but in their ignorance they often don't know what to do. So they simply toss money at popular problems by donating a portion of their profits to charities and public causes. The cynical side of these efforts is evident when the charities and public causes for which contributions are made are selected largely with the intention of looking like a good citizen and hopefully engendering consumer good will, political support, increased profits, and tax write-offs.

The second restriction being described here, however, suggests that most corporate philanthropy today does not provide a useful approach in trying to become socially responsible because it typically exhibits little or no understanding of the actual operationally based social problems created by a business. At least with regard to contributions of corporate money to nonoperationally based problems, I would agree with Friedman that such contributions constitute improper use of investor/owner profits.

It is occasionally argued that, because businesses are dependent on so many sectors of society, virtually all social problems are of concern to businesses and should be addressed by them. For example, the Committee for Economic Development, which includes top business leaders from around the country, suggested that businesses should become responsible for quite an extensive range of social problems because, as the Committee puts it:[2]

> *people who have a good environment, education, and opportunity make better employees, customers, and neighbors for business than those who are poor, ignorant, and oppressed.*

It is impractical to expect businesses to take socially responsible actions on a wide array of social issues. Rather, the second restriction suggests a simple rule that would require corporations to clean up their own social messes and to avoid destructive behavior with regard to other sectors of society. The rule does not hold that businesses necessarily should clean up problems created by other sectors of society or become society's police officers and social workers.

Responsibilities of Other Sectors to Businesses

A third principle of importance to this discussion concerns the social responsibilities of other sectors of society to businesses. From a sociological perspective, organized society is possible only when all parts of society work together to support the operations of each other. This is true even if one or more parts are more dominant than others in these relationships of mutual dependency, as is true for businesses in society today. I described this principle of interdependence in Chapter 1 and tried to dramatize it in Chapter 2 when I described the rise of the cult of the business-oriented society and its ramifications throughout society in changing social phenomena to accommodate business needs. If, as is patently the case today, we are going to place such great value on the role of businesses in our society and to orient so much of our lives toward businesses, then it follows that we will want all sectors of society to promote the welfare of businesses as much as possible.

Thus, this third restriction holds that not only do businesses have social responsibilities to work toward avoiding or alleviating problems they cause for other sectors of society, but these other sectors also have reciprocal social responsibilities to work toward avoiding or alleviating problems they cause for businesses. Actions by other sectors of society that threaten the vitality of businesses threaten the vitality of society as a whole and the lifestyle that you and I have. The importance of this point will be highlighted in Chapter 7, where I describe adverse effects of government regulations on businesses.

Brief History of Social Mechanisms Fostering Business Social Responsibility

Operating in the world as it actually exists, in contrast to the ideal world posed by Friedman and the market model, business leaders themselves have spoken out in favor of increased social responsibility in business. Much of the interest by the business community in this issue has arisen within the last few decades and is driven by the increased pressures placed on them by governments and by special interest groups during this period.

An early example was voiced by Frank W. Abrams in 1951 while he was chairman of the board of the major oil company which today is known as Exxon. Abrams put it this way:[3]

> *Businessmen are learning that they have responsibilities not just to one group but to many. . . . The job of professional management . . . is to maintain . . . a harmonious balance among the claims of the various interested groups: the stockholders, employees, customers, and the public at large. . . . [No] corporation can prosper for any length of time today if its sole purpose is to make as much money as possible, as quickly as possible, and without concern for other values.*

Concerns such as expressed by Abrams were sufficiently widespread in the business community by 1971 that the Committee for Economic Development, which includes leading business executives from across the country, produced a position paper for the business community entitled, "Social Responsibilities in Business Corporations." Their report stated the following:[4]

> *Today it is clear that the terms of the contract between society and business are, in fact, changing in substantial and important ways. Business is being asked to assume broader responsibilities to society than ever before and to serve a wider range of human values. Business enterprises, in effect, are being asked to contribute more to the quality of American life than just supplying quantities of goods*

and services. Inasmuch as business exists to serve society, its future will depend on the quality of management's response to the changing expectations of the public.

Some examples of responsible business contributions to society that were suggested in 1971 by the Committee for Economic Development included the following: giving aid to schools or assisting in managing schools, training disadvantaged workers, improving transportation systems, developing recycling programs, helping in community health planning, and improving management practices in government.

By the early 1980s, when a survey asked chief executive officers of major U.S. corporations whether they agreed that business already has too much social power and should not engage in social activities that might give it more, 77 percent disagreed. In contrast, 92.2 percent agreed that responsible corporate behavior can be in the best economic interest of the stockholder.[5] Also in the early 1980s the Business Roundtable, a group of 200 chief executive officers from the largest U.S. corporations, issued a report in which they stated:[6]

Business and society have a symbiotic relationship: The long-term viability of the corporation depends upon its responsibility to the society of which it is a part. And the well-being of society depends upon profitable and responsible business enterprises.

Why have we seen such growing support from business leaders themselves for the concept of businesses becoming socially responsible? The motivating factors in engendering this support will be described in this section through a brief historical review of business social responsibilities in the United States and of the attendant societal pressures that make businesses assume these responsibilities.

In this section and throughout this book I shall use the term social control mechanisms when referring to the societal pressures that force behaviors, thoughts, and emotions into a moral pattern more suitable for the expression of concern for the well-being of others. Such mechanisms are critical for holding any society together; but, as societies change, previous social control mechanisms may lose their effectiveness and new ones must be invented. The following historical review describes two major historical phases in the development of business social responsibilities in the United States and of the attendant social control mechanisms in our society that influence businesses.[7]

The Entrepreneurial Business Phase

The first phase, which I call the entrepreneurial business phase, occurred during the early history of this nation. At the beginning of this phase, typical businesses were, with some exceptions, small and closely identified with one, two, or a very few individuals who owned and operated them and who lived in the communities in which their businesses were situated. These small businesses were entrepreneurial in the sense that they were extensions of and were closely identified with the individual business persons who owned them.

Several social control mechanisms were present during the early part of this phase to foster business social responsibility among these small businesses. One mechanism was based on the typical business need to maintain the good will of customers to ensure a steady flow of repeat business and profits. For very small businesses operating in a community, this good will is built up through face-to-face relations between owner/operators on the one hand, and customers on the other. Such face-to-face relations provide a social control mechanism that fosters socially responsible business behavior toward customers insofar as it acts as an immediate check on possible wayward practices in pricing, advertising claims, or in the quality or safety of goods or services. The smaller the community and the more everyone knows each other, the more effective this social control mechanism becomes in fostering responsible behavior among businesspersons.

A second, closely related social control mechanism concerns the public reputation of the businessperson and of his or her family. Reports of wayward business practices toward customers, employees, property, or the community, would tarnish the public reputation and prestige of the businessperson involved and could be quite stressful to family members and friends. Again this mechanism was most effective in smaller, stable communities where everyone knew each other.

A third social control mechanism fostering business social responsibility also operated for businesspersons who were residents of the community in which their businesses operated. Being a resident of the community, the businessperson had ample reason to be concerned about public issues that affected quality of life in the community. Furthermore, successful businesspersons had the resources to do something about these issues. It was common, therefore, for the community to look to wealthy businesspersons to serve on community boards, to make donations of money for worthy community causes, and to influence others to do likewise. In a sense, the successful businessperson was partly forced into, and partly a willing convert to, a position of trustee or steward for the public good. Furthermore, if businesspersons did not hold public office themselves, they frequently were the campaign patrons and political consorts of those who did.

Other social control mechanisms that we find today for fostering social responsibilities were far less evident during the early part of this phase of business development. In particular, governments played a far smaller role during this phase relative to the multiple roles they play in our own time in pressuring businesses to become socially responsible. In addition, during the early part of this phase, unions played either little or no role.

This early phase of the social responsibility of business was really one of the social responsibility of the individual entrepreneur, because the individual entrepreneur for practical purposes was the business. Note that I am not trying to imply that business entrepreneurs during this early phase did not engage in corrupt practices injurious to their social surroundings. In every era we see corruption (a point I discuss in some detail in Chapter 8 where I develop a framework for promoting ethical practices in business management). Furthermore, not all communities were small, and certainly many were not stable in population during the early history of our nation. So ample opportunities for corruption and irresponsible behavior existed. What I am saying here is that we do see social control mechanisms during this phase that would work against such corruption and irresponsible behavior for many businesses, even if not always successfully.

To summarize the brief description I have given here, we see three forms of responsibility in evidence during the early part of this first phase: (1) the responsibility to run an honest business by not cheating community customers, (2) the responsibility to engage in philanthropic contributions to local charities, and (3) the responsibility to be a trustee for the public good by serving on local community boards. In addition, we see three major types of social control mechanisms fostering social responsibility: (1) the need to maintain repeat business through face-to-face relations with community customers, (2) the need to protect personal and family reputations in the community, and (3) vested interest in promoting the quality of life of the community in which one simultaneously lived and operated a business.

Changing Business Role

We still see these forms of social responsibility and attendant social control mechanisms evident in society today, particularly for the small businessperson at the local level (and, to a lesser degree, for some very well-known, large business owners and senior managers). But society has changed, and the small business, which is owned and operated by local community residents, is no longer the dominant business structure of our time.

Toward the end of this first phase, certain entrepreneurs succeeded in creating gigantic business empires that began to play increasingly dominant roles in our economy (e.g., in steel, shipping, oil, and other industries). With the increasing size of these businesses, the three mechanisms described here became ineffective because of the great social distance that large businesses create between entrepreneurs on the one hand and their customers and the communities in which their major facilities were located on the other. Consequently, neither customer reaction nor community opinion could have direct or immediate impact on the behavior of these entrepreneurs. Furthermore, such large scale entrepreneurs may not in fact live in any of the communities where their major business facilities are located; consequently they would have little reason to care about the quality of life in any of these communities. Under these circumstances, entrepreneurial corruption and irresponsible behavior became possible on a large scale. Indeed, many of these entrepreneurial "captains of industry" came to be known as the "robber barons" of their time.[8]

Though social mechanisms were largely lacking to bar these large entrepreneurs from wayward business practices or to foster in them concern for the communities in which their businesses operated, the media attention they received made them publicly visible in a way that did produce some concern among them for their reputations (and for those of their families). As a result, many of them donated money to create publicly visible organizations, such as universities, libraries, museums, hospitals, and so forth, that would serve as monuments to their own reputations. At least in these acts we see the continuing emphasis on entrepreneurial social responsibility in the form of philanthropy, if we do not otherwise see much regard for the public virtues of running an honest business or of serving as a trustee for the public good.

The Corporate Business Phase

The second historical phase, which I shall call the corporate business phase, occupies the period of time from roughly the late 1800s to today. During the early part of this phase, many very large corporate businesses appeared and increasingly came to dominate the U.S. economy. With the increasing appearance of these large corporate businesses, previous social control mechanisms for fostering social responsibilities were simply no longer workable.

In the typical large corporate business, ownership is split among a great many share-holders. For example, IBM today has over 800,000 shareholding owners. Most sharehold-ing owners of large corporations are but nameless, faceless abstractions to the managers and employees who operate and work for these businesses, to the consumers who purchase goods and services from these businesses and to the communities where major business facilities are set up. Indeed, the owners of these businesses may live a full continent away from where their major business facilities are located, or "the owners" may, in fact, be money funds that are managed by trustees. Furthermore, the owners themselves may know very little or nothing at all about the operations of the businesses they own, and they typically exercise no direct control over how these businesses are run.

Because corporate businesses typically create great social distance between owners and the concrete social reality of their businesses, businesses become to these owners sim-ply remote paper investments intended to yield good quarterly returns and hopefully to appreciate in value. Shareholding owners who do not live in the communities where the principal facilities of their businesses operate have no particular incentive to return a por-tion of their profits to the local charities of these communities or to work to promote the public good of these communities. Furthermore, being anonymous, no forces of moral op-probrium of these communities can impugn the reputation of the owners.

One new form of social responsibility that developed during the early part of this sec-ond phase resulted from pressure by community organizations for corporations themselves to contribute to the public good. An example is the community chest movement of the 1920s, wherein companies were pressured to encouraged their employees, from senior managers on down, to donate money through payroll deduction to community chests for distribution to local charities. This is somewhat like a voluntary tax that is collected by busi-nesses for the local public good and that serves as an alternative to governments collecting taxes for the same purpose. Through such programs a business made its presence in a com-munity felt as a force for public welfare. In a sense, these programs were forms of charita-ble philanthropy by large businesses, though they derived their funds from employee donations rather than from business profits and they did not extend to the notion of trustee-ship for the public good. The idea for such programs became the forerunner of our con-temporary United Way campaigns.

Social Distance

Of the three principal social control mechanisms that operated to promote social responsi-bility among small business individuals, the concern for repeat business of course contin-ued to hold importance for the business corporation. But its potential influence was seriously limited by the lack of personal immediacy in the relations between consumers and owners or between consumers and managers. To senior managers, consumers have become merely weekly or monthly sales figures on sheets of paper, and to owners they have no tan-gible character at all. Therefore, while the need to maintain repeat business has continued to serve as a possible check on business behavior, it nonetheless has become very limited in its potential impact. Indeed, profit losses due to customer dissatisfaction can be counter-balanced by finding new markets of customers, by diversifying to new products and ser-vices, by creating a monopoly on existing products and services, by buying and selling other corporations, by short-term strategies such as downsizing to temporarily reduce labor costs (see Chapter 14), or by employing accounting "tricks."

In this phase, removed as they are from the concrete social reality of their businesses, both owners and managers of large businesses find it only too easy to focus their attention on short-term profits and not on the larger context of tensions that exists between business and the other sectors of society. The temptation is for owners to buy and sell shares of stock of different corporate businesses with a concern only for quick returns on investments, while top managers look only for short-term profits to trumpet in the next quarterly report to justify giving themselves hefty bonuses and perks and to elevate their sense of prestige among their management peers. Neither owners nor managers see themselves as being wedded to their business over a long term, so immediate self-interest tends to prevail over long-term planning and over concern for employees, consumers, the communities surrounding their facilities, or for any other sector of society. Under these circumstances businesses have become, in essence, rational business machines; they are money-making enterprises that entrepreneurial owners and managers may manipulate to make the biggest short-term profits and managerial bonuses they can and without concern for the larger public welfare or even necessarily for the long-term health of their companies.[9]

The attitude exhibited by the very large-scale entrepreneurs in the latter part of the first historical phase and exhibited by giant corporate management in the early part of the second historical phase all too often took the following form: "I'm going to grab as much as I can, any way that I can, and I don't care about the consequences." Now, this is hardly an unusual attitude in the history of human affairs. What made it problematic is that it was being expressed around the beginning of the twentieth century by business leaders whose businesses had become the most powerful forces in our society. These businesses were gigantic in size and their influences were correspondingly extensive, both on the marketplace and on other sectors of society. And in keeping with the old saying that power corrupts, here, with such extraordinary concentration of social power, was the possibility of corruption on a truly grand scale.

Social Checks and Balances

The framers of the U.S. Constitution were well aware that checks and balances built into the structure of government itself were important for the restraint of governmental power. With the rise of very large entrepreneurial and corporate businesses, however, we see a massive center of power appearing in society and operating largely without restraint. Under the circumstances, the resulting potential for extensive corruption becomes a serious threat to social order. And corruption there indeed was, including price rigging, stock market manipulations, monopolies, vote buying, government bribes, employee abuse, consumer fraud, defective and unsafe products, environmental pollution, and so on. Without effective social control mechanisms to serve as moral restraints, big businesses became vehicles for shady deals and corruption on a scale undreamed of by small businesspersons.

What was needed was a set of counterforces powerful enough to pressure big businesses into socially responsible behavior. Needed were mechanisms to ensure that products were safe, of good quality, and fairly priced, that employees were treated fairly and provided with safe working environments, that the quality of life was maximized in the communities in which major business facilities were located, that pollution was controlled, that our marketplaces were not manipulated and abused and that government itself was not subverted. But what in society could serve to provide these much needed checks and balances to the power of big businesses and thereby pressure them into greater social responsibility?

The social and economic crises that big business practices created in our society and the eventual collapse of our economy in the Great Depression forced us to come up with such mechanisms. The most important sectors of society that arose during this time to serve as social control mechanisms pressuring for business social responsibilities were governments and unions. Although labor movements in the United States date back to before the mid-1800s, they typically carried no legal force, and their actions were often thwarted or crushed by both business and government action. In 1935 in the midst of the Great Depression, however, the federal government passed legislation (the Wagner Act) giving employees for the first time the *legal right* to form unions in order to bargain collectively with employers. I discuss this worker movement in more detail in Chapter 9.

The federal government also expanded its own operations and its involvement in business affairs during this period of time. Some major regulatory agencies that were formed during this second historical phase to oversee business practices included the Interstate Commerce Commission (1887), the Federal Reserve System (1913), the Federal Trade Commission (1914), and the Securities and Exchange Commission (1934), as well as many others that I shall describe in more detail in Chapters 6 and 7.

Both World Wars were important events during this second historical phase that fostered more responsible relations between big businesses and other sectors of society. In preparing for these wars, it was critical that businesses, government, labor, and all other sectors of society be pulled together to create the military capacity necessary to win these wars. This was especially true for World War II, which served as an experience in which a generation of business leaders learned to become attentive to and to work supportively with other sectors of society toward goals related to the larger public good.

With government and labor already having their foot in the door to pressure for more responsible business decision making, the later entrants through the door were special interest groups for consumers, civil rights, the environment, ethical investors, and others. The 1960s and 1970s saw the emergence of many pressure groups of these sorts. What we see today in business decision making, therefore, is a situation approximating the pluralist model that I described in Chapter 3. To borrow and expand on John K. Galbraith's[10] term, these are the "countervailing powers" that have organized themselves in society in an effort to hold businesses in check and to pressure for more socially responsible business behavior.

Navigating the Pluralistic Environment

These pluralist pressures combined with other dynamics I described for the first historical phase. Although small businesses today continue to experience the pressures of the social control mechanisms of phase one, corporations today experience primarily the pressures of the social control mechanisms of phase two. Among the phase two pressures on businesses, those exerted by communities for charitable contributions have now extended beyond the idea of employee donations to include as well the idea that some corporate profits should be donated as gifts to benefit the communities. Furthermore, in lieu of entrepreneurs sitting on community boards, senior managers are now called on to do so, and this suggests a new form of business trusteeship for the public good. Indeed, the necessity to monitor and influence the public concerns of powerful community members has become so vital in the corporate management effort that service on public boards has become a common prerequisite for managers seeking promotions into senior corporate positions.[11] In short, top managers have learned that they have to be influential with powerful members of other sectors of society in order navigate their business through the pluralistic environment of today. Top managers feel these pressures, and their public statements, especially since World War II, have reflected the increased effect that these pressures have on their ability to run their businesses profitably.

If we were to draw a moral from this brief history of business social responsibilities in the United States, it might take the following form: So long as businesses are small in scale and are not central to the well-being of society, business social responsibilities and business corruption are of little importance to society as a whole (though they are obviously important to local communities). But as businesses grow large in size and come increasingly to dominate society at large, the control of business corruption and the fostering of business social responsibilities become critical societal concerns. When businesses do not themselves become socially responsible, countervailing powers will arise as large-scale social control mechanisms to force them to become so, typically at the cost to businesses of loss of autonomy in business decision making. To avoid the further development, growth, and intrusion of these countervailing powers into business affairs, businesses must remove the need for these countervailing powers by developing the means within themselves to become socially responsible.

In Chapter 8 I discuss how businesses can set up their own internal social control mechanisms to initiate socially responsible behavior on their own. Chapters 9 through 13 describe specific problem areas for business social responsibility. In preparation for these discussions, the next three chapters provide an historical perspective on the evolving relations between businesses and other major sectors of society.

Part II

Businesses and Their Social Environments in Historical Perspective

The second part of this book consists of three chapters that provide an historical perspective on the social and moral foundations of businesses in society. Each chapter focuses as much on the social environment of businesses as it does on businesses themselves. This dual focus is necessary because businesses are inherently dependent on their social environments both as a source of support and as a source of moral justification for their activities. As you will see, until fairly recently in human history, societies typically provided neither the social support nor the moral legitimacy for the development and spread of business activities.

The chapters of this part of the book are organized as follows. Chapter 4 focuses on the prebusiness-oriented societies of antiquity, including food gathering and hunting societies and agricultural societies. Chapter 5 examines the business-oriented societies of mercantilism, colonialism, and early industrialization. Chapter 6 considers businesses and their social environment in contemporary industrial society in the United States.

Chapter *4*

Life in Prebusiness-Oriented Societies

Business in Prebusiness-Oriented Societies

There are many ways to classify historical periods, and each way that it is done necessarily involves simplification. The approach I take classifies history into several major economic eras. This approach also involves simplification, but it has the advantage of bringing into sharp focus the most important relationships that businesses have with their social environments.

In classifying economic eras, we must first consider what is meant by an *economy*. In using this term, I refer to the set of social scripts that people use in organizing their behaviors, thoughts, and emotions to create a regular social pattern for the production and distribution of goods and services in a society. Correspondingly, an economic era is defined as a time frame over which a particular set of social scripts for production and distribution is predominant among the world's most powerful societies. Using these definitions, I identify in Figure 4.1 four major economic eras in human history.

One cannot say with precision exactly when the major eras identified in Figure 4.1 began or ended; the time frames specified for each of the economic eras are only suggestive. As rough as the estimates of these time frames are, a comparison of them does help us get a sense of the relative lengths of time during which our ancestors lived in very different economies, having very different life-styles.

For example, one of the things that stands out in Figure 4.1 is the great gulf of time over which human affairs were carried out in economies that were not business oriented. Indeed, almost all of human history (approximately 39,500 years of the estimated total of 40,000 years, or nearly 99 percent of human history) occurred in societies in which the economic pattern did not center on businesses and business needs as it does in our society. Across this great gulf of time approximately 75 percent of human history occurred in societies in which the basic economic means of production involved simple food gathering and hunting;

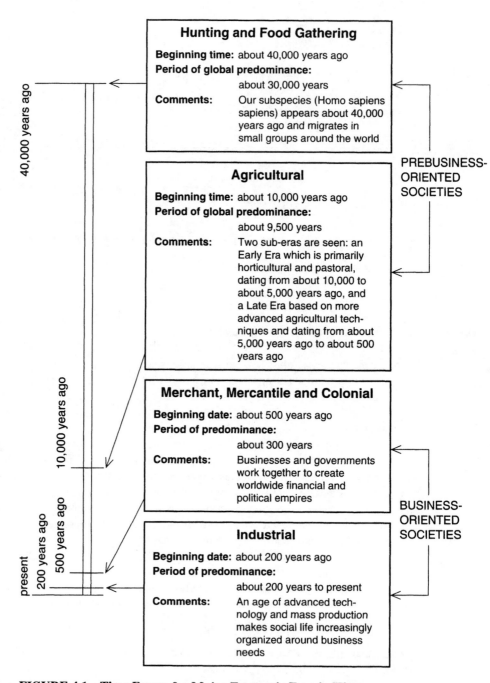

FIGURE 4.1   Time Frame for Major Economic Eras in History

roughly an additional 24 percent occurred in societies in which agricultural production dominated the economy. Only a little over 1 percent of the most recent human history has occurred in the context of business-oriented societies. In the remainder of this chapter I consider in some detail the first two types of prebusiness-oriented economies in which most of human history has occurred.

Food Gathering and Hunting Economies

We don't know exactly when our subspecies, Homo sapiens sapiens, began, but about 40,000 years ago is a reasonable guess based on archaeological evidence. Slightly earlier subspecies of sapiens, such as the Neanderthals, date back to more than 100 thousand years ago. The earlier species of Homo erectus and the genus of Australopithecus date back to 1.6 million years and more than 3 million years, respectively. The evidence we have suggests that our ancestors among the Homo sapiens sapiens lived much as did the earlier Neanderthals, Homo erectus and the Australopithecines: in small, nomadic groups referred to as *bands*. Their primary economic mode of production was food gathering and hunting; their primary economic mode of distribution was communal sharing or gift giving.[1]

The great gulf of time over which human history was dominated by food gathering and hunting economies might be dramatized by thinking in terms of the generations of our ancestors who have come and gone over this period. If we define a generation as 20 years, so that by the time persons have reached the age of 20 they would have had children, and their children would have had children by the time they, too, reached the age of 20, then the entire history of our species across 40,000 years consists of only 2,000 generations. Of this total, 1,500 generations of our ancestors lived communal food gathering and hunting lives. Furthermore, evidence suggests that, controlling for regional and climactic differences, the basic lifestyle and standard of living for our ancestors changed little over these 1,500 generations. Thus the 1,500th generation of our ancestors, 30,000 years after our subspecies began, probably experienced much the same lifestyle and standard of living as did our ancestors in the first 100 generations of human history.

It is hard for us today to appreciate what the lifestyle was like for the 1,500 generations of our food gathering and hunting ancestors. The closest we can come to experiencing this lifestyle and standard of living for ourselves is to go camping in the wilderness. For example, have you ever gone camping overnight where you had to sleep on the ground and were very far away from any populated area? Can you imagine what it would be like to camp out on the ground not just one night or two, not just a week or a month, but for the rest of your life? Can you imagine doing so with no tent or sleeping bag; no jacket, pants, shoes, socks, or underwear; no heater, grill, propane lamp, flashlight, or matches; no jug of purified water, ice chest, or canned or packaged foods of any kind; no medicine kit, insect repellent, "port-a-potty," toilet paper, soap, towels, or deodorant; and no vehicle, radio, reading material, gun, metal axe, metal hatchet, or metal knife? Now that would be a primitive existence! And these were the conditions under which our ancestors lived every day, for their whole lives, throughout most of human history.

Daily Life in a Hunter-Gatherer Society

We can assume that our forefathers and foremothers among the food gathering and hunting societies, being of the same subspecies as us, must have had the same intellectual abilities and same emotional proclivities as do we, their descendants. But their life expectancy was only about 20 to 30 years; disease, parasites, disability, and pain would have been fairly common experiences for them. Furthermore, their high death rates would have required equally high fertility rates to provide a continual replenishment of the membership of their band. Consequently, depending on prevailing cultural conventions, females might be expected to be either pregnant or nursing or both from their mid-teens until, for many, their early death. Also the bulk of the people in these societies would have been children (under the age of 20). Food supplies were uncertain, so our ancestors led a nomadic existence, moving on whenever the means for daily sustenance were exhausted in a particular area.[2]

The bands that our ancestors lived in were small, typically numbering no more than 20 to 40 people, so the relationships between band members were fairly close and personal, much like those between members of an extended family. Indeed, the harsh circumstances of their lives required band members to maintain strong communal bonds with each other much like those of a family in order to maximize the chances of survival for each individual and for the band as a whole. By organizing their economy communally so that people cooperated in food searches and in sharing the resulting day's find, each individual was afforded maximal protection against the risks of starvation or threats by either enemy bands or carnivorous animals.

In searching for the origins of business practices, we find very little potential for such practices in food gathering and hunting societies. Indeed, a market mentality would be difficult to imagine among people living in food gathering and hunting bands, given the great importance to them of maintaining strong familial-type bonds with each other. As is true, I am sure, of your own family, familial bonds make it a violation of human decency to treat your parent, child, sibling, or other close relative as though he or she were a potential customer to whom you could sell something with the intent of gaining from the transaction a profit for yourself. Rather, what binds us together into families foremost are patterns of gift giving and mutual support. These patterns, as best as we can tell, are what held our ancestors together as members of a band. Therefore, the interpersonal relations in these early societies provided little social basis on which to develop either market mechanisms or businesses.[3]

Gift Giving as a Forerunner of Business

On the other hand, at least in its structure if not in its intent, mutual gift giving among band members may have served as a forerunner for the later development of the business trade agreement. Although the trading of items or services as mutual gifts was common in these early bands, such trades required general public approval over the terms of the trade so as to avoid any possibility of conflicts that might be detrimental to the band. More modern business trades follow a similar structure, with both parties giving something to the other, and typically doing so against a background of general community approval for such activities. Of course the modern business intent is to maximize profits, or to get the best of the deal. And the sanctioning of such an intent requires a social distance between traders which, as suggested here, was not socially possible because of the familial-type bonds that held members together.

Gift giving also took place between bands and provided yet another possible forerunner for the future development of the social relations involved in business transactions. A number of neighboring bands sharing the same language and culture constituted a tribe, and bands in the tribe would regularly share resources and come together on special occasions for ceremonies and feasts. However, because these bands were nomadic and were partly in competition for the scarce resources to be found in the environment, their relations were necessarily shifting and political in nature. Therefore bands needed some social mechanism of alliance in order to reduce possible conflicts with each other. Gift giving again was the typical social mechanism at that time (as it still is today) for cementing these alliances by symbolically treating the neighboring band as extended kin. Indeed members of the neighboring bands typically were in fact extended kin. One major form in which gifts were given was through the arrangement of marriages of young females and males to members of a neighboring band for the purpose of forming political alliance.[4]

It is arguable whether instances of gift giving provided the structural forerunners of business trading practices. What was lacking to make them into true business activities was a social order that would facilitate conducting transactions between persons in an impersonal way with the sole intent of obtaining and accumulating tangible, personal profits. It is only with the emergence of agricultural economies that such a social order began to appear.

Agricultural Economies

I regret devoting so few pages to describing the bulk of our ancestors' history, which occurred in food gathering and hunting societies. But very little of the story of the origination of businesses can be drawn from these 30,000 years of human experience. Rather, it is in agricultural societies that businesses arise as increasingly common social phenomena. Consequently I shall devote much more attention to the last 10,000 years of human history, and particularly to the most recent 5,000 years, than I have to the first 30,000 years.

As I undertake in the rest of this chapter to describe key features of businesses and their social environments in agricultural societies, I must point out that agricultural societies vary enormously in their social characteristics. They vary, for example, in sizes of populations (which may number from scores of people to millions of people), in their principal economic production techniques (which range from pastoral and horticultural to advanced agricultural), in their religious practices (which range from pantheism and polytheism to monotheism), in their political structures (varying from having simple "head" persons with no actual authority to having republican democracies of the elite or to having pharaohs, emperors, or monarchs), and in the degree of their business development (with variations ranging from essentially none to the operation of far-flung commercial empires). However, certain features tend to be common among agricultural societies, and I shall highlight these and describe variations only when useful. In general, the brief account I can give in this chapter must involve much simplification to focus on the main features of the most typical agricultural societies without listing and cataloging all of the variations and unusual cases.[5]

To begin to appreciate the implications of the rise of agricultural economies as a dominant feature in societies, consider the following. Homo sapiens sapiens is the world's most intelligent life form. That is why it took us only 30,000 years, or 1,500 generations, to figure out how to plant seeds in the ground and domesticate animals in order to have a ready supply of food near at hand instead of continually beating the bushes each day for each new meal.[6] Actually, human discovery of elementary horticultural and animal husbandry techniques probably occurred much earlier in time, but it was only in the last ten thousand years that many societies became organized around these new modes of economic production.

Furthermore, it has only been in the last 5,000 years that agricultural techniques in some societies reached a stage of development as advanced as that of using a plow to turn soil and of using large animals to pull the plow rather than tilling and planting fields by hand with sticks.

The Early Era of Agriculture

The first 5,000 years of the agricultural era are what I call in Figure 4.1 the early era, a time when simple horticultural practices prevailed and were often little more than "slash-and-burn" operations. That is, forests were cut and burned to provide an unshaded field covered with a layer of ash, which served as a fertilizer. Then holes were poked in the ground with sticks and seeds were dropped in. This primitive procedure, if weather permitted, could create a bounty of food ready at hand. But the fertility of the land was rapidly depleted, so new forests had to be slashed-and-burned frequently.

Later Agricultural Era

In the later era of agricultural societies, which began about 5,000 years ago, plows were used to turn the soil to bring nutrients to the top and draft animals were used to pull the plows. These procedures could vastly increase the productivity of the land and the amount of land that could be cultivated. Furthermore, by the use of fertilizers, irrigation, and a system of letting some fields lie fallow or of rotating crops, it became possible for the same land to be used repeatedly so that people could remain in the same area relatively permanently. Thus, in agricultural economies we see arising for the first time in human history large, sedentary societies that were capable of producing great amounts of food near at hand.

The earliest of the more advanced agricultural societies probably developed around the Tigris and Euphrates Rivers of Mesopotamia (where Iraq is today) and around the Nile River in Egypt. Yet others developed elsewhere in Asia around the Indus, Ganges, and Yellow (or Hwang Ho) Rivers (and there were early developments as well in the New World in areas now a part of Mexico and Peru).

The area of Mesopotamia was especially fertile 5,000 years ago, but it also was unique in another way because it served as a land bridge between Asia, Africa, and Europe. Thus many nomadic bands migrated through this area and much cultural intermingling and diffusion resulted. But, although the area was ideal for producing abundant food, large populations, and all the other typical features of the agricultural lifestyle to be described in more detail here, this area also, unfortunately, was positioned to come under frequent military attack. Many of the earliest written documents (including the Old Testament) are from this area, and they are replete with tales of warfare and tribute.

Lost Links with the Past

Agricultural societies constituted the most powerful societies in the world for about 475 generations (in contrast to the preceding 1,500 generations of hunting and food gathering societies and the most recent 25 generations of human history when business-oriented societies began to dominate world affairs). Though we are much closer in time to agricultural societies than to those of food gathering and hunting, few of us living in industrialized societies today have any way to appreciate what life was like for the average person in agricultural societies of the past.

For example, how many of us today know the feel of soil between our toes; the smell of cows, hogs, sheep, or goats in a pasture; the sight of fields of grain and vegetables; the continual vigilance necessary in watching for the effects of weather, wild animals, and pestilence on crops and livestock? Animal husbandry without fences, without rapid means of transportation (horses or jeeps) and without a storehouse of animal feed and water ready at hand required continuous attention and effort. It was not a job for the dainty or prudish. The cultivation of crops likewise required continuous attention and periods of great effort, as in the initial clearing of fields, in cultivation, in irrigation and fertilization, in control of weeds and pests, and eventually at reaping time. Farming was hot, dirty work. One would be bent over in the fields, with hands calloused and muscles aching. Very few of us know life in this way today, yet most of our ancestors knew it very well for almost 10,000 years. From their toil and sweat came the surplus of food that made civilizations possible.

Questionable Improvements in Lifestyle

Agricultural societies presented a very hard life for most of their inhabitants.[7] The life of our average ancestor under these conditions was little better off, and possibly worse, than it had been in the food gathering and hunting era. Despite the bounty of food their agricultural production systems created, increased population sizes and ruler prerogatives in laying claim to most produce meant that an inadequate subsistence diet was generally the rule for most of our ancestors. Furthermore, famines, plagues, parasites, pestilence, wars, and inadequate public health measures also posed continuing threats to our ancestors' well-being. Consequently life expectancy was no greater than twenty-five to forty-five years. Indeed, mortality and fertility rates were so high that the bulk of the population of these societies consisted of children, who were fully expected to labor all day in the fields and pastures. Disease and pain were commonplace experiences for them.

Social Consequences of Agriculture

The development of agricultural economies occurred very slowly (requiring thousands of years) and brought about a complete transformation of the way of life of our ancestors. The new sedentary lifestyle that occurred in agricultural societies and the new abundance of foods made possible by increasingly advanced agricultural techniques had at least eleven dramatic social consequences for the structure of society.

Increased Population Size.   An expansion of food production made it possible to support a much larger population in a small geographical area. Agricultural societies, therefore, grew in size to include tens of thousands and eventually even hundreds of millions of people.

Impersonality in Social Relations.   Unlike a food gathering and hunting society, which typically functions as a single clan/community, agricultural societies grew sufficiently large to include many clans and communities. Although social relations within one's immediate clan and community could remain personal, other relationships in society became increasingly impersonal as a result because one simply could no longer know and have intense personal relations with everyone in the society.

Accumulation of Food as a Form of Wealth.   With a non-nomadic lifestyle and the ability to produce an abundance of foods, it became possible for the first time to accumulate and store foods and other types of goods as forms of wealth. This situation is in contrast to the physical conditions of life for food gathering and hunting societies in which the accumulation of goods was impractical and undesirable. In the context of their nomadic lifestyles, when campsites continually had to be changed to follow migrating game or to be ever near new supplies of fruits, grains, vegetables, and other food products, it simply made little sense for food gatherers and hunters to accumulate and haul things from place to place. Indeed, such accumulations would have been burdensome and would have slowed the band down when in retreat from enemies or when rapidly pursuing migrating game.

Most goods were simply consumed or put to use immediately by food gatherers and hunters. With few exceptions, tools, utensils, and shelters could be made at any time from materials readily at hand, so there was no need to obtain more than was needed for the moment or to stockpile or transport anything. Human vanity could be served by food gatherers and hunters in more easily portable ways (e.g., by tattooing, painting, or scarifying their skin; by attentiveness to hair styles; by carrying small amulets, totems, or other symbols of prowess; or by the special knowledge one held of magic, the forces of nature, or tradition).

However, with the invention of agricultural and animal husbandry techniques and the consequent rise of the type of sedentary lifestyle that is characteristic of agricultural societies, it became feasible for the first time to accumulate foods. After having consumed as much from among the crops and domesticated animals as required to satisfy hunger, or at least as much as rulers permitted for a subsistence diet, the remainder could be held as a surplus to meet future needs either in the form of larger herds of animals or as public granaries. For the first time in human history, an economic system had been set in motion that produced a surplus of foods that social conditions permitted to be stored as a form of wealth. As a corollary, for the first time in history it became necessary to ask how such wealth was to be distributed, and to whom.[8]

By far the most common manner of accumulating wealth occurred collectively, by households or by clans, tribes, kingdoms, or churches. Although some persons, to be noted later, typically held first claim to the accumulated surplus, all participating persons (except slaves) had at least some legitimate claim to it in times of want.

Social Differentiation.   Both the creation of a surplus of food and the expansion of population sizes made it possible for the first time for some people to be supported in the pursuit of specialized activities in life other than daily food production. Although most people toiled in the fields and pastures, the surplus foods they produced could be used to support others who could now engage more or less full time in such activities as artistic or craft work, religious leadership, war, political leadership, bureaucratic functions, or trade. In short, it became possible for the process to occur that sociologists call the *social differentiation* of society. In food gathering and hunting societies, by contrast, we see largely undifferentiated activities, with each person being sort of a "jack-of-all-trades," simultaneously providing political, military, religious, educational, health care, and other specialized services in addition to their regular food search activities.[9]

New Forms of Durable Wealth.   A settled lifestyle, a surplus of food, and the rise of social differentiation made it possible for a great variety of new durable goods to be produced and accumulated as new forms of wealth. Thus in agricultural societies we see for the first time a flourishing of art and craft work in metallurgy and in the creation of large scale structures, fine homes, and home furnishings. The accumulation of these new durable goods made whoever laid claim to them a "wealthy" person. Again the distributional question arises of who is to have priority rights over these goods. In contrast to food products, these goods were generally not produced and accumulated for collective purposes, but rather were reserved for the privileged few whom I describe in the next few sections.

Stratification by Occupational Status Groups. Social differentiation of people into specialized work activities made it possible for the first time for society to become stratified by occupation. A stratification system is a set of social definitions that identifies who is to be granted prestige, power, and privilege in society, including the privilege of priority rights to existing forms of wealth. Typically social stratification is based on an array of status groups, ranging from high status groups to low status groups, with each group being socially defined and distinguished one from another by the specific privileges, power, and prestige each is accorded. The appearance of occupational specialties made a convenient framework for stratifying society; people performing each specialized work activity could be regarded as constituting a status group. In what follows I shall describe several important occupational status groups that appeared in the social differentiation and social stratification processes arising in agricultural societies.

Religious Authorities as a Status Group. One of the status groups that arises in agricultural societies includes persons who specialize as religious mediums, guides, prophets, divines, and healers. Through their use of awe-inspiring rituals and through their promulgation of a common set of historical and ethical beliefs, these people play central roles in society by providing the symbolic bonds that help to tie the increasingly larger and impersonal populations of agricultural societies together. Control over sacred religious emblems, relics, absolutions, and ceremonies is a source of social power that gives religious authorities high standing as a status group in the typical stratification system. Thus they are in a strong position to make priority demands on society's wealth and, as I shall note later, they often did so.

Military Authorities as a Status Group. The protection of wealth in the forms of surplus foods and durable goods requires at a minimum a voluntary militia. But the presence of a surplus makes it possible to go further than this by supporting a standing army of professional warriors as a new status group. A standing military is a form of power in society, and leaders of the military are in a position to exert considerable political influence over society or even to take over political control of society, which they did with some frequency. Thus they too were able to claim strong priority rights over society's wealth.

Political Authorities as a Status Group. In agricultural societies we see the rise of another status group consisting of political leaders who serve a number of important roles in society: they raise and support a military to protect cultivated land and other forms of wealth from outsiders; they create and support a policing force and judiciary system to ensure domestic order in an increasingly large, impersonal population; they provide for the public welfare by supporting local religious groups, by staging important ceremonies, and by providing food for the population when needed from the surplus that is held in official granaries; and they also represent the society in relations with neighboring societies.

Of course, being in the specialized status group that is in control of the surplus of society gives one enormous power relative to persons in other status groups, who quite naturally will look to you for favors. And it is very tempting to go from being an adjudicator who uses the collective surplus for the good of the community to laying claim on it for one's family or clan (often subsequently conceptualized as being "nobility" who are divinely sanctioned to control the resources of society and to rule over society for its own good). It is equally tempting to move from laying claim on surplus food to laying claim on the lands from which the surplus foods are obtained. Hence we see in this era the rise of landowning aristocracies. Not too surprisingly, given the sources of power they controlled, the political authorities, religious leaders, and military leaders were at the forefront in efforts to lay claim on the wealth of agricultural societies, and they frequently worked out cooperative arrangements in exercising control over it.

The Rise of Empires, Vassalage, Serfdom, and Slavery.   The need for political alliance between societies holds even greater importance in the agricultural era than in the food gathering and hunting era. A band of nomadic food gatherers and hunters could always run away to new hunting grounds if gift giving failed to placate neighboring bands, but people of agricultural societies had to stay where they were to protect the land they cultivated. Thus, as noted here, a militia was necessary (and eventually so, too, were walled cities and castles).

But if one felt one's military to be superior to that of another neighboring society, why engage in mutual gift giving to build political alliances? Why not simply conquer the neighboring society, either murder or enslave its inhabitants, then lay claim to its lands as your own? Or why not simply create of it a vassal from which tribute could be exacted, and in this way expand your wealth and holdings into an ever-larger empire of such vassals? Certainly when confronted with food gathering and hunting tribes or with small adjacent agricultural societies, murder and enslavement seem the simplest courses of action. Most food gathering and hunting societies no doubt eventually met this fate at the hands of agricultural societies. But for societies further away, where the great distance would make their lands more difficult for you to cultivate under your control, a system of vassalage and tribute seems most appropriate. Ancient records, including the Old Testament, are filled with tales of such "noble" struggles and related political intrigue. And it is in the agricultural era that slavery becomes for the first time a useful economic tool for producing wealth for privileged status groups.

Artisans, Service Providers, and Merchants as Status Groups.   The existence of a surplus made possible the formation of powerful status groups of nobility, religious authorities, and warriors. Collectively these people comprised a "leisured class"[10] of persons who did not have to work directly with their hands as manual field laborers and yet had the power to demand as their privilege the finest of foods, goods, and services that society had to offer. This demand for luxury goods and services can be met, and was met to some degree, by plunder, confiscation, slavery, piracy, and extortion. But it also could be met in the form of a market demand that brought artisans, service providers, and merchants into increasing prominence as new status groups.

The artisans and service providers who were not slaves could sell their skills in wood carving, pottery making, metal working, baking, writing, healing, administration, and a variety of other arts, crafts, and services for which a market demand existed. Merchants, likewise, could find profit in setting up small production, service, or retail shops or in engaging in long distance trade to import exotic goods. In these status groups we see the first appearance of business activities. Their markets were driven primarily by demand from the leisured class, which held most surplus wealth and, therefore, was most in a position to purchase goods and services. But to the degree that at least some personal wealth was accumulated by what we might call the "laboring class" of farm workers, artisans, service providers, merchants, and others, they too could provide at least a minimal market demand for these early business activities.

What standing should artisans, service providers, and merchants hold as status groups in the prevailing stratification system? Artisans and service providers were more like farm laborers than were religious, political, or military leaders because they had to work with their hands daily, which is typically considered among status groups to be a debasing thing to do. Therefore although their prestige and privileges were greater than farm laborers, they were certainly inferior to the "leisured" status groups.

Merchants Posed a Different Problem

Merchants, by contrast, posed a different problem altogether. If they sold products or services that they labored over themselves, then to all intents and purposes they were artisans or service providers and could be treated accordingly. But if they served as "middle-persons" to sell the products or services of others, then their standing was much more ambiguous.

On the one hand, merchant activities as middlepersons were non-manual, so their standing in the stratification system should be above artisans or service providers and possibly at the level of the leisured class. On the other hand, although the activities of the leisured class could typically be justified morally on the grounds of their "nobile" or "divine" motives for the good of society as a whole (or of the deity), merchants could make no such comparable claims. Rather, merchant activities had no higher justification than that they were undertaken for self-interested, profit-seeking purposes. This, of course, violated the ancient norms for cooperative, personal bonds that had traditionally held societies together. Consequently, merchants were often seen as being to some degree corrupt or debased because their actions were anti-family, anti-clan, or anti-community. Thus their prestige as a status group in agricultural societies was much lower than that of political, military, or religious leaders. Correspondingly, their social powers and privileges were less.

For example, it often was the case in agricultural societies that merchants were barred from voting, holding public office, or owning land. They also typically had to register with political authorities and were closely monitored by them. In addition, they sometimes were subjected to special sumptuary laws barring them from using their wealth to create for themselves a lifestyle comparable to that of the local nobility. Indeed, the status group of merchants was so stigmatized that often only foreigners undertook such activities because they were already marginal to the societies in which they did business and, therefore, were already stigmatized.

To the degree that artisans, service providers, and merchants were able to accumulate wealth, they gained a social potency that derived from a new source of power in society: namely, market power. Furthermore, to the degree that they gained wealth, they served as new sources of demand for goods and services in the developing markets of society.

Business in Agricultural Societies

Conditions That Fostered Business Development

What did the first businesspersons need to make it possible for them to run businesses? By way of a summary, here are some of the most important needs of newly emerging businesspersons that were met by agricultural societies.

1. They needed a society in which a surplus of food was available to free some people, themselves included, from the daily chore of food production.
2. They needed social differentiation to make it possible for skilled artisans and service providers to be able to devote themselves to the production of goods and services that could then be sold.
3. They needed social relations among people in society to become sufficiently depersonalized so that transactions could be made at least in some places in society based solely with the intent of profiting from the other person and not based on mutual support and gift giving.
4. They needed a political system that maintained domestic order and provided intersocietal protection so that market transactions would be enforced by law, business property could be protected, and intersocietal trade routes would be safe.
5. They needed a leisured class, or at least some pockets of wealth, to create a market demand for goods and services. The largely subsistence lifestyle of the farm laborers could not otherwise have provided for much of a market demand around which to develop businesses.
6. A point I have touched on earlier is that businesspersons also needed an ideology that provided a moral justification for their profit-seeking actions in society. Unfortunately for them, such an ideology took a long time to develop and rarely found a place in predominantly agricultural societies.

Lack of a Moral Justification for Businesses

From an ideological perspective, both nobility and religious authorities were ideally situated to enlist general support for their actions because both were able to claim to be working on behalf of the "public good." Churches possessed the ultimate ideological justification for their actions because they could ascribe them to "divine will." Nobility, on the other hand, could use the brute force of police and military to some degree to bend others to their will, but typically also relied on "divine will" as a justification for their activities, either by pronouncing themselves to be deities or by asserting that their rule was divinely inspired.

When public representatives were elected by popular vote (e.g., by the citizens of ancient Greece or Rome) and held some power in policy making or as advisors, political rulers frequently could manipulate these persons to obtain public sanction for their favored policies. Or, through use of favors or appeals to the public-at-large, political leaders might succeed in inciting a public outcry of support for their actions despite what representatives had chosen to do.

In contrast, merchants were in no position to claim divine sanction for their actions. Nor could they claim to be undertaking their actions by popular demand or for the noble purposes of serving the general public good. Instead, as noted above, merchants typically were seen as greedy and debased because their profit-motivated exchanges violated the traditional basis for cooperative bonds of kinship and alliance. Furthermore, their commercial transactions served no larger public good in the context of societies in which most people lived at a subsistence level and few depended on markets for their sustenance. Thus, though the increasing depersonalization of social relations in agricultural society made it possible for business persons to exist and prosper to some degree, no moral justification arose to legitimize business interests as a force in society (or even more extreme, to legitimize business interests as a force of sufficient magnitude to override the power of political or religious interests).

History of Business in Agricultural Societies

Though businesses slowly began to play a role in agricultural societies, particularly more so in the later era after about 3,000 B.C., it is important to stress that their role in the overall agricultural economies of societies across the first 5,000 years and much of the next 5,000 years was, with a few major exceptions, either nonexistent or small and peripheral. Even when business activities became important in urban areas, they typically had little impact on the vast majority of the people in society, who lived short lives laboring in the fields.

Rather, at the center of the agricultural economy was the agricultural production system, in which most of the population worked as serfs, slaves, or tenant farmers and received in return for their labor provisions of food and supplies that were at a level close to subsistence. Few such persons would have had a personal surplus with which to create a market demand for businesses. The central powers directing economic and public affairs in almost all agricultural societies were, therefore, not businesspersons, but were the political, military, and religious authorities. Thus we can say of these societies that they were government-oriented, church-oriented, or military-oriented; but, with few exceptions, they certainly were not business-oriented as our society is today.

Nonetheless, while most people labored as farm workers and lived at a subsistence level, substantial development of a business sector did occur in a few advanced agricultural societies which serve as ancient forerunners to today's business-oriented societies. These exceptions are worth noting. For example, during certain periods of antiquity the area of Mesopotamia was thriving with commercial activities, particularly those related to the trade routes that passed through it. For this reason, many of the early written records found in this area refer to businesses.

King Hammurabi's code, for example, was written in Babylon about 3,750 years ago (about 1,750 B.C.) and is an example of one of the earliest written legal codes designed to regulate a society and its businesses. In it are found penalties for wine merchants who allow patrons to engage in riotous behavior in their facilities, penalties for poor workmanship by masons, minimum wages to be paid to field workers, and other governmental regulations for business. In addition to early records that refer to business, a good many early written records are accounts of commercial transactions. So we can conclude that businesses flourished in at least some of the ancient agricultural societies during the late agricultural era.

Crete.   A number of other developments occurred elsewhere. For example, in the third millennium B.C. the Minoan kingdom of Crete, an island near Greece in the Aegean Sea, arose as a maritime commercial power. An unknown disaster destroyed most of Crete in 1,450 B.C., and Mycenaeans from Greece took over the commercial empire. But the Mycenaean maritime empire, too, collapsed a couple of centuries later.

Phoenicia.   By 1,000 B.C., Phoenicia had become a major business-oriented society with an economy substantially centered on business commerce. With its center at Tyre (located in present-day Lebanon), Phoenicia built a maritime empire of commercial colonies around the Mediterranean. This was certainly one of the most extensive business empires of ancient times and served as an ancient forerunner to the more recent merchant, mercantile, and colonial societies that I shall discuss in the next chapter.

Greece.   The eventual collapse of the Phoenician commercial empire was hastened by conflict with a new maritime commercial empire of Greek colonies rimming the Mediterranean. In the new Grecian empire, fundamental business principles in accounting, banking, business law, the uses of credit, and the coinage of money became highly developed; business partnerships, joint stock companies, and stock exchanges could be found; and businesspersons gained considerable influence, if not always respect, in society.

Furthermore, beyond the traditional forms of commerce in luxury items, slaves, minerals, and metals, trade expanded to include foods and other nonluxury goods.[11] Geographic specialization in the production of certain items for international trade also occurred, with certain areas of Greece focusing on exports of wine and olive oil and eventually giving up most other types of farming.[12]

The extensive role of commerce in this Grecian economy, however, was made possible only by the enormous numbers of farm workers to be found in the Grecian colonies and among the trading partners of Greece who produced the surplus foods that Greek citizens purchased and consumed. Thus a purely commercial way of life was lived by only a tiny minority of people from among the full population of the Grecian maritime empire and its trading partners. This situation severely limited the prospects for the development of a complete transformation of social structures to the type of business-oriented, market-centered form that is more typical of our society today and that I shall discuss in the next chapter.[13]

The Grecian maritime empire itself also eventually fell apart. As a result of the conquests of Alexander the Great (356 B.C. to 323 B.C.), the former colonies and trading partners of the Grecian empire in the eastern Aegean, in the Middle East and in Alexandria now became the major centers of commerce in the subsequent period of time that is known as the Hellenistic era.

Rome.   These centers of commerce were subsequently conquered by Rome, a military- and government-oriented society, which built a military empire around the Mediterranean and into northwestern Europe. For a few centuries Mediterranean-wide commerce was severely reduced as Rome conquered, plundered, and destroyed or made vassals of many of the great trading cities of the time. However, with the passage of time, Roman commerce itself developed to a very high level in selected urban areas.

Late Roman Empire.   In the later years of the Roman Empire, three major developments resulted in a drastic reduction in the level of business activities in Rome and throughout its Western empire in Europe. First, and most importantly, internal corruptions in Roman society and foreign ("barbarian") threats to Rome and its empire made Rome no longer able to protect its trade routes over land or through the Mediterranean. Since it was no longer safe to engage in long distance commerce, the commercial ventures of Rome and its Western empire in Europe were greatly reduced.

Second, because of the intolerable social and political conditions in Rome and the corresponding dwindling of commercial opportunities, people in Rome's western empire of Europe began to settle into the relative safety and order of small, self-sufficient, closed, agricultural economies. Thus land became increasingly concentrated in the later years of the Roman Empire into self-contained "estates" that were controlled by manorial lords and that became the mainstay features of the subsequent feudal era of the Middle Ages.

These small estates produced almost everything that was needed on their own premises (including food and clothing) and operated their own mills, wineries, bakeries, and smithshops. Only for a very few items that were usually obtainable locally were there needs to look beyond the estate for purchases (such as for salt, iron, glassware, and pottery). Commercial demand, therefore, dwindled to very low levels, and without commercial demand there was no incentive to develop industries even for local markets, let alone for export.

As always, there were exceptions. A few cities, for example, did not follow this trend and instead developed considerable trading practices (e.g., Venice, Pisa, Genoa). Furthermore, small commercial fairs and markets continued to be evident in many rural areas of Europe.

Rising Church Influence.   The third major development working to reduce the level of business activities in the decaying Roman Empire was the rising social influence of the Roman Catholic Church. The elite of the Roman Empire in its later years turned from their ancient polytheistic religious beliefs to build closer relations with the Roman Catholic Church. In 312 A.D. Emperor Constantine was converted to Christianity; by the fifth century the entire Roman Empire was officially declared to be Christian, and no other religions were tolerated.

This development greatly increased the power of the Roman Catholic Church in society and left it alone as the central source of social order after the political and military collapse of the Roman Empire in the West. The Roman Catholic Church, however, held a low opinion of several core business practices, which can be seen, for example, in its doctrines on usury and on pricing.

Usury (i.e., the charging of interest on loans) was condemned as evil by the Roman Catholic Church because it seemed unfair to take advantage of someone who needs your financial help by charging them for your assistance. Usury had been a widely abused practice in the Roman Empire, and political leaders also on occasion had attempted to control it. But you can imagine what a dampening effect a general religious proscription against interest on loans would have on capital development and on business commerce in general in the very strongly church-oriented societies that survived after the fall of Rome.

The Roman Catholic Church also held that is wasn't moral to set prices on goods based on supply and demand market factors. Setting prices on such a basis could take advantage of people who are in desperate need by gouging them for the most money possible; this, of course, would hardly be appropriate for persons expected to treat each other in a "brotherly" (i.e., family) fashion. It was reasoned instead that there must be only one "just price" that the deity intends to be set on each type of good. As you can imagine, this doctrine too presented a drag on business development.

The combination of the decreasing safety of trade routes, the agricultural movement toward the formation of self-sufficient feudal estates, and the strong influence of a church opposed to key business practices resulted in a drastic reduction in commercial activities in

Europe. Consequently, by the year 800 A.D., the strongly church-oriented, manorial societies of Europe that arose from the collapse of the Western Roman Empire exhibited far less business activity than Rome had exhibited 800 years earlier and probably little more than could be found in typical agricultural societies three to four thousand years earlier.

With few exceptions, the limited commerce that did occur in these church-oriented societies tended to be conducted not by followers of Roman Catholicism, but by foreign peddlers from the Middle East. The most advanced commercial societies around the Mediterranean at this time were in the still remaining Eastern Roman Empire, with its center of power in Constantinople (where Turkey is today) and in the subsequent empire created by the Muslims in the Middle East, North Africa, and Southern Spain. The ensuing centuries of the later Middle Ages (particularly the twelfth, thirteenth and fifteenth), however, saw a general rise in industry and commerce in Europe, resulting eventually in the more business-oriented societies of the merchant, mercantile, and colonial era. I'll describe these developments in the next chapter.

The Kingdom and Church as Business Models

Earlier I suggested that the social patterns of gift giving that occurred within and among bands of food gathering and hunting people for purposes of communal and political alliance might have served as forerunners to the later development of business trades as social phenomena. In some respects, kingdoms and churches both operated in agricultural societies as early models for business profit-making activities, and they invented social phenomena that proved eventually important to business development. I shall describe some of the more important of these inventions in this section.

In view of the central power that they held in society, it is not surprising that kingdoms and churches could direct production processes and distribution arrangements in ways that brought a great wealth of benefits to themselves. Kingdoms, for example, could be operated by nobility much like large family-run businesses[14] for which there were two basic markets. A home market was created for service delivery to local people, principally in the form of military protection, food, and favors in return for labor, taxes, interest on loans, tribute, and gifts to the nobility. In addition, nobility might set up monopolies on public offices, on trade in certain items, and on certain industries such as mines, wineries, or mills and then require people to use and pay high prices for these goods and services. A second, external market might also be created by nobility for exchanging military protection and services to vassal societies in an extended empire in return for their tribute. From both types of internal and external markets, nobility could accumulate considerable wealth.

The church also could operate in some respects the same as a large business. In cases of theocracies, the church authorities and nobility were the same. Where they were separate, the church could independently expand its material holdings by exchanging its services as divine intermediaries in return for tithes, public collections, and donations and by direct sale of absolutions and sacred emblems. In some cases churches, because of their great wealth, took on several of the functions of banks by lending and exchanging monies. The wealth amassed by churches occasionally was colossal. For example, in Europe in the Middle Ages, the Roman Catholic Church had become the largest landowner on the continent and occasionally set up and operated its own mills and factories.

Rise of Bureaucracy.   In addition to operating like prototype businesses, political and religious activities in some agricultural societies led to the development of several social phenomena that figured importantly in the later development of large-scale businesses. One of these developments was bureaucracy, which is a social mechanism for organizing the efforts of many unrelated people to achieve large-scale collective ends. Bureaucracies were essential to the administration of large kingdoms and churches, and they served as a model for the later creation of administrative structures for private corporations, including business corporations.

Development of Graphic Arts.   A second development that arose in response to the needs of political and religious authorities was the graphic arts of writing, arithmetic, and bookkeeping.[15] The collection of rents, taxes, tributes, and tithes, as well as the necessity of communicating among large numbers of bureaucrats (occasionally over long distances), required a means of writing and of keeping track of payments. The resultant development of the requisite graphic arts needed for these activities figured greatly in facilitating subsequent business practices in accounting and contract writing.

Establishment of Schools.   A third development is that of specialized education, particularly in graphic arts. The need to read and copy sacred documents as well as to construct and maintain tax rolls made the creation of an educational system important to political and religious authorities. Churches often served as the provider of this education for specialized practitioners in graphic arts, including priests and scribes, and later including administrators and lawyers. Again, such specialists became of great importance in meeting subsequent business needs for commercial correspondence and for legal redress.

Developing Concept of "State."   A fourth social development is the means to legitimize the growing impersonality in relations among people. As noted earlier, impersonality is a corollary outcome of increases in population size. Political and religious authorities provided ideologies to bridge such impersonality by promoting the view that all persons, regardless of family, clan or community, were bound together as subjects to the same rulers or as children to the same deities. This legitimized having ongoing patterns of relations with strangers. It also legitimized working together with these people toward ends that were not personal, but that were alleged to have been set by noble or divine will to serve some larger public purpose.

   The invention of a means to legitimize impersonal relations is an important step in the direction of business development because impersonality is critical for the conduct of profit-making exchanges in markets and for the use of business necessity as a principle in the hiring and discharging of employees. However, the community of relations that is legitimized by political and religious authorities tends to make people feel some loyalty to each other as abstract religious brothers or sisters, as political citizens or comrades, and so forth, and these ties may impede the full development of the type of relations needed by businesses in market transactions. Consequently, as I shall discuss in Chapter 5, it is the more recent splintering of political and religious structures into a plurality of factions, such as parties or sects, that has set the stage in the modern business-oriented societies for the fostering of a community of relations among people who are bound together predominantly by market ties. It is this new market-oriented community that makes possible a fuller expression of business interests.

Development of Law.   A fifth social development is law, both secular and religious. The laws formulated in agricultural societies often served to impede business practices, while at the same time serving the interests of political and religious authorities. However, the effect of emerging legal structures on business development was otherwise positive. For example, as abstract laws came increasingly to serve as social control mechanisms for processing people's claims and complaints on an impersonal basis, they fostered the type of impersonal relations among people that is needed for business development. As a consequence, bonds of personal relations increasingly gave way to legal agreements as a means for holding people together. This, of course, set the stage for people to become related through mere business contracts, written or implied, and for actions to be judged against abstract law rather than through personal emotional bonds. Again this is handy for fostering personnel decisions based on abstract business necessity or for forming sales contracts based on abstract market demand rather than on immediate personal bonds between the persons involved.

In addition to providing an impersonal mechanism for enforcing business contracts, secular laws in particular also greatly facilitated business activities by setting and enforcing standards for weights and measures and eventually for the coinage of money. Without a uniform, officially enforced system of weights, measures, and currencies, the growth of business activities was severely hampered.

Are Businesses Evil?
A Moral Review of Prebusiness-Oriented Societies

Having briefly surveyed the history of businesses and their social environments in prebusiness-oriented societies, I wish to devote the final part of this chapter to a discussion of the moral foundations for business practices.

Businesses are social phenomena in which human behavior, thoughts, and emotions are organized in a *market context* around profit motives. As such, as we have seen, businesses are relatively recent and controversial social inventions in the approximately 40,000 years of human history. The basis for the historic controversy surrounding businesses centers on the morality of the business profit motive. The type of profit motive that is typical of secular or private businesses has been regarded historically in a negative way by most of our ancestors, as though it represented an evil, destructive influence that defiled and debased us as humans and threatened social order. To better understand why our ancestors held this view and to address the question of whether businesses are indeed inherently evil, I shall need to consider first how the human nature of our species is related to profit-seeking motives.

Human Traits and Profit Seeking

All too often our human nature is viewed as consisting of characteristics or traits that are genetic or psychological in origination. Yet we know from cross-cultural research that traits often ascribed to human nature are in fact strongly related to social forces; so prevailing social pressures either may call out and accentuate particular traits in the organization of our behavior, thoughts, and emotions or may suppress them almost altogether. In this section I shall describe two particular traits of our human nature that will help us to understand better the role of profit motives in the organization of human behavior.

Any effort to plumb the depths of human nature must necessarily be speculative and simplified. My effort here is no exception. As is true for any such undertaking, its merits must be judged in terms of the "fit" it presents to our experiences and in terms of the light it sheds on the issues at hand, which in this case concern the social and moral foundations for businesses in society.

Urge to Cooperate

The first of the two traits of our human nature that I shall discuss is evidenced by our great willingness to coordinate our behavior, thoughts, and emotions together with those of other people to create larger social phenomena. This trait makes us social creatures, as are chimpanzees, wolves, geese, ants, bees, tuna, the cells that form sponges, and a great many other life forms. By banding together in cooperative arrangements rather than by being wholly on our own, we maximize opportunities for finding and maintaining ready food supplies and for perpetuating and proliferating our species as a whole.

I shall call this trait our "urge to cooperate." It appears to be a powerful and fundamental trait in the human species that can not be overridden without great threat to established social order, to our species and to our individual welfare. Indeed, the force of our urge to cooperate is so great that we find people would rather live together even under the most miserable conditions than to live alone. Furthermore, we find that among the severest of social punishments that can be administered to a person are ostracism, excommunication, banishment, and solitary confinement. It is important to note, however, that, unlike the other social life forms mentioned earlier, our urge to cooperate is highly flexible in how it can be expressed, and the resultant structures of cooperation (i.e., the scripted social phenomena we create) are enormously varied and do not appear to be bounded by instinctive (i.e., genetic) restrictions.

Urge to Be Self-Seeking

A second fundamental trait that can be seen in our human nature typically works harmoniously with our urge to cooperate, but may occasionally work in opposition to it. I shall call this second trait our urge to be self-seeking, and it pressures us to seek both to create a self and to gratify this self. Our urge to be self-seeking is reflected in many experiences: in our experience of the sensations of our hands, arms, legs, and other body parts as being uniquely ours; in our sense of the unity and independence of our own body as an entity apart from the bodies of other people; in the intensity with which we feel both our personal hunger, pain, sexual tension, or pleasure and the satisfaction of these physical cravings; in our cognizance of the biographical uniqueness and immediate personal relevance of our birth, death, and other events that occur to us; in our awareness of our unique talents, skills, and the fortunate events that befall us individually and that set us apart from others; and in our solitary meditations on our perceptions, thoughts, memories, and dreams.

Collective and Individual Gains

Human nature, then, makes of us creatures who are simultaneously self-oriented through our urge to be self-seeking and collectively oriented through our urge to be cooperative. Not too surprisingly under these circumstances, the social phenomena we humans create typically serve both collective and individual ends simultaneously. This can be seen, for example, in the social phenomenon of foraging by members of food gathering and hunting societies. In fanning out to cover a geographic area that is as large as is possible, opportunities are maximized for lucky discoveries of food, which are then shared among all band members at day's end. Both the collective and each individual gain from this cooperative social strategy. On the other hand, some forms of social phenomena we humans create are not mutually beneficial, so either the individual or the collectivity may suffer as a result. This is a point to which I shall return in a moment.

Motives for Profit Seeking

Each of the two traits I have identified can serve as a motivator for profit seeking. For example, profit seeking driven principally by the urge to cooperate is intent on producing wealth for some collective purpose. It brings people together into cooperative working arrangements to achieve this purpose, and in this way creates and maintains social order.

By contrast, profit seeking driven primarily by the urge to be self-seeking is intent on producing wealth only for the self-gratification of the individual profit seeker. This form of profit seeking cannot create social order on its own because the cooperation of others is necessary to sustain an ongoing social phenomenon. Robbery is a good example of such profit seeking. In robbery we see tangible profit seeking that is driven only by the urge to be self-seeking, and cooperation from others is not necessary for an individual to obtain profit. Far from creating social order, profit seeking that is driven only by self-seeking, as in the case of robbery, destroys it.

It is this form of profit seeking, based primarily on the urge to be self-seeking, that historically has been reviled as evil. Collectively oriented profit seeking has otherwise been widely practiced and highly esteemed. An example once again was the communal economy of food gatherers and hunters. Other examples include the creation of public granaries in agricultural societies and the creation of magnificent temples and other religious buildings. As noted here, however, such collectively oriented profit seeking frequently also serves simultaneously to satisfy self-seeking interests. This would occur, for example, to the degree that cultural conventions permit cooperating individuals to make use for themselves of collective sources of food or of the collectively constructed religious facilities.

Extensive, Beneficial Relationships

Now let's expand this discussion to consider businesses. No economy can function unless it ties the people of a society together into cooperative production and distribution arrangements. Consequently, business activities that were based only or principally on self-oriented profit seeking could never become a central part of a society's economy. It is for this reason that the form businesses have taken as they have grown in importance as a structuring agent in society is based not so much on self-oriented profit seeking as it has been on the development or creation of extensive, cooperative, mutually beneficial relationships with other sectors of society. Thus, although self-seeking profit motives do play some role in businesses (as they do in many types of human endeavors), and businesses historically have been condemned for these motives, all too often the role of self-seeking profit motives in businesses has been greatly overestimated.[16]

An overemphasis on the role of self-seeking profit motives in business can be seen in two very popular conceptual models that are often used to describe our human nature. I shall critique these two models at this point to show that the business sector is based far more on a motivation to be cooperative than it is on a motivation to be self-seeking. From these insights we will be in a good position to conclude our assessment of the moral foundations of businesses in prebusiness-oriented societies and in our own business-oriented society.

The "Economic-Person" Model of Human Nature

A very common misrepresentation of business profit motivation is found in the popular concept of economic man (and of course we may speak also of economic woman or more generally of economic person). Economic person presents a model of human nature (either for people in general or for businesspersons in particular) that places great stress on the priority of the urge to be self-seeking. In this view, human nature is wholly dominated, is almost wholly dominated, or, as viewed by more fervent believers of this model, *ought* to be dominated by this one urge. The urge to cooperate often is deemed to be of far less, and possibly even adverse, significance to social order.

Economists who hold this view, for example, typically regard businesses to be natural and appropriate social instruments for individuals to create to satisfy their urge to seek profits for themselves. By contrast, societies that do not include businesses in their makeup or that restrict business activities are regarded from this point of view as being in violation of human nature because they do not allow its citizens full rein to seek their own self-interest. Furthermore, people who do not dedicate themselves to seeking their own interests or who urge others to seek collective or selfless ends are regarded as foolish or wrong or as in violation of human nature.

Economic person certainly is not a sociological concept. It regards each person as confronting every situation in life with the goal of maximizing what he or she as an individual can gain or profit from it. What is to be gained is seen differently by different proponents of this view. Some biologists and psychologists, for example, postulate a hedonistic-person version of this model, in which a person is bent only on maximizing his or her individual pleasures while minimizing his or her pains. What constitutes human pleasures and pains, however, is surprisingly and notoriously difficult for followers of this model to specify in an objective way.

By contrast, in the economic-person model each person is seen as being dedicated to maximizing his or her individual profits in the form of social rewards (or benefits or values) while minimizing his or her social costs. For simplicity, economists typically use money as the yardstick for comparing social rewards to costs. Unfortunately, just as there is no simple way to define pleasure and pain in a hedonistic model, there also is no simple and agreed on way to define objectively what the social rewards and social costs are for any given social activity when using the economic-person model.

Because economic person is a model of human motivation that is based on only one aspect of human nature, namely the urge to be self-seeking, its application to most social phenomena is severely limited. To understand why, let's look at this issue from a personal point of view.

Have you *ever* sacrificed your personal interests for the greater good of your family, friends, church, community, country, or for the good of the organization or company that employs you? Of course you have! Who hasn't? But are you foolish or wrong for having done so? Have you violated your human nature by doing so? Is it foolish or wrong to be loving, devoted, loyal, patriotic, or faithful? Perhaps from the point of view of your personal interests, and even occasionally from the point of view of the collective good, some of your sacrifices may indeed have been foolish and wrong. But probably most were not, and you probably would stand willing to make most of these same sacrifices again if you believed them to be needed. We sacrifice ourselves everywhere in social life because of our urge to cooperate. It is from this urge, as I argued earlier, that collective support for social order derives.

But suppose, consistent with the model of economic person, that we really were principally devoted only to maximizing our personal rewards. What would social order look like then? Suppose your parents were committed to getting as much out of you as they could while giving up as little as possible. Surely the social order of family life would disintegrate within such a motivational framework. As a baby you would likely not be fed, because it is costly to do so and you have nothing of monetary value to offer in return. Unpleasant chores such as changing your diapers would be avoided by your economic-person parents, and you would be allowed to sit in your own filth, preferably outdoors so as to not detract from the pleasantness of the house. Under the circumstances, why even buy diapers for you? Indeed, if someone were willing to pay more for you than the accrued costs for your care, your economic-person parents would readily sell you for a nice profit! But who would want to buy you? The costs of raising you, even cheaply, would surely be great. A profit might be had only if you could eventually be sold into some form of bondage.

Furthermore, why should your economic-person parents form a marriage together, or why should you as an economic person seek out a person to marry? Why spend energy, time, and money in support of another person? Why put up with another person's quirks, foul moods, or wants? And certainly why put up with them if they are ill or unable to bring an income into the house? Where's the profit in it?

Family structures would certainly collapse if economic person were the correct model of human nature. But what about other social structures? Well, what has God done for you lately? Why should we as economic persons tithe ourselves to build churches to honor God if we don't see our pockets filled with greater wealth than we give up in the transaction? Why should we as economic persons fool with religions at all; they only take, take, take, while offering at most an oral contract promising us spiritual fulfillment, which itself has no cash value.

Or why should we economic persons form governments, pay taxes, or bow down to law? Why not just buy a gun and barricade the windows of our homes? Do you get back from our governments as much value as you pay in taxes? If so, as an economic person you should be all in favor of government; if not you should be ready to secede. And what do we personally gain when government uses our tax dollars to create public education if we are not currently in school or do not currently have school-aged children? What do we gain by governments using our tax dollars to create welfare programs for the poor if we are not direct recipients? Why should we personally go to fight in a war or see our tax dollars spent to fight wars that we personally are not going to profit from? Why should we care a twit whether our country is conquered by another and our political structures taken over by foreign rule if our assets are not diminished in the process? Indeed, as economic persons we should cheer for our conquerors if we stand to profit from the whole operation.

Why should we as economic persons have friends unless we can take advantage of them? Why should we be honest, trustworthy, respectable, faithful, fair, or dependable, if in taking advantage of others we can get away with a profit as a result? Indeed, why exhibit any concern for anyone but ourselves unless paid to do so?

Is it really possible for society or for any organized, ongoing social phenomena to exist when the performers that create these phenomena are economic persons? I don't see how. Among the most self-centered, selfish, and self-absorbed persons in our society are young children. Could you imagine them creating and sustaining a social order?

But what about businesses as social phenomena? Surely the economic-person model applies in the business sector. Here we do see calculations of net profit being used as a basis for decision making, but how much of the full dynamics of decision making in the business sector is actually driven by such a self-seeking orientation? Again, not much.

As I described earlier, businesses shade into the phenomena of other sectors of society and are not independent of them. Consequently, all the diverse motivations that create and sustain these other sectors also undergird and support business as social phenomena. Therefore, businesses must count on a great deal of cooperation throughout society. For example, how does one make and keep a profit in business if cooperative arrangements elsewhere in society have not created effective governmental systems for enforcing contracts or for protecting property? How does one hire and keep employees if family members are not cooperating to raise and support children as a future pool of laborers and if spouses and children don't support family breadwinner efforts? How does one trust one's subordinates, superiors, or coworkers if religious codes have not fostered in them a sense of decency, fairness, and trustworthiness? In short, how can businesses operate without being surrounded by social phenomena that are created and sustained by our urge to cooperate?

But even beyond how it shades into other social phenomena and thereby relies on the motivational frameworks of these other phenomena, businesses fail to follow an economic-person model in ways intrinsic to themselves. For example, how can business leaders manage subordinates if everyone is out for themselves? How do you get the allegiance to the company and the team spirit needed to meet large-scale organizational goals? Furthermore, how do you get financiers to back your business ideas? All of the shrewdest calculations based on the best available evidence cannot predict future sales, though this evidence is typically demanded and considered by prospective financiers; ultimately the decisions come down to whether they believe in you and in your ability to organize a patch of social life and the people in it into a cooperative operation that, over time, will overcome unforeseeable adversity to return a profit. And they are counting on the larger social structures of the marketplace and the other sectors of society that impinge on both the marketplace and on your business to provide the supportive environment that will make your efforts successful.

The successful businessperson cannot merely be an economic person focused only on maximizing his or her profits. Instead, the businessperson must be a social person who depends everywhere on the human urge to cooperate in creating a social order. Our collective urge to cooperate makes it possible to create a business as a social phenomenon, to manage it, to obtain financing, and to succeed in establishing regular markets of customers.

In short, the unleashing of self-interest or self-seeking from social restrictions cannot by itself result in businesses, markets, or a society. Nor, as classical economics would have it, could it possibly lead to the maximization of wealth in a society. Any model of human nature that seeks to account for human behavior in social life, including that which occurs in the business sector, will fail unless it includes as much, if not more, emphasis on the urge to cooperate as it does on the urge to be self-seeking.

The "Rational-Person" Model of Human Nature

Another popular way of viewing human nature is presented in the model of rational man (or, by logical extension, rational woman or rational person). In this model people are seen as basing their actions wholly or almost wholly on rational considerations, or it is held by fervent believers that they *should* be doing so. The conjunction of this model with the economic-person model has given us the peculiar concept of enlightened self-interest, which holds that people may rationally decide to act against their immediate self-interests if they can envision a logical framework that indicates a greater gain to be returned to them in the long run or from some other source as a result of short-term sacrifices.

For example, a salesperson might decide to treat customers fairly rather than gouge them for immediate maximal gains if the salesperson can rationally come to the conclusion that the sacrifice of these short-term gains will result in a greater profit over the long term, such as through repeat business or by developing a positive public image that attracts other customers. Similar arguments can be formulated for why businesspersons might choose to treat employees fairly, to develop safe products, to avoid polluting the environment, to not bribe government officials, or so on.

In the concept of enlightened self-interest we see to what lengths human ingenuity can be stretched in order to provide rational justification for our doing the right thing in life. Because this concept rests partly on the economic-person model, in which humans are seen as motivated primarily by self-interest, and because I have already shown the economic-person model to misrepresent our human nature, enlightened self-interest necessarily fails to be either an adequate account of human behavior or an appropriate means for inspiring people toward increased moral behavior. But this concept also fails because human nature is neither wholly, nor almost wholly, rational; nor are there any plausible grounds for urging that it should be.

Many intellectuals love to believe that humans are rational animals, or that humans should base their actions entirely or principally on rational considerations. To these intellectuals, reason holds a place in life comparable to that of a divine force: it creates clarity and order out of confusion and chaos, it sheds light where there is darkness, and it provides certainty of action in an otherwise uncertain world. To them reason is worthy of our awe and possibly our worship. Often they undertake an austere regimen of personal discipline by withdrawing themselves from the uncontrollable features of life and by organizing their round of existence instead in a fashion that is as consistent as is possible with some particular rational framework that they favor. Such intellectuals are not party animals and are not fun to be around. It is to these people that the rational-person model holds so much allure. But how rational are people?

How rational are you? How rational are the people you observe around you? How rational were your mother and father? How rational are your feelings toward them? How rational were you, or are you likely to be, in picking a spouse? How rational have your friends been in picking spouses? How rational are your children or your friends' children? How rational are your relations with your children, your siblings, or your cousins? How rational are your neighbors? How rational was your career choice? How rational is your boss, co-workers, or subordinates? How rational have you been as a consumer in the last dozen or so purchases you have made? Of all social phenomena, bureaucracies are characterized by the most rational of organizational structures and rules, yet how rational are the overall goals of each bureaucracy, how likely are their best laid plans to go awry, and who among us enjoys working for or being served by a rational bureaucracy?

If you reflect upon these questions for a while, you will see that almost everywhere we look in society we find rationality to play but a minor role in human decisions. Even when rationality plays larger roles, such as in bureaucracies, we find such settings to be rather unpleasant and frequently to lead to undesired outcomes. Rational person is a model that neither fits what we see in social life nor is there any indication that we would be better off if social life were made to conform more closely to it, as it does in bureaucracies. As is true of the economic-person model, the rational-person model is not an accurate description of human motivation. Therefore, the concept of rational self-interest, which derives from both the rational-person and economic-person models, necessarily must fail as an account for moral behavior or as an inspiration to it. Indeed, our society would surely be in great trouble if it were necessary that we were rational and found personal profit in an action before any of us would do the right thing.

An account that is better substantiated empirically and is far simpler for why we often do the right thing is because our urge to cooperate with others makes us want to do so. This urge typically expresses itself irrationally and without concern for self-interest. It is found everywhere in social life (in our families, communities, religions, politics, and even in our businesses and markets), and it forms the basis for social order.

Are Businesses Evil?

Based on the considerations discussed here, we are now able to answer the question posed initially about the moral character of businesses: Are businesses evil? Our answer must be that businesses are evil to the degree that their motivation to be self-seeking expands beyond their motivation to be cooperative, in a way that threatens existing social order.

For example, any attempt in food gathering and hunting societies to set up an internal market for conducting business trades among band members certainly would have been destructive of the close, interdependent relations that held these societies together. Any efforts to create such business activities would have had to have been suppressed as forces of evil.

By contrast, the increasingly impersonal relations that arose in agricultural societies made self-interested motives for business activities more tolerable. Nonetheless, to the degree that they continued to threaten the basis for kinship or community bonds, and more particularly to the degree that they threatened the government- or church-oriented structures that held agricultural societies together, they would still be seen as evil. However, insofar as they became a source of luxury goods for the leisured class and others who could afford them, businesses increasingly became a desirable feature of society. In other words, they became necessary evils that brought benefits to at least some sectors of society. In this context, though they continued to be vilified as evil, at least in principal, they were nonetheless tolerated as "necessary" in practice.[17]

But what about in U.S. society today? Businesses in our society now play substantial roles in holding society together and in fostering collective ends. Thus, far from being evil forces that destroy social order, they have become in our time the central forces that create and maintain order. Therefore, in many, though not all, respects they have come to be seen as forces of good.

Businesses are so central to the structure of our society today and so munificent in the bounty we collectively derive from their presence that, in many respects, we revere them almost as though they were deities of a new secular religion. But, as appears to be true for most deities, businesses do have their dark side. Thus whenever self-seeking profit motives lead them into socially irresponsible actions that detract from the collective well-being, they continue to operate as modern day forces of evil.

Based on this discussion we must conclude that the purging of evil from the business sector need not entail the purging from it of self-seeking profit motives. Rather it is a matter of better channeling and blending self-seeking motives with collective motives so the resulting actions of businesses best serve both collective and individual ends. This is a realistic goal toward which this society has been moving.

In summary, if a better society and a wealthier nation are desired, such ends will not be achieved through naked self-interest turned loose. This would only result in anarchy. Rather these ends are achievable, if at all, only through our cooperative efforts to build relations from which we can all profit. If you are in business, or wish to be, in which business environment do you think you would find most satisfaction: one in which your co-workers, subordinates, financiers, suppliers, customers, and the community-at-large benefit along with you, or one in which you benefit regardless of what happens to others? Which environment do you think provides a more moral framework for the operation of businesses in our society? In which environment do you think a business is most likely to become a successful, ongoing venture?

Of course these are rhetorical questions. No business can remain viable without building and maintaining cooperative relations with its social environment so benefits accrue to all participants. Failures to build these relations, however, can cause considerable damage to other sectors of society (as the third part of this book will describe) and make businesses into less viable social phenomena as a result.

Chapter 5

The Rise of Business-
Oriented Societies

This chapter briefly summarizes the history of businesses and their social environments through what I have called the merchant, mercantile, and colonial economic era and into the industrial era. It is during this time frame that we see the rise of societies that are increasingly business oriented, and it has become common for scholars to call this process the modernization of society or the rise of capitalism.[1] Both modernization and capitalism, however, are terms that evoke a great many ideological connotations that can easily influence our thinking and emotion in ways that carry us well beyond what we actually see occurring in businesses and in their social environment. Therefore I have chosen to use a more neutral term, business oriented, for describing the trends related to how societies have come to be organized around business activities and business interests. Business oriented is a term that is as descriptive of the underlying social transformations as is the term capitalism and is more descriptive of these processes than is the term modernization.

In Chapter 4 I described how the shift from hunting and food gathering economies to agricultural economies entailed a dramatic transformation of society as a whole, giving rise for the first time to distinct political, military, and religious authorities and making these authorities central to the organization of society. In this chapter I shall show how the shift to the merchant, mercantile, and colonial economic era, and eventually to our own industrial era, involved equally dramatic social changes and resulted in the increasing prominence of businesspersons, business interests, and a general business orientation throughout society.

Although the shift to agricultural societies began about 10,000 years ago, hunting and food gathering societies did not altogether disappear in the transition. A few such societies still could be found in remote areas of the world even as recently as at the beginning of the twentieth century, so some of our very distant cousins never left this earlier lifestyle.

Likewise, as the merchant, mercantile, and colonial era arose among major European powers beginning about 500 years ago, prior agricultural societies elsewhere around the world certainly did not disappear altogether as a result. Indeed, most of the world's population today still lives in societies in which the economy is predominantly agricultural, such as India, China, and the countries of Africa and South and Central America.

When merchant, mercantile, and colonial economic processes arose in Europe during the past 500 years, they appeared first as a thin layer of development over the top of a vastly larger agricultural economic basis. Then over the ensuing centuries these newer economic processes grew substantially in magnitude and importance relative to the existing agricultural basis so that these societies became increasingly business oriented. In this way the merchant, mercantile, and colonial economic era constituted transitional or early stage developments in the rise of more advanced business-oriented societies. As I shall describe shortly, it is in the modern industrial economy that we see the foundations for the far more developed version of the business-oriented society that confronts you and me today.

Topics to be considered in this chapter include the following: the nature of merchant, mercantile, and colonial societies; the social forces that took shape over a number of centuries to give rise to industrialization; the historic role of the entrepreneur in society; the forces that gave rise to individualism and personal freedom in society; the growing importance of markets both in tying us together as a society and in giving us a sense of personal identity; and the question of whether we are better off, both on material and moral grounds, by living in a business-oriented society.

The Merchant, Mercantile, and Colonial Economic Era

In the era that I call merchant, mercantile, and colonial, we see the growing importance of businesses and commercial practices in the overall economy of society. In this section I sketch out the central features of the merchant, mercantile, and colonial subcomponents of this era.

Early in the merchant subcomponent of this era, we see only a limited number of businesspersons who engaged principally in long distance commerce. As the era progressed, however, the numbers of these merchants grew substantially and their commercial practices extended increasingly to the production and distribution of goods in local economies as well.

In the mercantile subcomponent of this era, by contrast, we see efforts by political leaders to develop strong national economies, which became a central part of their general nation building efforts during this era. As I note shortly, these efforts frequently involved political protection and political support for merchants in their home country. The colonial subcomponent of this era is a natural corollary to mercantilism, as political leaders and merchants joined forces to establish commercial ventures worldwide in the search for profits and riches for themselves and their home economies.

I noted in Chapter 4 that some of the ancient societies around the Mediterranean (such as Phoenicia, Greece, and Rome) exhibited through their maritime empires considerable development of the commercial side of their economies relative to their agricultural bases. So there were many ancient forerunners to the types of societies that are to be found in the more modern merchant, mercantile, and colonial economic era.

As of 800 A.D., however, commercial activities had dwindled to minuscule roles throughout most of Europe. No definitive date can be pointed to as the beginning of the modern merchant, mercantile, and colonial era in Europe, when commercial practices again began to become widespread. I have selected the sixteenth century somewhat arbitrarily to serve this purpose because it was a time during which considerable efforts were made by some European societies to find and develop trade routes around the world and because it is generally viewed by historians as marking a social departure from the Middle Ages.[2]

Merchants

Despite its greatly diminished role in Western Europe following the collapse of the Roman Empire, a substantial amount of commerce could still be found prior to the sixteenth century. For example, merchants, as a status group, have been in existence since before 3000 B.C. and have held varying degrees of influence in societies during the succeeding millennia. After the collapse of Rome's Western Empire, the Eastern Empire, with its capital in Constantinople, continued for many centuries to engage in extensive commercial activities. Then too, the rise of Islam in the sixth through tenth centuries resulted in the formation of a Muslim empire that involved much commerce in the Middle East, the north coast of Africa, Spain, and Sicily.[3] Those goods that did come into Europe during this time came from Muslim traders or from traders in the Eastern Empire.

During this period, Venice rose as a major trading city that carried on commerce with the Eastern Empire and with the Muslims and was followed into maritime commerce by Pisa and Genoa. Economic development also flourished during this time in northern Europe around the Baltic and North Seas. The "Northmen" (or Norsemen or Vikings) were seafaring people who engaged both in plunder and commerce throughout the Netherlands, northern France, the British Isles, Iceland, and as far west as North America (where they landed in about 1000 A.D.). Meanwhile, the Swedes developed a trade route to Constantinople down the Dnieper River to the Black Sea.[4]

Sufficient commercial development had occurred by the eleventh century so that the merchant guild or hanse had become fairly common in Europe to control local markets and to gain commercial privileges in many towns. Towns too occasionally banded together in commercial pacts, such as the northern European Hanseatic League of the thirteenth century, to ensure the safety of trade routes and to protect their own interests.[5]

The European crusades of the eleventh, twelveth, and thirteenth centuries to "free" the Holy Lands from the Muslims of the Middle East were partly plundering raids and partly commercial ventures intended to safeguard and gain dominance over trade routes. In the defeat of the Muslims, Mediterranean trade again came to be controlled by Europeans, and the ensuing Mediterranean commerce brought great wealth to European merchants.

By the fifteenth and sixteenth centuries A.D. some well-known families of European merchants had accumulated enormous fortunes, including the Medici of Florence and the Fuggers of Augsburg. Not surprisingly, the wealth of these great merchants placed them in positions of considerable influence. All merchants needed good relations with political leaders to ensure the safety of trade routes, the protection of their property, and the formation and implementation of laws favorable to their commercial activities. In some of the major commercial cities, the merchants themselves came into governance positions so they could control the legal system in ways favorable to their interests.[6]

Political leaders also found it in their interests to work with merchants to foster and protect commercial activities under their domain. In doing so, these political leaders stood to gain in several ways: by an increased availability of luxury items and an elevated local standard of living, by increased tax revenues flowing into governmental coffers and an increased movement of wealth into their growing local economy, and by an expansion of their personal influence and public renown to larger and larger parts of the world. The mutuality of interests served by good working relations between merchants and political leaders provided the foundations for the rise of mercantilism and its corollary of colonialism.

Mercantilism

In mercantilism, political leaders and businesspersons actively worked together to promote common political and economic ends.[7] In general, the "mercantilist" perspective held that international trade could increase the wealth of the political leadership, the merchants, and the growing home economy itself, if monopolies on trade were established and tariffs and restrictions were set both to protect home industries and to ensure a favorable balance of trade with other countries.

Chartered Companies
For example, political leaders might grant a charter to a merchant, a group of merchants, or a commercial company that would provide them with a legal monopoly to carry on international trade of a certain sort. By such an arrangement the political leaders could gain several advantages: they might be able to expand their political influence and prestige in world affairs; they might be able to increase their fortunes through kickback arrangements, "returns on royal venture capital," or through taxes on imports; and they might be able to increase the standard of living in their developing home economy through the increase of wealth and luxury goods that these ventures made available.

Protective Strategies
As a corollary to the granting of these chartered monopolies, political leaders often sought to protect the industries of merchants in their homeland from competition from abroad which, if left unaddressed, might detract from the economic development of the home country and result in a net flow of wealth out of the home country. Protective strategies used for this purpose included placing heavy tariffs on imports, carefully regulating commercial practices, and requiring the public to engage in consumption patterns favorable to home industries.

This era became one in which the great merchants, typically in collusion with political leaders, created trade routes throughout the then-known world and into the unknown world. But it was only a short step for them to go from cultivating trade partners around the globe to setting up a colonial empire. For what better way can one assure oneself of favorable trading terms than to set up political authority over a trading partner and to control their society as an extension of your business? Monarchs had reason to desire such an arrangement because it enhanced the sovereign's worldwide power and prestige and could result in a great flow of wealth back to the home country. The ensuing colonial era, then, was but an extension of the fundamental principles of mercantilism in which political and business leaders worked cooperatively both to stimulate the home economy through trade and to build worldwide commercial and political empires in the process.

Colonialism

Venice had for some time controlled the trade route for spices coming into Europe through the Mediterranean and Middle East, so mercantilists in other European countries had to find other routes for their trade. For this reason the Portuguese sailed around the southern extremity of Africa in 1498 and proceeded to set up Portuguese colonies in the spice-growing areas of the Far East. By contrast, Spain sailed west in hope of reaching the Far East by circumnavigating the globe. The result was the discovery of the New World in 1492, where Spain proceeded to set up its own colonies. The Netherlands, England, and France followed not too long thereafter to sail around Africa to establish colonies in the Far East and to sail west to establish colonies in the New World in the hope of exploiting its resources and laying claim to its territories.

Many great trading companies were formed during this era. Examples include the East India companies of England, France, and The Netherlands; the West India companies of France and The Netherlands, and the Virginia, Massachusetts Bay, and Hudson Bay companies of England. Companies such as these engaged in business ventures worldwide and in some cases did much both to stimulate the production of goods and to make available a larger array of goods in their home societies.

As implements of colonial power, these companies also often served as a military force in their efforts to create and perpetuate their commercial empires. The typical result was that they disrupted or destroyed the family, religious, economic, and political structures of the societies in the lands they colonized. Furthermore, their efforts often essentially enslaved the native peoples of these countries and subjected them to brutal treatment in order to gain profits from the colonial expeditions. Especially in the New World, companies resurrected the ancient practice of slave trading in order to work the mines and plantations of their colonies.[8]

As noted here, the New World was discovered during this era by accident in the search for quicker and more profitable trade routes for spices from the Far East. Spaniards were quick to send conquistadors to the New World in search for gold and silver in South and Central America, Florida, and the Southwestern part of what is now the United States. They also saw opportunities for developing plantations for sugar cane and other products desired by Europeans. France and England sought both a Northwest Passage to the Far East through the North American continent, and opportunities in agriculture, fishing, and hunting. French fur traders reached far into the midsection of North America along the Mississippi and St. Lawrence Rivers. England, by contrast, concentrated its agricultural and fishing efforts along the Atlantic seacoast, where it found particular success in tobacco plantations. England also sent expeditions to the Hudson Bay area to seek furs and a Northwest Passage.

Maryland was given by charter to Cecil Calvert by King Charles, to be run as a colonial enterprise fostering both the interests of the King and Calvert. Calvert and his family were to receive from this arrangement any profits from land rents or sales, and the King got a colonizing effort that placed royal subjects in the New World to legitimate and protect the King's interest and control of this part of the world and any resources it might have to ship back to England.

Likewise, Virginia was set up as a chartered commercial enterprise by the Virginia Company, the territories of North and South Carolina were granted by charter to a syndicate of eight proprietary colonizers, the pilgrims' landing at Plymouth was financed by an English merchant, and much of the rest of Massachusetts was colonized by the Massachusetts Bay Company. To the north, the Hudson Bay Company was given a charter to do pretty much as it pleased in exploiting the commercial possibilities available in what is now Canada. The principal commercial interest for the Hudson Bay Company was beaver fur, from which fine hats that were fashionable in Europe at the time, could be made. The political interest, of course, was to fight France for control of this land and its resources. The Native Americans on the lands of the New World either died in droves because of European diseases (for which they had no immunity), or, particularly in the Spanish and English colonies, were either slaughtered or driven off.

Wherever the merchant trading fleets went, they were followed by colonial efforts around the world; India, many countries of the Far East, the Middle East, Africa, and South America eventually became parts of worldwide colonial empires that served the commercial, political, and religious interests of European countries.

In previous agricultural societies, businesses were peripheral to society; political, military, and religious authorities were central. By contrast, in the merchant, mercantile, and colonial era, we see business leaders increasingly joining political, military, and religious authorities as co-equal partners in the central positions of society. In the process of industrialization, which I discuss next, organized religion moved decidedly to the periphery of society, and political and military authority typically were fragmented and shifted to a position dependent on business interests, leaving businesses as the dominant force in the center of society.

Why did business interests arise to become increasingly central players in society after the long period known as the Dark Ages that followed on the fall of Rome? What forces were at work to carry us through the social transformations involved in the merchant, mercantile, and colonial era and eventually into industrialization? These forces are described in the next section.

The Social Forces of Industrialization

Colonial empires created a flow of wealth into several European countries, but these empires were costly to maintain. There were substantial costs involved in outfitting and providing continuing supplies to the colonizers at very long distances from home. There were also significant costs involved in providing the military support needed both to fight off rival colonizers from seizing these colonies and to subdue the native populations of the colonies. The colonial empires had yet other adverse impacts of significance: their military needs represented a cost in human life and battle disabilities, which are always politically unpopular on the homefront; they threatened the moral fabric of society whenever slavery was used in the colonial efforts because slavery otherwise was held in the home country to be illegal and immoral; and there was always the risk of loss of all investments if a colony should revolt or be stolen by other colonizers.

Rising Industrial Forces

At work over a number of centuries, however, were a set of forces that eventually proved able to produce enormous amounts of wealth without many of the costs of maintaining political domination over colonial empires. These were the forces of industrialization, and industrial economies were eventually to replace the great colonial economies as the dominant economic form of production and distribution in the world's most powerful societies.

An industrial economy is one in which a set of social forces operate to vastly speed up and expand the production and distribution of a wide variety of goods and services in society. These forces have a long history, and one or more of these forces played key roles in the successive rise and development of agricultural, merchant, mercantile, and colonial societies.

For example, in the invention of the plow and its novel application—having it pulled by a beast of burden—we see early industrializing innovations that vastly expanded the production of food in agricultural societies and made advanced civilizations possible. We do not, however, say of these agricultural societies that they were industrialized, because few comparable industrializing processes could be seen elsewhere in their economy. Likewise, the development of better ships and navigational procedures played critical roles in making possible the era of merchant, mercantile, and colonial societies. But only a small part of their economies was industrialized, so again we do not wish to refer to these societies as industrialized. By contrast, we can say that our economy is industrialized because the production and distribution of goods is everywhere accelerated in our society.

Two Sources behind Industrialization

The process of industrialization rests on two major sets of social forces: one technological and the other social structural. The first force concerns the creation of production and distribution technologies that involve new energy sources, machines, materials, and a new form for organizing labor. Frequently analysts focus only on these technological developments in describing the process of industrialization.

Technology, however, is not by itself the source of industrialization. One cannot, for example, just hand new technologies over to an agricultural society and expect industrialization to occur. A second, corollary set of social forces also must be in operation to transform the major social structures of society in ways that both permit and facilitate the use of innovative technology for the purposes of mass production and distribution.

In the following sections I review briefly the history of changing technologies in the forms of energy sources, machines, materials, and the organization of labor. Then I shall describe the history of the corollary set of social forces that have altered the major social structures of our society to create a social environment more conducive to the use of innovative technologies. As you will see, the collective effect of these forces has been to free the businessperson from constraints by other sectors in society and to move business interests to linchpin positions in holding our social order together.

Energy Sources

An industrial society, of course, cannot operate without ample, inexpensive energy to drive its mass production and distribution processes. But the history of energy development in human societies reflects very slow progress on this score.

Throughout most of human history, our ancestors used the muscles of their bodies as their primary energy source. However, a few early means were developed to magnify or supplement this energy. For example, an early device to magnify personal energy was the throwing stick, which magnifies the energy in the rotating motion of the arm and wrist to permit spears to be hurtled with considerable force over great distances.

In somewhat more advanced developments, the early Egyptians set up irrigation and fertilization systems that operated naturally by the energy of the Nile River, as the annual flooding of its banks resulted in deposits of fertile silt and water. Later civilizations, such as the Romans, built aqueducts that used gravity to move water over long distances in pipes and troughs. As you can imagine, this was much easier than carrying water in buckets by unaided human muscles. Though early mariners relied largely on human rowing power, boats with sails were developed by at least 3000 B.C. to use the wind as a source of energy. The wind was also important in ancient wheat growing societies for separating chaff from grain. The earliest use of large animals in at least some limited applications as beasts of burden occurred more than 5,000 years ago, and animals continued to be the most important energy supplement to human power until very recent times. For many people around the world, animal power is still the most-used supplement to human power.

Rise of Power Sources
It is only relatively recently in human history, during the last 500 years or so, that we see inanimate sources of power becoming increasingly significant in production processes. For example, by the later Middle Ages both wind- and water-driven mills were found in many places in Europe for grinding grain into flour and eventually for running sawmills, trip hammers, and other types of machinery. If you have ever tried to grind grain by hand with a pestle and mortar, you know the task is monotonous and tiresome. Oxen- or mule-driven mills are invaluable as labor-saving devices for this purpose, but these creatures require food and tending and can be quite smelly and annoying. Water and wind as sources of power to drive a mill are considerably cleaner and nicer.

Unfortunately, however, wind and water have their limitations too, if one tries to use them seriously as energy sources to expand production processes. Wind power is, of course, subject to the uncertain availability and speed of wind; water power requires streams, canals, or rivers with rapidly running water, which greatly limits the sites at which production plants can be located. Nonetheless, watermills continued to be an important source of energy until well into the 1800s in the United States.

Advent of Steam and Electric Power
A major advance for the development of industrial production and distribution systems was the invention of the steam engine. The steam engine can be operated anywhere to drive many kinds of machinery, making possible steam-driven locomotives, ships, farm implements (thrashers and reapers), factory machines, and pumps for removing water from mine shafts. Of course, since the turn of this century, the steam engine has been superseded by the electric motor and internal combustion engine, making possible all sorts of lighter weight, labor saving gadgets such as automobiles, washing machines, sewing machines, food mixers, electric toothbrushes, and so on. The great importance to our economy of the internal combustion engine and electric motor has made oil and electricity into valuable commodities as sources of energy.

Other controlled applications of electricity have themselves become of great importance in this century, making possible inexpensive mass lighting, heating, and mass information devices (telephones, radios, televisions, and eventually computers). In what shape could we imagine industrial businesses to be in today if we did not have electricity as an energy source to facilitate and speed up production, and if we did not have combustion engines to make possible the transport of goods to mass markets? Clearly, innovations in energy sources have been critical to the formation of a mass industrial society.

Machines and Materials

In addition to ample and inexpensive energy sources, industrial economies also require a great deal of machinery and materials in order to set up mass production systems. The history of the development of machinery necessarily overlaps with that of the development of energy sources because machines are driven by energy or serve to transfer one form of energy into another (e.g., when the force from a series of explosions in a combustion engine is used to drive gears that create circular motion).

A machine is an assemblage of materials that has been put together specifically for the purposes of carrying out actions that we desire. The most rudimentary of machines are hand tools, and the earliest of these tools date back to the food gathering and hunting societies in which stones were shaped into axes and knives to become mechanical extensions of our fists, fingernails, and teeth.

However, tools are not very interesting examples of machines. Slightly more sophisticated machines can be created by the addition of moving parts to tools, as in the creation of bows and arrows that work together for use in hunting or in drilling. Other early machines that involved moving parts include wheeled carts, which date back to advanced agricultural societies of ancient time, and rowboats and sailboats, which date back to a comparable time period.

The materials used in production systems also have slowly evolved from wood, plant fiber, stone, bone, skin, sinew, horn and antler (as used among food gathering and hunting and early agricultural societies), to the later use of gold, silver, copper, tin, iron, bronze, steel, clay, porcelain, and glass. More recent developments in chemistry have provided us with fertilizers to increase agricultural production, artificial fibers to facilitate cloth making, and plastics and solvents that have been put to use in a wide variety of industrial applications.

A critical factor in the lifestyle of any era is the availability of diverse machines, inanimate energy sources, and inexpensive, plentiful materials. It is the meager presence of machines, inanimate energy sources and materials, for example, that is most characteristic of what we call the primitive living conditions that prevailed for food gathering and hunting societies generation after generation for 30,000 years. As noted before, the lifestyles of persons in agricultural societies were altered dramatically, simply by the introduction of plows and beasts of burden and from the bounty of foods that resulted. However, subsequently looking over the roughly 4,500 years of advanced agricultural societies, from about 3,000 B.C. to about 1500 A.D., we see very little change in the quality of life for the average field laborers who constituted the bulk of the populations in these societies.

How different our quality of life is today in industrialized societies. A hallmark feature of an industrialized society is the widespread availability and use both of artificial materials and machines driven by inanimate energy sources. These are the things we find everywhere in our society. Consider for example their presence in our personal lives, including our washing machines, clothes dryers, electric and gas stoves, refrigerators, microwave ovens, indoor electric lighting, central heating and air-conditioning, electric kitchen utensils, electric home carpentry tools, combustion engine lawn tools, automobiles, televisions, VCRs, radios, computers, telephones, trains, and airplanes. Take away all of these machines and related materials and energy sources and the quality of our lives would certainly be severely diminished.

New materials and machines driven by inanimate power sources have changed our everyday life dramatically by making everything so much easier for us, and they have greatly facilitated the production processes of our economy. This too is a hallmark feature of an industrialized society. For example, the complete handcrafting of an automobile with nothing but hand tools powered by human muscles would be an extraordinary accomplishment and would result in a product far too expensive for most of us to own. But with machines to make and assemble most components, with cheap sources of energy to power these machines, and with cheap materials to use in the assembly process, the cost of producing cars has become reduced to such a level that most American families today can afford to own one and possibly two. This same situation has occurred for an enormous variety of goods that we enjoy, resulting in a vast increase in their availability at decreased prices, and making for a greatly enhanced standard of living for us all.

Organization of Labor

Some of the critical developments in industrialization have to do with the technological issue of how labor is organized. A particularly important development in this regard is how labor is organized to facilitate the production and transport of foods, a development which both industrialized agriculture and freed farm laborers to turn to other types of work. Such a process of organizing and marshaling labor occurred in the early movement to slash-and-burn technologies, in the use of the plow and draft animals, in the creation of irrigation systems, in the use of fallow periods, and eventually in the careful use of crop rotation, fertilizers, animal breeding, and mechanical equipment for planting, harvesting, and food processing. The resulting bonanza of foods produced by these labor organizational principles eventually freed most laborers to engage in other lines of specialized work. As a consequence, societies with a fully industrialized agricultural sector, such as ours today, can be fed with a domestic farm labor force of less than 5 percent of the population.

Changing labor patterns also are seen in industry. A factory organization of work forces, a division of labor, and assembly line procedures all served to speed up production, so that fewer and fewer workers were needed to produce the goods we purchase. As a result, laborers again have been freed to move increasingly into service occupations. Mass production requires mass distribution services, and this need too is reflected in the reorganization of labor into such services as mass transit (ship, canal, rail, air, and road), mass merchandising (chain retailers and mail order), mass financial systems (banking, insurance, and stock exchanges), and mass business control systems (the modern bureaucratic corporate structure). All of these changing labor patterns have greatly facilitated the production and distribution of goods, making possible our industrialized society.

A Social Environment Conducive to Innovation

The second set of social forces driving industrialization concerns the reconstruction of the social environment so it both facilitates technological innovation and is able to continue to operate despite the disruptions and changes that technological innovation requires. As is clear even from a cursory review of history, flexibility and openness to change were not at all characteristic of most societies in the past.

For example, one of the things that is remarkable to us today about the history of our ancestors is the great lengths of time over which they lived exactly the same way, generation after generation, making and applying the same types of tools, using the same types of hunting and gathering or agricultural practices, and living at the same standard of living in terms of food, housing, clothing, health care, and so on. Why, for example, would it have taken them roughly 30,000 years to discover how to set up an agricultural system that involved planting seeds or herding livestock? Or why would it take roughly an additional 5,000 years to discover how to make a plow and to harness an animal to it rather than poke holes in the ground with sticks? Then too, why would it take almost another 5,000 years to discover how to use the steam produced by boiling water to drive a piston, and from this simple principle create a steam driven tractor for the plowing of fields?

Certainly our ancestors were intelligent. Indeed there is no reason to believe that human intelligence has undergone any change over the 40,000 years of our species. Instead we must assume that, if we could obtain culturally unbiased IQ scores from our ancestors at any time during the past 40,000 years, the distribution of these scores would be indistinguishable from what we see among people today. One major difference distinguishing us from our ancestors, however, was the social restraints that were placed on the creative use of their intelligence.

Resistance to New Ideas

Why would our ancestors (or we for that matter) be slow to accept new ideas? Well, consider the following arguments. Why should we make changes if life is going along pretty well as things are? Why try something new when the old, established ways of doing things are known to work reasonably well? And why run the risk of potential loss of one's current privileges, prestige, or power by setting up a new system for doing things?

The basic problem is that new technologies can and often do threaten prevailing social order. Why, for example, should people living a food gathering and hunting way of life go to all the work and bother of herding smelly animals around or toiling in the hot sun to cultivate crops if traditional hunting and gathering strategies have worked reasonably well in meeting their needs with far less effort? Furthermore, the shift to the use of agricultural techniques, when it came, resulted in the destruction of their entire lifestyle, including their nomadic and communal practices. Can there be any doubt that the people involved might have resisted these changes with great intensity, and that many no doubt died trying to defend their old ways of living?

Or consider too the vast transformation of social relations occurring during the more recent industrialization of society. As I describe in the rest of this chapter, these changes disrupted families, religions, political structures, communities, and nations and were strongly protested by social critics at the time.

In these two examples the existing systems of supportive social relations that held society together were destroyed with the introduction of new technologies, and new systems of relations were created with a resulting reallocation of power, prestige, and privilege. In each case, after the social order had been changed to accommodate these innovations, the new social order may be seen in retrospect by some, many, or most people as being preferable to the previous order. But all too often this was not the point of view taken by persons in the previous social order, who felt safe and comfortable in the system of supportive social relations they already had.

Personal Experiences with New Ideas

You can begin to appreciate how potentially disruptive the effects of innovation might be on the scale of society as a whole by considering its effects on a smaller scale in your life. For example, you may already have experienced or will experience the disruption that occurs in your lifestyle when you marry and must learn to create and share a home with a new spouse. Then too, most of us have experienced the disruptive effects on our lives when a new member is added to or subtracted from our family through birth, divorce, or death; when children grow up and leave home; or a relative moves in with us. Whether seen as joyful or sad events, such occasions require a redefinition of the social order of relations, rights, and privileges in the family. And this process of redefinition may be stressful until it is completed.

Similarly, you may know from personal experience that the new ideas of a person coming into an organization are often suppressed by superiors because they may threaten the authority of the superiors and may disrupt existing working relations. When the new person coming into an organization is a superior, his or her new ideas often are resisted by subordinates, who see such ideas as potentially messing up a good thing and making less enjoyable the working arrangements to which they have become accustomed.

If you want to see firsthand how resistance to innovations works, try suggesting to your parent, spouse, son, or daughter a new idea for improving their personal habits. Or try suggesting a new idea on theology at church, a new idea on community relations at a community group, or a new idea on education at a school board meeting. Try suggesting to an administrator a new idea on bureaucratic organization or try suggesting to your boss or to your co-workers a new idea for the reassignment of work responsibilities. Or try suggesting a new idea for customer relations or service delivery improvement to the manager of a small business. You probably know what will happen. At best the new ideas will be ignored or responded to with a brief expression of courtesy and then passed over. At worst, you'd better be wearing a suit of armor when you offer your new ideas. Most of us learn from such experiences not to have (or at least not to express) creative ideas. All too often new ideas are something we all believe we want provided that no one is injudicious enough to offer us one.

Despite the resistance to new ideas that we see in our society today, our current social structures make us remarkably more open to innovation than were our ancestors throughout most of human history. What was needed for industrialization to occur was for social restraints on creativity to be reduced so that technological innovation could become possible. Looking back at the development of Western civilization, there is no single turning point that dramatically reduced these constraints. Instead, there were a great many turning points spanning several centuries that collectively facilitated creativity and technological innovation. In outline form, I consider a number of these turning points with regard to political structures, religious structures, art, philosophy, science, and education.

Political Structures

One turning point was the rise of democratic governmental structures to replace the monolithic power held by the church, by hereditary nobility, or by the two jointly. Historically, both nobility and churches have sought to perpetuate themselves by controlling social order, particularly the economy, in ways that fostered their own interests. As a consequence, any social changes that might challenge their authority, such as the creation of trade routes or of local markets by enterprising private businesspersons, had to be suppressed or at least subjected to careful scrutiny and regulation.

As I noted before, however, businesspersons could prove useful to political and religious elites by supplying luxury items, by being taxed and tithed, and by lending their financial support to political and religious causes. Furthermore, the rising affluence of businesspersons placed them increasingly in a position of social power to make demands for political and religious policies that would be more supportive of their interests. But the thing that would be especially favorable for business interests would be a complete transformation of religious and political structures to make them less of an impediment to business activities and, better still, more of a *facilitator* of these activities. Indeed, the most useful political transformation from the point of view of fostering business interests would be if the political power concentrated in the hands of the land-based, hereditary nobility could be invested instead in a democratic structure where power could be better controlled by businesspersons themselves.[9]

Review of Democratic Structures

Democratic structures are no doubt as old as our human species, and a brief review of their appearance would be useful. Many food gathering and hunting bands arrived at political decisions by democratic agreement within councils.[10] Such elementary democratic structures permitted many points of view to be expressed and heard, and through the resulting dialogues two principal purposes could be served. First, this process helped to avoid unnecessary mistakes by ensuring that all available experience was drawn on in considering each issue and in identifying and evaluating alternative courses of action. But even more important, it helped to build collective support for putting the final decision into action.

When tribal chiefs and eventually monarchs and emperors appeared in agricultural societies, they typically continued to depend on councils of advisors or on councils of policy makers to ensure that decisions were arrived at that would receive support from powerful individuals or groups in society. The democratic structures of many of the city states of ancient Greece followed a somewhat different model, with political decision making split among an aristocracy of landowners and a popular assembly of citizens. The aristocratic landowners tended to hold most real power, however, and merchants, no matter how healthy, wealthy, and wise, typically were held in low repute. By contrast, in some ancient societies, such as Phoenicia, businesspersons had considerable political influence; this was true as well in the commercial cities of Venice and Genoa in the Middle Ages.

In many parts of Europe in the later Middle Ages, towns grew to become important commercial centers. Ruling lords profited considerably from this development through taxes placed on the businesspersons in these towns. Therefore, they had good reason to try to attract and keep these persons in the towns within their political domain. Significantly, one way this was done was by granting considerable civil liberties and power of self-rule to persons in these cities, and thus arose in the later Middle Ages the political power of the burghers or the bourgeoisie (i.e., the city businesspersons).[11]

Rise of Wage Laborers and Civil Liberties

In other developments over the same time frame, labor shortages forced ruling lords to grant charters of self-rule to many manorial villages in the hope of retaining and attracting free persons as laborers.[12] Attempts by lords in the growing commercial economies to make money by raising cash crops resulted in efforts to settle European wilderness areas and to reclaim marshes. For the free settlers that the lords relied on, these ventures fostered a frontier mentality including decreased political restrictions and increased personal freedom.[13] Efforts as well to turn the old manors into profit-making enterprises likewise required a freeing of serfs from traditional obligation, which happened with increasing frequency and resulted in their becoming wage laborers.[14]

Yet other political developments were occurring during this time to increase political participation. In 1215 King John of England was forced to sign the Magna Carta, guaranteeing a number of historic civil liberties. Parliaments appeared throughout Europe in the twelfth and thirteenth centuries as advisors to nobility, and burghers began to gain growing influence in these bodies.[15] The Puritan Revolution in the mid-1600s gave parliament considerable political control in England, and eventually an English Bill of Rights was granted in 1689. Then in the eighteenth century, revolutions resulted in the formation of democracies in the United States and France.

Contemporary Democracies

In contemporary United States democracy, we have a system in which all adults (with a few exceptions) have the right to hold public office and to vote for persons to represent them in political decision making. Our political system is organized in a way that intentionally splinters and spreads political power throughout society so that it will not bunch up in any one place to a degree that might make it oppressive or autocratic. Thus our system includes checks and balances in the distribution of power between federal, state, and local authorities and between legislative, judicial, and executive authorities.

Democracies that have appeared in the past few hundred years not only have brought to an end the autocratic political control previously exercised by a heredity, land-based nobility, but also have created a social distance between religious interests and political decision making.[16] Thus, religions have been made into increasingly peripheral forces in society, so that far from being major powers in the political decision-making process, as they had been in many societies in the past, today they have almost no influence over this process.

A Political Environment Conducive to Business Interests

As a result of the shift to democratic governments, a more open political environment has been created in which the interests of businesspersons can play a far larger role than was previously possible. Thus under the contemporary party system, which is the mainstay of democracies, business interests typically play major roles in most, if not all, parties. It is also typical for one party to take the lead role as the principal champion of business interests, while the other parties may emphasize other societal interests in addition to business interests.

The openness that a democracy exhibits to ideas from a variety of sectors of society is what makes it a suitable vehicle for fostering the industrial development of a society. This is seen in two respects. First, in a democracy no single authority has the monolithic power or vested interest to bar innovation in economic production systems. And second, businesspersons who favor technological innovation as a means of making or increasing profits not only face no monolithic political barriers in doing so, but have ample avenues for shaping national policies in ways that facilitate their commercial ventures. The significance of democracy to industrialization can be highlighted in the following observation: though all societies in the world possessing democracies are not necessarily industrialized, all industrialized societies have some form of democratic structures that have ended exclusive political control by land-based, hereditary nobility and by the church.

Religious Structures

A second major turning point that created a more open social environment and facilitated the movement of business interests into more central positions in society was the Protestant Reformation. For a variety of reasons to be described later, this movement played an important role, along with the emergence of democracy, in reducing the restrictive influences of religion on society. Prior to the Protestant Reformation and throughout the Middle Ages, Roman Catholicism was the major religion of Western and Central Europe and was a central power in the order of everyday social life. Its positions on business were restrictive because, as noted earlier, it opposed a number of basic commercial practices, including the charging of interest on loans and the fluctuation of prices based on market demand.

Now, as I noted earlier, new ideas typically are not welcomed; the history of Christianity has seen many reformers with new ideas who all too often were executed as heretics. Martin Luther's (1483–1546) attack on Roman Catholic practices, however, hit a respondent chord among three groups of people in North Central Europe. First were the wealthy burghers who controlled the political structure of a number of the commercial cities. Second were the nobility who wished greater freedom from the control of the Roman Catholic Church. And third were the masses who felt oppressed by religious leaders who often themselves were property and serf holders and frequently worked cooperatively with the nobility to keep serfs in a subordinate position. The collective support of these three groups made Lutheranism and other versions of Protestantism into lasting movements.

The doctrine of Lutheranism held at least two attractions to business interests. First, an emphasis was placed on God's great approval for the active working person in the world (versus the ascetic religious life, for example, of a monk). Because businesspersons had always been viewed historically as working persons, this doctrinal emphasis elevated their standing in the divine order of things and provided at least some hint of divine sanction for their efforts. Here at last was the beginning of an ideology that might justify the worldly orientation of businesspersons on divine grounds.

Second, Lutheran doctrines de-emphasized the importance of the Church as an intermediary between God and each person, so one did not have to conform to church rituals or follow church doctrines to find God's grace. This was certainly a desirable state of affairs for businesspersons because it meant they could violate church doctrines that restricted their business activities and yet still might go to heaven.

Of course, businesspersons are no more rational in pursuing their self-interests, nor necessarily more willing to change, than are any other persons. This is as true in terms of their reaction to the rise of democracy as it is for the Protestant Reformation. So business-persons did not rush en masse to support Luther or the religious reformation movement. Still, they played increasingly supportive roles over the century or so of the reformation to ensure that it was not just another minor skirmish within the Church resulting in a quick execution of the heretics.

The Protestant Reformation includes many subvariants (Lutheranism, Calvinism, Methodism, and so forth), including the creation of Anglicanism as a political ploy by the King of England in the mid-sixteenth century to end Roman Catholic Church political control in his domain. The Protestant Reformation was itself a set of major innovations in social life, but it also fostered further innovation by typically holding people to be responsible individually for finding or for creating their unique pathway to heaven, instead of relying on traditional prescriptions of the monolithic Roman Catholic Church.

In its influential Calvinistic form, Protestantism even went a step further than Lutheranism toward building an ideology that glorifies and justifies business activities. In this latter form it held that earned wealth could be a divine sign of having been elected to go to heaven. What a wonderful, religious-based impetus for fostering and sanctifying business interests.[17]

By splintering the previously monolithic power of the central church into many factions, Protestantism fostered a pliable social environment that is ripe for the sort of innovation and change needed for industrialization to occur. We see the long-term effects of this process in the world today; thus countries in Western Europe and the Americas that are most industrialized are, with few exceptions, predominantly Protestant,[18] and all of the least industrialized countries remain predominantly Catholic.

Art, Philosophy, Science, and Education

The pressures acting over the centuries to dispel the church and the land-based hereditary nobility from central places of power in society also are indicated in trends in intellectual and artistic efforts. Some of the early turning points in this process of transition derive from the redevelopment of commercial trade routes in the Mediterranean.

Europe descended into the Dark Ages following the collapse of Rome, but the Middle East continued to witness sustained intellectual achievements. Not only were the written records of intellectual accomplishments by the ancient civilizations stored and protected in Middle Eastern societies, but major new advances in mathematics and science also occurred. European contacts with Muslims in Sicily and in Spain and commercial ventures to the Middle East by some of the great trading cities of Italy provided important opportunities for the ideas of the ancient civilizations to become available to European intellectuals.[19] No doubt this process played some role in the subsequent flowering of the Renaissance (fourteenth to sixteenth centuries), which was a time of freer, humanistic expression in European art and literature.

Rise of Education and Scientific Inquiry

Other developments also were important. By the twelfth century, burghers in some cities had created schools to teach their children reading, writing, and arithmetic, which were important skills in business and market practices, and in some cases they were successful in shifting the cost of these schools to public taxpayers.[20] By 1300 there were at least a dozen universities in Europe, including Oxford and Cambridge, and there were almost a hundred universities by 1500.[21]

The increased availability of ideas from ancient civilizations, the stimulus of the Renaissance, and the growth of independent secular education all served to provide greater freedom to intellectuals from the constraints of religious and political ideologies and to stimulate innovation in their thought. This process found expression ultimately in the Protestant Reformation (for freedom in religious thought) and in the rise of democracy (for freedom in political thought). It also found expression in the rise of science and the general intellectual era referred to as the "age of reason," when individual scholars turned increasingly to reason and individual experience as their guides for interpreting reality, rather than to religious dogma or political dictate.

This freeing of intellect was very important in fostering the sort of careful studies of the materials, energy sources, and mechanical principles of nature that were needed to provide the basis for industrialization. It made it possible for the first time for a significant number of intellectuals to devote themselves to the pursuit of science and technological innovation rather than to aims set for them by nobility or church leaders. Thus we see the works of Copernicus (1473–1543) and Galileo (1564–1642) in astronomy, the empiricism of Bacon (1561–1626), and the discoveries in chemistry by Boyle (1627–1691), in physiology and medicine by Harvey (1578–1657), and in physics by Newton (1642–1727).

The ensuing age of enlightenment tied together the emphasis on reason and empiricism with the political ideals of human freedom, inalienable human rights, equality, private property, and progress. These were the ideas that excited the founders of the United States. But it is the enlightenment concept of progress that has served so often as the justification that we give for industrial innovations and for their many disruptive effects on social life.

Section Summary

In this brief account of many of the turning points that facilitated industrialization, we see that business interests have been served at each step, even if businesspersons did not directly plan for, engineer, or even in the short run necessarily support each change. At the same time that central religious authority was losing power due to the Protestant movement, and as the central political authority of a land-based, hereditary nobility was diminishing or disappearing altogether in the movement toward democratic political structures, businesspersons were growing in wealth and influence in society.

The fragmentation and removal of the nobility and church from their traditional dominant positions as sources of power in society left businesspersons as the only sizable status group whose interests transcended families, communities, and nations. Therefore, business interests came increasingly to serve as the common framework for defining relations between people in society (including relations of power, prestige, and privilege) and for defining relations *between* societies. Business interests became the new linchpins that held society together, and social order subsequently developed ever more tightly around these interests.

This restructuring of society around business interests spanned several centuries. From this process, modern cities arose to serve as mass markets for industrial products and as labor pools for industrial production systems. From this process, family structures became increasingly fractured, mobile, and fluid—in part to facilitate business needs for a mobile workforce. Mass education also arose out of this process as a means of training people for the increasingly bureaucratic and specialized employment that is characteristic of an industrialized economy. These are but a few examples of the reorganization of society that has occurred around business interests.

The decline of nobility and church as power sources and the rise of business interests as the dominant force in society contributed significantly to the process of industrialization. In the search for profits, businesspersons could find ample reason to foster industrialization while no longer encountering collective power to oppose them in doing so. The production of goods was greatly facilitated, and profits expanded, through innovations in energy sources, machinery, materials development, and the reorganization of labor. The potential profitability of industrialization attracted people capable of making capital investments in the construction of machine-based factory production processes and in research and development efforts that were directed toward creating new technology. Business interests, therefore, came to play central roles in promoting and expanding the industrialization process and in creating industrial society. Business interests are so central in this process that we may say of industrial societies that they are the most fully business-oriented societies history has yet seen.

In summary, it was the creation of a social environment conducive to innovation that made the appearance of an industrial society possible and that freed the businessperson to become a major factor in promoting industrialization. The result is a flexible social environment in which innovation and continual social change are possible and in which all of us have become freer. The significance of this freedom for businesses and for the rest of society requires further discussion. Therefore, the next several sections of this chapter will consider how this freedom appears for businesspersons in the form of an entrepreneurial spirit, how it appears to everyday people, and how it appears in markets.

The Spirit of the Entrepreneur

The many turning points in history that transformed the social environment into one that is conducive to innovation resulted in the freeing of what I call the entrepreneurial spirit as a force in society. In Chapter 4 I showed how two traits in human nature were reflected in businesses: the urge to cooperate and the urge to be self-seeking. In examining the role of the entrepreneurial spirit as a force in the industrialization of society, we need to consider an additional trait, the urge to create.

The Urge to Create

An urge to create sets Homo sapiens apart from other species. It is evidenced by the great plasticity or variability in how we respond to our environment, and examples of it abound almost everywhere in social life. We see this urge in the playful babbling and cooing of babies, in the impromptu games of children, in day dreaming, in home crafts and cooking, in art and science, and, foremost, in our ability to ad-lib script changes in social life. And, as is true for the urges to cooperate and to be self-seeking, prevailing social scripts may either facilitate or suppress our urge to create.

We can define the entrepreneur in general terms as an individual who creates business activities as new social phenomena. Obviously, not all businesspersons are entrepreneurs, because many persons involved in businesses do not create new business activities; instead, they manage existing businesses or carry out specialty functions as salaried employees. Note also that by this definition, the creations of entrepreneurs are social phenomena. It follows that the entrepreneur cannot act entirely on his or her own because social phenomena require the coordination of the actions of several people. Therefore, unlike the creative products of the theorist, the sculptor, or the writer, the entrepreneur must create cooperative arrangements with other people.

In the popular view, the entrepreneur is believed to be motivated by self-seeking motives and is held up as the ultimate example of individualism. Yet following from the discussions of Chapter 4, we can see from a sociological perspective that it is the urge to cooperate, rather than the urge to be self-seeking, that is essential to the entrepreneur's creations. Unless an individual has a strong urge to cooperate, the expression of his or her urge to create will not result in new business activities or in any other social creations.

For example, the entrepreneur must develop cooperative arrangements with customers to sell a product or service; if you have ever worked as a salesperson, you know how much interpersonal skill, tact, and customer management this requires. The entrepreneur also must develop cooperative arrangements with suppliers to maintain an adequate inventory of goods or materials at favorable prices; again, successful relations with wholesalers require creative social skills that few people master with proficiency. The entrepreneur also must manage both financiers and employees with great adroitness. Neighbors surrounding a business must be placated, and the demands and concerns of political authorities likewise must be addressed with timely care. In short, the entrepreneur's challenge is a social one from beginning to end, and a person lacking in the social skills of getting other people to cooperate can never be an entrepreneur no matter how creative he or she is.

The melding of the urge to create with the urge to cooperate is seen, of course, in many places in social life, including in the development of new churches or religious movements, in the creation of political movements and in developing voter support for a politician, in the creation of new family units, in the creation of new educational institutions or curricula, in the development of new public services, and so on. In a sense, we might say that the general spirit that motivates the entrepreneur is found everywhere in social life when individuals seek to create new social order. However, it is the specific application of this spirit to the creation of business activities that we wish to refer to with the term entrepreneur.

It would be useful at this point to consider how the urge to be self-seeking relates to entrepreneurial activities. The ultimate self-seeking person is the economic person; but, as I discussed in Chapter 4, such a person could hardly function successfully in business or in any other sector of social life. Thus, regardless of whether an entrepreneur does or does not have self-seeking motives, he or she must be motivated even more so by urges to be cooperative and creative. The desires to be creative and to get people to go along with an enterprise are what principally motivate entrepreneurs, and the fulfillment of these desires is likely to give the entrepreneur the greatest personal satisfaction.

The Rise of the Entrepreneur

Having now considered the nature of the entrepreneur from the perspectives of three traits of our human nature, let's draw on prior discussions to conclude this section with a brief account of the rise of entrepreneurs in society. Obviously, social order must *permit* business activities before entrepreneurs can come into existence. But for entrepreneurs to gain ascendancy in society, social order must go further than merely permitting business activities to occur; it must *encourage* them. As described in the previous chapter, the conditions faced by our food gathering and hunting ancestors neither permitted nor encouraged the appearance of entrepreneurs in their societies, as business actions would not have been consistent with their social order. In such societies the creative, cooperative spirit that otherwise might have found expression through entrepreneurialship was likely instead to be channeled into other endeavors, such as organizing hunting expeditions, staging special tribal events, or representing the band in negotiations with other bands.

The conditions of agricultural societies did permit expression of an entrepreneurial spirit through the creation of some business activities, but the political and religious authorities typically suppressed these activities whenever it appeared that the innovative activities might threaten their control of the economy. So the business sector remained small in scale and the entrepreneur typically held low status. As will be highlighted in the last section of this chapter, however, business entrepreneurs faced the ideal conditions for their ascendancy in society when the social structures of society were changed both to permit and to encourage innovation. In the newly freed entrepreneurial spirit—in its scrambling to create and apply new technology for purposes of facilitating production, expanding output, and increasing profits—businesses came to play a central role in the industrial revolution.

Individualism and Personal Freedom

Individualism and *freedom* are often held to be hallmark characteristics of business-oriented societies. There is much truth to this view. The major social structural changes described earlier that resulted in a business-oriented society and that removed many traditional restraints on the entrepreneur also removed many traditional restraints on all persons throughout society. The removal of these restraints "individualized" ordinary people; for the first time in human history, ordinary people were expected to take action as individuals and to make free choices, on their own, concerning many significant issues in their lives. This expectation was not placed on our earlier ancestors; it is an expectation that does not leave us feeling altogether comfortable today.

New Problems for the Individual

These points can be made more clearly through the following illustration. We are expected to "stand on our own two feet" in making free decisions about many major life events, and we are expected to be able to make a number of these decisions during our adolescence. Let's contrast the situation today with what would have confronted one of our typical ancestors in an agricultural society who perhaps was an adolescent serf bound to the land. Let's say that this person is your distant grandmother or grandfather from many generations ago living in about the year 1000 A.D. Consider some of the major questions that face an adolescent of our own society today, then ask yourself how this typical ancestor would have responded to them.

Occupation.   First, "What will you 'be' when you reach adulthood; that is, what occupation will you choose?" This is a perfectly sensible question to us today, but what sense could it possibly have had to our ancestor, when all his or her ancestors had worked the land, all his or her relatives worked the land and all his or her friends and neighbors did likewise? For our typical ancestor, there simply would have been no expectations that individual decisions were supposed to be made about occupations or careers. Not just serfs and slaves worked the lands, but most freepersons did likewise and had little alternative to doing so. A question about future career, a major question confronting our adolescents today, simply would not have been asked because the social order of our ancestors was not structured in a way to make this question meaningful.

Life Partner.   Now let's consider marriage.

"Will you marry?" "When will you marry?" "Who will you marry?" All of us today face these questions, but these too were questions for which individual decisions were not expected of our ancestors. The elders played major roles in making these decisions, as did religious and political authorities. A marriage had too many religious, political, and family implications for decisions to be left in the hands of the individuals directly involved.

Residential Choice.   "Where will you live as an adult?" This is a sensible question today, but what sense could it make to our ancestor? Our ancestor would have been born, lived out his or her life, and died within a geographic radius of ten miles or less.

Education.   Think about education. "Will you go to college?" "What college will you go to?" "What will be your 'major'?" These questions would surely be incomprehensible to our ancestors. Education would have been for only a select few and was conducted in places far away. Our typical ancestor would never have attended a day of schooling and would not have expected or wanted to.

Church and Politics.   What about church and politics? Let's ask: "Which religious faith will you accept as your own, and which political party will you eventually join and vote for?" For our ancestor this kind of talk would have been heretical and treasonous. These were not questions to be decided by individuals, or even to be asked. Even idle talk about such topics might result in being tortured, imprisoned, or burned at the stake.

Lifestyle.   Let's consider lifestyle. "What kind of car will you buy?" "What style of clothing will you wear this year?" "Where will you spend your next vacation?" These certainly would be foolish questions for our ancestor. Although there were no cars, there were horses and carts; but our typical ancestor would not have been able to afford such luxuries. It is unlikely that our typical ancestor had any money or much in the way of valuable items for trade. Furthermore, markets where he or she could spend money or engage in trades were rare and offered little in the way of goods and services. Opportunities to make individual choices in creating a personal lifestyle by purchasing goods or services in a marketplace were therefore rare. Consequently there were few opportunities to live differently than any of the surrounding field-laboring families.

Historical Lack of Choice

As these illustrations indicate, the situation confronting our typical agricultural ancestor made few demands for individual choices, and in most cases it suppressed individual choice. In other words, it not only did not encourage free choice, it often did not *permit* it. Social life in agricultural societies, in short, did not rely on individual choices and, therefore, did not make inhabitants into individuals who possess ranges of options from which they had the freedom to choose.

Current Choice Overload

Contrast this situation with what we see in society today. The adolescent or young adult today is expected to find within his or her own self the ability to make a great number of major life decisions as an individual by freely choosing from among a staggering array of available options. He or she is expected to win his or her way through school based on individual accomplishments; to select and court from all possible persons a marital partner on his or her own; to choose whether to go to college and which of many colleges to attend; to choose his or her own career path from a myriad of possibilities; to choose where, from Key West, Florida, to Nome, Alaska, to live; to make as an individual a personal commitment to a complex religious faith; to choose as well which among many politicians and complex, political views to support; and to construct a personal lifestyle from the enormous diversity of products and services that our markets make available to us.

Is it any wonder that teenagers in our society feel stressed by the many demands made of them to be self-directed, free individuals? Is it any wonder that uncertainty, anxiety, and a sense of existential void are widespread, and arose as societies became increasingly business-oriented?[22] And is it any wonder under these circumstances that a common response has been to create escape mechanisms by refusing to make decisions: by not voting or by voting for people based on no other consideration than that their names seem recognizable, by not attending church or by paying little attention to church doctrine, by delaying marriage or by handling it badly and then getting out of it through divorce, by letting prevailing fad or fashion dictate lifestyle, and by generally bumbling along in life, letting luck and whimsy determine our occupational career path and our decisions about money, marriage, lifestyle, and places to live?

Complete Freedom Socially Impossible

It should be clear from the foregoing illustrations that individualism and freedom refer to social structural arrangements in society which emphasize individual decision making in the many forms I have highlighted. The possibility of social structural conditions being formed to foster complete individualism and freedom is, of course, unthinkable for at least three reasons.

Physiological Constraints.   First, as noted in the Chapter 1, the physical conditions of our environment and of our physiology place limits on the freedom of what we can do, and these limits may be difficult or impossible to modify or remove. For example, we cannot grow wings and fly away just because we choose to do so. Nor will individual choice allow us to run foot races from New York to London.

Social Restraints.   A second restriction on individual freedom concerns the necessity of social limits on our decision making if we are to maintain social and moral order. Should we, for example, allow incest, drug peddling, truancy from school, price fixing in the marketplace, private ownership of nuclear weapons, vote buying, vigilante justice, or the dumping of toxic wastes into public rivers just because individual people want to do such things? There are limits on the degree to which freedom and individualism can be permitted, and beyond which society would collapse into political anarchy and social chaos.

Psychological Constraints.   A third restriction, as suggested here, concerns the fact that increasing conditions of individualization and freedom quickly overtax our limited cognitive capacity for decision making. In response, we seek out ways to escape from freedom[23] through alcohol, drugs, or sexual excess; through entertainment such as television, movies, organized sports, books, and magazines; or in compulsively slavish devotion to family, job, career, school, church, hobbies, cults, fads, political ideology, and so forth.

The extent to which freedom of choice is physically, socially, and cognitively tolerable is unknown. Much passionate debate occurs in our society over the need for each proposed, newly implemented, or existing public policy that limits freedom of choice. For the business sector, government control over business decision making is the most frequently debated issue; the next three chapters consider this issue.

I have said that individualism and freedom are hallmarks of our business-oriented society. Nonetheless it should be clear from the preceding discussion that we neither are ultimately free as individuals, nor shall we ever become so. Rather, business-oriented societies have made us freer and more individualized in decision making than have agricultural or food gathering and hunting societies.

Also note: I do not claim that business-oriented societies make all of us equally free or equally individualized. Freedom of choice is a privilege; as is true for all privileges, it is unequally distributed in society, so the prevailing social stratification system constrains some status groups more than others. Furthermore, increased freedom for some in society may come at the cost of decreased freedom for others. We'll consider these issues further in the next two chapters.

Markets

As societies have become increasingly business oriented, they necessarily also have become increasingly market oriented. This follows from the definition of businesses given in Chapter 1: businesses are social phenomena that organize behavior, thoughts, and emotions into a profit-making pattern involving regular exchanges in a market. Finding and developing a market is therefore a critical component of business activities. And free enterprise and the free market are terms that express the freedom of individual decision making in the market in general. This section will discuss how markets in a business-oriented society have come to tie us together as a society, how they provide us with personal identities, how they are controlled by businesses, and how they influence social inequality and social tolerance in society.

Markets Bind Society

To a remarkable degree, markets in a business-oriented society shape our everyday lives and our relations with others. Markets did not exist for our food gathering and hunting ancestors. Furthermore they were small, infrequent, and peripheral to the lives of our agricultural ancestors. But for people in business-oriented societies today, markets have become the central mechanisms that tie us together as communities and as a society. This is especially important as common religious and autocratic political authorities no longer serve this purpose.

Through markets, you and I are able to interact with anyone in our society regardless of their family, religion, political views, gender, race, ethnicity, age, or any other characteristic. A common set of market rituals binds us together as a society despite our great diversity. For example, though you and I may not know any particular steelworker, banker, hospital administrator, trash collector, or any person performing any of several of thousands of different types of jobs in our society, we know that we need these people to do their jobs so our lives will continue to include the wide array of goods and services that we enjoy and that make our standard of living high. And as consumers of goods and services in the market, we also know that our own occupational activities contribute to the array of goods and services.[24]

The Role of Markets

To appreciate the role of markets in our lives, consider the following. If markets somehow were to disappear overnight from our society, the effects would be catastrophic because we would no longer have a common basis for holding society together. Without markets, businesses could no longer function and would have to close. Consequently, all persons employed in businesses would be out of work and without means of support. The effects on our democratic governments would be equally severe because, without revenues from corporate taxes, sales taxes and income and property taxes from business employees, governments would not be able to sustain their operations. Without these sources of revenues, public services would be greatly disrupted and probably halted altogether, including schools, sanitation, military, police, public health, public assistance, and so forth, resulting in widespread loss of jobs for public employees. Furthermore, without markets, private suppliers of these same services would also disappear. Disappearance of markets also would destroy the small, nuclear family structure and force us to return to larger, clan-based structures which are more appropriate for scavenging for food and for mutual care giving.

In short, our society would collapse if markets were to cease to exist, because markets in the business-oriented society hold us together. This is a fact that was not true in prebusiness-oriented societies, where the disappearance of markets would have had relatively little effect on society. Markets not only tie us together, they also are central forces in providing us with personal identities. Most of "who" we are is "what we do," and what we do in life today is market-centered in two critical respects: in our employment and in the pattern of consumption that constitutes our lifestyle.

Markets Provide Personal Identities

Ask most adults in the United States who they are and, after giving their name, their next most likely response is their occupation. Most of us spend our childhood dreaming about what we will "be" when we grow up, and then most of the rest of our life trying to be the occupational specialist or succession of occupational specialists we have chosen. The loss of a job, therefore, is a great blow to us partly because we lose at the same time a major part of our identity and legitimacy as a person. If markets were to disappear overnight, the major mechanisms in our society for employment would disappear and we all would be left with less crystallized and less legitimate personal identities.

Our identities derive as well from the market products and services that we consume in creating a lifestyle. Look around you right now at all the parts of your immediate environment that derive from markets and collectively characterize your lifestyle. Just about everything you see comes from a market. This book is one example. But also coming from markets are the other things you see around you: chairs, tables and other furniture; rugs and floor coverings; sheetrock and paint; moldings, doors, windows, curtains, window shades, and light fixtures; paper, pencils, and pens; and food and clothing.

Your home or apartment structure itself comes from a market, as do your household appliances, your car, and quite possibly even the grass and trees on your lawn and your family pet as well! Markets also provide an enormous array of services that we enjoy: hair trimming and styling; entertainment in the form of television shows, movies, plays, or sporting events; restaurants and overnight lodging; banking, financial assistance, and insurance; health care and legal assistance; repair services of many types; and so on. If markets were to disappear overnight, the source of virtually all goods and services that constitute our lifestyle would be gone and our standard of living would be diminished as a result to—at best—a subsistence level. If this were to happen, *then* "who would you be"?

All of this is in great contrast to the lives of our ancestors. Whereas they drew their identity principally from family or clan, church, and (possibly) political authority and were bound together through their common orientation to these entities, our identity and social ties hinge instead directly on business markets. Such is the nature of our lives in a business-oriented society.

The Control of Markets

The concept of a free market as an ideal is much courted in theoretical rhetoric, while remaining friendless in everyday life. Free markets, of course, would by definition be unpredictable. But as our current social order and our personal identities are directly dependent on markets, we all have ample reason to wish to control markets to make them more predictably to our advantage, and to reduce the level of risk that unpredicatability in the market presents.

Golden Egg Analogy

Consider the following analogy. If there really were a goose that laid golden eggs and this goose were left totally free to go where it wished, we might never obtain a golden egg from it. At a minimum, therefore, we would want to know at all times where the goose was, what the goose was doing, and whether there were any threats to its health and safety. This would require oversight and intervention whenever needed.

Like a golden-egg laying goose, our markets are capable of providing great wealth, but if they were left on their own *we* may not get any of the wealth. It should come as no surprise, therefore, that both the business and government sectors practice considerable oversight and intervention in markets. The business sector intervenes through monopoly, price fixing, and a variety of other techniques; government intervenes through a great many regulatory processes.

How Businesses Control Markets

Let's consider here several ways in which businesses control their markets. It is often said of the free market that it is driven by consumer demand; but though there is some truth to this assertion, it is very much an overstatement. In reality, businesses have been able to gain control over many parts of the marketplace either by restricting market choices or by stimulating and channeling consumer demand.

The free market is a concept that is attractive at an abstract level only to theoreticians, statisticians, ideological zealots, and a few other persons who are removed from actual markets. For those directly involved in markets, it is a concept that has no allure. Rather, business efforts to control their markets are the most natural of actions to expect of them, and examples of their successes in these efforts abound throughout our economy. In controlling their markets, businesses, so to speak, control the goose that lays golden eggs and thereby ensure their access to these golden eggs.

Socially Sanctioned Monopolies.   Consider the following examples. Businesspersons have often sought to control their markets by creating monopolies so they can set prices at levels that return a level of profit deemed reasonable to them. We see this in the merchant and craft guilds of several centuries ago which were established to certify competence, to regulate and limit competition, and to set prices and standards for quality. We also see it in the legal monopolies on trade routes given to businesses during the mercantile era. More recently, legal monopolies have been created in our society in local gas and electric service, phone service, and some forms of mass transportation. Usually these arrangements are quite profitable for the companies involved (though they give up considerable freedom in decision making to a government-imposed regulatory oversight group).

Market Concentration.   Another contemporary way to monopolize markets is through market concentration, a phenomenon I'll describe in detail in the next chapter. In market concentration, the market for a product or service comes increasingly to be controlled by fewer and fewer companies. Thus, when a few big automakers in the United States controlled the U.S. market (before the flood of imports), consumers had little choice but to buy their products regardless of whether they were satisfied with the quality or price of these products. A similar situation exists today for washing machines, clothes dryers, refrigerators, and a great many other products. Research indicates that, in a situation of market concentration, prices may cease to reflect fluctuations in market demand. Instead prices may actually increase when demand falls, in order for large companies to maintain their desired profit levels.[25]

Domination of Related Markets.   Very large companies are often in a position to dominate related business markets. For example, their size may allow them to force suppliers to sell to them at favorable prices; they may use their large advertising budgets to create brand loyalty to keep new competitors from forming; their size and existing large-scale financing may place them in a better position to conduct and make use of research and development efforts in creating new products and markets; they may be able to dominate the skilled labor market by attracting and retaining the best engineers, managers, and other skilled workers; and they may be able to dominate the market on capital because of their creditworthiness resulting from their size and their control of their consumer market.[26]

How Professions and Service Providers Control Markets
The professions and several other service providers illustrate a number of other legal means for controlling markets.

Policies and Licensing.   One way they do this is by lobbying for the passage of laws or for the establishment of legal policies that will require consumers to purchase their services. Through lobbying they also may succeed in setting up licensing procedures that bar other providers from competing in the market through the delivery of similar services. Thus, for example, licensed physicians have a legal monopoly on providing prescriptions for many types of drugs, and they and licensed pharmacists have a legal monopoly on the dispensation of these drugs. Even if you personally know what kind of prescription drug you need, you are required by law to pay for the service of these two types of professionals to get the drug. Furthermore, no competitive professionals can enter the marketplace to offer these services at potentially cheaper rates. Under these conditions, it should not be surprising that physicians (and to a lesser degree pharmacists) are among the highest paid service providers in our society.

Price Leadership.   Yet another strategy used by service providers to control their markets is price leadership. This is an informal price-fixing arrangement in which service providers set and hold their prices based on prevailing practices and on serving their own interests, rather than in responding to actual supply or demand levels. For example, real estate agencies in a geographic area typically all will charge the same percentage rate for their commission. You will likely find no variation in these rates among them, no variation in these rates over time through good or bad housing markets, and no variation in their rates based on the actual difficulty or lack of difficulty in selling your house. Buyers of homes don't care what the commission rate is because they get the services of the real estate agency free. As buyers flock to the agencies, sellers who pay the commission are forced to list with the agencies in order to find buyers. In addition to the informal fixing of commission rates, this process of funneling supply and demand is a very nice way to control the market for the good of the real estate agencies.

How Producers Control Markets
There are a great many strategies for producers to use in exerting control over their markets.

Pricing Patterns.   First, for example, they too can control their markets through price leadership, wherein they set up informal pricing patterns that keep prices high enough to return high profits for all while avoiding real competition.

Planned Obsolescence.   Second, planned obsolescence and just plain shoddy workmanship guarantee a captive secondary market for consumers who are forced to seek repairs typically at highly inflated prices for replacement parts or for factory service labor charges.

Unnecessary Complexity, Usability, or Maintainability.   Third, products can be made unnecessarily complex; they can be designed with key components that easily malfunction or that require routine maintenance but that are located in inaccessible places; or they can be provided with incomprehensible manuals. These strategies ensure that company repair people or company specialists will be called on, typically at inflated prices, to provide repairs, routine maintenance, or technical assistance.

"Take It or Leave It" Pricing.   A fourth way to control prices derives from the increasingly bureaucratic character of many of our markets in which prices on items are fixed and not subject to haggling. In the classic model of the free market, the buyer and seller are supposed to negotiate over prices based on supply and demand factors. Yet in our largely bureaucratic markets, most prices (except for houses, cars, and a few other big ticket items) are pre-set so that goods are displayed with price tags affixed to them—take it or leave it. Try going into a department store to haggle over the price of a shirt, a hammer, or a toaster. You know what would happen. In such contexts marketing becomes less a matter of salesmanship than it is of inventory control, and the consumer loses direct influence on pricing as a result. If a particular consumer has the time, energy, and transportation resources to shop around, he or she might find a better price, but even when this happens it typically provides little or no direct influence on how the item is priced.

Controlling Consumer Information.   A fifth way to control markets is by controlling the information consumers have about products or services.[27] One example, is the use of advertising to create markets and to expand markets by getting people to believe that they need unnecessary and possibly ineffective, but high-profit, products (e.g., mouth fresheners, or feminine hygiene sprays) or even products that are hazardous to one's health (e.g., cigarettes or alcoholic beverages). Advertising can foster a belief among many people that one product which is quite expensive (i.e., has a high profit margin) is superior to another[28] or may get some people to believe that their personal identities are of low status unless they possess a particular high profit name brand item (e.g., a name brand pair of tennis shoes or jeans).

Another example of the control of consumer information is for businesses to rely on the complexity of their products and services or on the lack of information about them to steer consumers toward the purchase of products and services with high profit margins. In the ideal vision of the free market, intelligent comparison shopping by consumers is supposed to improve quality and drive down prices. Yet how can this happen if products or services are technically complex, if information is severely limited, and if the demands of life leave little time for fact finding? For example, suppose you have your car towed to a dealer who tells you that some very costly repairs are needed. How do you know if these repairs are really necessary and reasonably priced? Are you going to have your car towed to another garage for a second opinion? How much time can you devote to fact finding, given your need for a car. You probably do what almost everyone else does in these circumstances—you pay.

Suppose you do try to engage in serious comparison shopping for a washing machine, a camcorder, physician services, a mortgage lender, or even a can of shoe polish. How do you get the information you need? Try asking the service providers and sales staff for comparative information. Chances are you will have a hard time finding someone who is knowledgeable about the service or product he or she is selling. Even if you find such a person, he or she may not be willing to discuss seriously the pros and cons of their services or products. Try going to the library for books or publications on the product or service you are interested in. Chances are you will find that the brand or model you are most interested in either is not described in library sources (such as *Consumer Reports*) or is not directly comparable to competing brands or models. For many purchases you will not be able to make a knowledgeable decision. Rather, you must buy on faith or whimsy, and no doubt you provide healthy profit margins to businesses that rely (consciously or unconsciously) on you being unable to do otherwise.

Import Restrictions, Trade Tariffs.   Businesses also will attempt to shield themselves from competitors in a market by getting governments to set import restrictions or tariffs that limit or keep out foreign competitors. This, for example, has happened in the United States for automobiles, for steel, and for a very great many of other products.

Summary: The Control of Markets
The history of markets in business-oriented societies is one of unending attempts by businesses to exert control over them. This contrasts with the attempts by land-based nobility and religious authorities to control markets as occurred in the past. The practices I have described, are just some of the *legal* ways that businesses try to control markets in contemporary society. Bribes, kickbacks, cut-throat competition, explicit price fixing, and other illegal practices are discussed in later chapters. Governments have, in fact, defined as *illegal* and have attempted to stop only a few of the various ways that businesses go about controlling markets, and usually they have done so only when these practices have been so troublesome as to have brought public outcry. The ending of business controls over markets is *not* a general concern of governments; instead, as some examples here show, governments may assist businesses in setting up these controls. This is all to be expected in a society in which democratic governmental processes may be used by business interests and by other interests to foster business control of markets. The next two chapters discuss some of the efforts that governments undertake in our society to control markets.

Effects on Social Inequality and Social Tolerance

Free markets play a significant role in decreasing social inequality and in increasing social tolerance in our society.

Social Inequality

Markets cannot expand to "mass" proportions to include and tie all persons together in a society unless money circulates through the pockets of all participants. As this circulation happens, social inequality is decreased.

For example, in the typical agricultural society the nobility and church held almost all wealth, while the average person could be expected to have no money and little in the way of valuable items for trade. These societies were constituted, then, in such a way that they were able to function and persist for great lengths of time under conditions of enormous social inequality and with little in the way of markets. But how long could our markets today exist under the same conditions of extreme inequality?

The mass production and mass service systems that lie at the heart of our industrial economy require mass markets. If only a tiny minority of persons in society had the resources to purchase goods and services, as was true in agricultural societies, then our current industrial economy could not have developed or survived. Therefore because of their dependence on mass markets, business-oriented, industrial societies necessarily require a reduction in social inequality. Inequality became diminished in business-oriented societies in several ways.

First it was reduced when farm laborers were freed to become wage earners, with their labor converted to marketable cash. More importantly, however, inequality was further reduced as pressures that resulted in increased wages were brought to bear in the industrial era from many, often overlapping sources: by the changing occupational structure that decreased the availability of low skilled, low paying jobs while increasing the availability of higher skilled, higher paying jobs; by the increased productivity of machines, energy sources, and factory assembly processes which made more gross profits available for use in pay increases for workers (should businesses decide to use profits for such a purpose); by the increasing level of education of the population that has resulted in people expecting to be treated better; by shortages in the available labor pool for some types of work; by union demands on businesses; by government regulatory processes that reduce and control business competition within certain industries (e.g., railroads, trucking, or airlines) and thereby diminish business concerns over keeping labor costs down; by increasing numbers of government jobs with pay scales that compete with those of businesses; by a few industrial leaders who, for different reasons, offered higher pay to their employees with the result that other industries were forced to raise their pay scales in order to compete for employees; and by the increasingly bureaucratic structure of industrial businesses, which tends to deemphasize profits relative to a variety of bureaucratic goals that occasionally include maintaining a happy workforce.

Had inequality continued at the level exhibited in the early 1800s when industrialization was in its early stages, industrialization would not have progressed far. I do not wish to overstate this argument, however. While a reduction of inequality was necessary and did occur in the rise of an industrial economy, significant inequality nonetheless remains in our society, a fact which I discuss in detail in Chapter 6.

Social Tolerance

Markets also have increased social tolerance in society. Although the splintering of religious and political authorities has permitted the development of religious and political diversity in society, it is the impersonality of the mass market that allows us to relate to each other despite this diversity. Being bound to each other through mere market relations makes many social attributes less significant, though it clearly has not done away with all forms of discrimination and intolerance. In particular, social tolerance has been increased for such social differences as are to be found among religious and political beliefs and, to some degree, for ethnicity. However it has not been equally increased for physical differences such as race, gender, age, and physical disability. Continuing discriminatory practices based on physical differences are discussed in Chapter 10.

Is Life Better in a Business-Oriented Industrial Society?

The merchant, mercantile, and colonial eras represented an intermediate step in the development of business-oriented societies. In those eras, governments and religions formed working relations with businesses to foster their joint interests in world empire building. In the industrial era, however, religion receded significantly in authority and is no longer central to society. Autocratic political authority has been replaced by democratic governmental structures, and businesses have gained more control in society. Innovation and change have become the order of the day, typically prompted and evaluated in terms of potential profits for businesses. Are our lives better than those of our ancestors? Should we be proud and glad that we are business oriented?

There are a number of dimensions we could use to evaluate societies of the past to decide if we are better off living in ours. I cannot undertake a comprehensive evaluation here, but will restrict myself to considering several key dimensions, including gross national product per capita, standard of living of the poorest sector of society, health and longevity, and moral turpitude.[29]

National Plenty

Though he never used the term capitalism, Adam Smith (1723–1790) could be called the father of capitalism, as he became very influential in promoting the idea of a free market and of the critical role it should play in society. In essence, Smith argued that the wealth of society would be vastly increased if businesses were set as free as possible from governmental constraint (and, by logic extension, from constraints by religions, unions, or guilds) to produce and sell products based solely on market demand and competition.[30]

Smith reasoned that in a free market only products that people wanted to buy would be produced, and they would be produced in quantities suitable for prevailing consumer demand. The search for profits, coupled with the pressures of market competition, would drive business entrepreneurs to set up operations to produce goods ever more efficiently and cheaply, and then to sell these goods at lower and lower prices. As businesspersons scurried to respond to market demand by producing the most goods as cheaply as possible, the result would be a great elevation in the total amount of wealth in society, far more than had been obtained by noncompetitive mercantilist monopolies.

Although business-oriented societies never have exhibited the level of market freedom that Smith proposed, it is clear nonetheless that the relatively freer markets of industrialized societies have produced far larger gross national products per capita than have the relatively less free markets that were typical of nonindustrialized societies. So we can conclude that the free markets of industrialized societies are superior as sources of a national plenty.

Among contemporary societies, this pattern of differences can be seen in the following illustrative list of GNPs per capita in 1993: United States ($24,580), Japan ($34,160), France ($21,530), Germany ($21,020), Canada ($18,940), and United Kingdom ($16,180). Contrast this to Brazil ($3,528), Thailand ($2,077), China ($1,738), Algeria ($1,646), Columbia ($1,339), Egypt ($651), Ghana ($325), India ($282), and Kenya ($189).[31]

The Poorest Sector

It can be misleading to judge a society based only on GNP per capita, because inequality in the distribution of goods and services might be so egregious as to leave most people desperately poor even in a society with a large GNP. In judging societies, we therefore want also to consider the minimal standard of living experienced by the poorest segment of a society.

Relevant to this issue, we can easily see that typical members of our working class live in far greater luxury than did most nobility in earlier times. Furthermore, the average person in our society who lives below the poverty line generally fares far better than the lowest sectors of agricultural societies or the average person in food gathering and hunting societies. This is true largely because of our welfare programs, and reflects opportunities in education, health care, nutrition, housing, and clothing. The large surplus wealth that our economy creates, coupled with the politics of our democratic governments in redistributing this wealth in ways deemed politically appropriate, makes welfare programs possible. I discuss welfare in more detail in Chapter 6.

Health and Longevity

Another way to judge societies is to compare the health and longevity of their populations. Again we find industrial societies to be superior on these dimensions. Life expectancy in food gathering and hunting societies was only about 20 to 30 years, and it was little better in agricultural societies, at 25 to 40 years. As recently as in 1920 in the United States it was only fifty-four years, but by the mid-1990s in the United States it is 76 years.[32] The difference in life expectancies is largely due to our better health, which results from better nutrition and better public health measures. Improved nutrition and public health measures both are made possible by the great surplus wealth that our society creates, and by the political processes that redistribute this wealth.

Again this pattern can be seen in life expectancies for countries around the world. Life expectancy at birth in 1995 shows the following for selected countries: United States (76.0), Japan (79.4), France (78.4), Germany (76.6), Canada (78.3), and United Kingdom (77.0). This contrasts with Brazil (61.8), Thailand (68.4), China (68.1), Algeria (68.0), Columbia (72.5), Egypt (61.1), Ghana (55.9), India (59.0), and Kenya (52.4).[33] As these figures show too, in our modern world even predominantly agricultural societies have benefited in life expectancy from the diffusion of medical innovations from business-oriented industrial societies.

Morality and a Marxist Critique

A final dimension I'll use in this evaluation is morality. Is a business-oriented industrial society more moral than previous societies? Or have we merely replaced religious and aristocratic corruptions with business corruptions? I believe that the latter is the case.

Moral assessments always require a social context. If we simply used the morality of our time as our basis for comparison, our society would look good in such areas as maximizing individual freedom and in increasing our religious, ethnic, and political tolerance, as noted earlier.

But from the moral point of view of the agricultural society of modern-day Iran, we are seen (rightfully so from their perspective) as the "great Satan" for our refusal to behave in accordance with Muslim religious law and for our intrusion into the affairs of nations around the world in efforts to support governments favorable to our business interests. Communist ideology, on the other hand, has traditionally regarded us as being "decadent" because of our failure to restrain business interests in our society and thereby to free ourselves from their control. Food gathering and hunting peoples would likely be shocked by our indifferent attitude toward our ancestors and toward nature, by our refusal to share what we have with others, and by the insensitive and impersonal ways in which we treat each other. It appears, therefore, that we can neither say we are more moral or less moral than any other society without stacking the deck, so to speak, by judging ourselves by criteria that are central to how one society or another is constructed.

In considering the morality of the business-oriented industrial society, it might be useful to consider some of the major criticisms of it. Karl Marx (1818–1883), who might fairly be called the father of communism (though he did not invent the term *communism*), is the best-known critic of business-oriented societies, so I would like to consider here several of Marx's most important criticisms.

Marx's criticisms centered on economic and political issues, and he considered his own work as being scientific and, therefore, above crass moral concerns. Nonetheless, it is rather easy to see that moral concerns are at the heart of his criticisms. In particular, it is the moral question of fairness in how we all relate to each other through the structures of our economy that centrally concerned him. According to Marx, societies that I have called business oriented follow principles which he summarized under the rubric of capitalism; he considered the operations of capitalism to be decadent and grossly unfair.[34]

More than a social critic, Marx was also a crusty radical who sought to foster a revolution that would create a new world order to overcome what he saw as the iniquities of capitalism. This new world order would be an utopia he called communism, but neither the principles for how this utopia would operate nor the steps necessary to bring it about were described in any detail by him. Furthermore, his condemnation of capitalism in no way was meant to imply that he regarded agricultural societies to constitute a superior social form. Far from it, he held both agricultural and capitalistic societies to be equally corrupt. Marx was a better social critic than he was a prophet, so let's look at five of his principal criticisms of capitalism.

Unfair Distribution

First, Marx held that agricultural and capitalistic societies were both unfair in their distribution of wealth. In both cases great inequality occurs, so that the few families who laid claim of ownership of the means of production (land in agricultural societies, and industrial processes in industrial capitalist societies) held most of the wealth and lived grand lifestyles, while the rest of the population were exploited as slaves and serfs or as wage laborers and forced to live at, or close to, a subsistence level.

This criticism is partly true. Inequality was and is great in agricultural societies. And, as I shall show in the next chapter, it remains great in our own industrialized society, though it is less than what was seen in agricultural societies. If the morality of a society is to be judged based on inequality levels, then the business-oriented society doesn't look too good.

On the other hand, despite a considerable amount of inequality in our society today, we do not see the bulk of our population living at a subsistence level, as was otherwise the rule for the masses in agricultural societies and for most people during early industrialization (the period when Marx was developing his ideas).

Two principal shifts in inequality have occurred to elevate general living standards in our society. First, as I have noted earlier and will describe in more detail in Chapter 6, our current welfare system provides a floor to living standards that is above the subsistence level. Second, as I also described earlier, a general increase in wages has occurred in the later stages of industrialization as a result of a number of factors, including union contracts, the growth in numbers of government service jobs, the shift to more bureaucratic business forms that require more middle managers and specialists, and other factors. Thus if the morality of a society is judged based on the reduction of absolute material deprivation societywide, the business-oriented society looks pretty good.[35]

Concentration of Power

Let's consider another of Marx's criticisms. He charged that those who lay claim to the means of production (land or industrial processes) will control the government and all other sectors of society. Again, this criticism is partly true.[36] It applies best when we are considering agricultural societies, but a good bit less well, as I shall describe in the next two chapters, when applied to our contemporary industrialized society. If we envision this as a dimension of morality, we can say that the business-oriented society is apparently more moral than agricultural societies, but falls far short of reaching an ideal.

Economic Forces Alienate Us

A third Marxian criticism is that people in capitalistic societies are alienated by the economic forces that dominate all sectors of society. In other words, in societies in which economic relations define who we are and how we are to relate to each other, people are not allowed to be fully free to create a meaningful life for themselves: to do what they wish, to think what they wish, or to become what they wish. Marx believed that these constraints would be removed in the future utopia of communism as a result of at least two developments. First, automated industrial production systems would free us from the need to devote ourselves slavishly to work and should at the same time produce a bounty of goods that would make it possible for us all to enjoy any lifestyle we chose. Second, ownership of the means of production would no longer be tolerated, so the great bounty would no longer belong primarily to the few but could be distributed to everyone as they needed it to create a meaningful life for themselves.

This is a fair criticism to a degree, though it is difficult from a sociological perspective to imagine how any social order could be other than constraining. The economic relations of industrial societies do constrain us and, therefore, make us less than completely free. But as I argued earlier, industrial societies permit far more freedom than do agricultural societies. The central problem with this criticism is that any conceivable alternative social order would, of necessity, be constraining and, therefore, would be to some degree alienating.[37] To summarize, if human creative freedom is morally desirable, then business-oriented industrial societies are certainly more moral than agricultural societies, but fall far short of an ideal of total freedom (which itself is sociologically inconceivable).

International Exploitation

A fourth Marxian criticism is that capitalism fosters international exploitation, as capitalists scurry across national borders to expand their markets. This criticism is also true to a degree. But international domination and exploitation are hardly the social inventions of business-oriented societies. Conquest, exploitation, and empire-building were commonplace among agricultural societies. Among business-oriented societies, such efforts were most brutally applied during colonialism.

Modern industrialized societies, by contrast, find novel ways to carry out international exploitation.[38] We see this in the "banana republics" that are supported, defended, and economically dominated by the United States as ready sources of cheap foods and raw goods. We see it in the sweatshops of Asia that supply us with cheap clothing and novelties. We see it in the recent war with Iraq fought not to safeguard democratic liberties (Kuwait and Saudi Arabia being monarchies) but to protect our economic interests in the oil-rich Middle East. And we see it in bribes, payoffs, assassinations, and political manipulation undertaken by corporations that are engaged in international commerce (I'll discuss many of these issues in Chapter 13). In short, if it is moral for a society to avoid international domination and exploitation, then business-oriented societies fall short on this dimension, but no more so than agricultural societies.

Inherent Instability

A fifth criticism by Marx is that capitalism contains inherent contradictory forces that cause repeated disruptions of the economy and will eventually lead to its own collapse. Again this criticism is partly true, but it applies generally to all societies. All societies contain contradictory forces, all societies and economies experience disruptions, and all preceding civilizations have collapsed.

One of the central contradictions in capitalism that was proposed by Marx was that the pressures of market competition and increasing automation of industry would inevitably decrease business profits and consequently force wages and living standards down for the masses of laborers to a level that would be intolerable and would induce them to undertake a revolution to destroy the capitalistic system. This situation has not happened for a number of reasons, some of which I have described here (including the maintenance of high profits based on market control, the influence of unions, and the emergence of government welfare programs).

In Chapter 6 I describe several contradictions that have appeared in unrestrained capitalism, and I shall describe what we have done about them to keep our business-oriented economy healthy. Furthermore, in Part III of this book I shall consider how best to construct moral approaches to addressing a number of additional contradictions that have arisen in the business-oriented society and that threaten its future vitality.

Section Summary

In summary, though we are healthier and materially better off living in a business-oriented industrial society, we cannot say that business-oriented societies have provided a more moral basis for how people relate to each other. Instead it might be fairer to say that previous religious and political corruptions have simply been replaced with corrupt and socially irresponsible behaviors by businesses. The criticisms of Marx help us to identify a number of these areas of irresponsibility in business behaviors.

Chapter *6*

The United States in the Twentieth Century

Because it has become the world's most powerful country, the United States presents an especially interesting case example of a contemporary business-oriented society. One factor accounting for its current worldwide preeminence is the extraordinary size and strength of its industrial economy, as measured both in terms of its GNP and its GNP per capita. A second factor is its successful record of military strength. This record includes not only its major contributions to victories in the two World Wars of the twentieth century, but also the substantial military capacity and military presence that the United States currently has in the world.

In examining how the United States is organized as a business-oriented society, I shall describe several major features of U.S. businesses and of their social environment. First I describe the growing significance of corporations, market concentration, and bureaucracies in the U.S. industrial economy. Second I describe several major problems that the free market model encounters when applied to an industrial society such as the United States. Third I describe how, largely in response to these problems in the free market model, the U.S. economy has become increasingly government-regulated and government-aided during the twentieth century. Fourth I contrast the pros and cons of having an unplanned, free market industrial economy versus having one that is planned by governments. Finally I describe the nature and characteristics of social inequality in the United States, including both economic elites and the poor. The forces that bring welfare programs into being in the business-oriented industrial society also are examined.

Characteristics of the Business Sector Today in the United States

This section examines two major characteristics of the U.S. industrial economy that merit special attention as we seek to understand life in the business-oriented society. The first characteristic is the increasingly dominant role of corporate businesses in the organization and control of large portions of the U.S. economy. The result has been an economy with highly concentrated markets. The second characteristic to be examined in this section is the increasingly bureaucratic nature of businesses in our society. Because of the importance of corporations to our contemporary economy and because of their bureaucratic nature, we might fairly say that we now have a bureaucratic corporate economy.

The Rising Dominance of Corporate Businesses in the Economy

This section explores the pressures that led to the rise of big corporations as major players in the U.S. economy. First the corporate form for business endeavors are discussed. Then, pressures fostering the use of the corporate form and the growth in size of corporations and market concentration are examined. Finally the dominant role that corporations play in our contemporary economy are illustrated.

The Corporate Form

A corporation is a social entity that is granted the legal right to own property, to sign contracts, and otherwise to operate and to be governed in ways consistent with the laws of the political jurisdiction within which it is incorporated. Corporations may be created either to be for profit or to be not for profit; this distinction, of course, affects their taxable status and the political regulations applied to them. A for-profit corporation can be held either privately (with ownership held solely by one person or jointly among a few persons) or it can be held publicly (through the issuance and sale of shares of stock to the general public). These distinctions have legal and regulatory implications to ensure fair business practices and to provide a basis for judicial action in the event of civil suit.

As noted in Chapter 3, most businesses in early U.S. history were small, and corporations played but a minor role in our overall economy at that time. For example, the largest industrial enterprise in the United States before 1840 (the Springfield Armory) employed only 250 people.[1] Increasingly since the beginning of the twentieth century, however, the situation has changed dramatically, so that giant corporations have now come to play dominant roles in the operation of our economy. This trend too can be seen in employment figures. For example, by the mid-1980s, 14 million American workers (19 percent, or nearly a fifth of all U.S. business employees) were employed by only 500 U.S. industrial corporations.[2]

Industrial Pressures Fostering the Corporate Form

Intrinsic pressures within industrialization make for-profit corporations a convenient social form for organizing business endeavors.[3] It is worthwhile here to consider some of these pressures so we can understand why corporations are so important to contemporary economy.

One of these pressures derives from the fact that the industrialized production of goods often requires much start-up capital. Production expansion or the replacement of existing machinery also pose additional intermittent large capital outlays. The public corporation is especially useful for meeting these large capital needs, as the sale of corporate stock to the public raises substantial sums of money at little short- or long-term cost. Equivalent sums of money may not be obtained as easily or as cheaply from other funding avenues. Thus the financial needs of industrialized production systems make the corporate form a logical choice for business development.

A second pressure fostering the use of the corporate form in industrializing economies derives from the fact that industrialization relies on a mass production of goods. Such a capacity requires a corresponding mass market for the sale of these goods over geographic areas that potentially may be quite large. The large, capital-intensive, regional or area retailers that arise to serve this marketing need are, therefore, as much a part of an industrialized economy as are the large manufacturers who produce goods. Both the size and the capital requirements of these large-scale retail operations again make the public corporation an ideal social form for them to take as businesses.

In creating and maintaining mass production and mass marketing systems, industrialization also requires other types of mass services. As examples, it requires mass financing, mass transportation, mass energy production and delivery, and mass communications. The corporation also provides an ideal structure for the giant businesses that arise to provide these mass services, as in banking and insurance; in shipping by railroad, boat or truck; in the marketing of energy (e.g., coal, oil, gas, electricity); in direct communication by telegraph and telephone; and in mass communications (e.g., newspapers, magazines, radio, motion pictures, television).

The great importance that public corporations have come to hold in our industrial economy today is reflected in the growth in size and significance of our public stock markets. From a few investors dickering under the shade of a tree on Wall Street, the New York Stock Exchange has arisen to become, along with other smaller stock exchanges, a central indicator of the strength and health of our economy. Through the stock markets, the largest and most important businesses that have come to dominate our industrial economy are themselves made into mere commodities that are bought and sold by the share, minute by minute, day by day.

Pressures for Growth in the Size of Corporations and in Their Market Concentration

Not only are corporations convenient business vehicles for an industrialized economy, but there also is a natural tendency for industrial corporations to grow in size over time, so the markets of our economy become increasingly controlled by fewer and fewer corporations. One way this occurs is again driven by the nature of industrialization itself and of its capital needs.

To understand this principle, it is useful here to compare the industrial reality of the United States today with the ideal of a free market business environment as it was envisioned by Adam Smith in the late 1700s. In Smith's model, many small producers compete with each other in the sale of each type of good or service in an economy. When demand for a good or service increases, more producers should enter the market until their combined production meets existing demand. And when demand falls, enough producers should leave the market so that production falls to a level sufficient for the new lower level of demand. By aggressive competition among these many producers, the prices of products should be driven down to the lowest possible level.

Although Smith's model is appealing, it is simply unworkable for an industrialized economy. In an industrialized economy, mass production of goods is made possible by production systems that are highly capital-intensive. When one of these production systems is set up, it could conceivably meet all demand for a particular product on its own, provided that sufficient mass transportation and mass marketing systems are in place to get its goods to all consumers who demand them. By its very nature, therefore, the productive capacity of industrialization lends itself to the fostering of an economy that is filled with market monopolies or near monopolies.

Large-scale capital requirements pose an additional limit on competition in the industrial economy. Given the typically massive amounts of capital that are required to set up industrial production systems, and given limitations on the availability of capital itself, it is difficult for several producers to be formed to compete for the same industrial product. A related consideration also is important. The capital investment requirements for industrial production systems are greatest at start-up and may yield little profit over the ensuing short term. Thus already existing industrial production systems have an advantage, in that they typically have reached a point where their economies of scale produce substantial profit margins. As a consequence, they are in a position, if necessary, to sell a product more cheaply than any new producer of the product. In this way they can drive new competitors out of the market and retain dominance over it.

As a consequence of the productive capacities of industrialized businesses and of their related capital needs, industrial corporations tend to hold very large shares of their markets. Yet another way in which corporations become both large in size and dominant as a market presence, however, is by using the revenues derived from their mass sales to buy up other corporations. For example, if a corporation does find itself confronted with several competing corporations, it could purchase these corporations outright, with the result again of increasing its dominance over its markets. Or a corporation may buy its suppliers or retailers so it extends its control over the market (and price) for its products from the point of extraction of raw materials to the final point of sale.

Yet other concerns may lead corporations to purchase other corporations. Management may want to diversify corporate operations to counterbalance temporary profit declines from certain products or services with profits from high-demand products or services. To address these concerns, corporations may buy other corporations that sell entirely different products or services. The resulting corporate structure is called a *conglomerate.* Indeed, it is sometimes possible for corporations to obtain substantial profits simply by buying and selling other corporations or by buying and "cannibalizing" them. This may produce a larger short-term profit than could be obtained by all the mess and bother of actually using the corporations that are purchased to produce and sell goods to consumers.

A final point of importance is that antitrust laws give corporations good reason not to want to achieve complete monopolies over their markets by buying up or driving all of their competitors out of business. Instead, because of antitrust laws, two, three, or four major corporations typically will divide up a market for a particular product or service among themselves and not seek further market concentration through corporate consolidation. This situation of control exercised over a particular market by a few large corporations is referred to as an *oligopoly,* and, as I describe next, is a very common feature of our economy.

Corporate Dominance of the Economy

How much of our economy today is controlled by giant corporations? Consider the following observations. Fewer than one-fifth of all U.S. businesses are corporations (the remainder are proprietorships or partnerships), yet corporations account for 90 percent of all U.S. annual business receipts.[4] In addition, of the more than 3.8 million active business corporations in the United States during the early 1990s, a mere 2 percent accounted for 80 percent of all corporate receipts and 98 percent of all corporate net income.[5] Indeed, just a mere one hundred U.S. industrial corporations alone have sales that collectively are equivalent to more than one-third (37 percent) of the entire U.S. economy as measured by the GNP.[6]

Business concentration is especially great in manufacturing, the backbone of our industrial economy, in which only 407 giant corporations hold 72 percent of all U.S. manufacturing assets.[7] Market concentration in the form of oligopolies is substantial for most of the products that we use. For example, just four or fewer giant corporations control the U.S. market for steel, copper, aluminum, gypsum, soap and detergents, rubber tires, automobiles, turbines and generators, salt, chocolate and cocoa, breweries, roasted coffee, photo equipment, cigarettes, electric tubes and electric bulbs, breakfast cereal, prepared soup, telephone equipment, flat glass, synthetic fibers, and many more products.[8]

Market concentration is also the rule for the financial structure that is critical in supporting our industrial economy. For example, it is estimated that fifty banks hold nearly 60 percent of all U.S. deposits (just five banks hold nearly 20 percent), and fifty insurance companies hold 78 percent of all insurance assets (two insurance companies hold nearly 25 percent).[9] In the U.S. mass media, a social sector that greatly affects our understanding of the world around us, twenty companies own half of all U.S. newspapers, twenty companies own over half of all U.S. magazines, three companies control most of the revenues in U.S. television, ten companies control most of U.S. radio, eleven companies control most of U.S. book publishing, and four companies control most of the U.S. movie market.[10]

Another way to get a sense of the magnitude and financial clout of large corporations in our economy is to compare their annual revenues to the entire GNP of countries around the world. A GNP, as you will recall, is the total value of all goods and services produced by a country. Some relevant comparisons are shown in Table 6.1.

From Table 6.1, we can see that in 1993 the revenues of General Motors (GM) were greater than the entire GNP of the oil-rich country of Saudi Arabia. (Though this is not shown

TABLE 6.1   Comparison of Selected National GNPs and Corporate Revenues in 1993 (billions of dollars)

Country	GNP or Revenues	Corporation	GNP or Revenues
United States	6,348	General Motors	136
Japan	4,260	Ford	108
Germany	1,698	Exxon	98
France	1,239	AT&T	67
United Kingdom	938	IBM	63
Canada	526	General Electric	60
India	255	Mobil	57
Saudi Arabia	130	Wal-Mart	55
		Sears, Roebuck	51
		Phillip Morris	51

Sources: 1993 GNP figures are from U.S. Bureau of the Census, *Statistical Abstract of the United States: 1995,* 115th ed., (Washington, D.C.: Government Printing Office, 1995), Table 1373. The 1993 corporate revenue figures are from Standard & Poor's Corporation, *Stock Market Encyclopedia,* Vol. 18, No. 2 (New York: Standard & Poor's Corporation, May 1996).

in Table 6.1, they were also greater than the GNP of almost all of the non-industrialized countries around the world). Financially speaking, GM's revenues amount to more than half the size of the entire economy of India, a country with over 900 million people. GM's revenues are about a fourth of the size of the entire industrial economy of Canada, more than a seventh the size of the industrial economy of the United Kingdom, and about one-fortieth the size of the U.S. economy. General Motors corporation has more revenues than the entire gross state product of the economies of Maryland, Indiana, Wisconsin, or Washington,[11] and more revenues than any state government in the United States.[12]

Collectively, just ten giant public corporations (GM, Ford, Exxon, AT&T, IBM, General Electric, Mobil, Wal-Mart, Sears Roebuck, and Phillip Morris) account for more than one-ninth of our entire U.S. economy, an amount which is almost as great or greater than the entire industrial economy of the United Kingdom or of Canada. As you might imagine, when these corporations have something to say or when they want something done, whole countries (as well as states within the United States) feel obliged at least to listen.

Another way to get a perspective on the significant role of large corporations in our economy is to consider the many products they sell to us under different names. For example, PepsiCo is only of moderate size as major corporations go, with a mere $28.5 billion in revenues in 1994. You know PepsiCo for the carbonated, sugary, syrup water it sells (Pepsi). It is not clear why so many of us prefer such a concoction to ordinary, inexpensive water, but we do, and we are willing to pay dearly for each slug of it. But did you know too that profit margins on the sale of Pepsi have been so good that PepsiCo has purchased Pizza Hut, Kentucky Fried Chicken, and Taco Bell? Try ordering a Coke from these establishments. You can hardly drive down the highway anywhere without passing by, or possibly stopping in, a PepsiCo establishment.

Consider another example. If you smoke you know Phillip Morris. As our nation's (and the world's) largest cigarette producer, it makes and sells Marlboro, Benson & Hedges, Merit, Virginia Slims, and a number of other brands of cigarettes. Cigarette profits have been very good. So as Phillip Morris has grown in size to its more than $53 billion in annual revenues in 1994, it has bought up so many other businesses that it has now also become the nation's largest processor and marketer of packaged coffee, cheese, and processed meat products (including Kraft and General Foods brands, such as Post breakfast cereals, Jello, Maxwell House coffee, Velveeta cheese, Oscar Mayer meats, and Claussen pickles). Phillip Morris also is now the second largest brewer in the nation (including ownership of all Miller brands, such as High Life, Lowenbrau, and Lite). Even if you wanted to, it would be hard to escape the reach that this one cigarette company has in the U.S. marketplace.

The Role of Bureaucracy in Corporate Businesses

In addition to the growing influence that giant business corporations have over our economy, the other major characteristic of the U.S. business sector that I wish to discuss is the increasing role that bureaucracies have come to play in business management. In this section I consider the following issues: the rise of bureaucracies in corporate businesses, several well-known contradictions and sources of inefficiency in corporate bureaucracies, the split between bureaucratic managers and owners of corporations, and the resulting implications that bureaucratic corporations have for our economy.

The Role of Industrialization in Fostering Business Bureaucracies

To create a system of mass production or mass service, an industrialized business requires considerable planning and supervisory oversight to set up timely coordination among a great many specialized workers. The corporation serves this need through the development of a professional management system.[13] Management systems are, of necessity, bureaucratic in nature. Thus, just as industrialization brings into being an economy that is dominated by giant corporations, so too it brings into being an economy that is dominated by bureaucrats, bureaucratic rules, and bureaucratic paper trails.

As bureaucrats, managers divide complex corporate objectives into separate work tasks, assign workers to carry out these work tasks, set timetables for coordinating the efforts of these workers toward the completion of the tasks, monitor ongoing efforts, and make adjustments as needed. This overall management process takes a bureaucratic form in at least two respects: first it does so through centralized planning of corporate goals and work assignments, and second it does so through hierarchical structures of authority.

Bureaucracies are the best social means we humans have created for organizing the activities of many people toward the achievement of large-scale goals. If we define social power as the ability to make others do something even if they do not want to do it, then it is easy to see that a successfully organized bureaucracy provides a means for the exercise of enormous social power in society. For this reason, the successfully bureaucratized army is one to be feared, and the successfully bureaucratized government or church can survive over great periods of time while making large populations bend to its will. Similarly, successfully bureaucratized corporations have enormous power at their disposal in shaping and directing their respective markets.

Contradictory Pressures in Bureaucracies

Bureaucracies are the best means humans have for achieving large-scale goals, and successful bureaucracies provide for the exercise of great power; but bureaucracies often fall considerably short of meeting their stated goals. This happens because they carry within themselves several well-known contradictory pressures that can decrease their efficiency, sometimes to the point of making them almost wholly inoperative. The ample literature on management contains many books and articles that identify one or more of these pressures and claim to have found resolutions for them. Let's take a look, from a sociological perspective, at two of the most important of these pressures. The first concerns bureaucratic impersonality, and the second concerns bureaucratic goal setting.

Impersonality of Bureaucracy.   First, bureaucracies require a high level of impersonality in how people relate to each other. Such impersonality facilitates a rational approach in working with people so that workers can be viewed and treated much as though they were merely replaceable cogs in a large social machine. The humanity and uniqueness of each worker is de-emphasized; much attention is focused instead on how individuals perform a limited range of tasks assigned to them. In essence, people become mere objects to be used in achieving some desired end (and they become thereby alienated, in the Marxian sense, from the results of their labor, from the surrounding social order, and from themselves as creative, self-directed beings).

Needless to say, people don't enjoy being treated this way. Although the reaction of workers to this situation varies, rarely does it take the form of dutiful efficiency in task performance. In response to the impersonality of bureaucracy, many workers create an informal community of relations among their work peers that permits them to express a fuller range of human emotions while at work. This community of relations may further serve to set and enforce goals and rates for production that are at variance with those officially set by the bureaucracy.

It is also the typical case that personal feelings intrude in the relations between supervisors and subordinates, so that rational, task-oriented communications (including reprimands, directives, and coordination) are made difficult and occasionally impossible. Thus even the official management effort to apply rational control over subordinates is impeded by counterefforts by superordinates and subordinates alike to inject human warmth, feeling, and decency into their interpersonal relations.

Yet another common reaction to the impersonality of a bureaucracy is for workers to refuse to carry out assignments efficiently, or even to engage in covert sabotage. The power exercised in a bureaucracy is much like that seen in a totalitarian system: from the time a worker shows up on the corporate premises until the end of the work day, every expression, behavior, and mood is expected to conform to bureaucratic plans that are usually set without the employee's concurrence. As a consequence, passive resistance (if not outright sabotage and rebellion) often occurs despite the many years of bureaucratic preparatory training we have all received in our school systems. Workers, for example, may do as little as possible to get by, may sneak off for long breaks, may use drugs or alcohol, or may on occasion deliberately disrupt planned operations.

Bureaucratic Goal Setting.   A second inherent problem in bureaucracies lies in goal setting. Rarely are the goals of a bureaucracy simple, and many goals are unstated and contradictory. Furthermore, different factions of a bureaucracy may have different unstated goals. This possibility was mentioned earlier in considering how informal communities of relations among working peers may set production goals different from those specified by supervisors.

The unstated goals of management, however, are those that may pose particularly difficult problems for a bureaucracy. Being in the driver's seat, so to speak, of a powerful bureaucracy puts senior management in a position to steer corporations in directions that satisfy their personal objectives as much and possibly more so than the official objectives stated for the corporation. Thus when management deliberates over how best to use corporate resources, the enhancement of management job security, comfort, prestige, and compensation may come to figure equally with, or even take priority over, concerns for customer satisfaction, product quality, pollution control, worker safety, or even for profit maximization itself.

As management and subordinate workers both develop strategies over time either of passive resistance and sabotage or of redirecting corporate resources and work activities in ways that better meet their personal interests, the actual operations of bureaucracies may wander considerably from their original, official goals. Furthermore, the vested interests in these strategies by managers and workers alike make the bureaucracy considerably rigid, so that efforts to change or reform the bureaucracy are resisted at all levels and typically fail. When they do succeed, usually by a massive replacement of personnel or when external threats make everyone pull together to enact changes, a subsequent, new process of resistances and countergoals can be expected to develop over time to create a new system that is rigid and inefficient for meeting stated official goals.

Although bureaucracies are the best means we have for creating the large-scale business ventures that are characteristic of industrialization, they carry internal contradictions that make them inherently inefficient in their ability to respond to changing market conditions, to maximize productivity or profit over the long term, or to pursue innovative strategies for product or market development. Ironically, processes that we conceive of as being the result of poor management are actually inescapable consequences of a bureaucratized corporate economy.

The Split between Managers and Owners

Another interesting thing about the large corporate businesses that dominate our economy is that they split businesspersons into two very different types. First there are the nameless, faceless shareholders who together "own" these businesses as collective, public enterprises. Second there are the professional bureaucratic managers, also typically faceless, if not always nameless, who manage them.

With few exceptions, public shareholders have no direct relationship with the corporations they own and are in no position to provide oversight of them. Rather they behave as businesspersons to the degree that they buy and sell the stocks of these giant corporations in the search for profits from dividends and stock market price fluctuations. Nothing else about the corporations, including the inefficiencies noted here or even the quality, safety, or marketability of the products developed by the corporations are necessarily of the same order of concern to them as long as profits from dividends and from stock market price fluctuations are obtained.

Corporate managers, by contrast, are employees of their corporations, though at the most senior levels they also may come to own some (typically very small) fraction of the corporation's stock (usually as a result of awarding themselves stock bonuses or stock options). Managers behave as businesspersons to the degree that they either manage the operations that are under their control with the intent of creating a profit for their corporations or do so with the intent of creating a profit for themselves through "perks," pay raises, and bonuses.

If for no other reason than to justify their next pay raise, the making of a profit for the corporation is likely to be one of the central motivating factors for managers over the short term. However, a willingness to make profit sacrifices today in order to ensure long-term profitability is not likely to draw the same level of commitment. Indeed, the idiosyncrasies of each senior manager are the most important determinants in whether they will "marry" the company, with a personal commitment to the company's long-term viability and growth.

In short, the industrial corporations that dominate our economy operate largely as impersonal, short-term money making machines for shareholders and managers alike, and they lack well-developed, effective internal mechanisms for ensuring quality of products or long-term competitiveness or profitability. I discuss these issues in greater detail in the next two chapters.

Implications for the Social Environment

Given the importance that bureaucratic corporations have for our contemporary economy, it would be fair to use the term bureaucratic corporate societies in referring to advanced industrial societies such as our own. Three noteworthy consequences for the social environment follow from the shift that has resulted in our becoming a bureaucratic corporate society.

Dilution and Splintering of Business Interests.   First, insofar as the economy has come to be dominated by a few public corporations, which by their nature split their shareholders from their controlling managers, then the major means of production in our society are no longer controlled by those who own them.[14] This situation dilutes and splinters the power, interests, and influences that the business community has over other sectors of society. Under these circumstances, it simply is not possible for a small group of business owners to exert monolithic control over the rest of society.

Pressures for Social Responsibility.   Second, though no well-defined mechanisms exist within industrial corporations to foster social responsibility, the nature of corporations nonetheless makes it possible for some limited pressures to arise toward this end. One such pressure could come from the nameless, faceless corporate shareholders. Because they know little or nothing about the corporations they buy shares in, they may press for increased governmental regulatory actions on issues that concern them as individuals, but that otherwise run contrary to the interests of "their" corporations. Then too, some of these shareholders are actually funds that are managed by churches, employee pension programs, or other persons or groups with special interests in fostering certain socially responsible causes.

Furthermore, as noted here, managers also may come to their jobs with personal interests that may conflict with those of their corporations. As employees, for example, they have practical reason to be concerned about employee issues, particularly those concerning senior managers, but to a more limited degree extending to immediate subordinates as well. The creation of a pleasant working environment is of direct concern to them, and this concern can spill over into efforts to make subordinates happy.

The prestige and community reputations of managers also necessarily concern them, so there is motivation, to some degree, for them to be attentive to broader community issues. Likewise their unique personal commitments and concerns may meld together in their bureaucratic decision making to give their corporation a personality or culture that emphasizes customer satisfaction, employee welfare, product quality, and safety or environmentalism.

However, there is nothing unified or necessary in the appearance of any of these social interests among corporate managers and shareholders, and any such pressures for social responsibility among corporations may be diluted by the contradictory bureaucratic pressures noted earlier. In Chapter 8 I discuss in some detail how social mechanisms can be created to enhance socially responsible behavior within corporations.

Threats to Society.   A third implication of the growth of public corporations as the dominant forces in our economy are the threats that they may pose to our well-being as a society. One threat is that we might have to pay more and more for the same goods because of the increased control large corporations can exert over their markets. A second threat is that, because so much economic power is held in the hands of a few corporations, should one or more fail through poor planning, mismanagement, bad luck, or "what have you," we could experience massive economic repercussions. Third, if there are no social forces of comparable power to counter the actions of big corporations, then all sorts of abuses could be perpetuated against employees, consumers, or the environment without any means of stopping them. I discuss some of these abuses in this chapter and consider them in more detail in Chapters 9 through 13.

The End of Laissez-Faire

Several features of corporate businesses and their relations to our contemporary economy were described and critiqued in the preceding section. Now I would like to consider in more detail some problems with the free-market economic model and begin to describe how governments have come to address these problems in the United States.

The Laissez-Faire Economic Model

Adam Smith published his great work, *The Wealth of Nations,* in 1776, a year which coincided fortuitously with the signing of the American Declaration of Independence. As I noted in Chapter 5, Smith argued that the marketplace should be free of governmental control so participants could buy and sell goods as they pleased. He believed that, if markets were left unregulated, participants would naturally tend to follow a pattern of behavior that would result in businesses producing the greatest abundance and diversity of goods at the lowest possible prices throughout the society. This pattern of market behavior would work much like an "invisible hand," to use his term, to greatly increase the wealth of the nation. Smith's basic idea that governments should not regulate marketplaces is a central contention of fervent followers of the market model (as described in Chapter 2), and it is a concept that is often referred to by the French term *laissez-faire,* which can be translated as "leave alone."

Smith's emphases on the important role of business interests in society and on the freeing of business interests from governmental control found a receptive audience in the newly formed United States. At least two factors account for this receptivity: the history of the development of the colonies as commercial enterprises, and the unique circumstances of the early European–American immigrants.

First, from 1492 onward, business interests were the driving forces in shaping American history. This is seen in the European discovery of the New World as a result of searches for a trade route to the Far East. It is also seen in the subsequent history of colonial efforts to exploit the commercial resources of this New Land.

Second, many of the early European immigrants to the New World came in search of personal fortune and greater freedom from religious and political authority. They left behind the tightknit social control mechanisms that were found in kin, community, church, and governments of the European Old World. By contrast they entered the significantly freer social environment of the New Land, with few institutional constraints on them and many opportunities for obtaining personal wealth. Thus the circumstances of many early Americans would have made them highly receptive to Smith's ideas on the need to free profit-seekers from government intervention. Indeed, when English governmental restrictions increased, particularly on colonial trade but also on manufacture, these early Americans became so incensed by these actions that they revolted to create the United States as an independent country.[15] Under these circumstances it is not surprising that the early years of our development as an independent nation were filled with political struggles aimed at minimizing the powers of governments and maximizing individual freedom.

For the reasons given here, the United States provides a particularly good case example for examining the implications of Smith's ideas concerning a *laissez-faire* economy. In its history of colonization, in the lack of long-standing social institutions to constrain its citizenry, in the risk-taking character of the immigrants who populated it, and in its revolution from English governmental authority, the United States was born and came of age in a spirit of aggressive individualism and entrepreneurship.

In all fairness, though, a fully *laissez-faire* economy—one where there is no government involvement in the marketplace—has never been a reality in the United States. Even at the very beginning, the Continental Congress provided subsidies to industries during the Revolutionary War.[16] Subsequently, governments at all levels, from local and state to federal, have enacted legislation to regulate the marketplace and to protect and promote new industries in their jurisdiction by providing subsidies and special concessions and by setting tariffs on the goods of foreign competitors.[17] Furthermore, there was considerable early government involvement in the creation of turnpikes, canals, railroads, docks, and waterway improvements.[18]

Nonetheless, the total amount of governmental involvement in the market during the early history of our nation was small by the standards of most European countries at the time, or by modern U.S. standards. We might say of the early history of the United States that it came closer to approximating a *laissez-faire* economy than anything we have since experienced. We may use it, therefore, to illustrate the difficulties that are encountered in a society that is organized around a free market.

Five Major Shortcomings in the Laissez-Faire *Model*

There are five fundamental shortcomings in the ideal of a *laissez-faire* economy that in practical applications have forced governments to become involved in the marketplace.

1. Public Need for Adjudication Mechanisms
One problem is the general public need for a social means to maintain civil order by adjudicating disputes that arise over market transactions and by controlling those business practices that the public may consider morally offensive, such as slave trading, drug trafficking, piracy, prostitution, and so forth. At a minimum, this public need requires a set of laws to define fair and proper business practices, enforceable contracts, and the general public good. But more generally it also requires corollary policing and judicial systems. Thus the public good requires governments to be involved in the marketplace in defining, enforcing, and protecting fair business practices.

2. Public Need for Political Protection
A second problem is that the ideal of a fully *laissez-faire* economy ignores a basic political reality that underlies social order. In particular, people are going to want to defend their way

of life from possible collapse or from threat of economic domination by a foreign power. Yet in a fully free marketplace, major businesses may fail and in so doing utterly disrupt the way of life (as they did in the Great Depression). Furthermore, new industries may not be able to develop, and existing ones may be crushed by foreign competition. This latter situation would result in a net outflow of jobs and wealth from the United States and a reduction in our standard of living. It is a natural expectation that pressures will arise for governments to protect infant and existing industries that are judged to be important to our economy and to our standard of living. It is also a natural expectation that democratic governments will respond to these pressures through increased involvement in the marketplace.[19]

3. *Public Need to Control Undesirable Effects of Economic Concentration*
A third problem with the ideal of a *laissez-faire* economy is that it fails to take into account the reality of growing concentrations of economic power in an industrializing society. For example, what counterforce is there in the free market to stop a single corporation from becoming a monopoly—from running all of its competitors out of business or by buying them up and then setting prices on its products and services without regard to market demand? Likewise, what is there in the free market to stop businesses from forming coalitions, pools, or cartels to set or fix prices among themselves at levels higher than warranted by existing demand? Indeed, other than government, what social mechanism in society has sufficient power to stop these practices in the marketplace? How long could such practices continue before the public would demand a political response through governmental oversight and regulation? I describe in more detail in Chapter 7 the political actions that occurred in response to growing economic concentration of U.S. markets.

4. *Public Need to Control for Abuse of People*
A fourth practical shortcoming in the ideal of a *laissez-faire* economy concerns its potential abuse of people. When Smith's free market model is presented as a modern day cross-plotting of supply and demand curves, it is enthralling to the theoretician, it is elegant to the statistician, and it is so very inspiring to the market model ideologue. Indeed, devoid of real people it is a beautiful and alluring abstraction to behold. But what of the real people who might suffer long hours of hard work in dangerous working conditions and at low pay so that businesses can keep prices down and profits up in the competitive market represented by these demand and supply curves? What of the real families of these wage laborers who would suffer from the effects of low family income? What of the real employees who would be fired without benefits as a result of injury on the job, and what of the suffering of their real families? What too of the suffering of real people who businesses do not want to employ because of mental or physical handicaps? And what of the suffering of real people whose health would be destroyed as a result of unsafe products purchased in the free market?

The free market model, so elegant to contemplate and so appealing to American ideological sensitivities, hides within its abstractions a vast gulf of human suffering that begs for public redress. In real life, democratic governments are subjected to such pressures that they cannot fail to respond to this human suffering.[20] To bring this issue into sharper focus, I briefly describe below several ways in which the *laissez-faire* economic model may work as a social force to make more miserable the lives of employees, consumers, and society's disabled.

Humans Are Expendable.   To begin, I'll use a personal anecdote to describe how employees are affected. A number of years ago I was employed in an organization in which top management extracted as much from employees as possible; made demands that exhausted employees physically, emotionally, and intellectually; and, when employees could no longer keep up the excessive work pace demanded of them, fired those who hadn't already quit voluntarily. Workers were routinely expected to meet unreasonable demands by frantic work schedules requiring extensive overtime without compensation. Anyone who complained was immediately reprimanded or fired. Because this occurred during a recessionary economic period, there were plenty of people applying for each job vacancy, and senior management did not care about the turnover costs these practices created. I'd be willing to bet that you too have experienced a similar work environment at some time in your employment history.

Early in my experience with this particular organization, I was surprised to find a secretary typing furiously at a word processor while wearing two sweaters in an enclosed room which was positively frigid. I asked her why she didn't change the thermostat setting on the window air-conditioner. Without stopping her work, she replied as follows:

> It's the "human expendability principle": humans are expendable; machines are not. Mr. [boss] said I have to keep the room at this temperature for the good of the word processor.

Her boss had paid dearly for the word processing equipment (which was rather expensive at that time), and he had been told by the salesperson that it should be kept cool to avoid breakdown. The secretary, one of a long series, quit a few days later suffering from a cold and exhaustion.

The basic problem, as illustrated in this anecdote, is that, in a competitive, *laissez-faire* economy, there is considerable pressure to increase either profits or one's competitive advantage in the marketplace, or both, by getting as much work as one possibly can out of each employee without regard for their health or safety. For example, it was commonplace during the early history of U.S. industrial development for factories to demand that employees work an exhausting work pace over long work days (the seventy- to eighty-hour work week was the norm). It was not uncommon, too, for manufacturers to use child labor and to subject workers to highly dangerous working conditions.

The typical worker during the early industrialization of our society had little or no resources to fall back on if unemployed, so he or she had to take and hold any job at almost any cost. The industrial businesses, by contrast, had considerable capital and could weather along understaffed for quite some time, if necessary. Furthermore, the flood of European immigrants (who often were solicited to come to the United States by industries that were hungry for cheap employees) created an excess labor force of unskilled workers, so there were plenty of people available to accept almost any job. Under such circumstances, what social mechanism is there in the free market to stop businesses from abusing employees by applying what was called above the human expendability principle?

As described in Chapter 9, workers began to band together in the early to mid-1800s to create unions so they might attain a level of collective power equivalent to that held by large industrial businesses, thereby forcing reform. But this movement was not entirely successful, and, as I describe later, governments came to play the key roles in filling the social need for the protection of employees.

The Old and the Disabled.　There are several other issues related to the abuse of people by the free market economic model that are important. One issue is what to do with persons who become too old to work, who have been physically disabled by work, or who are otherwise mentally or physically handicapped. In the *laissez-faire* economy, people earn whatever the market is willing to pay them, but businesses typically are uninterested in hiring the elderly, the disabled, or the handicapped. So some other means must be found to make provisions for them. With the breakdown of family, community, and religious ties that occurs in industrialization to facilitate business needs, only government remains as a viable social mechanism for assisting these people. The public outcry over their plight and the resultant democratic governmental response to this outcry are altogether predictable. Thus the *laissez-faire* economy has forced governments to arise as providers of welfare programs to alleviate the human suffering that such an economy fosters. I discuss the rise of government welfare programs in greater detail at the end of this chapter.

Business Cycles and Unemployment.　Another issue related to the abuse of people by the free-market is what to do about laborers who are thrown out of work by business down cycles. In contrast to the situation in agricultural economies where the nobility were expected to use their wealth to aid laborers through lean times (resulting, for example, from poor harvests), there is no expectation that private wealth holders in business-oriented societies should do anything about persons made poor by business down cycles. Yet the misery of these people and their dependents can be quite profound and widespread, as it was during the Great Depression. Since the *laissez-faire* economy has no means of making provisions for people in these circumstances, such situations beg for political solutions. And governments are pressured to become the mechanism for delivering these solutions.

Abuse of Consumers.　Yet another issue related to the general problem of abuse of people by the free market is that of consumer protection. As the products brought to market become more and more complex, consumers find themselves incapable of judging quality, safety, or fairness of price. Who among us, for example, can tell from viewing a car on a showroom floor or test driving it whether it is safe or reliable? Who among us can tell which drug is snake oil and which is safe and effective? How can we know whether the labeling of products or the claims made in advertisements are honest? Given the hectic pace of our life-style today, split as it is between work and family demands, given the limited availability of information on most of the products and services that we use, and given the great technical complexity of many of these products and services, how many of us really want to live in a society where the *laissez-faire* motto reads: "Let the buyer beware"? The suffering brought by unsafe products is real (witness, for example, the thalidomide babies), but what social mechanisms can we turn to for protection from shoddy or unsafe products and services, from misleading advertising, or from unscrupulous business practices? Again, it is government to which we have naturally turned. I describe issues in government response to consumer concerns in Chapter 11.

5. *Public Need to Control for Environmental Pollution*

A final problem with the ideal of a *laissez-faire* economy is that of environmental pollution. I discuss this issue in detail in Chapter 12, but the problem, in brief, is as follows. Though all life forms pollute their environment, industrial production processes and the resulting goods that consumers use have made it possible for us to pollute our environment on a grand scale. In the *laissez-faire* economy, every business effort is expected to be aimed at holding down costs so as to compete successfully in the market. Any costs that can be avoided in this model will be avoided, and this includes the cost of safe disposal of industrial waste products (airborne, waterborne, or in solid form) and the costs of clean-up or remedy from wastes emitted by the products sold on the market (e.g., auto exhaust or freon leaks from refrigerators and air conditioners, etc.). What is there in the dynamics of the invisible hand's operation in the free market to prevent businesses from polluting the environment to the point of human extinction? Nothing. As the environment has become increasingly fouled, it is again governments to which the public has naturally turned to seek solutions.

The Failure of the Laissez-Faire *Economy*

If we look at U.S. history as though it constituted a grand experiment in the implementation of a *laissez-faire* economy, we can see all five shortcomings described here working to force increased government involvement in the marketplace. Both of the first two shortcomings concerning needs for a legal environment and for political protection of our economy and our standard of living were addressed early on through government involvement in the marketplace. By the middle to late 1800s it was obvious that the fourth shortcoming, concerning employee abuse, also had become a serious problem in the United States. It was during this time in Europe that Marx was writing his critiques of free market capitalism, and it was also during this time that early unions were beginning to demand redress of employee abuse. More lasting solutions did not occur, however, until the twentieth century with increased government involvement in the marketplace to legitimate and support unions and to force workplace reform by law.

The third shortcoming of the *laissez-faire* model (the growing concentration of economic power and its potential for massive abuses) became a serious problem by the late 1800s. The response cannot be surprising to anyone, with governments stepping in to undertake antitrust efforts in an attempt to address these problems.

But, even if none of the preceding four problems had occurred in the *laissez-faire* economy to require governmental intervention, the fifth shortcoming concerning environmental pollution would surely have sounded the final death knell for dreams of a *laissez-faire* economy. We may be able to survive somehow in the midst of wholesale abuses of employees, of consumers, and of the market itself by big business corporations; but we certainly cannot survive when our drinking water is poisoned and our air is contaminated by toxins. Government involvement in the market to reduce environmental pollution has become a necessary and quite predictable outcome of the *laissez-faire* economy.

If U.S. history is viewed as an experiment in the application of *laissez-faire* economic principles, then it is evident by the necessity of its expiration that the *laissez-faire* economic model fails to meet the needs of industrial societies. In its place we have created an economy that is both government-aided and government-regulated. The next section of this chapter examines in some detail the government-aided economy that we have created, while Chapter 7 examines a number of related issues in government regulation.

The Rise of the Government-Aided Economy

The Growth in Governments

Partly in response to the factors just described, the government sector in the United States has grown considerably in size to serve as a counterforce to the business sector by monitoring, controlling, and remedying the undesirable features of the free marketplace. How much growth has there been in the government sector in the United States? Consider these observations.

In 1890 the entire federal budget was 318 million dollars, with about a third of this budget ($107 million) devoted to military pensions.[21] There was no income tax or corporate tax at that time. By 1940 the federal budget was a little over nine billion dollars.[22] But, as of 1995, it was 1.5 trillion dollars (which is 1.5 million million dollars, enough to make 1.5 million Americans into instant millionaires).

The size of our government sector today is astonishing. For example, by the mid-1990s it cost nearly 3 billion dollars per year just to equip, staff, and operate the U.S. Congress.[23] Total spending of all governments (local, state, and federal) per person in the United States rose from about $467 in 1950 to more than $11,000 by the early 1990s.[24] Over this same period, total government spending as a percentage of the national GNP rose from 24.7 percent to over 41 percent.[25] Total government spending in the United States is now more than the entire combined GNP of the industrialized economies of both France and Great Britain put together, or of the GNP of the entire continent of South America or Africa.[26]

Government employment is also immense. From 1950 to 1992, total government employment rose from about 6.4 million to over 18.7 million people.[27] Current government employees constitute a group that is comparable in size to all of the people in the entire metropolitan area of New York City–Northern New Jersey–Long Island, and it is a group that is larger than the entire population of the metropolitan area of Los Angeles–Anaheim–Riverside.[28] It is a group greater in size than the entire population of Australia and about the same size as the entire population of Iraq (a country we recently went to war with).[29] It is more employees than all employees of the 500 largest U.S. industrial corporations,[30] and nearly as many as all employees who work in all of the states of the entire U.S. Pacific Coast (consisting of California, Oregon, Washington, Alaska, and Hawaii).[31] Furthermore, nearly a fifth (18.8 percent) of the national payroll comes directly from public operations at the national or local (e.g., military, schools, police, etc.), and total government purchases account for not quite a fifth (18.1 percent) of the entire U.S. GNP.[32] As these figures indicate, governments today clearly represent a towering presence in our society and play a significant role in our economy.

Brief History of the Rise of the Government-Aided Economy

In this section I describe briefly the history of how the United States went from being a society in which governments were small, to being a society in which governments were large and intruded extensively in the marketplace. Problems created by big business abuses of people and of the market played important roles in this history, but so too did the two world wars and the Great Depression.[33]

The rise of big businesses in the latter half of the 1800s resulted in a considerable outcry over their practices of price fixing and price gouging. These problems became especially serious in the railroad industry, in which farmers and small businesspersons were being squeezed mercilessly by railroad price discrimination arrangements. State efforts to end those practices met with little success, so it fell to the federal government to intervene. It did so by passing the Interstate Commerce Act in 1887, which created the first major federal regulatory agency (the Interstate Commerce Commission). Subsequent concern over the growing abuses by trusts and monopolies in the sale of products of all sorts led to the passage of the Sherman Antitrust Act (1890), the Federal Trade Commission Act (1914), and the Clayton Antitrust Act (1914).

By the early years of the twentieth century, the federal government had been pressed into action as a regulatory force in a few additional areas of national public concern. New legislation, for example, included the Pure Food and Drug Act (1906) to regulate the purity of foods and pharmaceuticals and the Federal Reserve Act (1913) to increase regulatory oversight of currency, credit, and banking. Still, the overall involvement of governments in the markets of that time remained small.

The world wars of the twentieth century, however, also played roles in increasing governmental involvement in the market. Both of the world wars, but most particularly World War II, required considerable cooperation between the government and business sectors to create the orchestrated industrial effort needed for victory. World War II in particular created a generation of business leaders, only now of retirement age, who by force of this experience became considerably more aware than were their predecessors of the important role that businesses might play in assuring the successful achievement of larger social goals.

Though considerable evidence can be found early in the history of this nation for the impracticality of a *laissez-faire* model for our growing industrial economy, the Great Depression more than any other event became the "final straw" for *laissez-faire*. It is hard for those of us younger than 55 or so to appreciate the Great Depression. You have to imagine a situation in which upwards to a fourth of the people in the workforce (nearly thirteen million people) were out of work, and there simply were no jobs. Many additional millions of workers were underemployed or were faced with severely falling wages. In short, the economic collapse left a vast number of families in the United States either without income or with too little to support themselves.

Our economy was a shambles. Preceding the Great Depression, a long period of overproduction and falling prices had left the agricultural sector greatly weakened, with many farm families living in desperately poor conditions as a result. Unbridled speculation in securities (much of it on borrowed money) had contributed to the collapse of the nation's stock markets, which seriously eroded the financial basis for industrial corporations and wiped out the savings of many people. An overextension of bank loans, which were now unpayable, coupled with runs on banks by fearful account holders, resulted in the collapse of our nation's banking industry; many people lost their life savings. Bank foreclosures on loans and mortgages, as well as the inability of many farmers, businesses, and homeowners to get their savings out of banks, resulted in bankruptcy for many. This was certainly a desperate situation.

Governments at the time of the Great Depression were still relatively small; fundamental programs we take for granted today did not exist, such as government-required unemployment insurance programs, Social Security, Supplemental Security Income, Aid to Families with Dependent Children, food stamps, housing assistance, Medicaid, Medicare, and so on. The desperate times would have been far more manageable if they had not lingered on so long, lasting over an entire decade. It was clear that the economy was in serious trouble, that no rapid self-correction of the fundamental problems of our economy was forthcoming, and that something had to be done soon to alleviate human suffering and stop any further economic hemorrhaging. A public problem of this magnitude places great pressures on democratic governments to provide a public solution; not surprisingly, governments began to respond to these pressures.

It certainly would be unfair to blame Herbert Hoover for a depression which gained first national attention with the collapse of the nation's stock markets less than a year after he took office. Rather, it appeared that the "feast or famine" cycles of previous agricultural economies had simply come to be replaced by newer "boom or bust" (recession–depression) cycles of an industrial economy. Hoover, an adherent of the *laissez-faire* model, assumed that this new depression was just another down cycle that would take care of itself (hopefully in short order, or at least before the next election). Unfortunately for Hoover, it did not take care of itself, and the depths of human suffering that it entailed begged for a political solution.[34] Enter Franklin D. Roosevelt.

Roosevelt, a man possessing a dynamic personality and a deep sympathy for human suffering, was voted into the office of President in the Fall of 1932 in an election landslide. As a Democrat, Roosevelt was a member of a party that, at least among Northerners, had long-standing political ties to the interests of working people. (By contrast, Hoover's party, the Republican party, had strong ties to the industrial sector and to other business interests dating back historically at least to the Civil War.) Roosevelt was a cousin of the irrepressible former Republican president, Theodore Roosevelt, who had sought to foster an image for himself as being a business trust-buster and who later bolted the Republican Party to form his own Bull Moose Party. All things considered, Franklin Roosevelt's personality, background, political support, and landslide victory made him more likely than Hoover to try to use government to get the economy moving again. Significantly, previous Republican presidents had been likely to regard a successful economy as one in which governmental involvement was minimal or nonexistent, but Franklin Roosevelt regarded it to be a duty of the government to remedy economic problems for the good of the average person. This shift in views constituted a "New Deal" for Americans, and the Rooseverters were "New Dealers."

This is not the place to describe in detail the entire alphabet soup of federal programs Roosevelt created to aid those who were suffering and in an attempt to reform the economic system (examples include the CCC, PWA, WPA, NRA, FERA, and many others).

Perhaps the most significant of the new government programs were those designed to address the sort of shortcomings that I described previously in the *laissez-faire* model. For example, the Securities and Exchange Commission (1934) was created to more closely regulate the stock markets; the Federal Home Loan Bank (created in Hoover's last year as President, 1932) went to work regulating home financing institutions; the Federal Housing Administration (FHA) was created to insure home loans; the Emergency Banking Act (1933) worked to create new confidence in the banking industry; the Federal Deposit

Insurance Corporation (1933, FDIC) was created to insure bank deposits; the Glass-Steagall Act (1933) dramatically altered regulations on banking; the Reconstruction Finance Corporation (1932, also a late Hoover creation) extended government credit to troubled businesses; the Agricultural Adjustment Act (1933, later declared unconstitutional) dramatically expanded federal regulation and support of agriculture; the dollar was removed from the gold standard and devalued to help farmers compete in international markets; the National Labor Relations Act (1935) created the National Labor Relations Board to provide legal recognition and protection for unions; the Fair Labor Standards Act (1938) set minimum wages, maximum work weeks, and minimum ages for employees; the Public Utility Holding Company Act (1935) and the National Gas Act (1938) set in motion regulatory processes designed to end abuses in the utilities industries; the Social Security Act (1935) provided an unemployment insurance system, and created programs to provide support for the disabled, widowed, elderly, and poor families with children; and a variety of public works programs were created, including the Civilian Conservation Corps, the Civil Works Administration, the Works Progress Administration, and the Public Works Administration.

In addition to direct programs of assistance for businesses, businesses were also assisted indirectly through the programs Roosevelt designed to reduce suffering among the unemployed. This indirect business assistance can be envisioned as follows. As more income becomes available in the hands of the poor through public aid programs, they should be able to spend more and thus create an increased demand in the market. This in turn should spur business expansion, business profits, and business employment. Then too, expanded business employment should make even more income available for spending and foster further business expansion. In essence, one might expect that the introduction of such relief programs should set in motion an economic spiral that, initiated by humanitarian efforts to reduce human suffering, would proceed under its own forces to bring the economy out of the depression.

Roosevelt's efforts to spur the economy were occurring at a time when an important English economist was becoming known to the American intelligentsia. In a book published in 1936[35] and in other writings and speeches John Maynard Keynes presented arguments justifying government spending as a remedy for economically depressed times. Keynes and his followers argued that government spending could play an important role in creating demand and in fostering employment in the marketplace. According to his theory, in times of recession or depression governments should increase their spending to serve as a corrective to reduced consumer spending. In essence, this strategy would constitute a government-generated demand-side solution to economic downturns; it would be a solution that seeks to increase market demand and employment through increased government spending.

The political reality of the collapse of the *laissez-faire* economy was such that Roosevelt's administration had already taken a number of actions that in retrospect could be regarded as embodying a demand-side solution of government spending. Keynes' arguments, therefore, served only to provide an intellectual justification for some of the programs that had already been set in motion. It would appeal to our moral sensibilities to be able to say that Roosevelt's demand-side programs were a Keynesian success story. That is, it would be very satisfying to be able to say that putting money into the hands of society's impoverished families, with the increased spending that resulted, did in fact stimulate our economy to the point of bringing us out of the Great Depression. All humanitarians, I am sure, would be most gratified if this were true. However the depression lingered on throughout the decade of the 1930s despite Roosevelt's humanitarian, demand-side solution programs.

The event that put our economy back on track was Japan's bombing of Pearl Harbor in December 1941, which resulted in our immediate entrance into the World War II. Here was an event that required a demand-side solution of government spending on a scale far more massive than politics would permit for mere humanitarian efforts. Furthermore, because patriotism in the face of an external threat to national security tends to override economic ideologies, this certainly was not a time to cleave closely to *laissez-faire* principles. The industrial economy had to be geared up in short order to support a major war effort, and both business leaders and government officials (especially from the military) had to cooperate to plan and carry out the production processes needed for this effort. Thus our entrance into the war forced governments to spend colossal sums of money and forced the government and business sectors to work far more closely together than they ever had before in the effort to achieve a collective social goal.

Federal outlays tell this story quite clearly. Between 1920 and 1932, the last year of Hoover's administration, total federal outlays as a percentage of U.S. GNP varied from 3.0 percent to 8.0 percent, with the percentage for most of these years (ten of the thirteen) falling below 4.8 percent. During the next nine years of Roosevelt's humanitarian government spending, prior to our entrance into World War II, federal outlays ran between 8.0 percent to 10.6 percent. During the war years between 1942 and 1945, federal outlays as percentages of GNP varied from 21.6 percent upwards to 46.4 percent. With entry into the war, we were now talking about some real federal spending.[36]

Our war effort had many favorable effects on the economy: it galvanized public cooperation, it put every available wage earner back to work (in either the armed forces or in the factories that supplied the war effort) and it vastly increased government spending. Here was a demand-side solution of government spending on a much grander scale and more easily defensible political grounding than Roosevelt's earlier humanitarian efforts. Although many people may complain about welfare programs and force politicians to set severe limitations on these programs, who will pinch pennies for national defense, especially in the midst of a war? Our entrance into World War II meant, in short order, that the Great Depression had come to an end.

Wars typically stimulate economies, but the usual tendency is for an economy to go into a slump after the war is over and the heyday of war-related spending has ended. This did not happen to our economy following World War II for several reasons. First, a large volume of consumer savings accumulated among wage earners during the war at a time when goods were rationed and hard to obtain. These savings, coupled with an immediate post-war tax cut, created a bonanza of consumer spending over the immediate post-war period that buoyed our economy.

Second, a variety of Roosevelt's welfare programs were now in place to provide a continuing demand-side solution of government spending for the unemployed. With much enhancement, the most important of these programs remain today to serve both as ongoing spurs to our economy and as palliatives for the miseries of the poor, especially for the elderly, disabled, and children. We might call this part of our government-aided economy the welfare-industrial complex.

Third, the war provided such a massive stimulus to the economy that there was very little enthusiasm for cutting defense spending after the war. Furthermore, such spending was much more acceptable politically than was welfare spending. So it was fortunate that a threat of communist designs over Europe could be identified as providing justification for continuing military preparedness and arms buildup. Thus we did not give up our war mentality; instead we entered the Cold War. As a demand-side solution to stimulating the economy though government spending, a "cold" war is much to be preferred to a "hot" one, both on political and humanitarian grounds. The cold war (with intermittent hot wars in Korea, and Viet Nam) and the perceived need for a worldwide military preparedness have provided us with many years of massive post-war federal spending as a stimulus to our economy. This part of our government-aided economy is typically called the military-industrial complex.

Again, federal outlays confirm this trend. As a percentage of the U.S. GNP, federal outlays between 1920 and 1941 never exceeded 11 percent, and for nearly half of these years it did not exceed 5 percent. However, at no time since the end of World War II have federal outlays, as a percentage of GNP, fallen as low as 11 percent. From 1947 to 1951 they varied from 12.8 percent to 16.8 percent of the GNP. From 1952 to 1974 they varied from 16.8 percent to 20.7 percent. Since 1974 they have never been below twenty percent of the GNP. As of 1993, federal outlays were 22 percent of the U.S. GNP, with three-fourths of all federal purchases of goods and services during that year going for national defense.[37]

In the early 1990s, the welfare-industrial complex and the military-industrial complex accounted for 57.1 percent and 21.6 percent, respectively, of all federal outlays, or a little over three-fourths of all federal outlays. The percentage of federal outlays devoted to welfare is an overly generous estimate, however, because it includes Social Security and Medicare as welfare programs. Social Security and Medicare together account for 31.8 percent of all federal outlays, with all other welfare programs combined accounting for 25.3 percent of federal outlays. Furthermore, these other welfare programs include veteran's programs, education, and a variety of other programs in addition to public aid program for the poor. Public aid programs for the poor by themselves account for only 10 percent of federal outlays.[38]

For both the welfare-industrial complex and the military-industrial complex there are many instances of abuse and fraud, as money falls into the wrong hands or as products that are purchased are misused, overpriced, or defective. Misuse of food stamps; welfare or Social Security checks going to ineligible people; overcharges to Medicare or Medicaid by physicians, hospitals, or nursing homes; and many other abuses abound in the welfare-industrial complex. The military-industrial complex also provides a great many examples of waste and fraud, such as grossly overpriced toilet seats and hammers, hundreds of millions of dollars spent on planes and other military equipment that are seriously defective or inoperative, and so on.[39]

Keynes once joked that an economy might be spurred by any government spending, even by having the government bury money and then having the private sector go to work digging it up again.[40] All government spending, even that which is absorbed through abuse and fraud, no doubt has some salutary effect for some parts of the economy. It does, after all, provide jobs and income for many people, and their spending trickles its way through the economy as demand in many markets.

All government spending, however, amounts to a transfer of money from those who pay taxes (or from debt), to those who are employed by governments, or to those who receive contracts, grants, or subsidies from governments. In some cases the people who are recipients in this exchange are seen as morally deserving; in other cases they are not. In any case, governments have now become collectively the biggest player in the development and sustenance of the U.S. market, and this is a far cry from the ideals of a *laissez-faire* economy. The contemporary importance of government to our economy is affirmed in the 1946 Employment Act, which declared that the federal government has a responsibility to foster employment in the economy.

In summary, if we may say of U.S. history that prior to the Great Depression we lived in a primarily "Smithian" economy, we certainly have come since to reside in a primarily "Keynesian" economy, with both of the government-sponsored military–industrial and welfare–industrial complexes playing leading roles in producing demand in our economy.

Major Ways Governments Help Businesses

In the rise of the government-aided economy, our governments have come to play many major roles in the economy to help selected parts of the business sector. Nine roles are described below.

1. Governments provide continuing demand-side spending solutions in the forms of military-industrial and welfare-industrial complexes. But in a larger framework, as noted earlier, governments at all levels stimulate many sectors of the economy through their combined market purchases, which amount to almost one fifth of the U.S. GNP. In addition to military purchases, some other areas of major government expenditures in 1992 were for education ($354 billion); interest on debt ($255 billion); public aid programs for the poor ($208 billion); health and hospitals ($119 billion); police, fire, and corrections ($87 billion); natural resources (including parks and recreation, $81 billion); highways ($67 billion), government administration ($67 billion); and sewage and sanitation ($32 billion).[41] In addition, government purchases reach out into almost every market, from paper clips to computers to shoe shines. These all represent governments' contributions to demand in our economy, and without them our economy would shrink considerably.

2. Governments give lucrative monopolies to some companies that provide certain services or products which political interests have determined should not be left open to free market dynamics. Examples include gas and electric companies, local telephone companies, and some mass transit companies. In return for being given a monopoly on these services, the companies that are involved are closely regulated by governments in an effort to ensure that the public good is met.

3. Governments pay for many "external costs," which are costs businesses would have to pay for themselves if they couldn't get someone else to pay for them. Some of these costs overlap with the general demand-side solution spending that was described earlier. Examples of external business costs that governments pay for include the costs of education so that each new generation of workers will have the skills desired by businesses; the costs of creating and maintaining a highway, airport, and water navigation system so businesses can transport their goods to markets; the costs of urban services such as mass transit, public health, sanitation, and so forth, so that a ready labor pool can be housed and maintained in easy commuting distance to the major production facilities of businesses and to their mass market outlets; the costs of cleaning up the environment from pollution produced by business production processes or from the use of business goods themselves; and the costs of maintaining a worldwide national defense system to protect United States business interests abroad and maintaining local police forces and judicial systems to protect business holdings at home.

4. Government use of tax structures and tax shelters can have an expansive effect on businesses in certain parts of the economy, such as in housing and office construction, oil exploration, and so forth, and on business investors in general, through favorable treatment for capital gains.

5. The federal government attempts to provide a stable currency in the economy through its control over the printing of money and through actions by its Federal Reserve System. Through these and other mechanisms it may at various times also attempt to reduce inflation in the economy or to stimulate capital investment and consumer spending.

6. Governments attempt to promote the vitality of the economy by regulating certain key parts of it so as to ensure that fair business practices are followed and that excessive abuses do not occur. Some major areas for these regulatory efforts include banking, insurance, antitrust, the stock exchanges, and the establishment of uniform weights and measures.

7. Governments subsidize research and development costs in the creation of the specialized technologies that are needed for such programs as space exploration and defense, but which often are subsequently applied by businesses to create products with a more general market appeal. For example, in 1994 the federal government provided funds to cover approximately a fifth of all industrial research and development costs in the United States.[42]

8. Governments provide subsidies, loans, and loan guarantees for business overproduction or to make up for business mismanagement in key industries, such as agriculture, banking (e.g., the bailout of Continental Illinois National Bank of Chicago and the savings and loan and banking scandals), automobiles (e.g., the Chrysler bailout[43]), defense (e.g., the Lockheed bailout), and for a number of other businesses through the Small Business Administration and the Export-Import Bank.[44]

9. Governments exercise a form of mercantilism in defending many U.S. businesses from foreign competition by restricting or taxing imports (see a fuller discussion of these issues in Chapter 13).

In short, governments have in a number of ways become friends to the business sector, and the presence of governments is felt almost everywhere in the national market. If the various forms of government assistance described here were to end overnight, the effect on our economy would be devastating. Collectively, we might say of all these forms of assistance that they constitute a government "wealthfare" system for the business sector. A summary of all the costs of this wealthfare system would reveal that it is far larger, far more elaborate, and far more costly than the government welfare system that we presently provide for the poor. Indeed, as I noted earlier and will discuss in more detail later in this chapter, the welfare system for the poor itself works indirectly as but a small subcomponent of the larger wealthfare system. However, the public dole always comes with a price. Thus just as the welfare system operates in large part by regulating the poor,[45] so does the wealthfare system operate by regulating businesses, investors, and the economy. The effects of government regulations on businesses is a topic I discuss in detail in Chapter 7.

The Planned and Unplanned Industrial Economies

In 1991 the Soviet Union, with its economy in shambles, dissolved. Thus ended the largest experiment of this century designed to see how well a government-planned industrial economy would work. Although government-planned economies have lasted successfully for very great lengths of time in agricultural societies, we have not seen a comparably successful effort in industrial societies, in which innovation and its prerequisite of individual freedom have historically been the rule. Figure 6.1 illustrates where several industrial societies would be placed on a continuum, with one extreme representing the ideal of the fully government planned economy (i.e., the command economy) and the other extreme representing the ideal of no government planning or intervention in the economy (i.e., the *laissez-faire* economy). The continuum between these two ideals represents varying degrees of government involvement and planning in the market.[46]

As I discussed earlier and as shown in Figure 6.1, the United States came closest to the ideal of the *laissez-faire* economy early in its history, though it necessarily fell short of the ideal. Since then, however, the United States has shifted considerably toward conditions which are identified in Figure 6.1 as economic pluralism, in which government planning and interventions, along with actions taken by other sectors of society, play significant roles in many, but not all, aspects of the economy.

Unlike the United States, other major industrial countries, such as France, Great Britain, Japan, Germany, and Italy, have very long histories involving agricultural economies and government involvement in the economy. Therefore, it was more natural for them to involve governments in their industrializing economies earlier and to a greater degree than it was for the United States. In these countries some industries were nationalized, such as Great Britain's ownership of steel, coal, power, transportation, and health care. By contrast, U.S. governments own very few services, such as public water and sewer treatment, while permitting heavily regulated monopolies in a number of industries, such as utilities. All of the countries practicing economic pluralism have a considerable government presence in their otherwise private sector economies, and all have created government-funded welfare-industrial complexes to attend to the human misery left unaddressed by the private business sector.

China and the Soviet Union attempted a different approach to industrialization by placing most facets of their economies under the central control of their bureaucratic governments. Though the initial ideological justification for this effort was based on concerns that businesses were too corrupt to produce a humane and just society, the ensuing governmental rulings and actions came more and more to be determined by what was deemed best for the current governmental ruling elite. Based on the poor economic results and oppressive social conditions that were obtained in these experiments, it appears that we may safely draw the conclusion that governments are just as corrupt and corruptible as businesses. Therefore, any hope of an utopia being brought into being through government planning and control is a pipe dream.

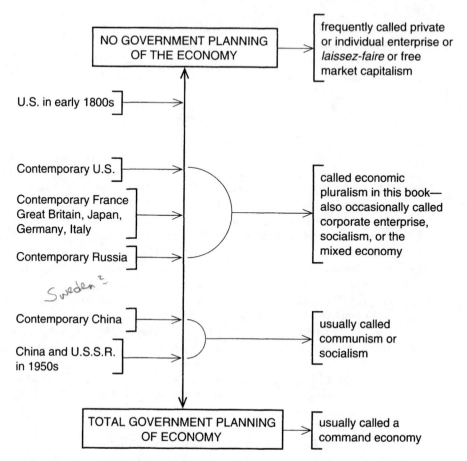

FIGURE 6.1 Continuum Representing Planned and Unplanned Economies

We may conclude from these discussions that the two great ideologies that have dominated international attention for more than 100 years appear to have run out of steam. Neither *laissez-faire* capitalism nor Soviet or Chinese style communism could deliver on the type of social and economic goals that their adherents promised.[47] In reality, countries starting out near either end of the continuum between these ideological extremes have moved increasingly toward the center, a pluralistic economic environment[48], which has shown itself over the past fifty years to work reasonably well in Western industrialized societies and in Japan.

The Failure of Rational Solutions

Why didn't the rational planning of the Soviet Union produce an optimally functioning economy? The failure of rationally planned solutions to social and economic problems is a never-ending source of annoyance to intellectuals. The intellectual would prefer to believe that the surest and quickest way to achieve any desired goal is with an organized plan. Yet, as a paraphrase of the old adage goes, "The best laid plans of mice and people typically founder and fail." It would be useful here to review a few reasons why rational plans fail.

Lack of Fixed Social Boundaries

First, as noted in Chapter 1, the phenomena of social reality do not possess fixed boundaries. From moment to moment they are never quite the same or independent; rather they are always changing and are extensively interwoven with other social phenomena. In such an evanescent context, how does one develop plans to make specific changes in particular phenomena? In actual practice one tries to do this by making many simplifying assumptions about social reality so as to make it possible to construct a well-organized, rational, comprehensive plan of action. Almost inevitably, however, the resulting plan founders on implementation because the simplifying assumptions it required for formulation fail to prepare the implementers to work with the actual complexities of social reality. This is as much of a problem for U.S. governments in their efforts to regulate businesses and the economy and for U.S. bureaucratic corporate managers in their effort to run their corporations as it has been for Soviet efforts to plan and run their economy.

Reliance on Bureaucracies

A second reason social plans fail is because they typically must rely on bureaucracies for their implementation, which of course was true for the heavily bureaucratized Soviet system of economic planning. As I described earlier for corporations, however, it is common in bureaucracies for internal counterpressures to arise that threaten official goals. We see this, for example, in the unofficial goals set by managerial bureaucrats and by workers that often are at variance with and override official goals in actual day-to-day operation, and we see this in the resistances and acts of sabotage engendered by the depersonalization and authoritarianism that are characteristic of bureaucracies. Thus in the Soviet Union, for example, bureaucratic managers (from the senior levels of the party elite on down) often were able to operate their respective governmental and economic functions in ways that served their own interests as much or more so than those set by official plans or ideology.[49] Then too, factory workers in the Soviet system exhibited their own forms of resistance and sabotage of these plans through absenteeism, drunkenness, unofficial rate-setting, theft, and so on.

Social Control and Social Resistance

Lastly, every planned social solution necessarily requires controls on human behavior, resulting in a decrease in human freedom. This is especially true in any effort to run a planned economy, as controls on capital, managers, line workers, markets, and consumers are all necessary. But just as persons in bureaucracies set their own unofficial goals and engage in resistance or sabotage to thwart official plans, so too do persons on the street. Thus in the Soviet Union a thriving black market played a major, if unofficial, role in the economy.

The Failure of Unplanned Economies

If a rationally planned economy is a folly, then what about a wholly unplanned one such as is posed by the ideal of *laissez-faire?* We know from our own history that this approach also does not work. Left mostly free of government controls, an industrial economy brings into being larger and larger corporations and thus places increasing proportions of the marketplace under the oligopolistic control of fewer and fewer businesses. Then too, business abuses of employees, consumers, the environment, governments, and each other all pose situations that beg for political solution. And so too do the emerging business cycles of boom and bust that periodically inflict much human suffering.

Economic Pluralism: The Middle Ground

By contrast, the middle ground of economic pluralism has included the solutions that industrialized countries have converged on and that have worked most successfully. In economic pluralism many special interest groups have a say in business decision making: shareholders, managers, consumers, consumer activist groups and class action suits on behalf of consumers, environmentalist groups, civil rights groups, employees acting independently or collectively through lawsuits or union contracts, assorted community betterment groups, business associations, and, of course, governments. Under such circumstances, the freedom of choice of businesspersons is constrained considerably as they face an array of often conflicting social environmental pressures. It is under these circumstances that our economy has generally prospered since World War II.

In a sense, economic pluralism is much like Smithianism *writ large*. In Smith's model the wealth of society is believed to be maximized, as if by an invisible hand, when free competition occurs among businesses in the market. Economic pluralism, by contrast, aims at maximizing the welfare of all sectors of society, as if by a much larger invisible hand, when free competition among the political interests of all sectors is permitted to be brought to bear in market decisions.

Advantages of Economic Pluralism
Pluralism poses at least four distinct advantages for an industrialized society.

1. Pluralism is best suited to societies that emphasize individualism. When political and religious power is splintered and people are expected to make their own choices about major life issues, there will naturally be a plurality of points of view on any issue. Under such circumstances, it is reasonable for people to band together with others who have made the same choices or who face the same conditions that restrict their choices so as to increase their influence on their surrounding social order. Thus workers may band together around common grievances; consumers, minorities, environmentalists, community members, and so forth, may band together into activist groups around issues that concern them; or politicians, public bureaucrats, or segments of the population at large may pressure governments into taking actions of interest to them.

2. Though economic pluralism decreases the freedom of choice for businesspersons, it otherwise maximizes freedom of choice society-wide by creating multiple avenues through which the interests of many persons can be brought to bear on marketplace decision making and on the economy as a whole. This is especially important in a society where, as I note earlier, economic power has become highly concentrated in the hands of a relatively few corporations that are in a position to dominate the economy and to engage in massive abuses, even if unwittingly, so long as there are no counterforces to highlight these abuses and prevent them from occurring. In short, economic pluralism maximizes freedom for the entire society by creating multiple checks on what would otherwise be the increasingly monolithic power of big businesses.[50]

3. Pluralism forces businesses to become more socially responsible because it provides avenues through which the interests of all sectors of society can be brought to bear on business decision making. In essence, it serves as a feedback process to bring businesses into more harmonious relations with other sectors of society for the good of all sectors and of society as a whole.

4. Pluralism sets the stage for more innovative and effective solutions to be proposed for collective problems in the economy or elsewhere in society, as it permits the expertise and political support of interest groups with many points of view to be brought to bear on social planning efforts, decision making, and implementation.

Shortcomings of Economic Pluralism

Of course there are shortcomings to pluralism as well. The most important is that it is not guided by an integrated purpose, so there is no social control mechanism to ensure the sort of continuous, consistent change in a short period of time that might be needed to deal effectively with serious problems, such as are posed by environmental pollution. Instead, it involves endless power struggles as people and interest groups scramble to create coalitions so as to better influence decision making. It is, then, a very inefficient, almost rudderless system for decision making; as a consequence, action on major issues may be stalled for decades or until catastrophe occurs. This is the situation that today confronts the U.S. Congress, major U.S. corporations, and many other parts of society (such as the educational systems, health care systems, correctional systems, and public assistance systems).

With no central power to press large-scale solutions onto society, the vying power groups can effectively stymie each other so that little or no action is taken until the foundations of social life decay perhaps beyond the point of remedy—or at least until catastrophe or external threat to national security or well-being forces all groups to work together. It would be desirable not to have to rely on such a greatly delayed decision making process, but in the twentieth century no better alternative to economic pluralism has presented itself for industrialized societies.

Inequality and Public Welfare in U.S. Society

Inequality in the United States

Sociologists love to study inequality. It is a controversial and interesting topic, and it is a phenomenon that pervades all parts of society, so there is no shortage of material for study. Three important social dimensions along which people are made unequal are: (1) prestige, or public esteem (and its corollary of subjective feelings of self-worth); (2) privilege, or access to society's most valuable resources; and (3) power, which is the control one has over others.

As I described in an earlier chapter, the creation of a surplus in agricultural societies set the stage both for the rise of civilization and for the rise of extensive social inequality in the form of privileged control over this surplus. Indeed, agricultural societies have exhibited the most social inequality of all societies. For example, even as recently as the mid-1700s, most of the land of Europe was held by nobility and the church. While virtually the entire population skimped by through their typically short lives on little more than a subsistence diet and an exceedingly deprived living standard, the privileged few landowners lived like, well, they lived like kings, or at least like well-off barons. From our perspective today, this system of inequality was unjust because of the heredity manner in which privileges were transmitted, the corollary lack of freedom of opportunity for everyday persons who were not nobility, and the widespread suffering this system inflicted on much of the population. Few of us, I am sure, would want to return to living under such a system. From our perspective, it was simply unfair.

However, the deprivation and suffering of most of the population made possible many features of what we call civilization. Through the deprivation of the many, the few power-holders were able to accumulate a sufficient surplus to cause the great structures, monuments, and works of art to be created that we so much admire today, including the cathedrals and temples, the castles and walled cities, the great art of persons patronized by the elite (e.g., da Vinci or Michelangelo), or the great works by thinkers such as Saint Thomas Aquinas.

Industrialization sets in motion an entirely new process for generating and allocating surplus wealth in amounts of extraordinary proportion. One way to view this process is through the way industrialization restructures occupations. For example, industrial techniques make large numbers of farm laborers unnecessary while making necessary large numbers of factory workers and, later, of corporate workers of all kinds. This restructuring has significant implications for social power. The social power that is entailed in the control of large numbers of people shifts in this process from landholders to persons who can lay claim of ownership to factories, and later to those who, although they do not own their businesses, have managerial control over them.

Not too surprisingly, those in power tend to set up rules of privilege that give themselves greatest access to social surplus. This was true for political and religious authorities in agricultural societies, and it is true for economic elites in business-oriented societies. However, the power of business elites today is not as monolithic as that which was exercised by political and religious authorities in agricultural societies. Consequently although social inequality in industrialized societies is substantial, it is not as great as it was in preceding agricultural societies. Let's look at some figures.

Surprisingly, very little data on the distribution of wealth in the United States has been collected, so we must make do with what is available. One of the best studies was done by the Federal Reserve System of all net assets (assets minus debts) held by households in 1962 in the United States, including asset holdings in businesses, securities, real estate, trusts, oil royalties, patents, homes, automobiles, and checking and savings accounts.[51] These data indicated that only a little over 1 percent of U.S. households held more than a third (34.6 percent) of all U.S. net wealth. The top 6.7 percent of U.S. households held more than half (56.3 percent) of all U.S. net wealth, and the top 20 percent held 76 percent of all net wealth. By contrast, the poorest 20 percent of households held only one fiftieth of one percent (that is 0.02 percent) of all U.S. net assets, and the next 20 percent of households held only 2.1 percent. These figures are presented in Figure 6.2.

If we imagine each percent of wealth in the United States as representing what any one percent of households should hold if all wealth were distributed equally, then the "super

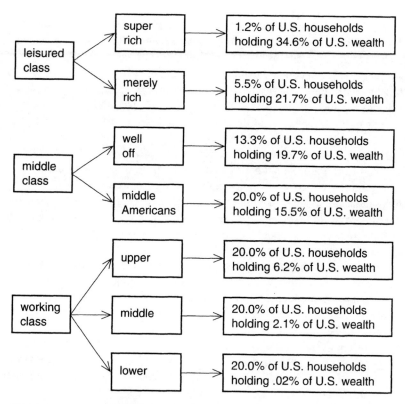

FIGURE 6.2   Distribution of Household Wealth in the U.S. in 1962

Source: Figures are drawn from Executive Office of the President, Office of Management and Budget, *Social Indicators, 1973* (Washington, D.C.: U.S. Government Printing Office, 1973), Chart 5/15; and from Frank Ackerman and Andrew Zimbalist, "Capitalism and Inequality in the United States," in eds. Richard C. Edwards, Michael Reich, and Thomas E. Weisskopf, *The Capitalist System,* 3rd ed. (Englewood Cliffs, N.J.: Prentice-Hall, 1986), p. 220, Table 6–D.

rich" (1.2 percent of households) hold nearly twenty-nine times (34.6 percent divided by 1.2 percent) more wealth than would be expected. The 5.5 percent of households that are "merely rich," by contrast, have holdings that are a little less than only four times better than would be expected of them (21.7 percent divided by 5.5 percent). Together, these two groups constitute what I shall call the leisured class of the United States. They consist of less than 7 percent of American households, but they hold over half (56.3 percent) of the wealth.

Society's surplus finds its way into the pockets of the leisured class in the United States without, for most of them, any need for personal exertion. Rather than being faced with the necessity of working for their living, a very distasteful prospect indeed, most of their income derives from unearned sources, such as from their holdings in corporate stocks, bonds, real estate, and trusts. For example, the holdings of this top 6.7 percent of households, when considered together, has been estimated to include nearly four-fifths (77.7

percent) of all U.S. assets that are income-producing.[52] Furthermore, just the top 1 percent of Americans have been estimated to hold 56.6 percent of all personally owned corporate stock, which might give them as a group considerable influence over the major corporations that dominate the U.S. economy. And just 1 percent alone own 60 percent of all corporate bonds and 89.9 percent of all trusts in the United States.[53] These few persons and their families are certainly in a very privileged position in the United States economy.

It is one of the great ironies of the American work ethic that we believe people's moral value and rewards to be determined by how hard they work. Thus, from this view, the poor are deemed to be morally defective because their impoverished condition obviously must have resulted from their not having exhibited enough of the virtue of hard work. By contrast, the well off are looked on approvingly as being persons who must have earned their elevated standard of living by having worked hard. The reality is, however, that the leisured class doesn't work, but relies instead almost entirely on the work of everyone else in the United States to keep the economy "humming" along so that unearned incomes continue to flow into their pockets. In a sense, the U.S. economy is itself much like a gigantic business enterprise that is run foremost to benefit this small leisured class. In this gigantic business enterprise most other persons work as high- or low-paid employees. Furthermore, by passing on their income-producing assets from generation to generation, this small leisured class forms an hereditary economic elite in the United States with some similarities to the nobility of the past.

In contrast to the leisured class, the well off of the United States are relatively poor, because they possess only about one and a half times (19.7 percent/13.3 percent) what should be expected for them if all wealth were equally distributed. Persons in this group tend to be the highest paid laborers in our economic system. If need be, they could use their accumulated savings to live comfortable life-styles for a number of years without working, but they could not do so indefinitely as could the leisured class. If we add the holdings of this group to those of the leisured class, we see that the top 20 percent of families in the United States hold 76 percent of the wealth.

This brings us to the 20 percent of families in the United States I have called the middle Americans. As a group, this 20 percent of households possesses somewhat less of the wealth that would be expected for them if all wealth were distributed equally (i.e., only 15.5 percent). Their lifestyles are comfortable, especially by working class standards, but in no way are they able to socialize as lifestyle equals with the leisured class. Together with the well-off we might say that they comprise the middle class who, if need be, could sustain a reasonable life-style during a protracted period of unemployment by living on their savings.

Another group I call the working class. This group consists of the 60 percent of households in the United States that collectively own only 8.3 percent of the wealth. These Americans own very little equity in their homes or cars, if they have either. Many may live very comfortable life-styles based on their current income, their credit purchases, and their mortgages; and so they often believe themselves to be a part of the middle class or may even have delusions of being well-off. But they have little or nothing in the way of a bank account or other equity and often have much debt. Their standard of living, no matter how visibly well-off at the moment, is almost totally dependent on their continuing receipt of a paycheck. Consequently a loss of employment would hit people in this group hard, possibly resulting in the loss of their home, car, camper, boat, health insurance, and other non-income-producing luxuries, if they have such things. This is why I call them the working class—they must work to survive.

On the bottom of the economic heap of the working class are those households in poverty (largely due to age, disability, or family circumstances). I discuss this group in a separate section.

How do you determine which group you are in? If your primary source of income derives from unearned returns from your assets and if your assets alone could support a family of four in a very comfortable life-style for the rest of your lives without working, you are probably a member of the leisured class in the United States. If so, you are very fortunate indeed. If, by contrast, you have sufficient assets to support a family of four at a reasonable standard of living for only a limited period of time without working, say one to two years, you are probably part of the middle class. Good for you. If, on the other hand, you would be in trouble if a month went by without a paycheck coming into your home and would be in serious trouble if three to five months went by without a paycheck, you are in the working class. You must work to maintain your life-style.

Social Mobility in the United States

Social mobility is the term sociologists use to describe movements of people from one status group to another. As I suggested earlier, the wealthier groups represented in Figure 6.2 have excellent prospects for passing on their privileges to their descendants. They can do this by the direct transfer of assets to their children through gifts, inheritance, and family trusts. They also can do this indirectly by the opportunities they make available to their children for exclusive schooling, marriages to suitably well-off mates, and the cultivation of contacts with powerful people. In some respects, therefore, the old agricultural system of hereditary nobility has been replaced in our industrial society with a somewhat more permeable system of hereditary economic elites. I say "somewhat more permeable" because there are in fact a few real-life "Horatio Alger"-type success stories in which persons of modest means, or more likely of well off or middle American means, accrue enormous fortunes in their lifetimes.[54]

Most research that has been done on social mobility has focused on how people move among occupations. Occupations are important status-bearing social phenomena to study because the incomes they provide are central for supporting the lifestyles of almost all industrial families (with, of course, the exception of the leisured class and the destitute—perhaps the only point of commonality these two groups share).

Research on occupational social mobility[55] shows that industrial societies such as ours are marked by considerable mobility relative to what is seen in agricultural societies. However, most of this mobility involves only small steps in terms of the prestige or privileges people gain or lose throughout their lives relative to that held by their parents. (Real-life "Horatio Alger" stories are the rare exceptions.)

Furthermore, occupational social mobility in our society has been mostly upward throughout most of the twentieth century, principally because the numbers of jobs available to successive generations in lower-paid farm and unskilled occupations have decreased while the numbers of jobs in higher-paid, skilled, and bureaucratic white collar occupations have increased. Therefore, to the degree that industrialization has made society into a land of opportunity, it has done so for most people principally through its effects on the types of jobs available to them in the occupational structure, essentially forcing successive generations of people to take higher-paying jobs.

Again, however, the general trend of opportunities has typically involved only small steps upward from the parent's generation to the children's generation. And because this trend holds only for persons who are wage earners in the occupational structure, there has been no significant threat to the nonwage earning leisured class of its having to share its wealth and privileges with large numbers of new members.

Does a Power-Elite, Governing Class, or Inner Circle Control Our Society?

Figure 6.2 highlights the fact that there is a small number of economic elites who have major holdings in the U.S. economy and who are in an obvious position to have considerable influence over the rest of society. The question then arises whether these people are in fact in control of the United States. This question can readily be answered in the negative because of the lack of a monolithic power base from which control over the United States could be effected. Rather, as I noted in Chapter 5, our political structures splinter power among jurisdictions (federal, state, local), among functions (executive, judicial, legislative), among political groups (parties and special interest pressure groups), and among bureaucrats (who often manage government agencies to suit their personal needs and who compete with politicians and fellow bureaucrats in their agencies or in other agencies for control of government resources and for control of the sector of society they are supposed to investigate, oversee, regulate, or provide with services[56]). As a result of this splintering, U.S. political structures do not permit monolithic control to be exercised.

Although no one may possess the means to exert monolithic control over the United States, at least some persons possess the power to exert considerable influence over selected parts of our society. In particular, the high degree of concentration of wealth in the United States provides a relatively few people with great potential power for influencing many facets of society, including government legislation, policy, and regulatory enforcement. Persons who possess great wealth tend to be regarded with awe by others, who want to hear, see, be around, and socialize with them, to make them happy, and to be favored by them.

The "Power-Elite" Concept

To what degree, then, might there be a U.S. power-elite, governing class, or inner circle of big monied interests that are in a position to greatly influence, or possibly control, what happens in the United States? C. Wright Mills proposed that a power-elite of top persons in business, military, and government has become organized around their mutual interests in the military–industrial complex to exert strong influence on government policy, military spending, and related business development.[57] Because the military–industrial complex accounts for more than one-fifth (21.6 percent) of the federal budget,[58] we are talking about an arrangement that can provide substantial profits for those involved. That there is an elite group of people, relatively few in number, who share common interests in the military–industrial complex and who profit from it, cannot be questioned. I would suggest that comparable elites in the business sector, the welfare and health sector, and the government also share common interests in and influence over the welfare-industrial complex, which works in part for their mutual gain.

The "Governing Class" Concept

A different concept is that of the governing class. G. William Domhoff has argued that, in essence, a small group of economic elites exerts extensive influence over our society.[59] In a classic study he selected the top fifteen banks, top fifteen insurance companies, and top twenty industrials which, as the earlier discussion of economic concentration indicates, dominate their respective markets in finance, insurance, and industry and consequently are the core business forces in our industrial economy. He then tracked down the names of the few people who served as interlocking directors on the boards of these top corporations (and therefore were in positions to control them). These persons were the core of what Domhoff called a governing class that has enormous influence over our economy.

Domhoff found that 53 percent of these elites were listed in Social Registers as the "cream" of society, and the rest were highly paid executives, consultants, ex-politicians, former government agency officials, and former members of the military elite. In this same study and in subsequent studies,[60] Domhoff traced out how social patterns of influence among such elites develop and are perpetuated by common experiences in exclusive schools, in exclusive social clubs, and through intermarriage. In addition, a circulation of these elites and their top-paid employees through key positions in society ensures that their common interests are well represented wherever policy is being formulated.

For example, Domhoff shows that these elites not only hold key positions in businesses, but also hold key positions in the White House,[61] in Congress,[62] and in the top positions of major government departments and agencies, such as the Secretaries of State, Defense, Commerce, and Treasury[63]; the top positions in the CIA and FBI; and in the major regulatory agencies and top leadership of the military. They also hold key positions on top public policy councils (such as the Council on Foreign Relations, the Business Advisory Council, on the Committee for Economic Development), top foundations (such as the Ford, Rockefeller, or Danforth Foundations), elite universities (such as the boards of trustees of Harvard, Yale, or Princeton), and in the mass media. On the whole, the evidence is convincing that business interests do coalesce and find avenues of expression in the manner described by Domhoff.

The "Inner Circle" Concept

In his concept of a U.S. inner circle, Michael Useem proposed a similar model for how managerial business elites meet, share interests, and influence each other and public officials through their interlocking directorate positions on the boards of major corporations and through their key positions on major national and international policy councils; major university, cultural, and charity boards; and major private foundations (such as the Rockefeller or Ford Foundations).[64] Because they are in powerful positions as business leaders, because they share common interests, and because their personal relations with each other on common boards allow them to influence each other's perspectives and the perspectives of top public officials, Useem argues in essence that a common, business-oriented world view, so to speak, coalesces among them and exerts considerable influence on government policy.

Limitations of the "Elite" Models

The three concepts of a power-elite, a governing class, and an inner circle overlap to some extent, but they are useful in describing slightly different ways in which business interests and individual business leaders influence governments and policy making in other parts of their social environment. These are real and significant influences, but the greatest influences, as I have described them in the three chapters of this part of the book, involve longer-term social structural changes that, although serving business interests, have not always been supported by business leaders. Within the larger framework that I have presented, the principal structures of society have become organized around business interests into a form that I have called the business-oriented society. In contrast to this much larger framework of business influences on other sectors of society, the effects of a power-elite, governing class or inner circle are comparatively slight (though real and worthy of study).[65]

A typical problem with the three concepts described here, and evident in the very terms used to refer to them, is that all too often they lend themselves easily to an assumption that some sort of conspiracy of monied interests is occurring to influence economic and political processes. It is one thing to detect mechanisms through which common interests arise and are expressed; it is quite another to assume that the whole process is a deliberate one involving collective, secretive planning and execution. The authors of these concepts do not subscribe to a conspiratorial view, but it is easy for others to do so.

The Problem with Conspiracy Theories

The problem with conspiracy theories for explaining social processes and outcomes is that they require us to assume that a group of people are capable first of rationally recognizing their common interests and then of coming together secretly to plan and coordinate their collective behaviors so as to bring about large-scale and possibly long-term social changes that are consistent with their interests. But, as I argued in Chapter 5, we cannot assume that people are rational persons who are capable of sustained rational deliberation, nor can we assume that they are economic persons who act only in their self-interest. Even if people were rational enough and self-interested enough to carry out a small conspiracy among two, three, or a very few people so as to secretly effect some limited action with the hopes of a desired outcome over a short time frame, it stretches credulity to imagine that dozens, hundreds, or thousands of people could or would conspire secretly to carry out a large number of coordinated actions over a period of many years to achieve ends that suit their collective interests. Much less feasible is it that they would succeed in such an endeavor.[66]

Business Interests Exert Control without Conspiracies

My argument is much simpler. Business interests are indeed central to a business-oriented society, even if they are not made so by conspiracies. Rather they are central because the marketplace has become the primary remaining mechanism that ties us all together. It is our relationships with each other through the marketplace that gives us all a stake in business performance: as owners, as employees, and as consumers of the good life that industrial business-oriented society has made available to us. This is not the result of a conspiracy among monied interests; it is, rather, the nature of social order and of social cohesion itself in a business-oriented society.

Poverty and Public Welfare in the United States

Having looked at the elites of our business-oriented society, I would now like to consider the poor. Every society must include mechanisms for supporting persons who are too young, too old, too disabled, or too ill to pull their own weight in the prevailing economic production system. The primary social mechanism for providing support has always been, and still is, the family, clan, or extended kinship system.

The Family in Agricultural Societies

In agricultural societies in which work was home based and tasks were plentiful and relatively uncomplicated, everyone (from toddlers to the very old and all but the most severely disabled and ill) could contribute at least *something* to the family unit. A large family was an asset under these circumstances, to maximize the potential number of able-bodied members relative to those who needed support at any given time. Life expectancy was short, in any case, so not too many elderly were around requiring support. If need be, neighbors, the community, the church, and nobility could be turned to for aid through difficult times. In the event of general crop failure, the public, church, or nobility's granaries were expected to serve as a source of public assistance.

The Family in Industrial Societies

In the shift to business-oriented societies, the old mutual obligations between nobility and farm laborers gradually ended, as laborers were forced increasingly into the employment of businesses. In this shift of employment, our ancestors no longer were in positions as field laborers to produce their own food, and they could no longer turn to the nobility for assistance through hard times. Instead, they became totally dependent on the market both for employment and for sustenance. Under these circumstances it became critical that at least one family member could bring home an income as a wage laborer.

As was true in the past, the family remains the principal welfare system in industrial societies for providing support to the young, the old, the ill, and the disabled. However, in industrial society all such persons become a greater burden for the family because there are no longer opportunities for them to contribute anything to the primary economic production processes of society, which now lay wholly outside the home. In the industrial society employers generally do not want to hire very young children (under the age of six or so), nor do they want to hire the physically or mentally disabled, the ill, or the elderly who are not able-bodied. Not able to contribute to the economic productivity of the family, these persons thus become a far greater drag on family resources than they had been in an agricultural era. Furthermore, those who need personal care and supervision either have to be left unattended at home, or an able-bodied person has to remain home with them, which further decreases the possibilities of improving family income for support of family members.

Provided that some income can be brought into the home, families might be able to skimp by. But if the "breadwinner" of the family falls ill, is injured at work, or loses employment, the family is in serious trouble. Furthermore, in periods of business downturns or busts, massive unemployment occurs, creating widespread human misery such as occurred during the Great Depression.

Changes to the Family Role

At least four changes occurred in industrial societies that further exacerbate the problems of poverty and the ability of the family to serve as society's principal welfare agency.

1. Longer life expectancy
2. Shrinking family unit
3. Disintegration of community ties
4. Failure of *laissez-faire* principles

These changes are further discussed below.

1. One of these changes was the effect that improved public health measures had on increasing life expectancy. As a result, society was confronted for the first time with growing numbers of elderly persons, who, as a group, require more health and personal care services. As more and more people lived to older ages, the capacity for traditional, family-based welfare services was strained in ways not previously experienced in human history.

2. A second change was the effect of industrialization on the shrinkage of the family unit. This shrinkage meant that there were fewer and fewer people in the family to serve in the home as care givers or to provide an economic base for the support of nonproductive persons, such as the disabled, ill, or elderly.

The family unit shrank during industrialization for at least two reasons. First, as field laborers left the land to take up industrial wage jobs, they often left behind their traditional networks of extended kin. The resulting mobile, nuclear family was the model best suited for industrial development, as people had to be made mobile to meet the labor needs of the changing industrial marketplace. Second, industrialization made children into an economic liability for the family unless the family could find employment for them as wage laborers so that they could bring in enough additional income to pay for their support. Under the circumstances of industrial society, having many nonwage earning children in the home could seriously degrade the standard of living and the viability of the family unit. We can see the full effect of this influence in the more mature industrialized societies, where typical nuclear family sizes have shrunk to a replacement size of two children per family.[67]

3. A third change exacerbating the problem of home-based welfare was the disintegration of tightknit community relations. The stable lifestyle of agricultural societies kept families in close proximity to each other over many generations so that people typically not only knew each other but knew all persons in each other's extended family as well. Furthermore, intermarriages made many families related in at least some distant way. Under these circumstances, families in a community shared emotional bonds that made it easier for them both to turn to each other and to obtain aid from each other in times of need. The mutual expectations of offering and receiving aid was an important part of the ties that bound these communities together, and it was an important part of the available welfare system that lay beyond the immediate family.

Industrialization, by contrast, required a mobile workforce and brought many previously unrelated nuclear families together into small geographic areas to serve as a supply of laborers. With no prior long-term relations among these families, and as families continued to move in response to the changing job market, the new model of community relations became increasingly characterized by anonymity, independence, and social distance.[68] Since this model provides a poor basis for the provision of community welfare, the family lost an important source of local support for hard times.

4. The fourth change, one which I have previously described, was the increasing inability of the *laissez-faire* principles to function properly in an industrial environment. The final straw was the collapse of the economy in the Great Depression, which left a fourth of the labor force out of work and forced many others into underemployment or decreased salary. The family structure simply was no longer able to cope with the massive welfare needs that resulted. Nor could families turn to the community, nobility, or a powerful church as their agricultural ancestors had been able to do in times of need. It became clearer than ever before that the business-oriented society was sorely in need of new social mechanisms to provide for the welfare of persons in need.

The Rise of Government-Organized Welfare

What was created in response to this need was a government-organized welfare system (a government safety net so to speak) to protect and support persons employers pass by and for whom our business-oriented society otherwise provides insufficient assistance. As it has evolved over the last sixty years, this welfare system has come to include the following major components for different groups who may be in need: Social Security, Supplementary Security Income, Medicare and Medicaid for the elderly; Social Security, Aid for Families with Dependent Children (AFDC), Medicaid, food stamps, and subsidized school lunch programs for children; AFDC, Medicaid, and housing subsidies for poor single mothers with small children in their home; Social Security and Medicare for the disabled; unemployment insurance for the temporarily unemployed; workers' compensation for those disabled on the job; and a system of state hospitals for the severely mentally disabled. These are some of the most important of the public welfare programs now available, but there are others as well.

The many welfare programs that have been created are a logical outgrowth of the rise of the business-oriented industrial society as we have had to grapple with the question of what to do with people who are not immediately employable. Although this fact is obvious, it is easily missed, downplayed, or ignored in popular antiwelfare rhetoric. The basis for this rhetoric derives from several often interrelated ideological sources. First, it derives from those who are opposed to big and potentially abusive governments and their corollary of big taxes, which effectively transfer money from one group of people (typically including the critics of welfare) to another (in this case, the welfare recipients).

Then too, antiwelfare rhetoric derives from those who fervently subscribe to the market model and see government efforts to create welfare programs as posing a threat to the economy and to personal freedoms because such efforts violate business market freedoms. Some examples of how freedoms are restricted include government requirements for businesses to pay unemployment insurance premiums and to make contributions to the Social Security retirement fund; government pressures on businesses to hire the disabled and elderly (and not to hire the very young); government pressures on businesses to create safe working environments for employees and to end pollution of the environment; recent legislation requiring businesses to have a family leave plan for employees; and so on.

Antiwelfare sentiment also derives from those who fear that government welfare programs will disrupt our work ethic by providing people with incentives to not work. From their point of view, the work ethic is a primary factor in our economic success as a nation and provides a badge of moral virtue to those who work.

Antiwelfare sentiment derives too from those who fear, loath, or are prejudiced against welfare recipients for a number of psychological and social reasons (including racism, ageism, sexism, and the fear that one's own social standing and self-esteem will be reduced if some of the lifestyle privileges and opportunities that are available to laborers as a status group are also made available to nonlaboring welfare recipients).

These various sources for antiwelfare rhetoric often interweave in practice, and the fervor of this rhetoric occasionally reaches the point of claims being made that we now live in a welfare state, despite the fact that government welfare programming is certainly not an autonomous, driving force in our society, but it is instead a force driven by the unfolding pressures of our business-oriented industrial society.

To appreciate better the plight of the poor in a business-oriented society, let's look at who they are in the United States. Poverty is, of course, defined under the pressures of politics, so the cutoff point for saying who is in poverty and who is not is determined partly based on how many people governments believe they can directly support, and partly on what level of lifestyle is considered—on political grounds—to be the minimal decent level tolerable for respectable persons in our society. As of 1993, a single person under the age of 65 with an annual income of $7,518 was considered by the federal government to be officially in poverty.[69] Someone with $7,600 in annual income (or $633 per month) was not officially considered to be living in poverty. Likewise, a family of four with $14,763 or less in annual income was officially in poverty, while a family of four with $14,800 in annual income (or $1,233 a month) was not. Using these federal criteria, 13.7 percent of the U.S. population in 1993 had annual incomes below the official poverty level, while an additional 8.4 percent would have been below the poverty level if not for government income support programs. Therefore, the total poverty figure for the United States is 22.1 percent or more than one-fifth of all Americans.[70]

How restricted are the lifestyles of the poor? You know what your income and expenses are each month. Suppose you woke up tomorrow to find yourself supporting a family of four with an income at the poverty line of $14,763 (or $1,230 a month), or suppose you woke up as a single person with an income again at the poverty line of $7,518 (or $626 a month). Now imagine what your lifestyle would be like. Would this level of income permit you to keep up your present mortgage or rent payments? If you tried to limit your monthly housing expenses to one-fourth of your income (or $308 for a family of four or $157 for a single person), what kind of housing do you think you could find? Could you keep up your current car payments and automobile insurance? Could you keep up your current health insurance payments (assuming here that your employer contributed nothing or little toward this cost)? What would you do when confronted by large health care expenses or large car or home repair expenses? Could you afford your current costs for electricity, gas, and telephone? What sort of food, clothing, or entertainment could you afford to provide to your children or enjoy yourself? Barring a major health care problem, you might be able to get by on this income, but it certainly would not provide for a pleasant lifestyle. These are the conditions faced by more than one-fifth of our population, and it is for this reason that we have instituted public cash transfer and other relief programs.

Here are some more characteristics of Americans who live in poverty. Even after figuring in public cash support payments (principally in the forms of Social Security, AFDC, and SSI), 39.3 million Americans in 1993 lived below the official poverty line. Of these people, 9.6 percent were elderly (i.e., age 65 and over). This percentage would have been much larger if not for the transfer cash payments of Social Security. Children are also frequently found to be living in poverty in the United States. Indeed, if children are our future, then this nation is in big trouble, because an additional 40 percent of persons in poverty in 1993 were age seventeen and under. Taken together, then, nearly half (49.6 percent) of our nation's poor in 1993 were either too old or too young to be attractive to employers.[71]

What about adults under the age of 65 who are in poverty? U.S. Census data from 1992 indicated that in more than two-thirds (68.6 percent) of the 2.7 million married-couple families living in poverty, the husband was working but was either receiving wages too low to raise the household out of poverty or was underemployed.[72] In another 15.1 percent of these households the adult male was unable to work because of illness or disability. This left only 16.3 percent of households in which the adult male was able to seek paid employment but was either unsuccessful in finding work, was in school, was keeping house and providing at-home child care, or was unemployed for other reasons. In female-headed households (with no husband present) 44.5 percent of female householders were working at low wages, 8.8 percent were ill or disabled, 35.4 percent were keeping house and providing at-home child care, and the remaining 11.3 percent were in school, unable to find work, or unemployed for other reasons. Thus, in most poor households that are headed by adults under the age of 65 (i.e., 85 percent to 88 percent of these households) the breadwinner was working, was ill or disabled, or was the primary care giver and supervisor for children and other dependents in the home. Under these circumstances, the typical antiwelfare rhetoric urging workfare as the solution to poverty is more than a bit presumptuous; it is either a very cynical political ploy, or it is just plain foolish.[73]

In considering who is likely to be poor, it is important to note that employment opportunities are not distributed equally in our business-oriented society. Rather, they conform to traditional patterns of discrimination. For example, one-third (33.1 percent) of African Americans are in poverty,[74] and unemployment rates are much higher for minorities. In 1993, 12.9 percent of African Americans were unemployed (vs. 6.0 percent of whites); 38.9 percent of African American teenagers were unemployed (vs. 16.2 percent of white teenagers); and 22.9 percent of African Americans between the ages of twenty and twenty-four were unemployed (vs. 8.7 percent of whites in the same age range).[75]

Being on welfare is no picnic for those unable to sell their labor to employers in our economy because of their age, disabilities, social circumstances, or employer prejudices. Public aid cash payments are typically low, so even with financial assistance those in poverty continue to have highly restricted standards of living. For example, the average monthly cash assistance under SSI to the aged, blind, or disabled in 1993 was $345. AFDC families received average monthly assistance of $377 that same year.[76] How grand of a lifestyle can you have with an income at this level? Would this level of cash assistance be sufficient inducement for you to seek to remain in poverty as long as you could?

Not including Social Security, which principally benefits the elderly, the combined cost of all other common forms of public aid that are aimed specifically at helping the poor (i.e., AFDC, SSI, Medicaid, food stamps, housing assistance, and other assorted smaller programs) was roughly $289.9 billion in 1992.[77] This was about 11.6 percent of the total budget of all governments and about 4.6 percent of our national GNP in the same year. It is equivalent to 15.6 percent of the annual income of the wealthiest 20 percent of Americans,[78] and is an amount comparable to the subsidies the federal government gives to the nonpoor each year through preferential tax treatment (i.e., tax breaks).[79] It is also about as much as consumers spent on recreation and amusements that same year.[80] Can our society afford the current costs of the public aid that we offer? I think so. What about you?

Antiwelfare sentiment is fairly common, but few people, including most critics, would want to see our nation's elderly, young, or disabled going without health care, food, housing, or other necessities of life. Furthermore, the welfare-industrial complex we have created has come to play a major role in our economy. First, by providing resources to those unable to sell their labor in the marketplace, it stimulates much economic demand (i.e., spending) from the poor that would not otherwise occur in many markets, such as for food, health care, housing, and so on. Second, it provides jobs to a large number of government and private sector welfare workers, particularly to women and minorities who are overrepresented in welfare jobs and who otherwise are discriminated against in the business employment marketplace. The spending of their income also increases demand in our markets. Third, and as a corollary, these programs pump large sums of money into the hands of certain businesses, especially health care providers and the drug industry, but also landlords, grocers, and many others. Indeed, if government welfare spending designed to help the needy were to stop today, not only would human misery be dramatically increased in our society, quite likely to the point of inciting public uprisings, but many sectors of our economy would suffer a considerable blow.

In short, government welfare programs have become a necessary by-product of the development of a business-oriented society. They are a palliative for some of the human misery the business-oriented society creates, while at the same time they help to keep the economy humming. They constitute, therefore, just one of the many (external) costs of doing business and of living in a business-oriented industrialized society.

Part III

The Social Environment of Contemporary Businesses: Selected Topics in Business Social Responsibilities

The third part of this book looks at how businesses relate to their social environments: Chapter 7 looks at both governmental regulation of businesses and the reciprocal influence of businesses on governments; Chapter 8 considers how the internal organization of businesses affects whether they become socially responsible; Chapters 9 and 10 consider employee welfare and equal employment opportunities; Chapters 11, 12, and 13 look at consumer, environmental, and international issues; and the concluding chapter, Chapter 14, considers the future of business-oriented societies.

Chapter 7

Government and Businesses

Ideological Confession

Sociologists try to develop an understanding of the social world as it actually is, rather than as current ideologies would suggest it to be. None of us, however, can become fully free from the ideological beliefs of our time. Therefore it is altogether fitting that I begin this chapter with an ideological confession.

I can make no pretense of being as articulate as Ayn Rand,[1] or as smart as Hayek[2] or either of the two Friedmans.[3] Furthermore, it is obvious that I do not share with them a common view on the role of economic phenomena in society on the one hand or of human nature and individual freedoms on the other. What I do share with them, however, is a deep distrust of governments.

As a sentiment, the distrust of governments has a very long and hallowed history in the ideological development of the United States. Indeed, to be opposed to the intrusion of governments into our lives is to be as patriotic as were the two Thomases (Jefferson and Paine).[4] I too am an exceptionally patriotic American in this regard. But my own antigovernment sentiment no doubt also derives from the fact that I came of pubescent age in the 1960s, a period of time that emphasized freer thought and expression and promoted opposition to authority in any form. Though the passing of time has reduced my once flowing hair to stubble, I retain this sentiment unabated.

Based on my confession that I am ideologically opposed to governmental authority, you can safely assume that I shall not propose in this chapter that governments will be, or *can* be, wise guardians of the public good or of the good of any individual or social entity. Nonetheless, as I described in the last chapter and will consider at many places throughout this part of the book, governments do provide social mechanisms that permit collective action to be undertaken on a wide array of problems and issues that confront us. Furthermore, it is only natural and to be expected in a democratic society that people will turn to governments for efforts to solve significant social problems, even if the cost of doing so is increased restrictions on their own freedom of action.

This book is not about governments, and I do not attempt here to make recommendations for improving the moral conduct, efficiency, or usefulness of governments in society. Also, because I have already discussed in Chapters 5 and 6 a number of specific issues concerning how governments and businesses interrelate, I do not wish to repeat those discussions here. This chapter focuses on two important issues not previously discussed: the scope, costs, and effectiveness of governmental efforts to regulate business activities; and business efforts to influence governmental decision making.

Governmental Regulation of Businesses

Governmental efforts to regulate businesses date well back into antiquity, as is witnessed, for example, by the early legal code of King Hammurabi (established in about 1750 B.C.). Throughout the long history of agricultural societies, governmental regulatory efforts were undertaken largely in an effort to ensure domestic tranquility and to maintain and enhance the power of the governing elite.

In modern business-oriented societies, however, governments have become peripheral, even if very powerful, forces in society that work largely to bolster and support business interests and a social order based on these interests. Governments today work to promote growth in the economy, protect business interests at home and worldwide, and clean up the social messes created by businesses (such as poverty and unemployment) that, if left unaddressed, might lead the citizenry to revolutionary actions against business interests and the business-oriented social order.

The *laissez-faire* model has many failings, both as a basis for the conduct of businesses in an industrial economy and as a means for ensuring the welfare and vitality of society as a whole. As a result of these failings, increased pressures have been placed on governments to develop regulatory systems to oversee business operations in general, and to reduce the negative impacts of these operations on other sectors of society. It would be worthwhile at this time to present an overview of the remarkable growth and diversity of the governmental system that we find currently in place to regulate businesses in the United States.

Current Legal Authority

Governments in the United States have ample legal authority to permit their regulatory involvement in the U.S. market. At the federal level this authority derives from several powers granted to the federal government by the U.S. Constitution. Among these powers, two are especially important: the power to regulate interstate and foreign commerce, and the power to promote the general public welfare.

Most governmental regulation of businesses can be justified on the basis of these two powers. For example, industrialization has fostered the development of an extensive web of commercial operations that cross state lines in the search for mass markets, so the federal government is able to justify the regulation of a very large part of our business sector on the basis of its responsibility for oversight of interstate commerce.

The power granted to the federal government to promote the general welfare provides an even larger basis for legitimating governmental involvement in the regulation of commerce. Indeed, with only a little imagination one can justify just about any governmental action on the grounds of promoting the general public welfare in some form (so long as the proposed governmental action otherwise cannot be shown to be explicitly prohibited by our Constitution). The exercise of determining which governmental actions are justifiable in the pursuit of the general public welfare (and which are not) is a matter for ever-changing political negotiation and judicial decision making.

Governments at state and local levels may justify business regulation based on the general power recognized in common law for governments to take actions in pursuit of the public good. Thus, one finds at all levels of government ample legal authority to legitimate as much involvement of government in our economy as prevailing political interests may wish to pursue.

Brief History of Growing Governmental Regulation

Governmental regulation of businesses during the early history of our nation was quite limited for two principal reasons. First, businesses were small and, therefore, were incapable of concentrated threat to social order. Second, our ideological commitment to a laissez-faire economy was relatively strong.[5]

Commitment to *laissez-faire* was shaken, however, in the late 1800s by the rise of large businesses that concentrated markets and engaged in abusive practices that threatened social order. The response to this situation was the organization of governmental antitrust efforts. This constituted a first wave of federal regulation of businesses in the United States.

The last straw for the commitment to *laissez-faire* was the economic collapse into the Great Depression. This event served to pressure governments to undertake a great number of new regulatory activities that collectively constitute a second historical wave of growth in governmental involvement in the U.S. economy.

More recently, with the maturing of our industrial economy, we have seen in the 1960s and 1970s yet a third wave of regulatory initiatives designed to modify business behaviors. I shall describe each of these three waves of regulatory developments briefly below.

Antitrust Movement

The first set of major regulatory efforts by the federal government came in response to the growth of big businesses in the late 1800s. These businesses typically operated across state lines and, with nothing to stop them from doing so, often engaged in outlandishly abusive practices. Many of the great family fortunes in the United States (such as those of the Rockefellers, the DuPonts, and the Vanderbilts) were formed by big business entrepreneurs at this time.

Consider the *laissez-faire* environment of the United States in the late 1800s. During this time John Rockefeller used cut-throat competition and price fixing strategies to set up an oil empire that at the time controlled more than 90 percent of the American oil market[6] (an accomplishment that must make today's OPEC cartel members green with envy). Jay Gould (called by some the "Mephistopheles of Wall Street") embezzled money freely, sold watered stock, and bribed government officials on his way to gaining control of the Erie Railroad and a number of other large commercial enterprises. Vanderbilt and many others, who are now know as the robber barons of the time,[7] engaged in similar practices to gain control over large business empires.

These and other business leaders participated in a variety of practices in restraint of trade that raised the ire of many, including each other. One example of an arrangement created to restrain trade is that of the formation of *pools*. By forming pools, business leaders within an industry agreed not to compete with each other and to charge uniformly high prices so that they could ensure ample profit for all. Both John Rockefeller and Henry DuPont set up pools of this sort in an effort to control the markets for their products.

Another arrangement in restraint of trade was the *trust*. In forming trusts, shareholders of several, often competing companies, allowed their company shares to be held (in trust) by a common board of directors, which then operated the various companies in a coordinated way that avoided competition and created substantial profits for all. Rockefeller was again a leader in the development of this form of market constraint. This arrangement became a very popular big business ploy, with trusts being developed in markets for a great many products, including sugar and whiskey.

A simpler monopolistic form for businesses, however, was for several competing businesses in an industry to be merged into a new single business that then could dominate the market for a product. J. P. Morgan was especially adept at creating these mergers. This strategy was used to create or expand several major U.S. corporations into positions of monopoly over their markets: examples include U.S. Steel, which was created in 1901 to control 62 percent of the steel market; International Harvester, which was created in 1902 to control 85 percent of the production of harvesting machines; Anaconda Copper, which was created in 1895 to control 39 percent of copper; and American Can Company, which was created in 1901 to control 90 percent of its industry.[8]

Among the most egregious of the abuses against small businesspersons by big businesses were the price discrimination arrangements widely practiced by the railroads. The railroads were the first truly big businesses in the United States, and they typically were in a monopolistic relation to their markets. Often they would overcharge small businesses for the transportation of goods on certain lines or on short hauls while providing price breaks to larger businesses on other lines or on long hauls. Hence small businesses were finding themselves being railroaded into subsidizing big businesses.

Railroad costs were a problem of national significance because, by the last half of the 1800s, our economy had developed to the point where the markets for many farmers and other small businesses depended on railroads for the transport of goods. However, railroad price discrimination arrangements were squeezing farmers and other small businesspersons; many were going bankrupt. The public outcry over these issues was itself part of a larger populist movement of the time that opposed big businesses. The situation decidedly called for path breaking collective action to end the abuses. But what social mechanism in society was large enough to confront the giant railroads and to stop the damage being done to small businesses?

After state governments failed individually to bring railroad abuses to an end, the federal government was eventually pressured into action.[9] The result was the landmark passage of the Interstate Commerce Act of 1887, which created the Interstate Commerce Commission as the first major federal agency designed specifically to regulate businesses. The Interstate Commerce Commission was charged with bringing to an end questionable pricing and service discrimination practices among railroads that crossed state lines, and it later was given authority to act similarly in regulating trucking, oil pipelines, shipping on waterways, and businesses involved in other modes of interstate transport.

The Interstate Commerce Act was only the first faltering step on a long and widening road of U.S. governmental efforts to end abusive practices by big businesses. Additional legislation was passed during the next three decades, expanding governmental regulatory efforts to end a great many business practices that restrained trade; these included the Sherman Antitrust Act of 1890, the Clayton Antitrust Act of 1914, and the Federal Trade Commission Act of 1914.[10] Antitrust legislation was further strengthened during this century by the Robinson-Patman Act (1936), the Wheeler-Lea Act (1938), the Celler-Kefauver Act (1950), the Consumer Goods Pricing Act (1975), and the Antitrust Improvement Act (1976).

How effective has governmental regulation been in deterring market domination and market abuse by big businesses? The current domination of our economy by a small number of large corporations and the recent buying spree of the 1980s, when giant corporations bought up many other corporations, does not lead one to the conclusion that the antitrust movement has been especially successful in the United States. On the other hand, given the natural tendency for industrialized economies to concentrate markets into the hands of one or only a few mass producers of goods and services, it is possible that the monopolistic features and business abuses of our current economy would be significantly greater, and competition as a feature of our economy significantly less, if not for the role played by government in the antitrust movement.

Great Depression

In the midst of the antitrust movement and prior to the Great Depression, a few additional important pieces of regulatory legislation occurred. One was the creation of the Federal Reserve System (1913) in the futile attempt to promote sounder business practices in the U.S. banking industry prior to its collapse in the Great Depression. The other was the passage of the Pure Food and Drug Act (1906) in response to public outcry over fears that the major meat packers were selling contaminated foods.[11] Pure food constituted a problem of increasing public concern in our industrializing society because fewer and fewer people lived on farms; therefore, more and more people were becoming dependent on the market and the meat packers for their daily food.

During the Great Depression there was a burst of governmental regulatory legislation, as the forces of government were pressed into action to seek ways to remedy the social and economic crises of the time. Under these circumstances, it was no longer possible to cleave too closely to *laissez-faire* ideology; governmental efforts to force businesses to engage in "fair" market practices were hurriedly developed in a great number of industries.

For example, this period saw the creation of the Federal Home Loan Bank Board (FHLBB, 1932) to regulate home financing institutions; the Federal Deposit Insurance Corporation (FDIC, 1933) to regulate and insure bank deposits; the National Labor Relations Board (NLRB, 1935) to regulate unfair business labor practices; the Securities and Exchange Commission (SEC, 1934) to regulate the stock market; the Federal Energy Regulatory Commission (FERC, formerly the Federal Power Commission, 1930) to regulate electric power and gas companies; the Federal Communications Commission (FCC, 1934) to regulate telephone, telegraph, radio, and eventually television; the now defunct Civil Aeronautics Board (CAB, formerly the Civil Aeronautics Authority, 1938) to regulate air transportation; and others. Collectively, this explosion of new regulatory activity constituted the second wave in the growing presence of government in our economy. It occurred so recently in the history of this nation as to be within the lifetime of some of us, or that of our parents or grandparents.

Recent Regulatory Legislation

A third wave of governmental regulatory initiatives occurred in the 1960s and 1970s in response to the maturing of our industrial economy and the perceived need for a great many new controls to be placed on businesses. During this period we saw more than fifty major regulatory laws enacted by Congress. This massive development of federal regulatory authority over businesses occurred within the lifetime of most of us or of our parents. Pause for a moment to let your eyes scan over the following list of examples of these laws:

Hazardous Substances Labeling Act (1960)

Oil Pollution Act (1961)

Air Pollution Control Act (1962)

Clean Air Act (1963)

Equal Pay Act (1963)

Civil Rights Act (1964)

Water Quality Act (1965)

Fair Packaging and Labeling Act (1966)

Traffic Safety Act (1966)

Flammable Fabrics Act (1967)

Age Discrimination in Employment Act (1967)

Consumer Credit Protection Act (1968)

Radiation Control for Health and Safety Act (1968)

Child Protection and Toy Safety Act (1969)

National Environmental Policy Act (1970)

Occupational Safety and Health Act (1970)

Lead Based Paint Elimination Act (1971)

Consumer Product Safety Act (1972)

Equal Employment Opportunity Act (1972)

Vocational Rehabilitation Act (1973)

Safe Drinking Water Act (1974)

Federal Energy Administration Act (1974)

Employee Retirement Income Security Act (1974)

Hazardous Materials Transportation Act (1974)

Energy Policy and Conservation Act (1975)

Toxic Substances Control Act (1976)

Department of Energy Organization Act (1977)

Surface Mining Control and Reclamation Act (1977)

Endangered Species Act Amendments (1978)

Emergency Energy Conservation Act (1979)

and others

Even persons highly critical of increased governmental regulation would be hard pressed, in looking at the array of issues covered by this list of legislation, to find very many issues for which they would wish all legal restrictions on businesses to be removed.

The Federal Regulatory Apparatus

From virtually no regulatory capacity at the turn of this century, the current federal apparatus for regulating businesses has grown to astonishing size and complexity. The executive, legislative, and judicial branches of government all now play significant roles in exercising oversight of U.S. businesses.

Executive Oversight

In addition to the major pieces of legislation listed here, a variety of new regulatory agencies were created in the 1960s and 1970s, including the Equal Employment Opportunity Commission (EEOC, 1964) to regulate employment opportunities in businesses; the Environmental Protection Agency (EPA, 1970) to regulate the effects of business operations on the environment; the Occupational Safety and Health Administration (OSHA, 1971) to regulate and reduce hazardous conditions for employees in the work setting; the Consumer Product Safety Commission (CPSC, 1972) to regulate the safety of products; the National Highway Traffic Safety Administration (NHTSA, 1970) to regulate the safety of motor vehicles and to reduce traffic accidents; the Pension Benefit Guarantee Corporation (created by the Employee Retirement Income Security Act [ERISA], 1974) to regulate and reduce fraud in employee pension funds; the Commodity Futures Trading Commission (1974) to regulate futures trading; the Mine Safety and Health Administration (1977) to regulate mine safety; and others. In all, there are now more than eighty major federal agencies[12] involved in regulating some aspect of business and the marketplace on employee rights, welfare, and safety; consumer protection; promotion of market competition, fair business practices, and market order; and on many other issues.

The President's cabinet has itself grown to include more and more regulatory functions, such as those undertaken by the Department of Energy (1977), the Department of Transportation (1967), the Department of Housing and Urban Development (1965), the Department of Health and Human Services (cabinet status in 1979, but originally created in 1953), and the more recent Department of Education (cabinet status in 1980, but originally created in 1953).

Congressional Oversight

The executive branch is not the only federal branch overseeing business activities. The U.S. Congress also plays a substantial role. On the Senate side there are several major committees providing oversight of business issues, including the committees on Banking, Housing and Urban Affairs; on Commerce, Science and Transportation; on Energy and Natural Resources; on Environment and Public Works; on Finance; on Foreign Relations; on Labor and Human Resources; and on Small Businesses. Each of these major committees has six or more subcommittees focused on business-related issues such as consumer affairs, economic policy, communications, energy regulation, environmental pollution, international trade, and so on. In all, there are more than fifty-five U.S. Senate subcommittees providing continuous oversight of one or more parts of the economy and of business activities. On the U.S. House side there are approximately sixty additional subcommittees also examining business affairs. Through these various committees, Congress is continually working to determine how best to formulate new legislation for the regulation of businesses.

Judicial Oversight

Besides the executive and legislative branches of government, the judiciary also has been actively involved in determining appropriate conduct by businesses. Especially since the middle of this century, the courts have increasingly ruled against businesses on complaints concerning employees, consumers, communities, and the environment. Occasionally court judgments against businesses have involved substantial penalties. For example, in 1983 an EEOC suit against General Motors cost GM $42.5 million. Of necessity, businesses must be attentive to the evolving body of court rulings on issues related to their operations if they are to avoid lawsuits and continue to be profitable. Unfortunately, the growing maze of court rulings is highly complex and not infrequently contradictory from one ruling to another.

The Costs of Regulation

From a situation at the turn of this century of almost no federal regulation or oversight of business affairs (and no income or corporate taxes), we face today a staggering amount of federal regulation and oversight. Of course, all such regulatory efforts require funding, and so we have subjected both our corporations and ourselves as citizens to substantial taxes to keep the whole governmental regulatory operation afloat in the hopes of cajoling or bludgeoning businesses into responsible behavior toward owners, employees, consumers, communities, governments, the environment, and other businesses.

The total governmental regulatory effort of today is truly massive. By 1991 a complete listing of the *Code of Federal Regulations* required 125,331 printed pages[13] and occupied about fifteen feet of shelf space. In 1991 the *Federal Register,* where new and proposed federal regulations are publicized, required more than 67,000 pages of fine print. The flood of regulatory paperwork is estimated to consume 4.5 million cubic feet of new storage space every year.[14]

The states are also heavily involved in the regulation of businesses. There are more than 78,000 state and local political jurisdictions capable of issuing regulations.[15] By one estimate, approximately a quarter of a million bills were proposed in state legislatures in a single year in the mid-1980s, with 50,000 of these becoming law and more than 37,000 new regulations being adopted at the state level.[16]

How expensive is this regulatory process, you may ask? Governmental expenses in creating and enforcing regulations are no doubt a pittance compared to what businesses spend responding to these regulations. For example, a study initiated by the Business Roundtable indicated that in just one year during the late 1970s, the regulations issued by six federal agencies alone added $2.6 billion to the cost of operations for forty-eight U.S. companies. To one company alone (Whirlpool Corporation), the regulations of just these six agencies added $20 million to its operating costs.[17] Yet another report indicates that in 1978 the regulatory costs imposed on GM amounted to more than $1.6 billion and added nearly 25,000 people to its payroll.[18] Dow Chemical Company spent $147 million in a single year in the 1980s to conform to federal regulations, including $5 million just to give testimony to regulators.[19] By one estimate, the Fortune 500 companies spend $1 billion a year just to comply with antidiscrimination laws,[20] and a federal estimate suggests that the cost *per year* in the 1990s of compliance with environmental laws is upward to $115 billion.[21] Yet another federal estimate puts the total cost of regulatory compliance in the 1990s at $430 billion per year, or about 9 percent of the GNP.[22] In short, when we talk about the costs of regulatory compliance, we are talking about a very substantial amount of money.

All of us pay for governmental regulatory efforts to get businesses to behave responsibly. We pay in higher taxes to cover the government's cost of issuing and enforcing regulations, and we pay in higher prices for products and services in order for businesses to respond to these regulations. By one estimate, for example, compliance with regulations in a single year (1975) reduced U.S. productivity by 1.4 percent.[23] Another estimate suggests that regulatory-related activities in a single year (1978) accounted for as much as three-fourths of a percentage point in the annual rate of inflation, and cost the average American family of four $1,200.[24] Then too, there are the hidden costs of jobs that are lost when plants close because businesses cannot conform profitably to new regulations, or when new plants are not built for the same reason. Apparently, these too are just part of the costs we must bear in order to live in a business-oriented society.

Newer Forms of Regulation

The federal regulatory agencies that were formed early in the history of regulatory development in the United States tended to focus on particular industries, such as railroads, waterways, electric power, banks, telegraph and telephone, agribusinesses, and so forth. By virtue of their industrial focus, personnel in these regulatory agencies were able to develop considerable expertise concerning the industries they regulated. As a result, they could craft their regulations in ways that recognized the realistic problems and needs of the businesses in the particular industry they regulated. In many cases the businesses that were regulated could not raise rates or drop or add services without federal permission and could not deny services to anyone. On the other hand, these businesses typically were shielded from competition and were assured of obtaining profits at levels conventional for the time. The relationship between "regulatees" and "regulators" in this earlier form of regulatory agency is occasionally described in terms of a *capture hypothesis;* that is, the regulators may become captured by the regulatees, who then use the power of the government to create market stability and profitability for themselves.[25]

This earlier form of governmental regulatory process might be called an industry-specific model for regulation. Examples include the Interstate Commerce Commission, the Food and Drug Administration, the Securities and Exchange Commission, the Federal Communications Commission, and the Civil Aeronautics Board. Many of the regulatory agencies conforming to this model remain with us today.

In contrast, a more recent regulatory model, which might be called the industry-universal model, has been added to the earlier regulatory structure. This newer model is found in many of the regulatory agencies that were formed during the 1960s and 1970s to set regulations for all industries on specific social or operational issues, such as consumer or worker safety, environmental pollution, discrimination in the workplace, and so forth. Examples include the Equal Employment Opportunity Commission, the Occupational Safety and Health Administration, the Environmental Protection Agency, and others.

Unlike the situation in the earlier industry-specific regulatory model, staff working for agencies following the industry universal model typically have no working knowledge of the unique problems facing any one of the vast array of industries they are to regulate. Furthermore, they often have little reason to care about how their regulations affect the viability of any particular industry. Needless to say, regulatory agencies following this newer regulatory model have created regulations that have brought the greatest outcry of protest from business leaders. By the mid-1970s, business distress, particularly over these newer regulatory agencies, had reached a point where political pressures arose for a change in regulatory directions: enter Gerald Ford, Jimmy Carter, and Ronald Reagan.

The Deregulatory Movement

As I discussed in Chapter 6, the *laissez-faire* economic model has a number of serious deficiencies which make possible many abuses of the social environment by businesses. It is in response to these abuses that governmental regulatory machinery has been set up to serve as a social counterweight to businesses in an effort to protect the welfare of society as a whole and the welfare of its many constituent sectors. There are, however, ample reasons for being displeased over the enormous growth of governmental regulations. A few of these reasons are considered next.

First, as I noted earlier, regulations cost you and me a lot of money in increased taxes and in increased prices on market goods and services. There is at present a lack of evidence to demonstrate that the benefits we gain from governmental regulatory efforts exceed the costs that you and I pay.[26]

Second, because centralized government regulators in the newer form of regulatory agencies often know and care little or nothing about the many different businesses they are regulating, their regulations may seriously damage the operations and viability of individual businesses, possibly forcing businesses to close, forcing them to go abroad where regulations are few, or creating barriers to the formation of new domestic businesses; the result is that foreign companies gain considerable ground in the marketing of products in the United States. As a consequence our industries may suffer lost productivity, lost profits, lost market share, and lost jobs; our entire economy may become at risk of falling into stagnation.

Third, governmental regulatory efforts are often unsuccessful for several additional reasons.

a. As noted previously for the captive theory, regulators and regulatees may work hand in glove primarily to serve the benefit of the regulatees. This was and still is a risk to be found in the occasionally cozy relations built up between industries and regulatory agencies under the industry-specific model.

b. Some regulatory agencies have been given little or no enforcement "teeth," so they cannot seriously achieve their stated objectives.

c. As regulations became increasingly complex and numerous and as they extend out to apply to more and more people and businesses, there simply is no feasible way to monitor and enforce compliance with them.

d. The state of art of our knowledge about the economy and the effects of proposed regulations is as yet so crude that governmental regulatory efforts, even with the best intentions, may nonetheless seriously damage the economy. Witness, for example, the recessions created by tight money policies to control inflation).[27]

e. Every regulatory process is of necessity a bureaucratic one. As a consequence, the typical problems of bureaucracies (including internal power struggles, rigidifications, goal drift, and self-interest) may develop to make personnel in the regulatory agencies commit resources foremost to please themselves and to follow paths that often carry them considerably afield from the stated objectives of their agencies.

f. There is no reason to believe that governments are less corrupt or corruptible than businesses. Therefore, asking governments to protect our economic and social well-being from businesses is a bit like asking the eagles to protect our chickens from the foxes.

In short, there are substantial reasons for being disappointed over governmental regulatory efforts. The frustration and anger that inevitably result from ineffective and counterproductive regulatory processes demand redress. Redress has come in the form of the recent deregulatory movement.

Executive "Footdragging"

The great burst of regulatory development in the 1960s and early 1970s generated so much opposition to regulations that, by the time of the Ford administration, the executive branch was becoming much more inclined toward developing a "footdragging" policy to control the development, issuance, or enforcement of regulations. Ford, for example, issued an executive order (EO 11821) in 1974 requiring federal agencies under his control to write inflation impact reports for each major, newly proposed regulation. The ostensible purpose of this order was to ensure that new regulations did not add so much to the costs of business operations that they became inflationary forces driving up the prices of goods and services. However, because we don't actually have the technology, knowledge, or resources to make such assessments in a sophisticated and convincing way, the unstated effect (and quite possibly the intent) of this executive order was to make the issuance of new regulations more difficult and therefore less likely.

Jimmy Carter campaigned for the Presidency on the grounds that he was a Washington outsider who, if elected, would throw the briefcases of regulatory bureaucrats into the Potomac (a visual image quite appealing for most of us, I am sure, but one that proposes actions that are unlikely to meet federal regulations on water pollution control). In 1978 he created the Regulatory Analysis Review Group (RARG) to review the economic impact of major regulations each year and to "call regulators on the carpet" for regulations the RARG didn't like. This vehicle for publicly humiliating regulators may have struck some level of fear into their hearts and made them less likely to issue regulations that would gain the attention and ire of the RARG.

Ronald Reagan campaigned for office in 1980 on the grounds that he was a Washington outsider who, if elected, would throw the briefcases of regulatory bureaucrats into the Potomac (by then a popular campaign pledge). One of his first acts as President in 1981 was to order a freeze on all new and proposed regulations for two months. During this time he issued an executive order (EO 12291) giving the Office of Management and Budget (OMB) authority to review all newly proposed executive agency regulations to ensure that they complied with the Paperwork Reduction Act of 1980.

This was a clever step. Regulators typically require a very great deal of paperwork from regulatees, but this executive order required regulators to spend enormous amounts of time and effort producing large volumes of internal paperwork explaining and justifying to the OMB their need for the large volumes of paperwork they wished to require of regulatees. Needless to say, compliance with this executive order quickly bogged regulators down in mountains of paperwork that they themselves had to produce in order to justify their regulatory paperwork requirements. As a consequence they had less time, staff, or other resources remaining to undertake serious efforts to monitor or enforce existing regulations or to develop many new ones.[28]

The executive order also required each executive agency to conduct cost-benefit analyses of the economic implications of existing and proposed regulations. Again, regulators were diverted in a direction toward spending a good bit of their time regulating themselves by writing reports to justify their regulatory efforts.[29]

In addition to his executive order, Reagan created a Task Force on Regulatory Relief, chaired by Vice President Bush and including many key members of the Cabinet. The task force was requested to critique new and existing regulations that might be burdensome to businesses and to oversee the development of related legislative proposals. The existence of such a task force may have intimidated some regulators.

Reagan's most effective step as a deregulator was his strategy of appointing people to head major regulatory agencies who were opposed to the missions of these regulatory agencies. Once in place, these people used their administrative power to cut regulatory agency budgets to the bone and to reduce or impede regulatory efforts wherever they could. As a consequence, the executive regulatory structure itself served to slow the regulatory movement to a crawl.

In carrying out this strategy, some of the "jewels" of Reagan's top regulatory appointments were James Watt as Secretary of Interior (to safeguard our nation's natural resources), Anne Gorsuch Burford as head of the Environmental Protection Agency (to protect our environment from pollution), and Clarence Thomas as head of the Equal Employment Opportunity Commission (to protect women and minorities from workplace harassment and discrimination).[30] Yet other antiregulators were appointed to head up (and to slow or stop regulatory action in) FDA, OSHA, NHTSA, the Justice Department (particularly in its antitrust division), FTC, the Department of Labor, the Department of Health and Human Services, the Department of Education, and elsewhere in the bureaucratic maze.

In his election campaign of 1988 George Bush could not campaign as a Washington outsider and had too many friends in Washington bureaucracies to make a campaign promise to throw their briefcases in the river. And indeed as President he made no special effort to appoint people to head regulatory agencies with missions they opposed. In 1990 he did, however, create the Council on Competitiveness, headed by Vice President Quayle, to examine and speak out on major pieces of regulation. This scrutiny might have played some minor role in making regulators more cautious in the regulations they designed.

Throughout the Bush presidency and into the Clinton administration, the deregulatory movement has remained alive, but it has lost much steam. To characterize the efforts, over the past two decades, of the executive branch to set in motion a deregulatory movement, we might say that it has been much like an elephant-hunting expedition in which the hunters were equipped with pea shooters. Bureaucratic government regulators have been annoyed, possibly befuddled, and occasionally stung by these pesky executive deregulatory efforts, but at most they have been temporarily bogged down and deflected from carrying out their regulatory work.

The executive branch, does not make the nation's laws and is empowered only to carry out and enforce these laws. Thus Presidents can at best ignore the laws of our land or drag their feet in enforcing them in their efforts to seek deregulation of businesses. Congress, of course, is empowered under the U.S. Constitution to enact laws, and Congress too became involved in the deregulation movement.

Congressional Deregulation

Congressional action tended to focus on industry-specific regulatory agencies. In a series of acts since the mid-1970s, Congress deregulated certain aspects of several industries including oil, gas, airlines, trucking, railroads, shipping, banking services, intercity buses, and communications. The long-term effect of these deregulatory efforts is not yet entirely clear. The subsequent crises and scandals in the banking and saving and loan industry certainly point to the need for a return to greater, rather than less, regulation of this industry. You and I, of course, are paying the rather hefty bill for cleaning up the mess made in these scandals. For airlines, deregulation almost immediately produced a price war, and the ensuing cutthroat competition has produced several adverse effects: many airlines have been driven into bankruptcy, some smaller communities have lost services, and workers in the airline industry in general have lost pay and benefits. Time will tell what will happen to consumer prices and services after the dust clears and those services that remain have become more concentrated into the hands (or wings) of a few giant airlines.[31]

Recent Regulatory Actions: Conclusion

Regulations provide a policing effort to ensure that businesses do the right thing. As long as businesses don't "behave themselves," it is quite natural that people in a democracy will use governmental means to insist that they do. Unfortunately, such efforts necessarily are bureaucratic, cumbersome, expensive, and, to a degree, counterproductive. Much resistance is to be expected, with resulting counterpressures for deregulation. It is unlikely, however, that many people seriously want to end all regulation of food and drugs, environmental pollution, workplace discrimination, worker safety, and a raft of other issues important to our lives. So regulatory efforts appear to be here to stay until such time, if ever, that businesses behave more responsibly on their own.

Businesses, of course, have not been passive observers of the regulatory and deregulatory movements. Rather, they have exerted influence in the political arena in a number of ways. I described several of these influences in Chapter 6. In the next section I focus on how businesses influence government through their use of political action committees.

Business Political Action Committees

It is natural in a democratic political environment for people with common interests to band together to influence public law and policy. These movements of people create political parties and special interest groups as social phenomena.

Political Parties

A political party serves to organize both voters and candidates, and it gains strength and influence throughout society based on the number of elective offices it can hold and the number of voters it can attract. Parties set their own public policy agendas, select candidates to carry their party's banner, assist in candidate campaigns for office, and attempt to get out the vote for their candidates. The rewards to faithful party members include sharing in the "spoils" of campaign victory, as they get the inside track on jobs, government contracts, and other special favors.

The ability to use government jobs, government contracts, and other favors as rewards to the party faithful has been one of the principal forces behind the creation and perpetuation of big city party machines. But the ability of parties to engage in patronage (i.e., control over the awarding of jobs) was reduced severely in the civil service reform movement. As a result, parties lost their principal mechanism for controlling large numbers of voters, a fact which may have contributed considerably to decreased voter participation in elections and to decreased party membership.

Without the ability to control voters, parties have become much less useful to candidates and have consequently lost control over their candidates. In the past, party control of voters put the party in a position to select candidates and to control their actions and votes; now party platforms have become increasingly meaningless as a guide for candidate decisions and the era of the big party bosses has come to an end. Candidates instead have been thrown on their own devices to figure out what positions they should take on major issues (or how to avoid taking any firm positions) in order to appeal to the largest cross-section of prospective voters; and how they should vote on major pieces of legislation.

Political Action Committees

The collapse of the power of parties has created a political vacuum that has made it possible for a wide array of special interest groups to gain increased influence in our political processes. As candidates scramble for funding and voter support from as many places as possible, special interest groups, with the pockets of money and voter allegiance that they possess, have gained a level of political importance they did not previously have when parties were strong. In this context we must consider the growing importance of political action committees (PACs).

Through PACs, businesses and other special interest groups are able both to provide campaign contributions to candidates who are favorable to their interests and to influence the legislative process itself. In view of the multiple and significant ways that governments now affect businesses and commercial operations, it is not surprising that businesses would want to exert influence over governmental decision making.

The Tillman Act of 1907 made it illegal for individual corporations to contribute directly to federal campaigns. However, in the past two decades, leaders of corporations have been able to maneuver around this law by forming political action committees as entities independent from their corporation. They then donate money to these committees and have the committees in turn donate the money to the desired candidates.

In legislation and in regulatory rulings issued in the 1970s, greater freedom was given to corporations to form their own PACs and to use corporate money directly in the organization and administration of these PACs. This body of legislation also restricted the amount of money a PAC could give to each candidate (no more than $5,000 per election), but had a giant loophole in allowing unlimited spending on behalf of a candidate. Under the guise of campaign reform, these laws had the ironic effect of producing an explosive growth in the number of PACs.

Thus although there were only 89 corporate PACs in the United States in 1974, by 1984 there were over 1,800, spending collectively close to $60 million in an effort to influence our politicians.[32] By 1978 PACs were giving three times more money directly to candidates for national office than to political parties,[33] which again emphasizes the declining significance of political parties.

As of 1992 there were nearly 4,200 PACs, which collectively contributed $178 million to U.S. House and Senate candidates in the 1991–1992 election year. These PAC contributions amounted to about a third (32 percent) of the 1991–1992 campaign funds for persons running for the U.S. House and about a fifth (19 percent) of the campaign funds for persons running for the U.S. Senate. Incumbents were especially sought after by PACs, with 51 percent and 38 percent respectively, of all campaign funds for incumbents in the U.S. House and Senate coming from PACs during that election year.[34] AT&T's PAC alone contributed nearly $1 million to U.S. House and Senate candidates in 1992. Tobacco PACs representing Philip Morris and R. J. Reynolds each contributed nearly one-half million dollars. Four defense industry PACs (Martin Marietta, General Electric, Lockheed, and General Dynamics) collectively contributed over $1.5 million.[35]

Recent research[36] suggests that corporate PAC contributions are designed principally to gain access to legislators (at the federal or state levels) and to maintain a continuing relation with them so as to influence the types of laws they will pass. The PAC contributions to legislators operate much as gifts traditionally do in our culture. That is, the recipient of the gift (the congressperson) is expected to feel thankful and more willing to listen to and respond favorably toward the concerns of the gift-giver (the corporation through its PAC). Much of the corporate influence that is exerted through this process is opportunistic in nature. It seeks to capitalize on opportunities (when available) to create loopholes in legislation that will exempt one or more corporations from having to pay particular taxes or that will water down regulatory initiatives that are adverse to corporate interests.

Research also suggests that corporate PACs tend to exhibit a unity in their support for specific candidates in contested elections.[37] As the figures given here indicate, this unity in recent years tends to center on support for incumbents, regardless of political party.[38]

As of 1994 45 percent of all PACs were corporate PACs; however, at least 8 percent of PACs represented labor organizations; 20 percent represented trade, membership, and health organizations; and about 26 percent represented other special interest groups.[39] Thus businesses are doing what many other special interest groups are doing in our society to gain influence in political affairs.[40]

Conclusion

Chapter 5 described how businesses and governments overlap in business-oriented societies, with governments playing substantial roles in supporting and promoting business activities. Chapter 6 described how governments have become friends of the business community in the United States, and how business leaders maintain substantial involvement in and influence over our governments through a circulation of business elites through key government positions.

Besides PACs, business influences on government take yet other forms. For example, most large corporations maintain Washington offices to keep track of newly proposed legislation and regulations and to lobby for actions favorable to their corporation's interests. Furthermore, more than 6,000 business trade associations, such as the United States Chamber of Commerce or the National Association of Manufacturers, perform similar functions.[41] In addition, several major business councils are influential in government policy formation; these include the Committee for Economic Development, the Business Roundtable, and the Business Council. Finally, offers of an "honorarium" to key congresspersons for services rendered (a speech, an article, or other trumpery) may have become a useful device for rewarding and influencing congresspersons and legislation.[42] Viewed across the board, then, we must conclude that PACS are at most a supplement to the already extensive influence that big corporations exert on government.

Looked at from a larger societal framework, PACs provide multiple avenues through which many groups of people (from people who like guns, to people who want more programs for the elderly) can exert an influence on our democratic governmental processes independent of the decaying parties. Furthermore, PACs and related lobbying organizations may promote greater attention to issues that do not otherwise have wide public appeal, and they may supply legislators and policy makers with the best technical expertise available for drafting legislation and regulations and for overall decision making. Thus PACs and lobbying organizations do serve several purposes that are at least potentially useful. Our historical alternative has been decision making in smoke-filled back rooms by party hacks or by under-the-table bribes. I do not believe that PACs provide a less moral vehicle for organizing political processes.

Chapter 8

Improving the Moral
Performance of Businesses

A Sociological Account for Corruption in Businesses

In this chapter I use a sociological perspective to explain why businesses in our society engage in so many unethical and socially irresponsible behaviors. Based on this perspective, I propose strategies for improving the moral performance of businesses.

Business as Crime

In examining the social landscape, one finds no clear dividing line between those social phenomena that we wish to call crime on the one hand and those that we wish to call business on the other. Indeed, it would be easy to argue that criminal behavior not only is not unusual among businesses, but it is a core feature of the business enterprise itself. Consider the following.

As defined in Chapter 1, a social phenomenon is a business if it consists of a repetitive pattern of efforts to make a profit in a market setting. At the point of sale, the act of making a profit involves getting the better side of a trade or getting more from a market exchange than does the other party to the exchange. The surplus value that a business receives from a market exchange relative to what it gives up is its profit. Therefore, the more advantages that the business can create for itself in controlling the dynamics of the market exchange, the greater its profits are from the exchange.

Prior to the rise of the business-oriented society, the social bonds that held most of our ancestors together would have been such that they would have considered it improper for their kin and neighbors to seek to create a profit-making relation with them.[1] The crime inherent in efforts to create such relations is that of continually trying to take advantage of, exploit, or cheat others. Attempts to establish such relations with others would have been regarded as not only unfriendly and unneighborly, but also as highly questionable on moral grounds and would have met with strong public disapproval and possibly adverse public sanction. For this reason businesspersons in earlier ages often were held in low repute; indeed they were typically regarded as being untrustworthy, treacherous, wicked, or corrupt; as being shysters; or as being social misfits or pariahs.

In contrast, the legal codes and supporting ideologies of our business-oriented society today lead us to a very different view of business activities. Far from being seen as improper, sinful, or criminal, we regard business profit making today to be a fully legitimate form of behavior for building relations among people in our society. Indeed our current ideological preferences go so far as to regard most business profit-making activities to be among the most highly valued of human endeavors.

Although being favorably disposed toward profit-making behaviors, people in business-oriented societies nonetheless are able to identify a small group of market organized profit-making relations that they do not wish to permit. Organized crime, for example, clearly fits the definition of a business, whether it involves drug pushing, prostitution rings, bootlegging, gambling, or protection rackets. In all such cases markets are established and recurring profits are taken. Why is it, however, that drug pushing is an illegal business enterprise (indeed it is a criminal enterprise), while the selling of other addictive substances such as alcohol or nicotine is a legal (noncriminal) business enterprise? Or why is it that loan sharking is an illegal business enterprise (again a crime), while the common practice of charging usurious interest rates on credit cards is not? Clearly, prevailing political interests are important in drawing lines between what we will regard as criminal businesses (or crimes) and what we will regard as legitimate businesses.

I shall leave aside any further consideration of the question of why some businesses are considered legitimate and others are considered criminal. Instead, for the remainder of this chapter I wish to consider only those businesses that are conventionally considered to be legitimate or noncriminal in our society. The question I want to pursue is why corruption occurs in these legitimate businesses and what can be done about it.

Corruption in Businesses

As I discussed in Chapter 7, when corporations operate in corrupt and socially irresponsible ways (even if they do so unwittingly or as a result of a lack of attention or commitment), they make necessary the development of external social control mechanisms to pressure them into doing the right thing. In a society with democratic political structures, governments become the logical social vehicle for applying these pressures. Unfortunately, as I also noted in Chapter 7, such a social solution results in decreased freedom for all of us, is costly, and meets with limited success.

How great is the problem of corrupt and socially irresponsible business behavior in our business-oriented society? Estimates vary considerably by study, depending on research definitions and sample.[2] However, all estimates point to significant and extensive business corruption.

In one study, nearly two–thirds (60 percent) of the 582 largest corporations in the United States were found in a single two-year period (1975–1976) to have been either charged or convicted with violations of federal laws by one or more of twenty-five federal agencies. Of those charged or convicted, an average of more than four violations occurred per corporation.[3]

In another study, 11 percent of more than a thousand large U.S. corporations were found during the decade of the 1970s to have been sanctioned by the courts for violations of federal laws related to just the following eight illegal practices alone: price fixing, bid rigging, kickbacks, bribes, illegal rebates, illegal political contributions, fraud, and tax evasion.[4] Companies with two or more violations included American Airlines, Bethlehem Steel, Firestone, PepsiCo, R. J. Reynolds, Tenneco, and many others.

Looking at the 500 largest U.S. corporations over a time frame from 1972 to 1982, another study found that twenty-three percent either were convicted of a major crime or paid a civil penalty for a serious infraction.[5] Imagine for a moment that there were 500 people living in your neighborhood and that nearly a fourth had major run-ins with the law. How safe would you feel in your neighborhood? Now recall that the 500 largest corporations have sales equivalent to more than a third of our GNP.[6] With roughly a fourth having been found to engage in serious legal infractions, how safe is our economy?

Although these figures on corporate crimes are disturbing, we can expect that, as is true for records on crime in general, the level of unreported or undetected business crime is much greater. Let's look at some more estimates.

Estimates suggest that fraud in the securities market may amount to one billion dollars annually, fraud in the pharmaceutical industry may amount to half a billion dollars annually, and home repair fraud may amount to another billion dollars.[7] In total, white collar corporate crime is estimated by the U.S. Department of Justice to cost perhaps as much as $200 billion annually,[8] and most of it goes unpunished!

Ethical problems are widely evident within corporations. More than half (57 percent) of managers in a 1976 study indicated that they have at some time felt that their role as a business manager conflicted with their role as an ethical person. One in ten executives reported being asked by their bosses to do something illegal. One in two (47 percent) reported having fired subordinates for unethical behavior. And nearly one in five reported having been approached by suppliers with kickback schemes.[9]

Here are some additional illustrations of the breadth and depth of corrupt and irresponsible behavior found in the business sector:

- Between 1977 and 1983 Beech–Nut Nutrition Corporation (a leading maker of drinks and foods for infants and a subsidiary of Nestle Corporation) sold as "apple juice" an adulterated sugar water concoction containing little or no actual apple juice. For this fraudulent practice, the company was fined $2 million.[10]
- In 1984 SmithKline, a giant pharmaceutical company, pleaded guilty to suppressing information about adverse effects of one of its popular blood pressure drugs, Selacryn™. During an eight-month period, 60 users of the drug died and 513 suffered liver damage.[11]
- In 1988 two employees of Ashland Oil successfully sued the company on charges that they had been fired for refusing to pay bribes to foreign officials.[12]
- In a national survey of 900 midsized and large companies in 1997, the American Management Association found that 63 percent use one or more techniques to spy on their employees in the workplace (including surveillance cameras, the recording of phone conversations, and the review of computerized records on employee computer usage). Of companies engaging in these practices, 23 percent do so without telling their employees.[13]
- In 1992 Sears, Roebuck, and Company announced that it would no longer pay its auto repair personnel commissions based on how many auto repairs they could find and talk

consumers into purchasing. This announcement came as a result of California's move to revoke or suspend all of Sears' auto repair licenses because of widespread repair fraud by Sears personnel. New Jersey and Florida had initiated similar investigations of Sears' auto repair practices in their states.[14]

- Depending on the estimate, between forty and sixty-three percent of all auto repair bills are inaccurate or fraudulent, resulting in almost $21 billion a year in consumer overcharges.[15]
- Corruption in small businesses appears to be widespread. A study of corrupt practices in mostly small businesses in the New York area found that over 71 percent of employees could readily identify deceptive practices undertaken by the business for which they worked.[16]
- Shortweighting (putting less of a product in a package than indicated on its label) was found in 26 percent of nearly a half million packages of vegetables, fruit, cheese, and other products sold in New York City markets. A survey of twenty-eight meat warehouses, also in New York City, found that all of them engaged in shortweighting and mislabeling of their products.[17]
- Over a third of 121 appliance stores in New York City were found to be selling used televisions as new. A national survey found that false repairs were suggested or made by 49 percent of jewelers and 65 percent of typewriter repair shops.[18]
- A study by the General Accounting Office of the U.S. Congress found that misrepresentation in the sale of gasoline and diesel fuel is widespread in the nation's gas stations, including the sale of regular gasoline as higher priced premium.[19]
- In 1976 Allied Chemical Corporation pleaded no contest to 940 counts of willfully polluting Virginia's James River with the highly toxic pesticide, Kepone.[20]
- The EPA estimates that 90 percent of toxic wastes are disposed of unsafely in the United States and that there may be 32,000 or more hazardous waste dump sites in the nation, with over 600 of them posing immediate health threats.[21] An example of a tragedy resulting from the unsafe disposal of toxic wastes occurred at the Love Canal. Between 1942 and 1953 the Hooker Chemicals and Plastics Corporation (later a subsidiary of Occidental Petroleum Corporation) dumped 21,000 tons of toxic chemicals into a fifteen-acre abandoned waterway known as the Love Canal in Niagara Falls, N.Y. Then, under pressure of condemnation, Hooker sold the dump site and surrounding area to the local school board, and a school and community were eventually built on it. Our ever-vigilant government officials, whom we expect to safeguard the public interest, were mute as usual on these developments. Twenty-five years later the community woke up to the problem. By that time eighty-two chemicals, including twelve carcinogens, were still to be found in the soils, air, and water of the community. A health survey of residents revealed extremely high rates of miscarriages, birth defects, cancer, liver disorders, and other serious health problems. In one affected neighborhood, only one of fifteen pregnancies in a twelve-month period reportedly resulted in a healthy baby.[22]
- In just fourteen states over a single three-year period (1979–1982), 124 corporations were convicted of bid rigging on highway projects.[23]
- In 1988 FBI investigations revealed a pattern of bribery, fraud, and bid-rigging among at least fourteen major defense contractors on government contracts that were worth tens of billions of dollars.[24]

- Between 1988 and 1992 the U.S. Justice Department brought seventy-three antitrust cases against thirty-nine corporations and forty-eight individuals involved in bid-rigging for school milk contracts. Grand juries were convened to investigate related charges in twenty-one states. Among litigants, Flav-O-Rich and Pet dairies have both settled their cases by pleading guilty and paying $13 million and $2 million, respectively, in fines.[25]
- Nearly thirty companies involved in the electric equipment industry (including General Electric and Westinghouse) were found guilty of working together to fix prices and rig bids throughout the latter half of the 1940s and the 1950s.[26]
- In the 1970s, paper companies accounting for 70 percent of the $1.5 billion market for paper boxes were convicted or pleaded no contest to price fixing.[27]
- A number of drug companies, including American Cyanamid, Pfizer, and Bristol–Myers, were found guilty of price fixing in the sale of antibiotics.[28]
- In the 1980s, more than twenty-five major oil companies agreed to pay fines and to set up repayment plans costing them several billions of dollars for having engaged in illegal consumer overcharges amounting to as much as $25 billion.[29]
- In 1992, four major airlines (United, American, Delta and USAir) agreed to pay $44 million and to issue $365.5 million in discount coupons to consumers to settle a price-fixing suit that resulted in overcharges to an estimated 12.5 million travelers over a period from January 1988 through May 1992.[30]
- By one estimate, price fixing among corporations costs consumers $60 billion annually in overcharges.[31]
- In the 1970s, Equity Life Insurance Company invented thousands of phony insurance policies to defraud investors of between $2 and $3 billion.[32]
- Revco Drug Stores was found guilty in 1977 of a double billing scheme to defraud Medicaid of Ohio of a half million dollars.[33]
- In 1985 a federal judge found State Farm Insurance Company to have discriminated against women in the hiring of insurance agents in California. In a 1992 settlement agreement, State Farm agreed to pay $157 million to the more than 800 women who had been refused jobs as agents simply because they were women.[34]
- During the 1970s and 1980s, more than 450 large corporations admitted to having made bribes to foreign officials totaling collectively over $1 billion. Most of these companies were offered immunity from prosecution in return for admitting what they had done. Companies admitting to having made more than $1.5 million each in illegal or improper foreign payments included Alcoa, American Home Products, R. J. Reynolds, United Brands, Chrysler, General Tire and Rubber, Armco Steel Corporation, Exxon, Gulf Oil Corporation, Mobile Oil, Shell Oil, ITT, Warner-Lambert, Upjohn, Boeing, United Aircraft, and Lockheed. Lockheed is a special standout in this distinguished list. Lockheed alone paid out $12.6 million in bribes to top Japanese officials (including Japan's Prime Minister, Kakuei Tanaka) in order to win contracts to sell twenty-one of its Tristar jets to All Nippon Airways.[35]
- In the 1970s, U.S. political candidates received illegal contributions from more than 300 U.S. corporations, including Northrop Corporation, American Airlines, Exxon, Ashlund Oil, Phillips Petroleum, Gulf Oil, Braniff, Goodyear, and Greyhound. Northrop alone agreed to pay back $2.3 million to the federal government in fees it had added

on to its defense contracts specifically to cover the costs of its illegal campaign contributions and for its entertaining of government officials.[36]

- By illegal use of insider information, Ivan Boesky and David Levine were able to "soak" the stock markets for hundreds of millions of dollars. Several large, prestigious Wall Street firms were involved. One report suggests that these practices continue to occur today, unabated.[37]

Holy cow! Such widespread corruption makes a person feel that it might be wise to have a police officer posted in every corporate office, at every employee workstation, in every small business, and in every market setting. It certainly would appear that there is something fundamentally wrong with businesses in the United States to foster corrupt and socially irresponsible behavior on such a widespread basis!

Corruption Society-Wide

Actually, before we conclude that businesses are the "bogeypersons" incarnated from our most fearsome childhood dreams, we should take note of the following fact: the corruption that we see in businesses is also to be found in substantial proportions in all major social institutions in our society. Consider the following examples:

Family

> About a fourth of all murders are committed by family members;[38] more than one-fifth of all married men and one-eighth of all married women cheat on their spouse;[39] each year over a million teenage girls become pregnant and more than one-third of all mothers under the age of twenty-four are unmarried;[40] more than 1.5 million abortions occur annually;[41] almost one-fourth of all births are out of wedlock, half of our nation's children grow up in broken homes, and it is estimated that between ten and twelve percent of female children in the United States are subjected to sexual abuse before the age of fourteen (perhaps as many as one-fourth are sexually abused by age eighteen).[42]

Religion

> Violations of central religious codes are widespread in society, including the use of verbal vulgarities, "taking the Lord's name in vain," fornication, adultery, and alcohol and drug abuse; only about 40 percent of Americans regularly go to church, and only 55 percent claim that religion is very important in their lives;[43] one survey found that some 400 Roman Catholic priests and brothers were reported between 1982 and 1992 for sexual abuse of children;[44] "media ministries" and cult leaders build financial empires while their leaders (e.g., Jim Bakker, Jimmy Swaggart, Reverend Moon) are arrested on criminal charges.

Governments

> Watergate, the Pentagon Papers, and the Iran-Contra affair revealed that U.S. Presidents and high level officials in government and in the military lie to the public and seek to use the official power they have to cover up their own illegal acts; "Koreagate," ABSCAM, the Keating Five, and other episodes show that Congresspersons and other high level officials can be bought; in the decade between 1972 and 1982, twenty-nine

members of the U.S. Congress were prosecuted for crimes;[45] in a single three-year period (1981 through 1983) forty-five high level officials in the Reagan Administration resigned under criticism for ethical violations or under investigation for criminal activities;[46] the CIA has been found to have engaged in wanton violations of its charter by engaging in domestic intelligence gathering, and the FBI has been used by insiders and by Presidents for political purposes;[47] both Harry Truman and Lyndon Johnson won U.S. Senate seats, a major step in their ascension to the Presidency, through election fraud;[48] Detroit's Police Chief William Hart was convicted in 1992 of stealing $2.5 million from the city.[49]

Education

As many as 60 percent of students are estimated to cheat on tests; by one estimate, almost a third of Illinois high school students have brought weapons to school for protection;[50] phony diploma mills grant college degrees in any specialty; colleges and universities lie about curricula and programs; and defaults on student loans cost taxpayers billions of dollars.

Health Care

The General Accounting Office of the U.S. Congress estimates that fraud in health care may amount to $70 billion a year;[51] unnecessary surgeries are frequently reported as being performed to boost hospital revenues and physician income; drug companies routinely offer bribes to physicians to get them to prescribe their medications;[52] and the overmedication of the elderly and women (particularly with valium) is widespread.

Charities

"Administrative expenses" are often outrageously excessive: for example, as president of the United Way of America, William Aramony's compensation package alone consumed nearly half a million dollars in United Way charity funds each year during the early 1990s;[53] a study of the one hundred largest charitable foundations in the United States in 1991 revealed that thirteen of their top managers received more than $300 thousand per year in salary, and another twenty-four received more than $200 thousand per year, proving once again that "charity begins at home" or at least in the charity's "home" office.[54]

Science

Fraud is repeatedly discovered in scientific research and reports (from my informal observations, I would estimate that at least a fourth of social science research is in some way fraudulent) and scientific research money is misappropriated for parties, yachts, and other luxuries (as was done, for example, at Stanford University during the 1980s).

Mass Media

"News" is presented in an entertainment format, typically with an obvious bias and based on half-truths, instant analysis, and sound bites; most television programs during the family hours are filled with violence, vulgar language, and fornication; in 1993 NBC's *Dateline* presented a phony newscast in which it had secretly attached explosives to a GM truck to ensure that it would burst into flames as a result of a side-on collision.

Everywhere we look in our society we find corruption and irresponsible behavior. Ours is the largest, most complex, industrial nation in the world. But we also rank number one or near the top on many dimensions of corruption, such as per capita murders, rapes, robberies, and a wide assortment of other crimes. For example, in the early 1990s in the United States, a violent crime occurred every 17 seconds, with a murder every 21 minutes, a rape every 5 minutes, a robbery every 46 seconds, and an aggravated assault every 29 seconds.[55]

In general, tendencies to do the wrong thing seem to be very widespread in the United States: we cheat on our spouses and duck out on family obligations; we engage in extensive amounts of employee theft (accounting for perhaps as much as $50 billion a year, with roughly a third of a million employees arrested for theft each year);[56] we pad our business expense accounts, shoplift, and cheat on our income taxes;[57] we fake illnesses in order to avoid going to work or school, infringe on copyrights (including making illegal recordings of audio and videotapes), and are guilty of a great many violations of traffic laws (including seat belt, speed limit, and drunk driving laws), and of many other laws specifying proper or decorous behavior in our society. Crimes against property (theft and vandalism) in the United States now occur at the rate of one incident every two seconds;[58] about a million Americans are arrested annually for drug offenses, another 600,000 for public drunkenness, and another 1.2 million for driving under the influence;[59] and in a large survey of teenagers in Illinois, a third admitted to having committed a serious crime, thirteen percent admitted to robbery, forty percent admitted to keeping stolen goods, and fifty percent admitted to engaging in shoplifting.[60]

If you think about it, it doesn't seem too safe for you and me to live in our complex, business-oriented society.

The Social Grounds of Deviance

How can we explain so much corruption society-wide? From a sociological perspective, corruption may be viewed as a normal part of social life.[61] Indeed, corrupt and socially irresponsible behaviors appear to be as much a part of society as are proper and responsible behaviors. Available evidence, for example, shows corrupt and socially irresponsible behaviors to be in ample supply not only in our own society, but in all societies historically and cross-culturally.

Emile Durkheim, one of the early great sociologists, is well known for his thesis that social deviance is a natural part of society.[62] I shall draw on and expand on his arguments in the discussion that follows.

Each society sets out moral boundaries on the range of behaviors that are to be permitted among its members. In doing so, some actions are defined as being out of bounds or as being deviant. If society did not have boundaries for defining acceptable from unacceptable behavior, then social life and society itself would be chaotic and impossible.

The punishing of transgressors of these boundaries (i.e., of deviants) also serves a vital role in society. It serves as a means to rally people together as a moral community and in this way to reaffirm their social solidarity. Thus public efforts to censure deviance help to hold society together. The significance of this process of setting boundaries and of censuring transgressors as a means for reaffirmation of social solidarity is very critical to social order. It is so critical that, even if all forms of deviance as currently defined were to be eliminated, new forms would have to be defined into existence so that we could continue to pull ourselves together into a coherent moral community through the device of defining and condemning deviance. In short, we need deviance and we need to punish deviants in order to establish and maintain social order.

Fortunately (or unfortunately), deviance is not in short supply. Rather it abounds everywhere for at least two reasons: we as individuals continually test the limits of what we can get away with (to ad-lib as it pleases us), and social settings themselves may be deficient in the means to call us back into social order. As Durkheim has noted, the lack of sufficient means to restrain us in a moral order is especially a problem in industrial societies, where the major social structures of family, community, church, and government have become increasingly splintered and depersonalized.

In Chapter 5, I introduced the concept of an urge to be creative as a part of our human nature, and I noted that such an urge leads us to make social script changes wherever we can. We can assume that propensities to be creative will not be found equally shared among persons in any given population. Some persons may possess a strong urge to be creative and be more inclined to deviate from social scripts; others may possess a weak urge to be creative (the stodgy "prim-and-propers" among us who probably deviate nonetheless in dreams and reverie).[63] Most of us, of course, fall somewhere in between, engaging in creative deviance whenever opportunities arise and when there is nothing to restrain us from doing so.

Thus at any given time there should be plenty of deviant behaviors in all sectors of society, and the amount of deviance should be greatest when social counterforces do not exist to serve as a barrier to such activities. With the splintering of family, clan, community, church, and political power, in the United States, we certainly have a fertile environment for the unrestrained production of deviance. And deviance we do have in great abundance. It should, therefore, be no surprise to find substantial amounts of corrupt and socially irresponsible behaviors within the business sector *or within any other sector* in society.

To summarize, deviance is a phenomenon that appears everywhere in society. It is held in check by social control mechanisms, such as are exerted by families, extended kin, neighbors, the community, or church or governmental sanction.[64] As these social control mechanisms have become increasingly splintered by the forces of business-oriented industrialization, an increase in deviance has been a natural corollary. Thus there is so much deviance in society today not because we are different as people from our ancestors, but only because the complexity of our society and its lack of adequate social control mechanisms creates an enormously rich environment for us to engage in creative deviance and for us to get away with it. This situation appears to be just one more cost (or opportunity) that derives from our living in a business-oriented, industrial society.[65]

Improving the Moral Performance of Businesses

When businesses were small and peripheral to the social order of society, corrupt and socially irresponsible business behaviors posed little threat to society at large. As I noted in Chapter 3, when such undesirable behaviors occurred, they typically could be held in check by informal public pressure brought by consumers, by clans, and by the community, or if necessary by religious and political authorities.

In business-oriented societies, by contrast, corrupt and socially irresponsible business behaviors gain far greater significance as a threat to public welfare. We have now come to be tied together around business interests. Consequently, corrupt and socially irresponsible behaviors by businesses have the potential to threaten the very foundations of contemporary social order. Furthermore, the enormous size and anonymity of many businesses today make it no longer possible to control business corruption through informal public censure. As a consequence, we have been forced to seek other social means to hold businesses in check. And in a democratic political environment, it has been quite natural for us to turn to government to provide that means.

However, government can enforce moral order (if at all) only by controlling us, and so our personal freedoms become reduced as a result. If we wish to remain as free as possible, a better strategy would be for businesses themselves to set up their own internal social control mechanisms to monitor and regulate their behaviors. In this section I shall discuss a number of possible social control mechanisms of this sort. I shall focus my attention primarily on large corporate businesses, because they dominate our economy, but I shall also comment briefly on small businesses.

At the outset I wish to make it clear that the social control mechanisms I shall propose do not rely for their effect on the voluntary goodwill of individuals. Left to their own devices, individuals voluntarily will engage in as much deviance as they can get away with.

By contrast, the social control mechanisms I describe in this section do not place the onus on individuals to volunteer to be better people or to do the right thing on the basis of their own strength of character. Rather the social structural arrangements I shall propose are social control mechanisms precisely because they pressure each person to increase their behavioral conformity to standards that are judged within the context to be socially responsible regardless of the person's strength of character or personal convictions.

All social control mechanisms result in a loss of individual freedom, as any effort to control deviance must, but the social mechanisms I shall describe allow pluralistic pressures operating at the decentralized level of corporations (and of corporate divisions) to specify, detect, and sanction deviant acts. Thus the social mechanisms I shall propose might be described as involving a process of decentralized, pluralistic compulsion.

I shall consider three major social forces in the business sector as potential social control mechanisms for corporations: the shareholding owners, the board of directors, and management.

Shareholder Owners

There is little to be said for pressuring shareholding owners to serve as a social control mechanism for fostering responsible behavior in businesses. In the typical publicly held business corporation, the shareholding owners are nameless and faceless; they are unknown to each other and typically are unknown as well to corporate management and to the corporate board of directors.

Shareholding owners typically have little or no direct control over the businesses they own and have little knowledge about the operations of these businesses. Rather their ownership is to them just a paper investment. Furthermore, the persons who hold positions as board directors and who allegedly represent shareholder interests are typically hand picked and appointed to their board positions by management through trumped up shareholder nomination and election processes that would have made the previously ruling Communist Party of the Soviet Union proud. As a result of the nomination and election processes, the board members hold more allegiance to management and to each other than to the shareholding owners, who they don't know and with whom they have no communication.

When corporate ownership is concentrated into a few hands or is private, owners often themselves serve on the board of directors or are top managers. Thus a managerial or board perspective is dominant in this situation as well. Because there is little to be said about the use of shareholding owners to foster improved moral behavior among businesses, I'll move on to consider the boards.[66]

Corporate Governance and the Board of Directors

Throughout history parents have served as the most important social force ensuring moral behavior. Parents set an example for us; ensure that we are properly dressed and groomed; monitor our every behavior and whereabouts; scold, nag, and cajole us on our manners; and punish us whenever necessary for bad behavior. Furthermore, because we have a desire for our parents to think well of us, we resist doing the wrong thing if we think our parents will find out.

In my reverie I have imagined proposing that no persons be appointed to senior management positions in a corporation unless they bring their parents to work with them each day. In fantasy I can imagine these parents demanding that their managerial children use limited corporate resources wisely; play fairly and nicely with others; not lie, cheat, or steal things; not hurt or abuse other people or vandalize the environment; take care to apologize and make restitution or fix anything they damage; and generally show respect for laws and for the welfare of others. Though I personally believe that physical punishment is inadvisable for children, in these reveries I have made an exception by providing each managerial parent with a yardstick as a teaching aid in fostering improved corporate management behavior.

But I suppose this whimsical plan would meet with some minor snag in actual implementation that would lead some to argue against it. And I suppose that an alternative plan of assigning a police officer as a permanent escort to each senior manager would also run into some problem or other that would lead critics to conclude it to be unworkable or unacceptable. Therefore, we are left with the board of directors itself to serve the disciplining role of parents and police officers to corporate management.

Corporations as Legal Entities
The various states in the United States provide the legal basis for allowing corporations to be formed and for defining their legal duties, rights, and restrictions. Private individuals, singly or in groups, are allowed to create a corporation because it is believed that a corporation might provide a useful social vehicle for collective action in service of the public good, or at least that it will not detract significantly from the public good in the pursuit of its goals. In the early history of this nation, each proposed corporation was in fact examined closely prior to approval or disapproval to ensure that the needs of the greater public good (or at least those of vested political interests) were to be met. Eventually, however,

with an increasing number of proposals arising for corporate formation, the process for approving new corporations became routinized, so that investigations of the impact of the proposed corporation on the public good were no longer required. Nonetheless, the general assumption still is that all corporations should either serve the public good or at least not detract from it.

Corporations may be formed to serve business or nonbusiness purposes. In the typical case when a large corporation is created to undertake significant business activities, the owners of the corporation are shareholders whose interests are directed toward personal gain from their investment in shares of the corporation. In accordance with the articles of incorporation, a corporate board of directors is formed to oversee management of the corporation on behalf of the shareholders. If there are few shareholders, the shareholders themselves may constitute the board of directors. However, in the business environment of large public corporations today, the directors of the board may hold no or few shares of stock in the corporation, and the social distance between the director and the typical shareholder is usually very great. How then do the directors serve either the interests of the shareholding investors or the broader goals of the public good?

The Structure and Operation of the Board of Directors

What were the corporate boards of directors doing when all of the scandals and corrupt business behaviors occurred that were described earlier in this chapter? Where was the board of directors when Allied Chemical Company was dumping Kepone in the James River? Where were the boards when Exxon, Goodyear, or Northrop were making illegal contributions to candidates in U.S. elections or when Lockheed was bribing the Japanese prime minister? Where too were the boards when major U.S. companies were engaging in price fixing, bid rigging, marketing unsafe consumer products, or engaging in discriminatory employment practices? Or where were the boards in the recent banking and savings and loan scandals that we taxpayers are expected to clean up? Were the boards protecting the investment interests of their shareholders? Were they looking out for the public good (i.e., the good of the consumers, the employees, the environment, other social institutions, or international relations)? Or were they perhaps simply "out to lunch" when these corrupt and socially irresponsible practices occurred.

It is easy to see that the typical structure and operation of boards of large, publicly held corporations today provide little basis for protecting shareholder interests or for protecting the larger public good. For example, a recent estimate indicates that boards usually meet only a few times each year (ranging between two and seventeen times, with most boards meeting five to ten times for two and one-half to three and one-half hours per meeting.[67] The estimated average total time per year spent by board directors in preparing for board meetings ranges from 0 to 330 hours, with most directors devoting for the entire year only between twelve and forty hours in preparation time.[68] Information distributed to directors prior to meetings may be scant, and in many cases even the agenda is not sent out before the meetings.[69] Under such circumstances, the influence of board members on corporate policy is minimal, and boards operate more as mere "rubber stamps" for top management plans.

What does it take to become a board member? Membership on a major corporate business board is a quite cushy job, paying an average of between $20,000 to $33,000 annually[70] for the minimal time that is involved. I am sure that I could spare some time for such an assignment. How about you?

But nomination and election to a business board (which essentially amounts to appointment by senior management and the current board members) generally goes to economic elites (often to top managers of the corporation itself, to chief executive officers of other corporations, senior law partners, senior investment bankers, or top former political office holders) who either are influential old friends of management and of current board members or who they would like to have as influential friends.[71] If you qualify on such grounds, lucky you.

Control of the board is almost always firmly in the hands of management. In the typical case (that is, 80 percent of the time)[72] the chief executive officer (CEO or top manager) is the chair of the board of directors and, therefore, calls all meetings and sets and controls the meeting agendas. In addition, a little under a third of all directors on the board are themselves senior managers of the corporation,[73] so management both controls and is amply represented on the boards that are legally supposed to oversee management in the interest of stockholders.

Considering how corporate boards are presently structured, they are not suitable social mechanisms for controlling the moral performance of corporations, or even for promoting the profitability of corporations. Whether they provide any useful oversight as presently constituted depends principally on the unique personalities and personal commitments of senior managers and of particular board members. Such fortuitous occurrences of individual interests and desires, even when found, obviously do not constitute an enduring social control mechanism for fostering high moral standards in corporations.

Steps to Transforming the Board into a Social Control Mechanism

A two-fold strategy is needed to transform the board into an effective social control mechanism for fostering improved moral performance among corporate businesses.

1. The membership must be changed. All senior managers (including CEOs) of the corporation that the board is expected to oversee should be barred from board membership, and this means, of course, that CEOs could no longer be chairs of their corporation's board. Obviously the CEO and other senior managers are essential resource people for boards, and boards might wish them to sit in on many or most meetings. Control of the board, however, must be removed from the CEO and senior management before the board can serve as a serious disciplining force over the behavior of the CEO and senior managers either in terms of the corporation's responsibilities to shareholders or to the public good.

2. All boards need to draw up mission statements that clearly set their principal function to be that of overseeing management in fact, rather than in theory. The mission statement should spell out how this is to be done and what subcommittees are to be formed for doing it.[74]

What are the subcommittees likely to be most useful to corporate business boards? Current trends are for corporate business boards to create nomination, audit, and compensation committees. I'll describe each of these. In addition I'll describe the need for other committees related to a fuller array of issues in corporate responsibility.

Nomination Committee.   One important board subcommittee is a nomination committee that serves to recruit new board members. By 1986, 89 percent of Fortune 1000 companies had a nominating committee, partly as a result of pressures placed on businesses by the Securities and Exchange Commission (SEC).[75] The effectiveness of this committee is at present limited because, as noted here, most CEOs are chairs of their own company's board and, therefore, have significant influence in determining both the membership and actual operation of the nominating committee. Until the CEO is removed from the board, the nominating committee cannot serve to recruit a board membership that will have the independence in fact to oversee management.

Audit Committee.   A second important subcommittee that is now widely found among large corporations is an audit committee to oversee and ensure the integrity of company books and of published corporate financial reports. Assorted practices that collectively amount to "cooking the books" have been common in accounting for a very long time. Because of the importance of corporate businesses to investors and to the economy at large, however, concerns over these practices have become especially great in the latter part of the twentieth century. Thus by 1974 the SEC issued a requirement that all corporations with proxy votes disclose to their shareholders whether they had an audit committee on their board to review the accuracy of their records. Furthermore, if they had an audit committee, the SEC required that they reveal the identities of the persons who served on this committee so shareholders might better judge the likely independence and integrity of the committee. In 1977 the New York Stock Exchange issued a requirement that each company listed on its exchange must establish an audit committee on its board consisting of directors who are not members of the management of the company.[76] As a result of these actions, by 1989 97 percent of large companies were estimated to have created an audit committee.[77]

Compensation Committee.   Another subcommittee that has become a popular addition to the board is the compensation committee, which sets senior management pay and perquisites (and may also determine board director compensation). This committee wouldn't be particularly important if it weren't for the present reality that management controls its own board. The compensation packages that have been awarded to top management of U.S. corporations over the last two decades have been increasing rapidly, even when there has been little or no gain in corporate performance (or even when the corporation has been losing money). Public outcry over the size of CEO compensation, coupled with action by the SEC and pressures from the business committee itself,[78] have been such that, as of 1989, 82 percent of large companies had created a compensation committee to oversee compensation practices.[79]

To date, the compensation committee has not been especially effective in holding down executive compensation. Indeed it may work quite in reverse to increase compensation further.[80] By its very nature the committee focuses attention on increased compensation (rather than decreased compensation) as a mechanism to motivate management to do their jobs and to not leave the company for greener pastures. In the race between companies to keep up with each other in CEO compensation so as not to lose a talented individual, CEO compensations continue to spiral upward. I discuss the issue of management compensation in greater detail in a later section of this chapter.

Other Committees. As the nomination, audit, and compensation committees have been set into place to provide increased protection for shareholders, other subcommittees would also be critical for disciplining the corporation to serve the public good (or at least to keep it from unduly detracting from the public good).

What additional social areas should the board consider through the formation of a sub-committee structure?[81] Obviously, the corporation has obligations to conform to laws and to governmental regulation. Management's responses to these legal requirements provide the first basis for a board's evaluation of the social performance of management.[82] But none of us can claim to be ethical by our mere conformity to the letter of the law, and so this is a necessary but insufficient basis for the board's evaluation.

Other major areas of corporate social responsibility for which the board may wish to form subcommittees for managerial oversight include the following: employee safety, welfare, and equal employment opportunities; environmental protection; fair practices in dealing with suppliers and buyers; community and governmental relations; and consumer protection and service. In addition, however, the board could evaluate long-term corporate vitality, including: plans for new products and new markets; plans for competing with other businesses in the market (including foreign businesses); plans for improving capital development and productivity; management's efforts to control its own management costs; and other areas of planning the board considers appropriate for the corporation in question. It is important that the board have the flexibility to select areas for managerial oversight and to create corresponding subcommittees as it deems most relevant for the nature and operation of the corporation itself.

The evaluations that the board conducts of management's efforts relative to each area of oversight that the board has selected need not take a great deal of time if areas for oversight are chosen judiciously, evaluations are spread out among board subcommittees, the specific issues to be evaluated in any given year are rotated through two- or three-year cycles, the onus is put on management to set objectives and to report on progress in each area of oversight, and if outside auditors are used when appropriate to verify management reports. The process of conducting such evaluations of managerial performance in all areas deemed important by the board and of having a board that is in fact independent of management should provide a very strong disciplining agent for corporations.

The Board as an Internal Control Mechanism

The use of the board as an internal mechanism for monitoring and enforcing socially responsible business behavior in corporations has important advantages. It focuses attention and effort only on those issues that are directly relevant to each corporation (and that may be defined differently from one corporation to another). Furthermore it permits strategies for improved performance to be worked out at the corporate level in ways that make sense for the vitality for that particular corporation.

With its subcommittees structured as it sees fit, a board could establish an annual system for evaluating the job performance of the CEO based both on trends in corporate net profits and on corporate social performance in as many areas of social responsibility as the board has deemed relevant for the particular corporation. The first bottom line for their annual evaluation of management would still be the profitability of the corporation. If the profitability of the corporation is eroding, the CEO should be "canned," or if profit declines stem from unforeseen market conditions, a portion of CEO salary could be withheld until management plans result in profitability being turned around (and as an inducement, all past withheld salary could be returned to the CEO at that time).

A second bottom line, however, would also be evaluated by the board. This second bottom line would consist of corporate performance in each area of social responsibility that the board has chosen as relevant to the corporation. Senior management salary increases or bonuses, if any, should be made contingent not only on acceptable corporate profitability, but also on a favorable record of social responsibility in corporate performance. Under this model, both the board's objectives and its actual operating performance would be centered on assessments of the corporation's profitability and its ability to be what the board conceives of as a good citizen in society. Continuing failures on either grounds would warrant replacement of senior management. In short, the board would become in fact a disciplining mechanism to force management to operate the corporation in a more socially responsible fashion.

A final evaluation step, however, is essential for every board. Every board must also evaluate its own performance against its mission statement and evaluate the performance of each of its individual members. Furthermore, these evaluations should be published in the annual stockholder report. Board members who fail to conform to the standards set by the board mission statement should be forced to resign. Failure of the board to conform to its own mission statement should result in a written plan of remedy and possibly a reconstitution of membership. These plans also should appear in the stockholder report.

Why Would Corporate Leaders Restructure Their Boards?

Why would boards and senior management change their old, comfortable, "good old boy" practices in order that boards in fact become internal social control mechanisms to discipline management? One factor, admittedly a minor one, may simply be natural human goodwill. From what we see all around us, we know that people often want to do the right thing, so long as they know what the right thing is and meet no barriers in doing it.

As I noted in Chapter 3, there is a developing appreciation among business elites of the need for increased social responsibility in corporate behavior. The many pluralistic pressures that have arisen throughout this century have forced business elites to become more conscious of the implications of business practices for the well-being of other sectors of society. Management and their boards cannot resist these pressures indefinitely. At least with regard to investor interests, as I noted earlier, the SEC and the NYSE have pressured for more board accountability. The first decade of the twenty-first century should bring pressures for board oversight of social issues ever more to the fore.

As an added inducement, however, governments could offer to reduce taxes on corporations that set up effective internal social control mechanisms to regulate themselves on social issues. If corporations successfully regulate themselves, as measured by observable reductions in unethical and socially irresponsible behavior, then we don't need extensive governmental regulatory and enforcement operations. Under such circumstances, governments have less need for revenues. Furthermore, corporate taxes are just passed on to you and me anyway as a hidden sales tax in the form of higher prices on goods and services, so we are the persons who ultimately pay them. Then too, in raising prices to cover corporate taxes, U.S. goods and services become less competitive with foreign corporations, so corporate taxes may contribute to lost markets and jobs as a result.

Another idea would be to require all corporations to become federally chartered (as noted earlier, they are chartered by states at present and typically shop around for the state with the least chartering restrictions, which is most often New Jersey or Delaware). A federal charter could privatize at least some of the current scale of federal regulatory operations by requiring corporate boards to serve as monitors of their own corporation's social performance. The proposal to institute federal chartering could be used as a threat to get corporations voluntarily to set up more responsible boards, but I am otherwise not in favor of this idea since I think it unwise to continue to expand the powers of the federal government if we can avoid doing so.

Controlling Management Compensation

As noted here, among the corporate problems that boards must resolve concerning management ethics are the current compensation practices that result in gigantic paychecks and "perks" for senior management. These practices serve only to promote greed and self-interest among senior managers rather than real commitment to the long-term welfare of the corporation. This situation presents an excellent illustration of the weaknesses of corporate boards as they are currently structured, and it would therefore be useful to discuss this situation further.

Rapid increases in compensation packages for top management have occurred for several reasons. First, managers typically control their own boards and consequently are able to exert considerable influence over the compensation they receive. Second, unquestioning board allegiance to an "economic person" view of management leads board members to believe that people can only be motivated to take on top management jobs and to manage well by making direct appeals to their naked self-interests, such as by offering them gigantic pay checks and "perks." Third, board members themselves are usually vastly overpaid for their board work[83] and, therefore, have a distorted view of what constitutes fair compensation. Fourth, board members frequently are themselves CEOs of other companies, and consequently they are inclined to regard high pay for CEOs to be appropriate. Collectively, these factors have led board members to dump very large sums of corporate money into the pockets of CEOs and senior managers regardless of corporate performance and sometimes even when a corporation is "going down the tubes." These practices are an insult to all other employees of the corporation and to its shareholding owners whose collective pockets are being picked in the process.

No one's services are worth a million or more dollars a year. Yet one study of large and medium size industrial corporations indicated that the CEOs of these corporations received an average of $1.7 million in annual compensation, with CEOs of the thirty largest receiving $3.2 million annually.[84] I could find you tens of thousands of people of no greater competence than the current lot of U.S. corporate CEOs who would do handsprings to have the CEOs' jobs for a tenth as much!

What we should want to promote in our CEOs is not self-interested greed. Rather the people we should want as our CEOs are those who enjoy motivating and organizing the work of others and whose concern for their corporation extends to bulldog efforts to keep management costs down.

The majority of CEOs are no doubt a good lot, nice to their aging parents and willing to help their neighbors (if they only had the time to do so), but the current compensatory practices would corrupt even a saint. Imagine if your pay were to be decided by a board that you chaired and that you filled with friends, with immediate subordinates whom you could fire, and with persons from other organizations who hold the same type of job as yours and on whose boards you or your friends sit in judgment concerning their compensation. Do you have that image in your mind? Now how high do you think your compensation would go? Even if you blundered badly, do you think that your compensation might not go up anyway? As moral as I would otherwise hope myself to be, in my reveries even Fort Knox does not hold as much wealth as I would cascade upon myself if college professors could set up such a compensation system for themselves.

A get what you can while you can attitude among top management contributes to short tenures in office, much job hopping, and a lack of commitment to the long-term profitability of the corporation. Furthermore, the ideal of "economic person" makes those hypnotized by it ashamed of their natural inclinations to want to "do the right thing" and makes them unable to coordinate people's activities successfully over a long period of time.

The "economic person" perspective operates much like a cult (a cult of the economic person) to infantilize its faithful followers. It does this by calling out within them all of the narcissistic inclinations typical of a child and then praising and richly rewarding these inclinations, while punishing and effectively suppressing any display of mature concern for the well-being of others and of the good of the larger social order. If we want our corporations to improve their moral performance, the last person we want to head a corporation is an "economic person."

Rather we need individuals who can balance self-interest with collective-interest, who are creative within the constraints of generally accepted moral order, and who are able to develop allegiance and cooperation from the masses of employees throughout the corporation. A CEO who cannot pitch in to help out with any task in the organization and who surrounds him or herself with vast perquisites and enormous pay fails to be a role model as the number one corporate employee and has become instead a modern-day emperor or demigod.

Two simple things could be done about this problem. First, boards could restrict top pay in corporations to no more than six or seven times the lowest pay that is given out to any full-time worker in the corporation. Employees (including CEOs) who want more pay than that would be hard pressed to find it anywhere. Let those dissatisfied with this restriction leave "in a huff" if they wish. Second, boards could, as a part of their formal evaluation of CEOs, evaluate management efforts to keep management costs down.

Ascension to the senior offices of the corporate businesses that dominate our economy has become much like a successful venture in piracy. Once it happens, the corporate treasuries are burst asunder to provide booty to enrich the lucky plunderers. I cannot see how boards can rectify this situation until they are freed from the direct control of the corporation's CEO and senior managers.

Management

With board membership and structure set as described here, both board members and senior managers could be expected to become significantly more attentive to and responsive to the social problems that are created or that are fostered by their corporations. In Chapter 3 I argued that a business should only be expected to act to rectify social problems that derive from its own operations, and the social mechanisms I have proposed thus far are consistent with this restriction. For example, corporations cannot be expected to end racism in general in society, but they can be expected to work toward ending racism in their own operations. Although they cannot be expected to end pollution of the environment society-wide, they can be expected to restrict significantly how their own production processes and products pollute the environment.

The board structures I have described should be supplemented with corollary structural modifications within management itself. A number of relevant ideas have already been suggested in the literature on management for improving corporate social responsibility along these lines. Four of the most important internal social control mechanisms that management can develop are codes of ethics, strategic planning, managing for ethical outcomes, and the use of ethical training. Each will be described briefly.

Codes of Ethics
One idea that has been in vogue for a number of years is for a corporation to adopt a corporate code of ethics that declares the standards by which the corporation wishes to live. This code of ethics, of course, should be consistent with the board's mission statement. Though the creation of a code of ethics is laudable, it may easily become a ceremonial ornament unless it does in fact reflect the board's mission statement, management is held accountable by the board for living up to the code, and additional internal social mechanisms are set in place by management.

Strategic Planning
A second popular idea in management literature is the development of strategic planning to take into account social forces outside the market in efforts to plan over the long term to achieve corporate profit goals. The original intent of strategic planning was to identify and develop strategies for dealing with social issues that may either impact on profits adversely or provide new opportunities for profit expansion, but it is not difficult to use the basic techniques to reach not only profit goals but also social goals that have been approved by the board.

The basic techniques of social planning include social forecasting, scanning the corporation's social environment, and conducting social audits or writing social reports on corporate social performance. There is an ample body of literature on these techniques, to which the interested reader may turn.[85]

Managing for Ethical Outcomes
If managers are removed from the board of directors and if the board in fact evaluates the CEO on the social performance of the corporation, then senior managers will have ample reason to wish to institute a management system for achieving social and ethical outcomes. Based on the concerns for corporate social responsibility that have been identified by the board, and after these concerns have been thoroughly examined and charted with strategic planning techniques, senior managers could specify management objectives and plans for each area of social concern. Then traditional management-by-objectives procedures could be used to set these plans in motion by creating an authority/responsibility system to monitor and enforce compliance. Because organizations behave ethically only if there is a

commitment from the top to do so,[86] this system should foster the greatest social responsibility at all levels of the organization (by contrast, if CEOs are seen as buccaneers in pursuit of their own self-interest, then there is no reason for other employees not to behave likewise).[87]

As a part of socially responsible management, subordinates must be made to feel free to discuss issues of ethics and social responsibility with their supervisors. Socially responsible management techniques would make such discussions mandatory and would leave no doubt as to management expectations.

Ethical Training

As a corollary to managing for ethical outcomes, employee training for social responsibility would be useful if applied on a regular basis for all employees, from the CEO on down. Because deviance is natural and is to be expected from any employee whenever opportunities arise for it, no one should be exempt from this training, and it should be repeated at least annually. The corporate code of ethics, assuming it is sufficiently elaborated, could serve as the core of positions around which ethical training could be undertaken.

Will It Work?

Will an in-house regulatory system involving both board and management actions actually succeed in making corporate businesses less corrupt and more socially responsible? It is hard to imagine that such a system would be less successful than the current system of governmental regulatory oversight, and it is easy to imagine that it would be more cost effective. With a board and management system in place that is attuned to being socially responsible, one should expect a considerable reduction in corporate business corruption to ensue. As a result, a reduction in the need for governmental regulatory efforts also should occur.

The degree to which governmental regulatory efforts could be reduced if these proposed changes were put in place would be determined, of course, on political grounds. But if businesses act more responsibly, there will be less impetus for the formation of special interest groups or for public outcry to arise to pressure governments into undertaking or retaining regulatory functions. In Chapter 6, I suggested that a pluralistic social environment is much like Smith's views *writ large* to include not only market supply and demand factors but all social forces to drive business behavior in directions that maximize the greatest good for society. If this is true, then the control mechanisms I have proposed here are likely to provide a better internal conduit for these social forces, and thereby to effect this greatest good, than have government regulatory efforts.

It is important to recognize, however, that not all problems can be addressed adequately by corporations acting on their own. Although increased social responsibility can be achieved in many areas without additional significant costs to the corporation, in other areas (such as pollution control or improvements in employee or consumer safety), costs may be substantial. Under these circumstances a corporation would risk loss of market share if the costs of its socially responsible actions required price increases on an order that would make its products or services no longer competitive with those of other corporations (including foreign competitors) that undertook no comparable efforts. The usual market dynamics, as described in earlier chapters, would work in these cases to ensure that no corporation undertook such responsible action unless it already controlled its market through monopoly, price fixing, price leadership, or other strategies.

Therefore, at least for some issues, a larger social regulatory mechanism is needed that is capable of setting broad standards on many corporations simultaneously, such as can be accomplished by governments (even if the need for detailed or extensive governmental regulations on many issues can be otherwise reduced from current levels by the proposals I have given). Furthermore, political lobbying for tariff controls or for export tax rebates might be appropriate if it can be demonstrated that socially responsible behavior by U.S. corporations results in products and services that are less competitive than those of foreign companies in the world market.

Another drawback, however, is that ethics, social responsibility, and good intentions typically are the first things discarded when the viability of an individual or organization is threatened. I described this point in Chapter 3. The social control mechanisms I have proposed, therefore, can be expected to work only in those economic good times when jobs are safe and corporate profits are flush. Whenever these conditions erode, prospects are not favorable for the implementation of these internal social control mechanisms in corporations as a replacement for government regulation.

Small Businesses

I have emphasized corporate businesses in this discussion because they already have the bureaucratic capability to create social control mechanisms internal to themselves that would foster improved moral behavior. They also hold central roles in our industrial economy and can seriously disrupt the economy through their corrupt and irresponsible practices. Consequently, they are an appropriate focus for attention.

Very small businesses, however, are another story altogether. Given their typically short life cycle, as most struggle to become profitable and to sustain themselves but then fail and go bankrupt, their owners/managers (who may be only one person) have little of the security that would foster a socially responsible outlook. Nonetheless, as I noted in Chapter 3, the relatively closer face-to-face contacts between these businesspersons and their markets provide considerable opportunities for disciplining mechanisms. Few small businesspersons, for example, can cheat community consumers for long and survive. The best opportunities for fraud among small businesses exist for those "fly-by-night" operations that are able to pick up and move on to new markets whenever the word is out about them in the local market, or for those providing goods or services that are too complex for the typical consumer to judge whether they need them and whether they are fairly priced (as is the case for auto repairs).

Potential abuse of employees by small businesses is a problem that is mitigated by the paternalistic/maternalistic attitude that often develops in the close working relations small businesses foster. Environmental pollution also occurs in the small business context, but in this and in many other areas of social responsibility, the dimensions of the problems, although significant, pale in comparison to damage that big corporations can do to our economy, environment, and society.

In short, there is very little that small businesses can do to create internal social control mechanisms, and corruption at this level is abated at best by existing interpersonal pressures from consumers, the community, employees, or by government regulation.

How to Know What Is Right

Ethical Relativism

Sociologists are generally reluctant to talk about ethics, though several interesting features of ethics are easily discerned from a sociological perspective. When observed empirically, rather than considered in the abstract, ethical frameworks in social life can be seen as social phenomena in every respect, with all of the characteristics of tentativeness, inventiveness, and overlapping boundaries that I described in Chapter 1 for social phenomena in general. We know from empirical observations that ethical frameworks not only vary among societies and over time, but they also can vary considerably within complex societies, such as in industrial societies, where their variations again reflect changing social circumstances and political interests.

These observations are all obvious upon empirical inspection. However, these observations are quite annoying to many philosophers and religious leaders and to a number of other persons who can be quite vocal in their claims that ethics (invariably meaning an ethical framework that they themselves publicly espouse) are universal and absolute. Social scientists who conclude from their observations that ethics are evanescent and multiple are branded as moral relativists and are made to feel that there is something immoral, or at least amoral, about them for having come to such conclusions.

Stung early by outcries from influential people, most of sociology as a discipline has simply avoided the whole issue of ethics. Thus ethics is not covered in standard introductory textbooks on sociology and is not taught in college courses in sociology or in preparatory programs for new sociologists. Little sociological research has been done on the topic, and most sociologists neither discuss nor even think about ethics as a social phenomenon. Some have gone so far as to adopt the philosophical view that another realm of reality exists that cannot be studied by empirical means and in which ethics resides as a universal, nonempirical absolute.[88]

Here are my views. That we humans at certain times encounter something in our experience that appears to us to possess an absolute or universal quality cannot be denied. Furthermore, when we feel great conviction in the absoluteness or universality of a particular ethical proposition or ethical framework, we may well feel motivated to behave in ways consistent with it, as though it were our "duty" or we found it to be the "desirable" thing to do. This experience and its subsequent effects on our behaviors are noble: they civilize and humanize us. We know of no other animal that has such an experience as a source of motivation for its behavior.

But the experience of something as being absolute or universal is itself socially useless if only one person has that experience. Some social forces (such as have traditionally been found in families or in the religions and the political structures of agricultural societies) must operate to call out this experience in a large number of people simultaneously so as to form a common moral community for collective action. As the number of people sharing a common experience of the universality and absoluteness of a particular ethical framework increases, the degree of "universality" and "absoluteness" of the ethical framework as a source for creating social stability and for creating predictability of behaviors in social life does in fact increase. The strength of an ethical framework as a social motivator, then, depends on the degree to which social conditions lead us collectively to believe in it.

Ethics then serve to tie us together as moral communities. And, even if shifting social conditions make these ethical bonds fleeting, they may still be experienced as universal and absolute by participants within a circumscribed social setting. In societies that are small and relatively simple in social structural design, prevailing ethical frameworks may be few in number, correspondingly simple in structure and commonly held among the people. However, growth in the size and complexity of societies is necessarily matched by growth in the number and complexity of ethical frameworks that serve to tie people together into morally "right" patterns of social behavior.

It should be expected that the dominant social structural pattern of any society necessarily will be rooted in, and supported by, some ethical framework. The dominant social pattern in the business-oriented society, of course, is its business orientation, around which the various social phenomena of society are tied together as a loosely functioning whole that is oriented largely by business values. Thus (as I argued in Chapter 4 and briefly at the beginning of this chapter) in the business-oriented society businesses no longer are seen as evil or even as a "necessary evil," as they often were in previous agricultural societies. Rather, in the business-oriented society businesses and business markets are the central social forces (scripts) that tie society together; therefore, they now are more often seen as forces of good. It is within this context that conventional wisdom in our society holds that capitalism or free market enterprise is a great positive force in human affairs serving to liberate us and to bring about the greatest good for the greatest numbers.

However, to the degree that businesses also continue to threaten other sectors of society, they continue as well to represent negative forces. These latter threats represent the ethical violations, the forms of unacceptable deviance, that draw most public attention and outcry for rectification. Because the ethical frameworks undergirding the business-oriented society are quite complex and continue to evolve, how are the boards of directors and senior management of corporations today to know what is the right thing to do?

Of course they must do what we all do to find the right path in life; they find clues about what is right and wrong from the reactions of others around them. At a minimum, corporations can find such clues in the great bounty of governmental regulations applied to businesses. But clues also are widely evident in the mass media (as I pointed out in Chapter 1, government and mass media are two of the most powerful forces that shape our understanding of the social world).

All one has to do is to read any newspaper and one will learn that corporations shouldn't pollute the environment, discriminate in employment, force employees to work in unsafe environments, sell dangerous products or services, bribe government officials, and so on. The sticky part comes in figuring out how to apply those prohibitions to one's own corporation. This requires knowledge about the specific operations of one's own company, knowledge about the social problem itself, and a commitment to figuring out some way of addressing the problem.

We can assume that corporate boards and managers already are in the best position to find out about the workings of their companies, if they bother to make the effort to do so. Also, if the social control mechanisms proposed here are put into place, a rather strong commitment should be engendered among senior managers for resolving social problems connected with the operations of their corporation. Additional detailed knowledge about the nature of social problems related to businesses can be gained readily from a growing body of technical literature. In the remaining chapters of this part of the book I review a number of these social problems.

There is no one path that all corporations should follow in behaving responsibly toward other sectors of society. There is, after all, no single, simple ethical framework with which to specify such a path. Rather I am proposing that corporations set up the internal social control mechanisms that will permit them to discern and begin negotiating their way through the ethical patchwork of society in order to find their best path toward becoming more responsible members of the social community. Such an effort was not necessary when businesses were small and peripheral to societies of the past; it is essential in the business-oriented industrial society of today.

Ethical Decision Making

Before proceeding to the remaining chapters of this book, in which a number of the major social problems and ethical dilemmas facing businesses today are described, I would like to pause for a moment here to discuss the role of ethical decision making in the resolution of social problems. Of course I will do so from the perspective of a sociologist.

A popular argument for the improvement of corporate social responsibility is that corporate managers should learn to use ethical decision-making skills in setting major policy and in making managerial decisions. I have no objection to efforts to do this, but there is little reason to believe that much will be accomplished as a result or that such efforts can or will be used on a regular basis.

The central problem is that ethical decision-making techniques require us to be rational, yet we know from observation that few of our decisions involve much in the way of cognitive exertion, let alone a rational state of mind. We make purchases of foods, clothing, automobiles, houses, and other items and services based typically on momentary whimsy, emotion, blind allegiance, or routine. Whimsy likewise plays an important role in selecting spouses, in setting most household rules for our children, and in many of our dealings with subordinates. Rationality of decision making is hardly the key to success as a parent, lover, boss, friend, neighbor, or anywhere else in social life. The ethics that infuses our social actions, therefore, certainly could not be attributed to our holding onto a rational frame of mind.

Furthermore it is hard to hold a rational frame of mind for as much as ten seconds, let alone for the hours or days that might be required to grapple with a serious ethical issue. When bureaucracies entail rationality in the forms of paper trails, books full of detailed procedural rules, fact-finding reports, group decision making, and so on, issues take seemingly (and quite possibly) *forever* to be addressed, and resistances are met all along the way both by decision makers and by the people ultimately expected to put the plan into action.

Philosophers (who are persons quite adept at sustaining a rational frame of mind for minutes at a time) have attempted to develop a variety of logical frameworks for determining the ethical character of an action. It has become popular to classify these into three groups. First are "ends oriented" (or *teleological*) approaches, which justify actions based on the desirability of the ends that result from them (even if the actions that have been selected are themselves odious). An example of this type of reasoning can be seen in Adam Smith's arguments about how the wealth of a nation will be maximized if individuals are allowed to compete with each other in a free market in pursuit only of their own self-interest. Even if self-interested behavior is itself morally repugnant, a greater good, according to Smith, is achieved by its unrestricted expression. This line of reasoning, as subsequently developed by Jeremy Bentham (1748–1832) and John Stuart Mill (1808–1873), is called utilitarianism. As an ends oriented ethical framework, utilitarianism seeks to advance as an end the "greatest good for the greatest numbers" of people.

A second type of ethical framework is represented by means oriented (or rules oriented or *deontological*) approaches, which posit a number of restrictions to be placed on the actions one can take regardless of the desirability of the outcomes that may derive from the action. The Ten Commandments of the Old Testament, for example, set restrictions on one's conduct regardless of the ends that one may seek. An especially important variation of means-oriented thinking postulates a number of "inalienable human rights" (perhaps deriving from divine will) that should not be violated if an action is to be judged ethical, regardless of the ends that are to be sought. Examples of this type of reasoning are found in the American Declaration of Independence, which appeals to our "inalienable rights," and the rights to be found in the U.S. Bill of Rights. Another example is the right of private property (as laid out in the fourteenth Amendment to the U.S. Constitution), which is often used in the business sector to justify business actions even if those actions result in ends that are otherwise held to be morally reprehensible by many people.

A third type of ethical framework includes the justice-oriented approaches, which hold that the rewards and costs of any action should be fairly distributed among all parties. Marx's critique of capitalism and his views on communism are examples of this type of reasoning.[89]

Ethical decision making can, of course, merge the three major approaches by posing three basic questions of any proposed action: (1) are the ends to be achieved by the action desirable, (2) does the proposed action violate any one's rights or violate any laws, and (3) will rewards and costs of the action be fairly distributed among persons or parties involved? This is a nifty framework on the face of it, but becomes tortuous to apply in practice. How do we know, for example, what ends (or outcomes) will ensue from any given policy, and furthermore, how do we know which of these ends will be good and which bad? How do we know what rights humans have, and how do we know which parts of a policy might affect those rights? How do we know what a policy's costs and rewards will be, and how do we know what constitutes a fair distribution of these costs and rewards? These are questions that require very great rational deliberation to resolve, and in the real social world such an exertion is very unlikely to occur. In actual practice, then, rational ethical decision making by individuals appears to provide a rather poor vehicle for either stimulating or enforcing moral behavior in a social setting.

The social control mechanisms I have proposed in this chapter do not require us to be rational or even especially apt at deliberation (no philosopher kings are required). Rather the board members may be ordinary people. They would be expected to identify critical areas for corporate social responsibility based on whatever knowledge they have (derived, for example, from their practical experience with the corporation, from corporate reports, from reading the newspaper, from talking to their friends and spouses, or "what have you," including even the reading of books such as this one). They then evaluate management plans and accomplishments related to these critical areas by whatever techniques they choose (including whether they personally like the CEO, have a "bur under their saddle" that leads them to be highly critical, or any other procedure they know how to use or want to use).

No longer being in control of the board and its evaluation system and no longer able to run the board and management to amass the greatest possible compensation for themselves, senior managers will likely do what any good bureaucrats do: they will scurry around trying not to look bad to superiors who have the power to punish them. I trust in human ingenuity for managers to come up with useful, workable ideas for addressing those critical areas of responsibility that have been identified by the board and to do so in ways that at least look good (regardless of how they may be judged by rational ethical decision makers). Creating codes of ethics, instituting strategic planning, designing management systems for ethical outcomes, and providing ethical training are the strategies I have proposed, but managers can do whatever they think will put them in the best light with the board. The net effect of this policy—even if bureaucratic dynamics cause it inevitably to fall short of what we might hope for—should produce more responsible business behavior at lower costs than is produced by current governmental regulatory oversight.

As an aid to thinking through how best to respond to a number of major social problems confronting businesses, the remaining chapters in this book look at issues of responsibility related to employees, consumers, the environment, and the international arena.

Chapter 9

Employee Rights and Welfare

This chapter examines our rights and our welfare as employees in a business-oriented society. It is natural that both of these issues should concern us because so much of our daily round of life is spent as employees. The following order will be used in discussing these issues. First, this chapter describes the transformation of our ancestors into wage-laboring employees who worked for commercial interests. Second, the ideology that justifies the priority of the rights of financiers over those of wage-laborers is examined. Third, recent developments in employment-related rights and welfare are discussed. Fourth, the special role of unions in fostering employee rights and welfare is considered. Fifth, contemporary pressures for improving safety and human relations in the workplace are examined.

Are Wage-Laborers Prostitutes?
Employees as Micro-Businesses

In Chapter 1 businesses were defined as social phenomena that operate to obtain profits from a market context. The Fortune 500 companies qualify as businesses under this definition, and so do the typical medium sized and small commercial ventures of our acquaintance. However each one of us who draws a paycheck also qualifies as a business under this definition. Consider the following.

For most of our ancestors in agricultural societies there was little in the way of a labor market in which they could sell their labor as a commodity. Instead, most of our ancestors were serfs or slaves who were bound legally to the land or to an owner. In the rise of the business-oriented society, however, our ancestors became freed from the bonds of serfdom and slavery[1] and became instead wage-laborers in what has become an increasingly complex market for labor (i.e., a labor market or job market).

Thus as denizens of a business-oriented society, we are in a situation in which we must scurry about seeking some means of selling ourselves as wage-laborers at a price that we hope will make possible a decent standard of living for ourselves and our families. In this regard we are very much like prostitutes. The difference is that, whereas prostitutes sell the service of their sexual organs for cash, we sell the service of our muscles, brains, and energy for cash.

Our prebusiness-oriented ancestors no doubt would have considered it morally demeaning to behave as we do, selling our own bodies for mere money. But we consider it to be a perfectly normal thing to do; indeed we consider it to be morally uplifting and mature. It is what we call finding gainful employment or growing up and taking on adult responsibilities. To the degree that you and I receive a return on the sale of our muscles, brains, and energy that is less than what is obtained by small businesspersons or by other professionals (such as lawyers or doctors), this difference arises because as wage-laborers we typically possess far less control over our markets and prices (wages) than they have over their markets and prices.

In the business-oriented society, then, we have all become micro-businesses, selling the only commodity we have—ourselves. And this is as true for wage-laborers in the public sector, such as in government employment, as it is for wage-laborers in the private sector. That business-oriented societies should make us into little micro-businesses is wholly predictable from a sociological perspective. As individuals we are very much like mirrors reflecting the larger social reality around us, and it is from society that the motivational frameworks that infuse us and guide our actions as individuals derive (as scripts). What is in society, therefore, is in us, and vice versa. Like it or not, you and I in a very real sense are the business-oriented society, and like millions of little mirrors of it, we perpetuate it through our actions.

Ideology and the Rights to Return on Our Labor

When we look back over time and consider how the many preceding generations of our ancestors were often pitilessly exploited over thousands of years in agricultural societies, many of us feel forced to conclude that our ancestors in the olden days must have been ghastly ignorant, child-like, and spineless. Consider for a moment their situation.

When a tiny group of nobility (or church leaders) claimed to be the only legitimate (often divinely sanctioned) owners of all land, most of our ancestors not only acquiesced to these claims, but most also appeared to believe these claims to be just and proper.

With almost all productive farm land owned by this tiny group of nobility (or the church), the vast majority of our ancestors settled for being slaves, serfs, or tenant farmers. This was not a temporary adjustment. It was a pattern that lasted for thousands of years.

Furthermore, the products resulting from our ancestors' toil did not belong to them. If they were fortunate, they were permitted to retain just enough to live on at a level of subsistence that we would consider depraved today. The rest of what they produced went to the nobility (or church), making it possible for these temporal (or ecclesiastical) lords to live at a life-style considered very grand for the times. By one estimate, for example, our peasant ancestors gave up each year as much as half of the product of their labor to the ruling nobility, who constituted less than 2 percent of the population, while they retained barely enough food for themselves.[2]

Why were our ancestors so dense? I don't know about you, but I almost feel shamefaced to claim them as my kin. They were stupid enough to become ensnared and enslaved or enserfed by an ideology that gypped them and bled them dry to the advantage of a small group of elites in society.[3] We do not know when the great turning point occurred in the evolution of human intelligence that sets us apart from them, but it is clear that today we tower over our ancestors intellectually. With our superior intellect, we could never be as mesmerized by a dispossessing ideology as they were. Or could we?

Consider this. As I noted in Chapter 6, a fairly small group of economic elites owns most of the assets of the United States. By one estimate, a little less than 7 percent of families in the United States own more than 50 percent of the wealth in the United States. Furthermore, their proportionate share of ownership of all productive property in the United States (that is, property that produces income) is a much higher percentage.

Now it is from this small group of elites that the bulk of financial capital derives for a wide assortment of commercial ventures in our business-oriented society, while most of the rest of us put up only our lifetime of labor (muscles, brains, and energy) for these ventures. Who then owns the products of these commercial ventures? You know the answer: the products legally belong to the financiers. Why? Because our modern ideology concerning property rights legitimizes the priority of their claims of ownership over all products resulting from these ventures. And most of us are so mesmerized by this ideology that we believe their claims to be only right and proper. I know I believe it; don't you?

Under these circumstances of disparities in wealth, most of us in the business-oriented society must settle for being wage-laborers, selling our muscles, brains, and energy in the existing labor market. As wage laboring employees a portion of the value of the goods and services that we produce is paid to us as wages and benefits, and another portion is paid out to cover the costs of materials, inanimate energy, rents, interest on loans, and other related operating costs. What remains then goes to at least three groups of people.

One part of the remainder goes to the financierial owners, an allocation which is fully consistent with our prevailing ideology. This portion constitutes the profits that we all believe belong justly and properly to them. The rake off to this small group of economic elites when considered across the many commercial ventures in the United States is, of course, very great. The U.S. Bureau of Census figures for the mid-1990s show, for example, that the top 20 percent of American families, which includes those who are among the economically elite financiers of business, received nearly half (46.2 percent) of all income in the United States while the bottom 60 percent of wage laborers shared among them less than a third (30.2 percent) of all income.[4]

Before the financial owners get their share, however, another share of the value resulting from the goods and services that our labor produces goes to those crafty employees in large corporations who have succeeded in separating themselves from the low status and limited rights of most other employees by virtue of holding titles as senior management. The share that these employees get from the production process has been growing in size throughout this century. However, our prevailing ideology does not justify the giant incomes and "perks" that they have been able to divert into their pockets, nor does it justify their corporate empire-building. It is only the power that they wield as top commercial decision-makers that has led most of us to view them as though they were some sort of quasi-owners and, therefore, as possessing some tenuously legitimacy in their claims on a larger share of the product of our labor.

The third major group receiving a part of the value of the goods and services that our labor produces is government, particularly through its corporate, employer payroll, and personal income taxing systems. The purpose of these taxes is to fund programs that are deemed politically to be important in a business-oriented society. At least some of these programs have to do with employee welfare, a point to which I'll return shortly.

From sociology we know that ideologies are powerful motivational frameworks that orient our thoughts, emotions, and behaviors. It is often easy to see how other people, such as our ancestors, were motivated by an ideology; it is typically much more difficult to see how we ourselves may be similarly motivated by an ideology. Ideologies may last a long time, but none are changeless. Our own has been undergoing some fundamental changes that have placed increasing emphasis on the use of productive wealth to foster the welfare of a wider array of sectors of society. This is represented by the movement for business social responsibilities. A growing emphasis on improving employee rights and welfare is reflective of this movement.

Contemporary Employee Rights and Welfare

As I described in Chapters 2 and 5, businesses and business markets orient most aspects of our lives and lend us a sense of identity. In the process, they also define our human rights and welfare. In this section I shall consider the contemporary development of employee rights and employee welfare in our society.

Businesses as a Source of Meaning, Identity, and Motivation

Most of us either have or will have spent the better part of each weekday for 12 to 20 or more years in pursuit of schooling credentials that we hope will enhance our marketability as wage-laborers. This is our youth, spent in the often mind-numbing and authoritarian routine all for the sake of conforming to the contemporary requirements of employment in our business-oriented society. After we have squandered our youth in this fashion, we then devote the bulk of each ensuing weekday for most of the rest of our lives, perhaps for upward to 45 years or more, selling our muscles, brains, and energy for a paycheck in labor markets that are largely dictated by business interests. This is what the meaning of our life is in a business-oriented society.

For most of us, to "grow up" means to become employed, capable of sustaining ourself and our family with a paycheck. Employment as a wage-laborer is at the center of our adult identity and gives meaning to most aspects of social life. It is for this reason, for example, that suicide rates are greatest for the unemployed, especially for the old and the young. It is also because of the importance of employment in our lives that we have created educational systems and that we endure their authoritarian control for so many years. It is for this reason too that we adults crowd ourselves and our children together into small geographic areas, creating the urban areas that facilitate business and market operations. And it is for this reason that we have increasingly held organized religion at arms length and that we have limited the power of governments, so that neither sector can severely challenge business interests. It is also for this reason that we have built canal, rail, pipeline, and highway systems sprawling across our continent to foster our business markets. It is for this reason as well that we have taken on a highly mobile life-style, ever ready to move geographically in search of jobs. And for this reason too our kinship structures, families, and communities have become increasingly fractured and fluid, leaving us more and more individuated and alone. These are but a few examples of how our becoming an employee to serve the business interests of our time has affected virtually all aspects of our personal identity and has given meaning and order to our daily social existence.

Employee Rights

In view of the centrality of business interests in giving our lives meaning, identity, and motivation, it follows that business interests would also have important implications for our rights and welfare as a people. *Rights* are powers or privileges granted to us on some basis (such as our citizenship, age, gender, etc.). *Welfare* concerns provisions that are made for our well-being. All societies have included some system for specifying human rights and for providing for human welfare.

For example, in hunting and gathering societies, rights varied among people based on their gender, kinship, stage in their life cycle, and demonstrated ability. Rights in this type of society might include being allowed to speak on a matter, being allowed to be a decision-maker in a hunting party, being the first in line for a share of the day's catch, and so on. Provisions for the welfare of all persons occurred through mutual patterns of gift-giving, as I described in Chapter 4.

In agricultural societies, by contrast, both the nobility and the peasantry had certain rights based on tradition. Both had the right, for example, to expect the aid and support of the other in times of emergency. Provisions for the welfare of all persons were made through the use of public, royal, or church granaries in the event of crop failures, through kinship and community support in the event of personal injury or illness, and through the availability of military and police in the event of attack.

But let's now look at the business-oriented society. We like to congratulate ourselves for living in a free society, by which we typically mean a society in which individuals are relatively free from capricious and autocratic governmental control. Our American Revolution, for example, was fought over what we conceived to be capricious governmental actions in violation of our natural rights. It was this concern that led us to create a constitutional government and a Bill of Rights as safeguards against governmental abuse of us as people.

Concern that we may have rights that could be capriciously trampled by businesses did not arise at the time of our revolution, principally because the vast majority of Americans lived and worked on subsistence level farms. Obviously this situation no longer holds today. The most powerful force influencing our lives today is that of business, and this force necessarily plays a significant role in determining our day-to-day rights.

Consider this. On a daily basis, how much time do you spend interacting with governmental officials? Unless you work for a government, you probably spend little or no time in such interactions. Rather, the majority of adults in the United States are at work for the bulk of each week under the direct supervision and control of potentially capricious and autocratic business supervisors. Living under such a situation, spanning most of the years of our adulthood, the actual rights that we have as a people are quite limited.

As employees we are told when we must show up, when we may leave, what types of clothing we may wear, how we may express ourselves to others, and what we will do at any given moment while at work. We may be subjected to psychological tests, physical and medical examinations, analyses of our blood and urine, and genetic testing. We have no right to freedom of speech or of expression, nor necessarily to privacy or due process as employees.

In short, the daily round of life of most people in the United States is lived out under conditions of little or no actual freedom.

Examples of Employee Rights

Just as we currently have a Constitutional Bill of Rights to define our rights and protect us from governments, the situation I have described above would suggest that the time may have come for the declaration of an employee bill of rights to define our rights as employees and to protect us from abusive employers.[5] What constitutes a fundamental human right, however, is a matter determined by political negotiation. Here are just a few examples of rights that employees might wish to be granted by their employers:

- the right to the privacy of one's person and possessions while on the job
- the right to the privacy of one's life outside of work, without surveillance or control by one's employer[6]
- the rights to due process for grievances at work and to just cause for termination
- the right to a safe working environment
- the right to be treated in a nondiscriminatory way regardless of one's gender, age, race, ethnicity, and religious or political beliefs
- the right not to be forced to participate in illegal or unethical behavior as a condition of employment
- the right to have some involvement in decision-making on issues that directly affect one's job
- the right to ensure that records an employer assembles and keeps on an employee are accurate and are not improperly used or disseminated inside or outside of the employment setting

To what degree are you protected from capricious and abusive behaviors by your employer? Do you have, in your current place of employment, the rights that I just listed? How would you know that you do? If you believe that you do have any of these rights, who has defined them for you and who enforces them? If you search for answers to these questions, you may be surprised to learn just how few rights you actually do have as an employee in your work setting.

In some cases, such as for worker safety and for discrimination in employment, it has been our governments that have defined and enforced a few employee rights for us. In other cases, unions have defined employee rights through labor contracts (such as for due process). In general, however, businesses have not made any great effort on their own to define and defend employee rights for us. This could easily be done in corporations by developing and enforcing corporate employee bills of rights, much as most large corporations now have written corporate codes of ethics.

Employment-at-Will and the Implied Employment Contract

The legal foundation for our present conception of employee rights derives from our hoary tradition of common law, and its centerpiece is the concept of employment-at-will. The common law right to employment-at-will applies to both employees and employers. In particular, employers have the right to hire or fire anyone at will and have the right to set the conditions of work for employees at will. Workers likewise have the right either to accept or to quit any employment at will. No one is forced to offer or accept a job. No employer is forced to retain an employee, and no employee is forced to remain in the service of an employer. The rights embodied in employment-at-will, therefore, convey freedoms to both employers and employees alike.

These rights may be specified and modified, of course, by mutual agreement in a written contract. The merit of forming a written contract is that all parties become legally bound to its terms and may sue for breach of contract if its terms are not met. This puts the power of governments as enforcing agents behind the rights of employers and employees as specified in the contract.

In negotiations over the terms of a written contract, however, the individual employee typically has little or no power relative to the employer. Consequently the terms of a written contract work principally to the advantage of the employer. Do you want to see just how discrepant the power relationship is between you as an employee and your employer? Try the following. See how far you get in the job market if you either write up an employment contract and present it to a prospective employer, or if you strike out certain conditions and substitute others you prefer on a contract that is supplied by the prospective employer. Or in your present job try writing up a new contract specifying conditions of employment more favorable to you and then present this contract to your boss for signature.

An Implied Employment Contract. Many U.S. workers, however, are hired by employers without written contract, and court rulings in the 1800s took an interesting turn by holding that there may exist an implied, but not written, employment contract between employers and employees. Whether an implied contract exists and what the nature of its unwritten terms might be, of course, were subject to the decisions of the courts.

This doctrine of an implied employment contract was used in court rulings in the 1800s to uphold employers in employee suits brought against them for injuries on the job. The courts ruled that they found no unwritten terms in the implied employment contract that specified that workplaces should be safe or that made provisions for compensation for workplace injury. Consequently workers worked at their own risk and had no right to collect damages for workplace injuries. Later court rulings, however, have tended to be more favorable to employees, as more and more unwritten terms favorable to employees have been discovered by the judiciary in the implied employment contract.

Two Forces Affecting Implied Contracts. Two social forces have played key roles in contributing unwritten terms to the implied contract. One of these forces is presented by unions. As unions have become successful in certain industries in obtaining written contracts that specify terms of employment favorable to employees, these terms have come to serve increasingly as the unwritten (implied) standards for other places of employment as well.

The second force is government, including major pieces of legislation, regulatory interpretations, and court rulings. Here, for example, are some illustrative governmental actions that effectively have defined unwritten terms in the implied employment contract:

1. Discrimination in the workplace
   - Civil Rights Act of 1964 (and subsequent amendments)
   - Equal Pay Act of 1963

- Age Discrimination in Employment Act of 1967
- Vocational Rehabilitation Act of 1973
- Veterans' Readjustment Assistance Act of 1974
- U.S. Supreme Court ruling on Griggs v. Duke Power Company
- and others

2. Occupational safety, injury and working conditions
    - Occupational Safety and Health Act of 1971
    - state worker injury compensation laws
    - legislation baring child labor, setting minimum wages and maximum work hours before overtime pay rates apply
    - and others

3. Job security and retirement pensions
    - the National Labor Relations Act of 1935 legitimizes worker efforts to bargain collectively
    - mandatory unemployment programs paid for by employers and administered largely by states
    - increased court rulings requiring just cause in the firing of employees
    - protected groups defined under the Civil Rights Act and court rulings
    - laws baring the firing of "whistle blowers" or of employees refusing to violate public policy or refusing to work under unsafe conditions
    - Social Security Act of 1935 creating a mandatory retirement pension program to which employers and employees must contribute
    - Employee Retirement Income Security Act of 1974
    - and others

Just a cursory review of this list suggests that the concept of employee rights is one that is continuing to evolve through political processes. It has become a critical issue as our business-oriented society matures, and it defines much of the actual day-to-day human rights that we possess. We can expect further substantial development of this concept over the next twenty to thirty years. Businesses can either take a more active stance in developing the standards for the rights of their employees or, as they have done in the past, they may wait to have these standards forced on them. For the reasons I have given in Chapters 7 and 8, it would be better for us all if businesses took this social responsibility on themselves, rather than waiting for governments to do it through increased government regulation of businesses.

Employee Welfare

As I noted in Chapter 6, the business-oriented society puts us in a rather difficult position with respect to provisions for human welfare. The splintering of governments, churches, communities, kin groups, and families has left us increasingly on our own to provide for our well-being as individuals. None of our ancestors had to cope with welfare needs under such circumstances.

Not surprisingly, we have used political means, both through the formation of unions and through governmental action, to force the business sector, which is the greatest holder of wealth in our society, to become attentive to our welfare needs as employees. Because the concept of welfare, as provisions for the well-being of people, overlaps somewhat with the concept of rights, some of what I shall say on this topic is redundant with several of my earlier comments.

Fringe Benefits as Employee Welfare

In addition to our paycheck, the principal means by which businesses express concern for our welfare is through our fringe benefits. Fringe benefits now account for almost a third (30 percent)[7] of payroll costs, and include by order of magnitude:

- employer matching contributions to Social Security (the federally organized retirement and disability program for employees);
- employer contributions to private health and life insurance plans for employees and to private employee retirement plans;
- employer coverage of costs for paid vacations, rest periods, holidays, and sick leave;
- employer contributions to workers' compensation programs and to unemployment insurance programs;
- and other smaller employment benefits.

For many of us the fringe benefits from our employment (particularly for family health insurance and for retirement) are now as important or more so to us than is our paycheck. In short, our well-being and that of our family have become very directly dependent on employer-financed welfare programs that are designed specifically for our benefit as employees.

In addition to fringe benefits, other efforts to provide for the welfare of employees have occurred. Frequently these are enforced by law, including efforts to improve the safety of the workplace, to restrict the hours of work, and to end abusive child labor practices. To appreciate the significance of these efforts to promote our welfare, consider the following. How many of us would wish to return to the earlier industrial era when the twelve-hour work day and six and one-half day work week were standard, when the health and safety standards in the workplace were almost wholly lacking, and when child labor was common? None of us, I am sure. Protection of our welfare as a people is clearly greater today than it was for our early industrial ancestors of two, three, and four generations ago.

A Private Welfare System

No society can sustain itself without some practical means of addressing the welfare needs of persons living in it. We may derogate the unemployed poor of our society for their circumstances and we may cut public welfare programs for them to the bone to express our moral condemnation of them, but for most of us our peace of mind and security rests squarely on the private welfare system that we (through unions and governments) have forced businesses to institute on our behalf. The costs for this employer paid welfare system are far in excess of those of the public welfare system and are passed along to all consumers, rich or poor, in higher prices. This is sort of like a private taxation system paid by everyone for the benefit of the employed. If you are employed, you are a recipient of these private welfare benefits.

Pressures for Expanded Employee Welfare

The issue of how many forms of welfare should be provided to employees, as with the question of how many rights employees should have, is one that businesses could play a greater role in determining, or they can wait for these issues to be determined by external forces (e.g., by unions and governments) and then forced on them by contract, law, or governmental regulatory oversight. Among current pressures on businesses are those pushing for the adoption of a whole slate of new employee welfare programs:

- employee assistance programs (EAPs) for drug and alcohol abuse, for retirement planning, or for other forms of employee counseling;
- flex-time, parental leave, job sharing, and in-house day care for employees with dependent family members;
- job redesign (enlargement, enrichment), organizational development (decentralized group decision-making with more involvement by lower level employees), and a variety of other human relations or quality of work life steps to make the work experience better meet the psychological and social needs of employees;
- increased in-house skills training and job retraining programs to educate employees for changing employment technology;
- and many other programs.

An increasingly aggressive business stance in defining and in setting in motion socially responsible programs for employee welfare is likely to expand considerably in the next few decades. There is no other realistic alternative for assuring our welfare (or rights) as a people in a business-oriented society.

The Rise and Fall of Unions

As I noted earlier, the power of a business is typically much greater than that of an individual employee or job applicant. Consequently businesses hold a decided advantage in coming to terms, at will, over decisions to hire, fire, or set salaries and working conditions. This situation of unequal power between employers and employees becomes especially problematic in an industrial economy, such as ours, which is dominated by large businesses. In particular, large businesses have the potential to survive understaffed for quite some time, and possibly indefinitely, but the typical individual in our society is unlikely to survive for more than a few weeks without a regular supply of paychecks. This imbalance of resources between consenting parties to written or unwritten employment contracts creates the potential for considerable abuse of employees, and such abuse has occurred. Indeed it occurred on a grand scale in the earlier phases of the development of our industrial economy.

In a democratic political environment, however, it is quite natural for individuals to band together into political coalitions when confronted with a common threat to their well-being. The intent of these coalitions is to create a collective social force of equivalent or greater power to the one that threatens them and in this way to end, or at least control, the threat. Of course this is precisely what wage-laborers have attempted to do in the formation of unions.

The purpose of unions is to provide a social means for monopolizing labor markets. Each individual wage-laborer operating as a micro-business in the sale of his or her own body in the labor market is at a distinct disadvantage in setting labor terms with a large employer. But when employees and job seekers in a common industry band together, they may be able to monopolize the market for the sale of their muscles, brains, and energy, and in this way they may gain an upper hand in setting the terms of their employment.

The union movement among American laborers, of course, was not welcomed by business owners and managers. One problem is that unions pose a direct and serious political threat to business autonomy of action. Furthermore their demand that increased business expenditures be made for employee wages and benefits places a new source of pressures on business profits. Then too, labor union pressures on profits do not easily fit our prevailing ideology, which holds that the suppliers of financial capital, not the suppliers of labor, have the right to ownership and control of the profits from goods and services that labor produces. Thus union activities that seek to allocate a greater share of this value to laborers are often seen as illegitimate infringements on the just and proper rights of financierial owners (much as peasant uprisings in the Middle Ages against the authority of the state and church were seen as illegitimate infringements on the just and proper rights of the nobility and church). Finally, union wage and benefit demands typically create an upward pressure on the prices of the goods and services that the laborers produce. The results of these pressures may be twofold. First, the business that accedes to union demands may become less competitive in the marketplace, and second, successful union demands in a number of businesses may create an inflationary effect on the economy as a whole.

By both legal and illegal means, big businesses fought the early formation of unions, including by use of legal injunction (under common law and initially under antitrust laws unions were considered to be illegal conspiracies); by use of public or private police to arrest, injure, or kill strikers; by use of organized crime to infiltrate and control unions;[8] by wholesale firing of union members; by use of "scab" (alternative nonunion) labor; and by other strategies. Until the 1930s, unions had little legal standing in the United States, and governments typically sided with businesses in an effort to break unions through prosecutions based on the Sherman Antitrust Act or on common law.

The growth of unions, not surprisingly, parallels the growth of big businesses and the corollary potential for abuse of employees by big businesses. There were a number of small unions in the early 1800s in the United States, but most of the important unions were created after the Civil War when industrial businesses were expanding in size in the United States. In 1869 the Knights of Labor formed, and in 1881 and 1886, respectively, the more powerful Federation of Organized Trades and Labor Unions and the American Federation of Labor (AFL) were created. In 1935 the Congress of Industrial Organizations (CIO) was created and eventually merged with the AFL to form the AFL-CIO. Other important unions were formed in the transportation industry (Teamsters), in mining (United Mine Workers), and in many other industries.

The maturing of our industrial economy, the increasing prospects for employee abuse, and the acknowledged failure of *laissez-faire* in the Great Depression combined to create the impetus for the most important pieces of federal legislation on labor. The Norris-La Guardia Act of 1932 greatly limited the ability of courts to intervene in labor disputes. Then the National Labor Relations Act (or Wagner Act) of 1935 provided legal recognition and protection to unions and to other efforts of workers to bargain collectively. This second act in effect held that all workers have a right to organize into unions and to bargain collectively with employers for their own betterment. The National Labor Relations Board was also created by this act to monitor unfair employer and union practices and to supervise union elections.

The effectiveness of unions as a political means for ensuring employee rights and welfare has been variable, but in general wages and benefits have been forced upward in unionized industries, and employees in these industries are better protected from capricious and abusive treatment by management and owners. Furthermore, there has been a spill-over effect, so that employers in other, nonunionized businesses have been forced to improve the working conditions and compensation they offer in order to keep their employees from forming unions and to continue to compete for prospective employees with business in which workers are already unionized and have these benefits.

The more critical driving force in creating and enforcing requirements for employee rights and welfare, however, has been government. In many of the European industrialized societies, labor interests have formed their own political parties and at certain times gained control of government itself. This happened, for example, in Great Britain and France after World War II. The labor movement in the United States, for reasons about which we can only speculate, never formed successful political parties.

In the few years following the Great Depression and World War II, union membership in the United States reached its peak, with nearly one in three (32.5 percent) of all nonfarm civilian workers belonging to unions. This certainly posed a significant social force in our economy. But union membership has been in a steady decline since then, so that by the mid-1980s only one in five (20.1 percent) of nonfarm civilian workers were union members, and by the mid-1990s not quite one in six (15.5 percent) were union members.[9] Why has this decline occurred?

One reason for the decline in union membership has to do with the reduction in the proportion of blue collar (or industrial production) jobs in our economy. This has hurt unions because, with few exceptions, unions have drawn their greatest strength from blue collar workers. The shrinking proportion of blue collar jobs in our economy is the result of several factors. For one thing, we have witnessed an explosive growth in white collar (or bureaucratic and service) jobs in our economy, and unions simply have not been as successful in organizing workers in these jobs. Then too, the maturing of our industrial economy has resulted in the increased use of robots and other automation techniques as replacements for blue collar workers. Finally, for a variety of reasons (including union-induced pressures on product and service prices and including deregulation), many manufacturers that employed large numbers of blue collar laborers either have gone out of business because of their inability to compete with foreign or smaller nonunionized competitors or have moved their blue collar jobs overseas (or to other locations in the United States) where unions do not exist or are a minimal presence.

In addition to the shrinking proportion of jobs for blue collar workers, a second reason for the decline in union membership probably derives from our increasing dependence on governments, rather than on unions, to force businesses to be more attentive to issues of employee welfare and employee rights. A third reason is the increased willingness of corporate businesses to act more responsibly in providing for the welfare of employees, even if only to make workers happy enough that they won't form unions or make new union demands.

A final reason for the decline of union membership is that unions have accomplished, even if with substantial assistance from governments, many of the objectives they initially had set. Consequently, relative to the situation in early industrialization, there is less current need for workers to create and use unions as a political force. Until some major change occurs in the balance of social powers between employees and businesses, unions can be expected to continue to attract reduced membership. However, we can expect that unions will surge back in membership should social conditions change so as to leave workers less protected than at present. The current trend toward corporate downsizing and corporate buyouts of each other for purposes of momentary profit enhancement is leaving a great many employees with less job security and may be a contemporary pressure toward a re-unionization movement (see Chapter 14).

Businesses can keep union sizes small well into the future by undertaking more socially responsible efforts to do well by their employees and to end adversarial relations between management/owners and laborers. Furthermore they could address the pressures that the costs of such socially responsible behavior may have on their prices and their market competitiveness by creating more aggressive profit sharing and profit-based bonus programs so that wage and benefit increases are not assumed to be automatic with each contract negotiation cycle but become tied instead to growth in business profits. This is a radical step that violates our ideological commitment to the priority of claims on profits by the suppliers of financial capital, and to date few companies have been willing to implement such programs.

Health and Safety in the Workplace

The production of goods and services has never been particularly safe. Among our food gathering and hunting ancestors the rigors of hunting expeditions likely posed many risks, resulting in broken bones, sprained ligaments, concussions, perforated skin, damage to internal organs, or worse. In addition to tripping, falling from elevated places, accidental drowning, accidental injury from one's own weapons or from those of others in the hunting party, one might also be attacked by angry animals, brush against poisonous plants, be bitten by poisonous animals or insects, and come into contact with parasites and many types of diseases (such as malaria). No doubt the many safety and health factors that were related to their mode of production played a role in accounting for the rather short life expectancy of our early ancestors.

The working situation is only marginally better in agricultural societies. If you think farming is a safe vocation, you haven't tried it. Animals used for draft, milk, or meat are unpredictable and occasionally may inflict considerable injury either out of orneriness or accident. Farming tools and equipment often have sharp and pointed edges which can cause great injury if mismanaged or by accident. The elements, marauding wild animals, and the seemingly ever-present wars fought for the benefit of higher ups who wished to lay claim to greater shares of land, all posed additional severe threat to worker health and safety in agricultural societies. The primitive conditions of agricultural work life made parasites and disease all too common. These work-related factors no doubt contributed to the short life expectancy of agricultural workers.

It should be no surprise to learn that there are health and safety threats to the producers of goods and services in industrial, business-oriented societies. The owners of early industrial production systems typically exhibited little concern for the health and safety of the workers in their businesses. Indeed the assumption, upheld by the courts, was that virtually all injuries or illnesses deriving from the workplace were the responsibility of the employees, not the employer. Following the reasoning of employment-at-will, the argument was that employees agreed at will to accept their jobs and their working conditions as is, with all of its threats to their safety and health. Consequently they must assume full responsibility for almost anything that happens to them on the job (this concept is known as the assumption of risk). In short, if you were injured on the job or fell ill from an unhealthy workplace, tough for you; you could expect to be fired without any compensation or consideration. This is what employment-at-will means: you are on your own.

If the labor market were sufficiently diversified and fluid to permit an employee to select from among many types of jobs, no one would take the high risk jobs (without a considerable increase in pay) and employers would be forced to reduce the risks in their workplaces in order to find employees. Unfortunately, the labor market was not so structured during early industrialization and, as noted above, employers had the decided upper-hand in at will employment decisions. Furthermore, employees often lacked sufficient information about the safety of a workplace. Thus, for example, employees may have taken a job and worked at it for years without knowing that it exposed them to high levels of toxic chemicals or other hazards. The *laissez-faire* market model simply provided no reasonable solution to the problem of abuse of the health and safety of employees. Enter the government.

Though unions had been pressing for workplace reforms related to employee safety and health since the 1800s, it has only been within the lifetime of most of us that governments have become deeply involved in these issues. By the 1960s most states had passed workers' compensation laws to establish compensation systems, paid for by employers, for workers who are injured on the job. These programs are often costly for employers, but they usually provide meager compensation to injured employees and in return often bar employees from suing employers for further damages. Some states have also attempted to regulate workplace safety, but to little avail.

How great is the problem of workplace safety and health in the United States? By the early 1990s the National Safety Council estimated that workplace injuries in the United States claimed the lives of 9,100 workers and disabled an additional 3.2 million annually.[10] Think about it for a moment, 9,100 people is equivalent to a fairly good sized small town in the United States being totally wiped out each year; 3.2 million people is equivalent to all of the people in an entire metropolitan area of a large city (such as of Atlanta, Miami-Fort Lauderdale, or Seattle) being injured each year. This is a lot of health and burial costs, a lot of human suffering and poses a great strain on many families in the United States.

In addition to on-the-job injuries and fatalities, however, a great many people experience long-term health risks as a result of workplace conditions. For example, the Occupational Safety and Health Administration (OSHA) estimates that there may be more than 100,000 deaths and 390,000 new cases of disability diseases every year in the United States as a result of exposure to dangerous substances in the workplace (including asbestos, lead, silica, carbon monoxide, cotton dust, chemical solvents, etc.).[11] The National Institute for Occupational Safety and Health has identified approximately 25,000 toxic substances in the workplaces of the United States.[12] Are there any in your workplace? Would you know if there were?

The ineffectiveness of state action on these issues resulted in pressures on the federal government to become involved in setting and enforcing national workplace safety and health standards. As a result, in 1970 OSHA was created to specify and enforce health and safety standards in the workplaces of America. The OSHA's regulatory authority is limited to businesses engaged in interstate commerce, which includes most large employers.

The OSHA has been controversial from its beginning for several reasons. First, many of its early safety standards were hastily put together and appeared (and were) foolish (such as specifications for safe toilet lids to be used by employees). Second, it focused most of its attention on safety issues related to injuries, and by its own admission, too little on long-term risks to health. Third, its limited budget and monumental, national enforcement task made its enforcement efforts spotty and grossly inadequate. For example, with more than six million worksites in the United States, it would take OSHA 1,154 years to review all worksites if it could review them at the rate of 100 per week. One study has found that for 75 percent of the worksites in the United States at which employees were killed or seriously injured in the mid-1990s, OSHA had not done a safety inspection in more than five years.[13] Fourth, even when finding violations, OSHA's penalty structure for safety violations are meager, offering little inducement for businesses to rectify safety problems. For example, a study of the OSHA's follow-up inspections in 1988 found that in 24 percent of cases employers had not made required corrections for safety violations.[14] As another example, when a Comtrak, Inc. worker was cut in half in a workplace accident in 1995, OSHA fined Comtrak $1,800.[15] In short, not only are businesses unhappy with the intrusion of the OSHA into their workplaces, but hardly anyone else has been happy with the OSHA's performance to date.

How much does OSHA's regulatory effort cost us? Cost estimates, as usual, are hard to come by. One estimate by the National Association of Manufacturers in 1974 indicated that the average annual costs of compliance with OSHA regulations (including filling out reports as well as making and maintaining necessary workplace modifications) amounted to about $35 thousand for small businesses with less than 100 employees, $75 thousand for businesses with 101 to 500 employees, $350 thousand for businesses with 501 to 1,000 employees, and so on, ending with average costs of $4.7 million for big businesses with over 5,000 employees.[16] You and I, of course, pay these costs in higher prices.

What have we gotten for our money? Statistics on workplace-related injuries and diseases have shown variable and inconsistent patterns over the decades preceding and following the creation of the OSHA.[17] Consequently, there is little reason to believe that OSHA as a regulatory agency has been an effective means for improving workplace health and safety in our business-oriented society.

A far more effective intervention strategy would be for businesses themselves to take these concerns seriously and to create a management system (as I described in Chapter 8) for addressing and resolving, health and safety problems unique to them. It would not be difficult to provide federal incentives for businesses to become more socially responsible for worker health and safety. Even without federal regulations or inspections, if significant fines were assessed against businesses for every worker who was injured or made ill by a job, it is easy to imagine businesses suddenly becoming more committed to reducing workplace health and safety threats. As an alternative or adjunct, corporate taxes could be adjusted based on employer safety records. The effect would be the same.

Humanizing the Workplace

As I noted in Chapter 5, industrialization has been driven in part by changing technology in the organization of work. These changes have not always been enjoyable for workers. For example, we Americans puff out our chests with pride over Ford's design of the moving assembly line as a means for vastly increasing the output of workers, but how many of us want to work on an assembly line, doing exactly the same thing, over and over, hour after hour, day after day, week after week, year after year? Ford, as it turns out, had a tough time retaining employees under these circumstances and had to offer wages that were extremely high for his time in order to keep his production lines staffed. Needing between thirteen and fourteen thousand workers for his production operations, Ford encountered turnover that amounted to 50,000 workers quitting in a single year. He found that, to retain 100 new workers, he had to hire 963.[18]

Not long after Ford's production system innovations, Frederick Taylor developed his ideas for the scientific management of employees.[19] Using time and motion studies of workers in a production process, he believed that he could modify worker and machine movements so as to achieve the greatest efficiency between them and to get the most from each worker. In this way, workers and machines were to become extensions of each other. Though initial productivity increases occurred from these techniques, many "ungrateful" workers figured out ways to sabotage the scientifically designed work plans (in some cases through informal rate setting and in other cases through union demands).

By the 1930s a human relations movement was in bloom among academic researchers who made the novel discovery that factory workers were in fact human beings and not machines or extensions of machines. People, they found, are motivated more by the emotional bonds that they form with each other than by wages, management plans, or by clattering machines. So the human relations movement emphasized meeting the human needs of wage-laborers in order to boost their productivity. Sensitivity to the psychological and social needs of employees was urged as the new management order of the day. Personnel departments became human resources departments and some increased attention to workers as human beings occurred.

We are still in the midst of a human relations movement as we struggle to find ways to create a more human production environment and to boost productivity in the face of growing international competition for markets. Business innovations in the past few decades, such as the creation of job enrichment programs, organizational development programs, attempts to change the organizational culture, applications of "Theory Z," profit sharing, and other plans emphasizing quality of work life (QWL) are evidence of this movement. An ample body of literature exists on these topics for the interested reader.[20]

Chapter *10*

Employee Equal Employment Opportunities

Chapter 9 considered employee rights and welfare in general, but this chapter focuses on the important issue of how patterns of discrimination in our society influence employment opportunities. This is a topic of great importance because, as I noted before, a person's standard of living and personal identity in a business-oriented society depend on the working conditions, pay, and benefits provided by their employment.

It is not pleasant to think about the racism, sexism, and other discriminatory "isms" that deny opportunities to people in our society. (If this has not been a good week for you, perhaps you will wish to skip this chapter and save it for a time when your emotional fortitude is greater.) None of us, however, can escape the consequences of discrimination. If we wish to hold firmly to the belief that people should be rewarded in our society based on their merit, then serious efforts must be made to end discriminatory "isms" in our society. It further follows that, because businesses are central social mechanisms through which discriminatory patterns in our society are perpetuated, one cannot escape the conclusion that businesses must play a major role in ending discrimination.

Businesspersons, however, cannot appreciate the role of their businesses either in the perpetuation of discrimination or in efforts to end it without understanding how discrimination itself operates society-wide. Therefore, I shall devote a good bit of this chapter to describing the ways in which discriminatory practices in our society deviate from an ideal of equal opportunity, particularly as a result of racism and sexism. After this description we will be in the best position to understand and critique the nature and intent of affirmative action programs in businesses.

Is the United States a Meritocratic Land of Opportunity?

A *meritocracy* is an ideal toward which we may wish to aspire. In a meritocracy, individuals receive rewards based on their individual merit. The determining elements of merit may include: (1) native abilities and personality traits such as intelligence, artistic ability, courage, fortitude, and so forth; (2) acquired skills such as the special skills learned in a trade, in a profession, or through schooling; and (3) the degree to which individuals exert themselves to get ahead—their hard work, including the special efforts they make to advance their education and to take advantage of opportunities.

In a meritocracy, people would be able to get from life what they deserve based on their innate abilities, pluck, savvy, and hard work. For this to happen, a meritocratic society would have to make available to all persons equal and ample opportunities for them to obtain the rewards that they merit.

Our belief in the ideal of a meritocracy is a central part of the ideology that we frequently use to explain and justify who gets ahead in our society and who doesn't. We frequently hear it suggested, for example, that people who are well off deserve to be so because they must have been smarter and worked harder than other persons. Likewise, people who are poor must deserve to be so because they have been stupid, ignorant, or lazy.

An American adage consistent with this meritocratic ideology might run something like this: "If you just have enough pluck and, yes, maybe even a little luck, by working hard and being shrewd you too can pull yourself by your bootstraps to achieve riches in America." This meritocratic ideology undergirds the great American dream that lured so many of our ancestors to this continent and that gave the United States the international aura of being a land of opportunity.

Who Wants a Meritocracy?

The ideal of a meritocratic society sounds really wonderful, at least on the surface. But nobody who already possesses some wealth, power, or prestige really wants to live in a meritocracy. To persons who are already wealthy and, therefore, do not need to work, talk about hard work must sound wearisome indeed. Furthermore, it would be rather frightening to think of hordes of people out to win away from you the wealth, power, or prestige you currently possess. A lack of complete commitment to the meritocratic ideal is not just to be found among the rich; it can be found as well among all of us who possess or can lay claim to even small amounts of wealth that we wish to protect. How many of us, for example, are willing to see our parents' assets handed over, upon their death, to the most deserving persons in our society based on their innate ability and hard work rather than to ourselves? You see, the cherished belief in familial inheritance of property violates the principles of a meritocracy.

In fact, I know of no society that has been organized entirely along the lines of a meritocracy (though all societies have some meritocratic elements). Instead, skin color, gender, clan or family, ethnicity, age, religious belief, and other social characteristics traditionally play important roles in determining "who gets what" in society.

The Race for the Prize

If we imagine a meritocracy as being a society in which everyone is brought together to run a great race, with the winners to receive the greatest rewards that society has to offer, then the following starting positions for such a competition might be observed in the United States. At the starting line, we place the racial minorities and all women. They will run the full race, including some swampy terrain, quicksand traps, and high mountains that are near the beginning of the race course. About half way along the pathway for the race, and after these early obstacles, we will have a different starting line for working and middle class

WASP males (i.e., White Anglo-Saxon Protestant males). The considerable head start we permit these people, of course, will ensure that many of them will be among the winners. They will, however, work hard enough and experience sufficient competition with each other over the latter half of the race course to believe sincerely at the end of the race that they deserve what they have achieved. On the other side of the finish line we will place all of the children of the leisured class; there is no point in their associating with the rest of us or in soiling their feet by having to run for the wealth they already possess.

To what degree does the United States deviate from a meritocratic ideal? Let's consider the competitive situation in the United States for people of different social classes, races, genders, ethnicities, ages, and religious belief.

Social Class Structures in the United States

In Chapter 6 I described class structures and social mobility in the United States in some detail. As a consequence I need only summarize that earlier description here to show how our society deviates from a meritocracy as a result of class structures.

The U.S. leisured class consists of about 7 percent of families. These families own about 54 percent of the wealth in this country. If we assume that newborns are equally distributed among families, then the average newborn in the United States has approximately a 7 percent chance of being born into a leisured class family and of being by this fact already across the finish line of the great American race for society's wealth. You too had this one-time-only chance to be born very rich. A 7 percent chance of being born rich is a likelihood that is far, far greater than that of winning the grand prize in a state lottery. Did you "blow your chance" as I did?

If you were not born into the leisured class, then you must try to win your fortune through the workworld. Research on social mobility indicates that there is a great deal of occupational mobility, but most of it consists of small, mostly upward, steps from our parent's generation. The chances of anyone moving from the lower working class to the heights of the leisured class are slim and likely to be no more than two or three percent. You had a much better chance of being born rich than of achieving it by your own efforts.

Now I know you may think that education is your ticket to riches, but guess again. Most self-made millionaires obtained their fortunes from real estate, from crime, or as entrepreneurs, and not from the types of jobs that require educational credentials. Furthermore, in both the educational credential market and the job market, you are at a distinct disadvantage if you are not from a leisured class background. The well-off are able to send their children to exclusive prep schools and to prestigious colleges and universities where they get high-status credentials. Regardless of how well or how poorly their children perform in the classroom relative to you, the high status of the educational credentials they receive will put them ahead of you in applications for the best jobs. In addition, they will have "rubbed shoulders" and made valuable contacts with a wide assortment of elites whose relatives and friends are in positions to give them a "leg up" over you in getting the best jobs and contracts (if they care to exert themselves by going after either).

In short, education is itself stratified along class lines, with schools for the rich, schools for the middle class, and schools for the working class. The prestige and value of the educational credentials these schools provide vary accordingly. The juiciest jobs simply are all but out of our reach if we are not born rich or in some manner able to get a high status credential or high status contacts. Across the broad spectrum of all remaining jobs, which comprise the bulk of all jobs, length of education does play some, though not by any means a *determining,* role in opening up or closing off job and pay opportunities for us. So sticking it out in school may give you some advantages over others in your current social class, but it is not by itself a ticket to success. Let's now look at some other factors contributing to your ability to sell yourself in the labor market of our society.[1]

Sexism in the United States

We have just seen that a major way in which our society deviates from the ideal of a meritocracy is in the way rewards are allocated across generations based on class structure. Another major deviation rests on the different ways we treat the two genders.

Sexism inside Us

Sexism is found in all sectors of our society and is deeply ingrained in each of us. Consider the following riddle that I first heard in 1972 as a young adult:

> *A man and his son are in an automobile when the automobile is involved in a terrible collision. The man is killed instantly, and the boy is rushed by ambulance to the hospital. When rolled into surgery, the attending surgeon takes one look at the boy and says "I cannot operate on this boy; this boy is my son."*

Why would the surgeon have said this? If you haven't heard this riddle before, please pause here to try to resolve it before reading the solution below.

When I first heard this riddle as a student in a college course I was young, radical, and freedom loving. My consciousness was raised to a height at least twice that of my physical stature. I believed firmly in removing barriers on opportunities for all races, for both genders, and for persons of all beliefs. I was firmly opposed to racism and sexism and believed that these were social injustices the roots of which lay "out there" somewhere in the social mists; I certainly was not part of these problems. I was not racist or sexist.

I cannot forget the shock I felt and the lesson I learned about myself when I heard the simple solution to the riddle. I couldn't figure out the solution in the few minutes the professor gave us to think it through. I could not see the solution that would be immediately obvious to any nonsexist mind: that the doctor must be the boy's mother.[2]

We think in sexist terms and react to the world in a sexist fashion because each of us, male or female, is a reflection of our society. And just as the business orientation of our society makes us as individuals into micro-businesses, so too the sexist orientation of our society makes each of us sexist. We need not be cognizant of either fact for society to have its way with us. Sexism (and racism and other "isms") is not just something "out there" in the social mists; it is also deep inside us in the crooks and crannies of the inner being that society has given us.

All known societies exhibit some means of allocating social roles and social rewards based on gender. All known societies, then, are sexist; which is not the same as saying that sexism cannot be reduced substantially or even ended entirely if we have the will to do so. But, historically, females have borne a very heavy toll as a result of sexism. Consider the following observations.

Gender Violence

Infanticide was a widely practiced means of population control until the industrial era. Because of the low valuation placed on females, female babies bore the brunt of this practice.[3]

We don't kill female infants today in the United States; however, the beating and raping[4] of women in the United States, especially by "boyfriends" and husbands, is widespread, as is sexual abuse of young girls in their homes. Therefore, violence directed against women remains a significant problem in our society.[5]

Ours is not the most sexist of contemporary societies. Indeed, one could claim that Japan, France, or Mexico are far more sexist. Nonetheless, we have a strong history of sexism.

Gender Rights

Our democracy was proclaimed in 1776. All of the signers of the Declaration of Independence were, of course, males. In our newly founded land of the free women were not granted the right to vote until 1920, roughly one and a half centuries after our democracy was formed. The right to vote in the greatest democracy on earth has been granted to women so recently that, depending on your age and gender, you, or your mother, or your grandmother or great grandmother were among the first women in the history of the United States to get to vote.

Until recently, women were considered to be the property of men, passed on from father to husband at wedding ceremonies where they promised to love, honor, and obey their new husbands. Wives could be beaten and abused by husbands, forced to move wherever husbands wished to go, and do whatever husbands wished them to do. The law stood behind these husbandly rights. Women, by contrast, possessed few legal rights, but had many legal obligations. Wife abuse remains a major problem in our society, with most of it going unpunished. Currently we are also dealing with the issue of whether it should be considered illegal for husbands to rape their wives.

It wasn't until the 1960s, within the lifetime of most of us, that many states gave women (particularly married women) the legal right to control property and to sign contracts. It wasn't until the 1970s that discrimination against women in educational opportunities and credit lending was declared illegal. Can you imagine how much opportunity you would have in life to get ahead if you could not control property, sign binding contracts, or obtain credit? Women were considered emotionally and intellectually incapable of handling such business transactions on their own. Again, depending on your age and gender, you or your mother, sister, your wife or daughter may be members of the first generation of women in the United States to have major legal restrictions removed from them in business and employment opportunities.

Gender Employment and Earnings

Removing official, public legal restrictions on women is not enough to place women on an equal footing with men in the race for society's rewards,[6] because there are many private and informal discriminatory practices that operate throughout the business and employment sectors to the detriment of women. Going all the way back to Biblical times, a female slave was considered to be worth 60 percent of what a male slave was worth (Leviticus 27:3–4). The valuation of the two genders in the sale of their labor in the job market of today is little different. By the mid-1980s, median earnings of full-time employed women in the United States were about 64 percent of what full-time employed men earn. This figure was no different than the percentage discrepancy between women and men thirty years earlier (roughly 64 percent in 1955), well before the "feminist revolution" and before major federal laws were passed barring discrimination in employment or in pay based on gender.[7]

As a result of deindustrialization, corporate restructuring, and recent recessions, earnings for men dropped in the 1980s and early 1990s. Largely as a consequence of declining earnings for men, median earnings for women in 1992 stood at 71 percent of that for men. If economic conditions for men improve in the near future (which is by no means a foregone conclusion), then the percentage differences between earnings for men and women may well drop back again closer to the Biblical level of 60 percent.

Some of the discrepancy between male and female earnings arises from the following circumstances: women are more likely to occupy (and typically be restricted to) the lowest paying jobs in our economy,[8] woman are more likely to have less job experience than males (due to the fairly recent opening of opportunities to them to enter many types of jobs they were previously barred from, and owing to continuing discrimination), and women are less likely to be able to maintain continuous careers of promotions since they (unlike men) find that they must leave and return to the labor market in cycles related to family needs.[9] Nonetheless, some of the discrepancy in pay is simply the result of unequal pay provided to women relative to men for the same jobs. For example, among all executives, administrators and managers in the United States in 1992, women were paid on average 65 percent of what men were paid; among all sales workers, women were paid 57 percent of what men were paid; among all administrative support and clerical workers, women were paid 75 percent of what men were paid; among all precision production, craft, and repair jobs they were paid at a rate of 66 percent, and so on.[10] A study of women with masters degrees in business administration (MBAs) in the 1980s found that, though their entry pay was comparable to that of new male MBAs, within seven years they were earning only 60 percent of what their male counterparts were earning.[11]

The evidence suggests, then, that being a man in the United States job market may be worth, on average, as much as half again or more in pay over being a woman. It can come as no surprise then that single parent, female-headed households are the poorest households in our society. The moral we can draw is that the shrewd person who wishes to get ahead in the United States would be well advised to be a male.

Education is not a magic ladder to economic success, but women should get all the education possible because each year of education is worth less for women in the job market than it is for men. In the early 1980s, for example, full-time employed women with five or more years of college (which is equivalent to a bachelor's degree and some work toward a masters or doctoral degree) were earning an average of $19,500, which was $2,600 more than male high school dropouts, and about $700 less than male high school graduates.[12] In 1991, women with five or more years of college were earning 69 percent of what men earned with a comparable education. Women with only a high school diploma also were earning 69 percent of what men with equivalent education were earning.[13] It is estimated that male college graduates can expect to earn about $1.5 million more in their lifetime than female college graduates.[14]

Even within the educational setting women often meet many obstacles and setbacks reserved especially for them. For example, research conducted by the U.S. General Accounting Office on students at the U.S. Naval Academy during the early 1990s found that new female students entering the Academy with SAT scores comparable to those of new male students could expect on average to receive lower grades, lower performance evaluations, and lower rankings for officer placement. By contrast, they could expect to be charged and convicted more often than men for honor violations (such as for lying, cheating, or stealing). Not surprisingly under these conditions, their attrition rate was 43 percent higher than for male students.[15]

Though women constitute more than 40 percent of our workforce, they hold only 15 percent of entry level management positions, 5 percent of middle management positions, and a mere 1 percent of senior management positions.[16] In the top jobs of the Fortune 500 companies, men outnumber women 600 to 1.[17] If not for affirmative action programs, many of these percentage figures would be much smaller. Indeed, in all high status jobs women are vastly under-represented. Despite representing roughly 50 percent of the U.S. population, women are unlikely to be found in the U.S. Congress (fifty-five of five hundred thirty-five in 1995) and U.S. Supreme Court justices (two of nine in 1995), and among doctors (16 percent), lawyers and judges (16 percent), dentists (6 percent), architects (11 percent), school superintendents (2 percent), and so on. Even of the 16,000 corporate board of directors' positions of the top 1,000 companies, women hold only 400 positions (which is a rate of less than 3 percent).[18]

Of course lower pay and fewer job opportunities are not the only obstacles women face in the race to get ahead in our society. Depending on the survey, between twenty-five and 60 percent of women report being sexually harassed at work.[19] Men might regard these actions as harmless or even humorous, unless they think about them happening to their mother, sister, wife, or daughter.

Racism in the United States

It certainly is not pleasant to think about the injustice, the loss of opportunity, the human suffering, and the degradation that sexism creates, but it is important for us to do so in order to understand the role of such programs as affirmative action in the business sector. For the same reason it is important to understand how racism operates in our society.

Our society is indeed racist and, like it or not, that means that each one of us is racist. We could not be otherwise as a product of our society. Sexism and racism are insidious social processes that creep into our inner being as individuals, creating for us identities and motivational frameworks that operate within us regardless of our awareness and regardless of our gender or race. Once inside us they work to perpetuate, through our discriminatory behavior, a system of unequal rewards based on sex and race.

The Origins of Race

So far as anthropologists and historians can determine, all known societies have practiced racism. Furthermore, it is conceivable, and quite ironically so, that the racist practices of our ancestors may themselves be a leading factor in the origination of the races. Here is how it may have worked.

Because we all belong to the same subspecies, our ancestors probably looked much alike at one point in human history. The derivation of the physical differences between contemporary human races, therefore, may itself have been the result of such racist practices as selective inbreeding and genocide (including infanticide and the murder of outsiders) based on physical characteristics that were perceived to be desirable or undesirable by our ancestors. Through this process it would have been possible, over a number of generations, for our ancestors to have bred purer and purer racial characteristics among their descendants. For example, through inbreeding and genocide it would be possible to breed successively lighter-skinned descendants, darker-skinned descendants, or descendants with particular facial features or hair textures.

Social isolation and environmental factors such as the effects of sunlight no doubt also played roles in the derivation of the races. Nonetheless, the skin color and facial features that you and I see when we look in a mirror may well be a reflection of the successful racist practices that occurred in the societies of our ancestors (this possibility gives even richer meaning to the assertion that we are but mirrors of our society).

As social phenomena, races are extraordinary nebulous, lacking in clear boundaries and overlapping considerably. Thus some people who are socially defined to be "Negroid" in our society have lighter skin, thinner noses, narrower lips, and straighter hair than some people who are defined as being "Caucasian." Our culture has tended toward a simple distinction among people as being "blacks" (none of whom are actually black in skin color) and "whites" (none of whom are actually white in skin color). It is hard to believe that this crude system of classification could result in a fairly well-organized system of racist allocation of opportunities and social rewards, but it has. In what follows I shall consider principally how racism has affected African Americans, but I shall also describe briefly the plight of the Native American.

Racism in the New World

The landing of Columbus on the shores of the Western hemisphere marked a significant event in Western history. Historians dispute whether this was the first discovery of the New World by Europeans, but there is no doubt that it was the last. To the excited Europeans of the Old World, the New World meant gold, crops, land, furs, and the possibility of a passage to the spice trade of the orient. The flood of European immigrants to the New World eventually Europeanized it, and treasures of the New World were reserved primarily for European descendants.

The founding of this Europeanized new world was based firmly on racist practices. Native Americans who did not die from European diseases, and a great many did, were slaughtered or eventually imprisoned in reservations, as Europeans (particularly in the northern continent) set out to create their land of the free.

With Native Americans dying from European diseases, and with many of those who did not die engaging in military counteractions against the settlers, European settlers had to look elsewhere for laborers to assist in their exploitation of agricultural opportunities in the New World (principally for sugar cane and later for tobacco and cotton). Slavery presented an easy means of obtaining this labor. Slavery refers to the historic practice of selling slavic peoples from eastern Europe into bondage to buyers in the Middle East. Female Slavs were especially desired as concubines. Unfortunately for the European settlers of the New World, the politics of Europe no longer permitted slavic peoples to be rounded up for use as slaves. So the Europeans had to look elsewhere, and the elsewhere was Africa.

Slavery in the New World

Intermingling of Europeans and Africans over the millennia had made them relatively immune to the diseases of each other. Consequently Europeans found that health conditions did not prevent them from using Africans as slave laborers in the New World. Furthermore, at least some Africans were accustomed to heat and to tropical climates, so they were able to do hard work in a similar climate in the New World. The European colonial efforts had already made considerable headway in destroying the great African civilizations. Consequently Europeans were in a strong political position to have their way with the African peoples.

Can you imagine being captured by a hunting party one day on your way home (maybe tonight after work or school)? Can you imagine being beaten, tied up, and hauled away to a holding area in which you wait many days with little or no food and with intermittent beatings? Can you imagine people with a different skin color than yours (and perhaps different eye and hair color too) appearing and directing that you and a number of other bound individuals be loaded into the hold of a gigantic ship? Can you imagine being bound flat on your back in this hold, to lie in your own excrement for weeks on end, and to be packed tightly together with others? Can you imagine, laying bound in this hold, the heat; the darkness; the dank, stale air; the stench from human excrement; the nausea from the rocking ship; the wailing, crying, and hysterical reactions from the scores of persons bound tightly about you; the sounds of people dying; the inability to understand the language of the persons who hold you in bondage; the uncertainty of where you are being taken, of how long you will be bound, of whether you will survive even this day let alone the next; or of what awaits you at journey's end? Can you imagine enduring this experience day after day for two months, the time it typically took ships to sail across the Atlantic? Can you imagine throughout this journey the aching over the loss of your family, and indeed the loss of your entire culture and way of life?

Perhaps as many as half of the Africans who were enslaved for shipment to the new world did not survive the trip to the New World because of disease, starvation, and suicide. Can you imagine the experience of those who did? Can you imagine the ship coming to rest in the new land and of your being unloaded, still bound, to be placed in a new holding area? Can you imagine being hauled up, stripped naked in front of the strangers of this new land, and sold on an auction block? Can you imagine having to learn the language of your owner, who claims to be your master? Can you imagine experiencing repeated beatings intended to break you, and of being ever under the threat of mutilation, branding, and the whip should you fail to comply immediately and with a cheerful demeanor to every order?

Can you imagine being in a situation in which whether you were permitted to marry or to have children was up to the person claiming to be your master, and this person could sell your spouse or children, whip them, rape them, kill them, or do anything else that pleased him? In the land of the free, in the great democracy of the United States, you had no political power and no protection under the law. Indeed, the law worked against you so that you could not run away without being hunted down, probably beaten, and certainly returned by the law. Nor had you any legal right to protect yourself or your family from attack by your master or from any other European American.

Though our democracy was founded in 1776, most, but not all, African Americans were still being bought, sold, and owned as slaves for almost a hundred years thereafter. By the mid-1860s, partly for humanitarian reasons, partly as a means of punishing the southern states for the Civil War, and partly to destroy the economy of the South, slavery in the United States was declared illegal.[20] This event, however, did not end this nation's history of abusive practices aimed specifically at African Americans.

An American System of Apartheid

Rather, following a brief period of "reconstruction," we embarked on a set of practices that constituted an American system of legal apartheid. The segregation of public facilities and of schools became enforced by law (the so-called "Jim Crow" laws). African Americans were often denied entry into restaurants, hotels, and many other places of business, and they were forced by discriminatory real estate practices to live in squalid, segregated areas.[21] Furthermore, they were not eligible for many types of employment and were typically paid a much lower wage than European Americans.

Though African Americans were legally given the right to vote in 1870, it was not until almost a century later, the 1960s, that the many ad hoc barriers set up to keep them from voting (such as intimidation, beatings, property damage, lynching, poll taxes, literacy tests, and other techniques) were largely ended and African Americans were finally permitted to vote in large numbers. This occurred so recently as to be within the lifetime of many of us. Almost all adult African Americans today are among only the first or second generations of African Americans to actually get to vote in the roughly 200 years of our democracy.

Given a history of more than two centuries of enslavement and an additional century up to our lifetime of an American version of legal apartheid, it should not be surprising that African Americans have made little headway in getting ahead in the American land of opportunity. The profound effects of a long history of American enslavement and legal segregation are quite visible today.

I recall in my early youth reading about African Americans still alive at that time who had been born as slaves. There may still be some African Americans alive today who are children of former slaves, and many more who are grandchildren of those former slaves who lived during the impoverished years of reconstruction following the Civil War. If we assume that each generation of descendants corresponds to 20 years, then most of the 3.0 percent of the African American population who were aged 75 or over in the mid-1980s were probably only two or three generations removed from slavery (i.e., had grandparents or greatgrandparents who were former slaves). The 8.5 percent who were between the ages of sixty and seventy-four were probably only three generations from slavery; the 17.3 percent between the ages of forty and fifty-nine probably were only four generations from slavery; the 33.7 percent between the ages of twenty and thirty-nine were probably only five generations removed from slavery; and the remaining 40.5 percent of African Americans under the age of twenty were probably six generations removed from slavery.

After slavery ended, how long should it take for its adverse effects to be washed out as impediments that would work against descendants in their efforts to get ahead in life? If a meritocracy were created on the day slavery ended, I should think we would see significant advancement of the descendants of slaves within two to three generations (forty to sixty years).

But the end of slavery in the United States introduced for most African Americans an additional century of widespread legal discrimination in which their educational opportunities were few and deficient, their employment and earnings prospects were very limited, and their political power almost nonexistent. Looking at African Americans adults as of the mid-1980s, roughly a quarter would have reached maturity (age twenty) under conditions of the highly repressive legal system of segregation that was practiced in the United States until the mid-1960s. These would be the parents and possibly grandparents of young African Americans growing up today.

If the ending of legal discrimination in our society meant finally the institution of a meritocracy, then the generation of African Americans just now in their early working years (late twenties) should be the first generation to have the opportunity to achieve significant progress relative to preceding generations of African Americans. As I show next, however, the processes of racial discrimination in our society today are far more profound and insidious than were the highly visible, legal restrictions that we have ended. Discrimination is very much with us today. Consider the following.

Race, Employment, and Earnings

African Americans in the U.S. job market today tend to be the last hired and first fired, with employment preferences being given to European Americans. As a consequence, the rate of African American unemployment today is two (and for teenagers, three) times higher than the rate of European American unemployment.[22] Depending on the city, between forty and fifty percent of young urban African American males cannot find an employer.

When they do find someone who will hire them, African Americans can expect to be paid less than two-thirds of what European Americans are paid. For example, median African American family income in 1988 was 57 percent of that of European American families, which is a substantial decline from 61 percent in 1970,[23] when affirmative action programs had just begun to get off the ground and antidiscrimination laws in employment were beginning to be actively enforced. In short, when selling oneself on the labor market, the market value of being white is a bit over 50 percent above that of being black. If you are a European American, could you imagine trying to support yourself or your family on 40 percent less pay than you presently bring home? Under these circumstances, is it any surprise that African Americans are three times as likely as European Americans to be living in poverty? Roughly a third of African Americans (32.7 percent in 1991) live in poverty. Almost half (45.9 percent in 1991) of African American children are growing up in poverty. With such a high rate of poverty among African American children, the prospects for African American to get ahead in life over the course of the next two generations looks very gloomy indeed.

Setting aside issues of poverty, research indicates that African Americans meet many special obstacles set just for them at each step in the race to get ahead in the United States. They must have higher scores on intelligence tests than European Americans to hope to get the same grades as European Americans in school; they must get higher grades than European Americans to hope to get as much schooling as European Americans; they must get more years of schooling than European Americans to hope to get the same jobs; and they must get better jobs than European Americans to hope to get the same level of pay.[24]

Far from being a ladder to success, educational attainment plays only a small role in assisting African Americans to get ahead in our society. For example, in 1987 African American families headed by a householder with four or more years of college (i.e., a bachelor's degree and possibly some work toward a master's or doctoral degree) could expect to earn only 71.8 percent of what European American families brought home when the householder had the same educational background. When families are compared in which the householder had no more than a high school diploma, African American families could expect to earn 65.4 percent of what European American families earned. Comparing householders who were high school dropouts, African American families could expect to earn only 53.7 percent of what European American families earned.[25]

Race, Punishment, and Institutional Genocide

There is one pathway in our society along which African Americans encounter fewer obstacles than European Americans, and that is on the road to prison. Research shows that African American children are more likely than European American children to be physically punished by school authorities and to be suspended from school.[26] African Americans in general are more likely than European Americans to be watched by police; therefore, when they commit a crime they are more likely than European Americans to be caught. Once apprehended, they are more likely than European Americans to be beaten by police and are more likely to be charged with a crime rather than to be let go. When both African Americans and European Americans are charged with the same crime, African Americans are more likely to be prosecuted, rather than to have the charges dropped. If both African Americans and European Americans are prosecuted for the same crime, African Americans are more likely to be found guilty; but if both are found guilty of the same crime, African Americans are more likely to be sent to prison, are more likely to be given longer prison sentences, and are more likely to be sentenced to death. Once in prison for the same crime, African Americans are more likely to be denied parole; and if on death row, they are more likely to be executed.[27] Is it any surprise, therefore, that African Americans comprise almost half of all prisoners in the United States and occupy 40 percent of all death row cells?[28] And is it any surprise that approximately a third of young African American men are serving a criminal sentence in this country (in prison, on probation, or on parole)[29] while only a fifth of African Americans males of any age are in college?

Our society is structured in ways that not only promote pathways to prison for African Americans, but also foster patterns of institutional genocide of African Americans. At birth, African Americans have a life expectancy that is seven years shorter than for European American newborns. Several factors contribute to this difference. Infant mortality for African American babies is twice that of European American babies. Nearly half (48.1 percent) of all murder victims in the United States are African Americans.[30] Furthermore, African Americans have a 37 percent greater chance than European Americans of sustaining occupational injury or work-related illness and a 20 percent greater chance than European Americans of dying from work-related causes.[31] Indeed the disadvantages and greater risks for African Americans in our society mean that roughly 59,000 more African Americans die each year than would be expected based on a European American mortality rate.[32] This is equivalent to everyone in a fairly large size small town dying each year in this country. Being black in America is clearly hazardous to one's health.

Other Discriminatory "Isms" in the United States

Of course our society discriminates against a great many types of people, including the young, Polish Americans, left-handed people, and many others. Prevailing political interests determine which forms of discrimination demand redress. Following are a few additional forms of discrimination that have received attention in our society.

If you are a white male under the age of forty you may feel greatly impatient with a lot of talk about racism and sexism. You may even feel that people who claim to be discriminated against are just cry babies who, if they just got off their duffs, could make their own opportunities and improve their lives on their own, as you perceive yourself as having done.

Ageism

But consider this. A forty-year-old person of either race or gender who looks for a new job can expect to encounter obstacles to employment. Or a fifty-year-old who loses a job, perhaps because of a layoff or for any other reason, will face even more obstacles when looking for a job. Much worse is the situation for a sixty-year-old who loses a job. Do you know what the job market looks like for sixty-year-olds? It would be better for us all to remain under forty (and it would be even better yet to remain under thirty) so as not to have to come face to face with the realities of ageism as a discriminatory "ism" in our society.

Anglo-Saxon White

Consider this too. The letters "AS" in WASP stand for Anglo Saxon. To hold the greatest advantage in the competition to get ahead in the United States it is not enough to be white, rather you must be Anglo-Saxon white. More generally, you should be of northern European ancestry (especially English or German); certainly you should not be of a swarthy Southern (or Mediterranean) European ancestry (including Spanish, Italian, Greek, or Turk). And it is also wise not to be of slavic or other eastern European ancestry. Even being of French ancestry has disadvantages.

Try to name some United States presidents who were not northern European white, perhaps some Mediterranean-American presidents, Slavic-American presidents, or even a French-American president.[33] Look at the sea of Anglo-Saxon faces in the U.S. Congress and in the board rooms of our biggest corporations. It is very evident that ethnic discrimination plays an important role in our society in determining who gets what. If you are a white male who doesn't care about the fact that discriminatory practices against African Americans and women are rampant in our society, perhaps your ethnic origins make ethnic discrimination an issue that affects and should concern you.

Protestants

The letter "P" in WASP stands for Protestant. Catholics, Jews, Muslims, and followers of other major religions face difficulties in securing high-status positions in our society. For example, though there were many Roman Catholics in the United States prior to the founding of this nation and Roman Catholics account for nearly one-fourth of our current population, only one U.S. president was Catholic. All of the rest were Protestant. Again, Congress and the board rooms of our major corporations are awash with Protestants; Catholics and Jews are greatly underrepresented in such positions. However, it is not even enough to be Protestant in our society. Among Protestants, Episcopalians and Presbyterians rank highest in receiving society's rewards. As of the mid-1980s, they are 50 percent more likely than Methodists or Lutherans and nearly three times more likely than Baptists to have incomes in excess of $40,000.[34] If you are a white Anglo-Saxon male, it might be wise to check your religious affiliation.

The Dynamics of Racism and Sexism

Racism, sexism, and other discriminatory "isms" operate through two social vehicles. One is prejudice, or our disparaging thoughts and attitudes about different types of people. And the other is discrimination, or the discriminatory behaviors we exhibit toward these people. It is a standard sociological observation to note that our thoughts and attitudes are only loosely connected with our behavior, and that it is very possible for us to think about the world around us in one way while behaving in another. Thus we may be prejudiced against a certain group of people, but exhibit little or no actual discriminatory behaviors toward them. Or we may be unprejudiced, but very discriminatory in our behavior against a group of people. And of course we may be both prejudicial and discriminatory, or neither.[35]

Given that racism, sexism, and other discriminatory "isms" consist of two parts, you and I cannot conclude that we are not racist or sexist simply by looking inside our hearts to see what feelings lurk there. We may feel little or no prejudice within us (or we may feel much prejudice). It is more important that we look at our behavior. What we find when we do so can be revealing and disconcerting.

Racism in Our Major Social Institutions

Recent history has shown that it is far easier to change prejudicial attitudes than discriminatory behaviors. Public opinion polls of attitudes have shown a substantial decline in prejudice over the course of the latter half of this century. However, discriminatory behavioral patterns related to sexism and racism remain nearly as strong in the United States today as they were forty years ago. And in all likelihood you are an active participant in these discriminatory behavioral patterns. Consider the following:

Families and Friendships

When both parents are present, families continue to be generally patriarchal in structure, with the husband considered to be the head of household (a fact which may account for our current high divorce rates, as women seek more control over their own lives); there are very few interracial marriages (if you are white, count how many of your relatives are black and then explain to me how you and your relatives are not discriminatory);[36] there are few close friendships between the races. (If you are white, count how many close black friends you have and how many times you have called on them in the past month to share an evening or friendly activity together; then explain to me how you are not discriminatory.)

Neighborhoods

Neighborhood segregation remains extremely high in the United States, with most neighborhoods being almost all European American or almost all African American. (If you are European American, count how many African American families live on your block and then explain to me how you are not discriminatory.)

Schools

Despite movements to desegregate public schools in the 1950s, 1960s, and 1970s, schools continue to be highly segregated, with many schools being almost all white or 80 percent or more minority. (Count your teachers and classmates or those of your children; if you don't find at least one in eight to be African American, explain to me how you are not participating in a discriminatory schooling process.)

Work Setting

Despite many years of affirmative action programs and resultant tokenism, women and blacks continue to be vastly underrepresented in higher paying jobs and are overrepresented in secretarial and janitorial jobs; unions traditionally have been more discriminatory than employers against women and blacks. (If one in eight of your co-workers, subordinates, or bosses are not African American, explain to me how you are not participating in a discriminatory work setting.)

Government

Women and African Americans are vastly underrepresented in positions of governmental power, including in Congress, in the courts, and in executive offices. For example, in 1989 women and African Americans each held only 6 percent of seats in the U.S. House;[37] in the U.S. Senate, women held only two of one hundred seats and African Americans none (if you have not cast your vote for a woman in 50 percent of the elections for political offices in which you have voted and if you have not been voting for African Americans in at least one in eight of these elections for office, explain to me how you are not participating in a discriminatory political system that stacks the governmental power structure in favor of white males).

Health Care

Doctors in the United States are 98 percent white and 84 percent male; nurses are 96 percent female; nursing home facilities tend to be virtually all white or all black; the overprescription of tranquilizers for females is common; African Americans have a shorter life expectancy than whites. (Explain to me how these outcomes in our health care system do not arise from discriminatory behavior.)

Mass Media

Mass media stereotyping of women and African Americans continues to be common; of roughly 500 vice presidents of the three major networks in 1982, only six were minorities, and only two of 500 commercial television stations in the United States that year had African American managers.[38] Although African Americans hold 40 percent of all laboring jobs in the broadcast industry, they hold fewer than 3 percent of the managerial and official positions in this industry and only 0.3 percent of news director positions.[39] Among the nation's newspapers in 1989, three-fifths did not have even a single minority member as journalist.[40] (Explain to me how these outcomes do not arise from discriminatory behavior.)

Churches

Many religions, including Roman Catholicism, bar women from top positions of church leadership; churches continue to be the most segregated of our institutions, more so than neighborhoods, work settings, health care facilities, or schools. Walk into almost any church in America and you will find the congregation to be virtually all white or all black. (Apparently we are unable even to pray to our deity together; if at least 12 percent of the pews in your church are not filled with African Americans and

88 percent filled by non-African Americans, explain to me how you are not participating in a discriminatory religious system.)

Castes and Master Statuses

As seen in these many examples of major social sectors of our society, discrimination is alive, widespread, and continuing to flourish today. Indeed, African Americans are placed in a position in our society that bears substantial resemblance to that of a caste of untouchables, whose very touch may be morally or socially polluting (e.g., European Americans may not want to buy or live in a house that an African American family has lived in; they may not want to live in a neighborhood that African Americans live in, have African Americans in their social clubs, be seen socially with African Americans, have an African American as a boss or close co-worker, attend a church with African Americans, or even be buried in a cemetery where African Americans have been buried. Indeed, like the untouchable caste in India, African Americans may become for European Americans mostly invisible, to be kept out of sight and mind.[41]

Sociologists use the term master status to refer to the plight of African Americans and women in the United States. Regardless of their social standing on other dimensions (such as social class, education, occupation, place of residence, or so on) their race and gender constitute statuses that override all others in social significance. Thus, irrespective of the other social statuses they may have achieved, they are treated as blacks and as women first, with all of the racist and sexist prejudice and discrimination this entails in our society (i.e., they are always viewed as the black lawyer or the woman vice-president or black or woman this or that, rather than simply being viewed as a lawyer or vice-president or "what have you"). There is no escape from the low status ascribed to them and the attendant discriminatory behaviors directed toward them by virtue of their race or gender no matter how much money or education they may achieve or how high their occupational standing.

Both the perversity of this situation and the great breadth and depth of discrimination that makes it a reality in our society operate regardless of our personal conscious feelings on the topic of prejudice. Indeed, prejudice is the least injurious of the two social vehicles (prejudice and discrimination) that constitute racism, sexism, and the other "isms" in our society. It is far less damaging to your self and family to know you are not liked than to be denied equal opportunities for housing, schooling, health care, employment, and pay, and to be singled out for special attention by our correctional system.

Overt and Covert Discrimination

One of the major problems, and an important one for understanding affirmative action, is the insidious nature of much discriminatory behavior; as the examples just given illustrate, much of our discriminatory behavior occurs without our being aware of it or even of our approving of it. To obtain a better understanding of how this process works, we need to differentiate between two basic forms of discrimination: overt discrimination on the one hand and covert (or latent or institutionalized) discrimination on the other.

In overt discrimination we are fully aware that our behaviors are discriminatory and we engage in these behaviors knowingly. Thus we may openly say that we will not hire a woman or a black person for a particular job and then behave accordingly. This is an example of overt discrimination. Such discriminatory behavior is easy to detect because people are aware of it and admit that they are doing it.

Covert discrimination, by contrast, occurs without our necessarily being aware of it. Indeed we may be unprejudiced and vocally opposed to discrimination and yet engage in discrimination and be affected by it. Covert discrimination works in many ways. One of its more significant variations is how it works on our self-image and motivation.

In our society, one witnesses from birth onward innumerable instances of the subservience of women and African Americans to European American males and the great attendant disparity in their relative opportunities and rewards. Exposure to an endless flow of such observations necessarily shapes how we conceive of our own identity, self-worth, and prospects in life. Young European American males, more so than women or African Americans, are confronted with ample evidence from what they see around them to confirm that they are valuable persons who can expect one day to hold power and wealth in our society. There is a confidence, an assurance, that experience tends to lend to them and that the same experiences decidedly do not lend to women and African Americans. Rather, women and African Americans may be left as a consequence of these experiences with a diminished self-image and a lowered sense of social potency. In short, covert discrimination can shape our identities and our feelings in ways that permit society's patterns of discrimination to flow through us, to be actualized, and to be reconfirmed by us, as we either reach out to take what we believe to be our rightful prerogatives or hold back from them in feelings of uncertainty and inadequacy. This process is covert because it operates without us necessarily being aware of what is happening.

Covert discrimination works in a great many other unseen ways and is widely found in the business sector. Another example would be for a white male, wanting the best new employee possible, to recruit for new senior-level managers from his old-boy network of white male friends. This person may be wholly unprejudiced against women or blacks and indeed may act wholly in a nondiscriminatory way if presented with a recommendation from his old-boy network to hire a female or an African American. The trouble is, the old-boy network is very unlikely to know of or to recommend a female or African American and consequently will very likely forward only recommendations for European American males. Such a recruitment strategy, then, works without our being aware of it to bring about an outcome that is covertly discriminatory. Or consider the impact of job requirements on applicants. The employer may be fully willing to hire anyone who meets the requirements specified for a job without any discrimination based on their ethnicity, race, or gender; nonetheless, the requirements may covertly weed out certain groups of people so that only European American males remain as being qualified for consideration. For example, if police departments require all applicants to be at least 5 ft, 10 in. to be considered for employment, this would exclude most women and Mexican American males. No one need say, "Let's discriminate against women and Mexican American males." The job requirements result in the same end without anyone necessarily being aware of it or desiring it.

Institutionalized Discrimination

Institutionalized discrimination is another specialized form of covert discrimination that works through the very relations between the different major parts of our society. A diagram depicting how institutionalized racism works in the U.S. is presented in Figure 10.1.

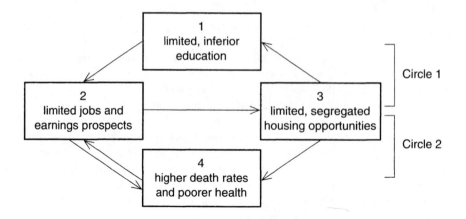

Efforts to break these two circles of
institutionalized discrimination:

1. busing and Head Start programs
2. affirmative action programs and laws
   barring discrimination in employment
3. fair housing laws
4. neighborhood health centers and Medicaid

FIGURE 10.1   Institutionalized Racism in the U.S.

An examination of this diagram brings us closer to understanding the role of affirmative action in businesses as a response to discrimination in employment.

Figure 10.1 illustrates two circular pathways of institutionalized racism that operate in and between several major institutional settings in our society to the detriment of African Americans. Overt and covert discrimination can be found within each institutional setting (e.g., within school settings and within work settings). However, of primary concern in the operation of institutional discrimination is how patterns of discrimination are sustained *between* major institutional settings. We need not be aware that our behaviors contribute to and reinforce these covert patterns of discrimination, nor need we be in favor of them for them to work as barriers in the efforts of African Americans to get ahead in our society.

The first circular pathway shows the institutional carry-over effects of discrimination that many African Americans encounter as they move from institutional setting to institutional setting in life. Any discriminatory effects carried away from the school setting (box 1 in Figure 10.1), including poor quality education in largely segregated schools, affect a person's job and earnings prospects as they move later into the work setting (box 2 in Figure 10.1). Limited job and earnings prospects, in turn, limit their housing prospects and fosters segregation in the neighborhood setting (box 3 in Figure 10.1). This situation in turn limits schooling prospects (given that most will attend a school close to them and this will effectively be a segregated school that is underfunded because of limited community resources). The whole pattern, then, constitutes a vicious circle of defeat that really has no starting point and that can continue generation after generation without any person willfully feeling prejudice toward African Americans.

This first circular pattern operates most effectively for poor African Americans (recalling again that about one-third of African Americans overall and about one-half of African American children live in poverty). However, as one moves around and around the circle, discrimination that occurs within institutional settings (such as giving African Americans lower pay for performing the same job as European Americans or steering African Americans into segregated neighborhoods) compounds the discriminatory effects to be found between institutional settings. Thus the whole pattern of discrimination, considering both its operations within institutional settings as well as between them, works quite well as a social engine not only to keep many African Americans in a disadvantaged underclass, but to press more African Americans into this underclass if they are not ever vigilant and more resourceful and hardworking than European Americans.

The second circular pathway shows a carry-over effect of limited jobs and earnings prospects on housing and health prospects, with limited housing prospects also influencing health prospects and limited health prospects further limiting one's ability to obtain and retain employment and earnings. Again, this circular pattern operates without any real beginning point and without any need for anyone to feel prejudice toward African Americans. Both circles are institutionalized: they are a part of the very way in which the social institutions of our society are related to each other.

Efforts to End Institutional Racism

What have we tried to do as a society to end these hidden circles of institutionalized discrimination? We have tried to change access to education, jobs, housing, and health care. For example, both Head Start and busing were programs designed to break the first circle of discrimination. By most accounts, Head Start, which is a program intended for poor children, has shown at least minimal positive effects in promoting later school performance. Busing, on the other hand, has been a failure. In the same time frame that court-ordered busing plans were being put into effect, a white flight was occurring from our cities that resulted in the European American suburban rings we now have around our inner cities. The inner cities have been left, by this process, increasingly African American in population. The result of this racial migration is predictable: most inner city schools are now overwhelmingly minority and have even less local funding resources as European Americans took their money with them to the suburbs.[42] In short, this pathway in the circle is quite alive and well today.

In response to segregation patterns in housing, our society has made it illegal for homeowners to refuse to sell property to someone because of their race, for landlords to refuse to rent to someone because of their race, for real estate agents to steer people to race-appropriate communities, or for banks and other lending agencies to refuse to lend money for mortgages to people based on their race. It is very hard to monitor or enforce these laws, however.[43] Furthermore, the nub of the problem, that limited earnings prospects also limit residential prospects for poorer minority members, is largely unaddressed. In short, our programs for breaking the circle here are too modest and are ineffective.

In response to health care needs, our society created neighborhood health centers and Medicaid (for the very poor). It is difficult to say whether the neighborhood health center movement was making headway in improving the health of minority members in neighborhoods where they were located, because politics and funding cuts plagued these centers almost from the beginning of the program. Medicaid has been a valuable program for the very poor, but the "means tests" used for it are very restrictive; many working poor who desperately need health care services can't get them through Medicaid because they are "overqualified," on the basis of their poverty-level earnings. Furthermore, the recent trend has been for governments to cut funding for Medicaid. Again our efforts here are too little and are ineffective.

This brings us to affirmative action and laws barring discrimination in employment. I describe affirmative action in more detail in the next section, but its specific intent is to open up employment possibilities for minorities and women. From my earlier comments on the very minimal progress of African Americans and women in the workplace over the past few decades, we can conclude that affirmative action too has had a negligible impact in breaking the two circles of institutionalized discrimination.

For African Americans, the real success story of affirmative action has been for the relatively few African Americans in our society who are well-educated. Among recent college graduates, African Americans receive incomes that come close to those of European American graduates, though still falling short.[44] In addition, however, some working class African Americans have seen gains as a result of additional blue collar and lower white collar opportunities becoming open to them that were closed in the past. Most African Americans, however, have gained very little as a result of affirmative action. For this reason, median earnings figures, as noted earlier, show no gain for African Americans as a whole. Also, as noted before, trends in women's earnings have been unimpressive.

The modest impact of affirmative action to date suggests that it has resulted in little more than tokenism in the increase of opportunities for women and minorities. Each workplace, for example, may feel pressured to have its token blacks or women; but once this goal is met, no further opportunities are made available. Clearly, much more needs to be done to expand employment opportunities in our society. The major patterns of institutional discrimination described here will have to be addressed if we are to achieve that goal.

To summarize, though we ended slavery 130 years ago and we ended our system of legal apartheid thirty years ago, we have made minuscule progress toward ending the hidden circular patterns of institutionalized discrimination that continue to pose major obstacles to the efforts of many African Americans to get ahead in our society.

Affirmative Action in Businesses

I have given a rather lengthy introduction to racism and sexism in our society because it isn't possible to appreciate the role of affirmative action without this background. The term affirmative action, of course, is an euphemism: that is, it is a nice way to say something that we don't want to say with more accurate terms. What it really entails is discrimination conducted in favor of certain groups who are deemed politically worthy of receiving special opportunities. It is in fact reverse discrimination (or affirmative discrimination) practiced primarily against European American males who, as I have documented, otherwise receive, without requesting it, most of the advantages heaped on them by the ongoing, widespread discriminatory patterns in our society. It is action, and it is action that follows what is politically deemed to be a positive direction toward balancing or overcoming existing discriminatory patterns. Hence it is affirmative action.

The Nature of Affirmative Action Programs

Affirmative action programs are designed to remove covert barriers to employment for categories of people that society has specified as deserving of protection (i.e., they have become defined as protected groups). African Americans and women are the two categories of people who have received most attention as protected groups in such programs.

It is critical to recognize that affirmative action is designed to remove covert discrimination. Overt discrimination is not at issue and is already outlawed under other legal provisions. For example, it is already against the law to discriminate openly in employment decisions against people because they are African American or are women. Affirmative action, by contrast, goes beyond addressing overt discrimination to seek to overcome hidden or covert mechanisms of discrimination in employment. At issue is not just the ending of discrimination in current employer decisions, but the remedying of the effects on potential job seekers of hidden patterns of institutionalized discrimination that make protected groups less aware of job opportunities or less qualified for these opportunities.

Consider the following situation. Suppose you are an employer in need of employees and you fully intend to discriminate against no one based on their race or gender. Indeed, you instruct that the Social Security number of each qualified applicant for your job openings be written on a slip of paper, all such papers be put into a hat, and the people to be offered a job drawn at random from the hat. What could be more nondiscriminatory than this? In no way have applicants been judged on racial or gender grounds in the employment decision.

Suppose, however, that after a year of this new, nondiscriminatory system you find that all persons who had been hired in the past year were European American males. What could go wrong with this overtly nondiscriminatory selection system to cause it to yield such results?

What may have gone wrong is that your selection system operates in a fashion that is covertly discriminatory. At least three possibilities exist. First, African Americans and women may never have had the opportunity to learn about your job opening and, therefore, never applied and had their names put into the hat. This is especially likely if you relied on your old-boy network to obtain applications. Second, even if your job openings were well-publicized, you may have set employment requirements that were in fact irrelevant to assuring that a candidate is qualified for the job, and that very effectively weeded out most African Americans and women (e.g., remember the earlier example of the effect for women of a height requirement). Therefore, the Social Security numbers of these people would not appear in the hat as qualified applicants. Third, even if the employment requirements you set are not irrelevant to being qualified for the job, the existing circles of institutionalized discrimination that were discussed earlier may have made it difficult or impossible for many African Americans or women to have met these requirements. Again, few or no African Americans or women would end up in your hat for selection. You may pat yourself on the back for not overtly discriminating against anyone, yet your hiring practices effectively continue to bar minorities and women from opportunities for employment.

What this illustration represents are three forms of covert discrimination that are operating to keep African Americans and women from being hired. If you do nothing about these covert processes, then you continue to contribute to ongoing institutionalized discrimination in our society. Affirmative action is intended to provide remedies for these and other forms of covert discrimination, including those related to promotion within companies. It would be useful to review some affirmative actions designed specifically for these three forms of covert discrimination in hiring practices.

Overcoming "Lack of Opportunity" Bias

First, employers seeking to act affirmatively with regard to protected groups should make special efforts to ensure that minority members and women in fact have an opportunity to know that the employer has jobs available. This principally would involve the advertising of jobs in widely read newspapers, rather than by simply spreading the word about an available job through an old-boy network. It is in keeping with this principle that employers today not only advertise positions in widely circulated newspapers and professional magazines, but also include in their advertisement the little line that reads, "An Equal Opportunity Employer," or EOE for short (this becomes their documentation to government regulators that they have acted affirmatively in getting word out about their jobs).

An employer, however, may go further in this affirmative direction by taking out additional advertisements in specialty magazines and newspapers that African Americans or women are especially likely to read. Furthermore, the employer may set up recruiting campaigns to let potential job applicants at predominantly minority or women's colleges know about their jobs (in addition to their typical recruitment campaigns at predominantly white colleges). The imperative is for employers to take action (affirmative action) to let protected groups know about available jobs so that members of these groups have the opportunities, often denied to them in the past, simply to be able to apply for these jobs.

In an active recruiting campaign, an employer should be able to find ample protected group members who are qualified to apply for most of their jobs. By ensuring that these protected group members know the job is available, the first action in affirmative action is accomplished. These persons may apply for the job or they may not as they please, and if they apply they may either be hired or they may not be hired depending on how they compare with other applicants. No one is guaranteed a job through this first step in affirmative action. The intent, once again, is only to let people know about a job so they have a fair chance to apply for it.

Overcoming Unnecessarily Restrictive Qualifications

A second major type of affirmative action is for the employer to assess very carefully the qualifications that are to be used in determining which applicants are qualified for the job. If these proposed qualifications make protected group members less likely to be eligible for employment, then these qualifications should be carefully assessed to ensure that they are indeed necessary for the job in question. In other words, the qualifications to be used in employment decisions (in hiring, firing, promotion, pay) must be clearly based on bona fide occupational qualifications or on business necessity.

For example, if a company does not want to hire anyone who might become pregnant or decides to fire anyone who does become pregnant, obviously a large number of women could be affected. But before using potential or actual pregnancy as a condition to determine who is qualified for the job, the business that is in pursuit of affirmative action should show that this qualification is a necessity for their business. Likewise if a business decides to hire only persons with a high school diploma, then minority member groups are more likely to be denied employment relative to European Americans because the institutionalized patterns of discrimination discussed earlier result in more barriers for them in the pursuit of education. Under such circumstances the business should show that a high school diploma is a bona fide or legitimate and necessary qualification for the job. The importance of this second action in affirmative action has been upheld in two important U.S. Supreme Court rulings: Griggs *v.* Duke Power Company in 1971 and Connecticut *v.* Teal in 1982 (it was reversed by the 1989 U.S. Supreme Court ruling in Wards Cove Packing *v.* Antonio, but reversed back again by the 1991 Civil Rights Act).

Providing Training to Counteract Historic Discrimination
In some cases, no (or too few) protected group members with the requisite, bona fide job qualifications can be found. In such cases, a third major affirmative action would be needed to break hidden patterns of institutional discrimination that keep women and minorities from gaining the qualifications that are needed for the job. Therefore, commitment to affirmative action may lead an employer to establish special training programs for protected group members so they can develop the qualifications needed to become eligible for a job—qualifications that were denied to them through their earlier (restricted) life experiences. In the typical situation when this action is called for, obvious previous obstacles can be identified that have worked to keep protected group members from developing the necessary skills required for the job.

For example, union discrimination in granting memberships to African Americans or women in some industries has meant that few African Americans or women have had the opportunity to learn on-the-job skills required to apply for skilled jobs. In response, a commitment to affirmative action would call for training programs to be developed to provide these skills to interested members of protected groups so that they then will become qualified for the jobs in question. It is critical to emphasize that this third action in affirmative action also does not mean the hiring of people who are unqualified for a job. Rather, such affirmative action training programs are intended to ensure that protected group members will have the opportunity to gain the necessary qualifications for the job and, therefore, will be able to compete on a level field with other people who apply for the job.

Affirmative Action and Quotas
The three actions just described sound good (positive, affirmative), but how do we ensure that businesses are making a serious effort to implement them? This is where the so-called "Philadelphia plans" come in. In Philadelphia plans, government regulators work with employers to establish affirmative action goals and timetables for the accomplishment of these goals. The easiest way to determine compliance, however, is by counting how many of the employees of a business are African American, women, or of some other protected group and to compare these counts to some standard. Herein lies the source of the notorious quotas.

One way to do these counts is to compare hire rates of protected group members to those of European American males. If affirmative action programs are working, the hire rates for protected groups should be the same as for European American males (stated as percents based on the number of applicants in each group).

This reasoning has led to the 80 percent rule, which holds that protected group hire rates should be no lower than 80 percent of the European American hire rate. Thus, for example, if 10 percent of the available European American labor pool is hired, then one should expect that no less than 8 percent (which is 80 percent of 10 percent) of the African American labor pool is also being hired if affirmative action is having its desired effects of making protected group members aware of the job, providing them the necessary skills to qualify for the job, and removing irrelevant qualifications as requirements for the job that serve no other purpose than to discriminate against the protected groups. If the 80 percent rule is not met, government regulators may become quite troublesome in their dealings with a business, and so businesses have ample reason to make sure that they are hiring specific minimal numbers of minorities and women relative to European American males to keep their hire rates roughly equal. This whole process, then, boils down to a quota (and, parenthetically, to tokenism).

Another way employee counts are examined by regulators is by requiring businesses to show that their proportions of current minority and women employees reflect the relative proportions of these people available in the potential labor pools from which employees can reasonably be obtained. Thus, for example, if the available labor pool from which employees could reasonably be obtained is 20 percent African American, a business would need to explain why only two or three percent of its current employees were African American. The percentage comparison required by this rule, known as Order No. 4, pressures employers to set up employment targets for the hire of minorities and women. Again, these are essentially quotas, as employees seek to ensure that the minimal numbers of protected group members are hired to yield proportions consistent with Order No. 4.

Employment quotas, however, are politically unpopular, and the U.S. Supreme Court has ruled against the use of quotas by public agencies (Regents of the University of California *v.* Bakke, 1978). Therefore, the counts used in assessing employer compliance with affirmative action are assiduously referred to as targets, which is an euphemism that apparently is less offensive in our political arena.

Does affirmative action discriminate against European American males? The answer is "yes." There is no comparable special effort to alert European American males to employment opportunities (though the publication of these opportunities in widely circulated newspapers does make more European American males aware of them than before this affirmative action step was taken). There is also no comparable effort to remove irrelevant job requirements that might discriminate against European American males under the age of forty. Furthermore, there is no special effort to provide training programs for European American males so that they too can gain the skills needed for better jobs. So affirmative action programs work selectively to provide favors to protected groups while not making similar deliberate efforts on behalf of European American males. The evidence I reviewed earlier on the lack of progress of African Americans and women during the last few decades, however, suggests that European American males as a group have not suffered from the effects of affirmative action.

Legal Authority for Affirmative Action

The legal authority for affirmative action programs derives from two sources. First is Title VII of the Civil Rights Act of 1964 (which was extended by the 1972 Equal Employment

Opportunity Act). This body of legislation created and empowered the Equal Employment Opportunity Commission (EEOC) to provide regulatory oversight for businesses and public organizations with fifteen or more employees. In addition to declaring it to be illegal to engage in overt discrimination in personnel decisions (including hiring, promotion, work assignments, performance appraisals, disciplinary actions, pay, benefits, and termination) the enabling legislation also permits, but does not require, businesses to set up affirmative action programs as aids in ending covert discrimination in employment. In actual practice, however, businesses are effectively forced to create affirmative action programs in order to avoid a lot of EEOC regulatory hassles and legal costs. For a business to have an approved EEOC plan is rather like its having an inoculation that helps to keep the EEOC from descending on it like a disease. An EEOC plan also helps to get court rulings on employment discrimination cases to go in favor of the business, as I discuss in more detail later.

The second legal source for affirmative action comes from an executive order issued by Lyndon Johnson in 1965 (EO 11246, amended by EO 11375, and itself an update and extension of executive orders by Franklin Roosevelt and John Kennedy) that barred discrimination by federal contractors. As it has been put into operation, Johnson's executive order requires all federal contractors and subcontractors with $50,000 or more in federal contracts and fifty or more employees to set up an affirmative action program. Needless to say, becasue so many businesses engage in sales to the federal government, this executive order covers a lot of the business sector.

Johnson justified the issuance of this order on the grounds that discrimination against the employment of minorities, women, or other groups may result in many qualified people being unable to find work in the businesses that the government patronizes. If these businesses instead are hiring less qualified people simply because they are white or males, then these discriminatory practices would likely reduce the efficiency of these businesses and make their costs and prices unnecessarily high. As a consequence the federal government would not be getting its money's worth when it purchased goods from these businesses. Efforts by these businesses to end their discriminatory practices should make them more efficient and, therefore, should lead to a better buy for government.

Unlike the Civil Rights Act, this executive order specifically requires that businesses set up affirmative action programs, at least businesses that want government contracts. The affirmative action programs established under this executive order are administered by the Office of Federal Contract Compliance Programs (OFCCP) of the U.S. Labor Department. And it is from OFCCP that regulatory Order No. 4 was issued.

No President since Johnson has had the temerity to end the executive order requiring affirmative action. Even Presidents Reagan and Bush, who voiced opposition to affirmative action, did not end the executive order, which they could have done with a simple signature. When Reagan proposed the ending of affirmative action, many major corporations, including IBM, AT&T, and General Electric, urged that it be retained.[45] Why? Well in my own opinion the nation's business leaders were simply more attuned to social responsibilities than was President Reagan.[46] But it should also be pointed out that approved and hopefully effective affirmative plans help big businesses to avoid lawsuits for employment discrimination. Lawsuits can otherwise be quite costly, as witnessed by the following settlements paid by companies charged with discrimination: $38 million by AT&T in 1973, more than $32 million by General Electric in 1978, and $42.5 million by General Motors in 1983.[47]

U.S. Supreme Court rulings, such as in the 1979 ruling on United Steelworkers of America *v.* Weber and the 1986 ruling on Firefighters Local Union No. 1784 *v.* Stotts, have generally been in favor of affirmative action programs, provided that the adverse effects on European American males are not great. However, new appointees to the high court by the Reagan and Bush administrations are likely to work to greatly decrease the role of the Court as a force in ending discrimination against minorities or women in the workplace. For example, the 1989 ruling (noted earlier) on Wards Cove Packing *v.* Antonio effectively reversed the court's 1971 ruling in Griggs *v.* Duke Power, which held that employment qualifications must be shown by employers to be bona fide or necessary. (The effect of the newer court ruling was itself reversed by the new 1991 Civil Rights Act.) A further defanging of the U.S. Supreme Court as a force for fostering civil rights can be expected as the 1990s draw to a close.[48]

In any case, affirmative action programs themselves have made, at best, but a minor dent in the widespread discriminatory practices in employment in the United States. As is true for any bureaucratic program, there are ample ways of getting around it. Indeed, as I noted earlier, earnings figures over the last three decades show no progress overall for African Americans and little progress for women. Though all of us are quick to point out examples of success stories—of minorities or women who now hold influential positions or receive high pay, these instances gain so much of our attention because they are exceptions. These exceptions draw our attention and lay hold on our memory in much the same fashion as if we were to see a few stalks of healthy corn in a well fertilized field of wheat, while all the time we failed to notice or to remember the rest of the corn plants, stunted and wilting in an unattended field across the road.

African Americans and women are not the only persons to receive legislative attention in efforts to remove barriers to employment opportunities in America. The Civil Rights Act (which bars overt employment discrimination) and affirmative action programs (which attempt to end covert employment discrimination) are just two of our efforts to provide protection to certain groups of Americans who are deemed by political judgment to need protection. The last three decades have also seen the Equal Pay Act of 1963 (enforced by EEOC) to mandate equal pay (and benefits) for women for doing the same or very similar jobs as men (but not necessarily equal pay for doing very different jobs that nonetheless have comparable skill levels); the Age Discrimination in Employment Act of 1967 (updated in 1974, 1978, and 1986 and enforced by EEOC) to protect persons over the age of forty from employment discrimination; the Vocational Rehabilitation Act of 1973 (enforced by OFCCP and EEOC) to protect those with disabilities from discrimination in employment; and the Vietnam-Era Veterans' Readjustment Assistance Act of 1974 (enforced by OFCCP) to protect disabled veterans. There are yet other important pieces of legislation that define protected groups.

If you dislike the idea of some people being protected or feel that the system is working against you, consider this. All of us fall into one or more protected groups if we live long enough. If you are not a member of at least one of these protected groups—a woman, an African American, a Hispanic, a Native American, a person with disabilities, a Vietnam veteran, or a person over the age of 40—then all you have to do is live to your fortieth birthday and you too will be a protected group member.

Conclusion

Is Affirmative Action Moral?

Affirmative action is reverse discrimination; there can be no doubt about it. But is discrimination itself always absolutely and universally wrong? A sociological perspective could not lead to such a conclusion.

All societies have discriminatory patterns, and ours is no exception. However, discrimination can be seen as evil or as just and proper, depending on the cultural environment. In our society we see it as just and proper to discriminate against people based on their age. For example, we do not allow persons under the age of eighteen to vote, drink, or purchase cigarettes. We don't allow persons under the age of sixteen to drive an automobile, or persons under the age of fourteen to be employed. At the other end of the age spectrum, we allow people over the age of sixty-five to draw monthly assistance checks and health care services from the Social Security and Medicare systems, all paid for by payroll taxes imposed on people who are almost all under the age of sixty-five. We also believe that it is just and proper to deny privileges to persons convicted of a crime, and we believe it just and proper to require by law that children be in schools for much of their childhood. I believe these actions (discriminatory though they may be) are all just and proper, and most adults probably agree.

After several hundred years we ended the practice of slavery in this country, but maintained for most African Americans thereafter an additional hundred years of profound and widespread legal segregation lasting up until the lifetime of most of us. This is a history of discrimination on a grand and ferocious scale that I am sure few of us today are proud of. Indeed I think we would be willing to say of it that it was evil.

If the widespread patterns of discrimination against African Americans had indeed been brought to an end in the 1960s with the ending of this country's version of legal apartheid, I'm sure we could feel much better about ourselves today. As I have described in this chapter, however, patterns of discrimination remain rampant and profound in all major institutions in our society and infuse and motivate our personal behaviors. Hence, the challenge of ending discrimination remains very much with us today.

It is a standard technique in fighting forest fires to set small fires in order to contain and hopefully put out large fires. The principle of reverse discrimination can be conceived analogously. Affirmative action can be viewed figuratively as a means of setting small fires of reverse discrimination in an effort to counter and, hopefully, put out the giant fire of discrimination against minorities and women that otherwise burns out of control society-wide, consuming and destroying the lives of so many people in its path. The more aggressively we pursue affirmative action strategies (and to date our efforts on this score have been lackluster), the fewer generations should have to pass from this time forward before we make significant inroads in breaking the pattern of institutional racism and sexism in our society. The goal that is sought is not, as is often claimed by opponents, the hiring of unqualified protected group members over other persons who are qualified for a job. Rather the goal is to increase the opportunities for persons to apply for jobs and to become qualified for those jobs who are otherwise currently greatly disadvantaged by the widespread racism and sexism of our society.

Given the context and the options available to us as a society, is the undertaking of affirmative action programs a more moral course of action for us than simply to end these programs and then do nothing? I think it is. What about you?

What Should Businesses Do About It?

Businesses did not create racism or sexism nor are such discriminatory practices the inventions of the business-oriented society. But the business-oriented society and businesses in particular certainly perpetuate and reinforce our major patterns of discrimination. If we as a people are to live in a business-oriented world where social rewards are largely controlled by businesses, and if we prefer that these rewards be more directly based on ability, skills, and effort rather than on race, gender, age, or other seemingly irrelevant characteristics, then these patterns of discrimination are very much a business problem.

In our democratic society it is only natural for afflicted or concerned people to turn to governments for remedies. However, governments within our lifetime have shown themselves fairly inept at providing remedies. And indeed, government efforts to end discriminatory practices in employment have been lackluster and quite unimpressive in their results.

Increased socially responsible behavior by businesses directed toward reducing discrimination in employment would dramatically reduce the pressures on governments to impose political solutions, including such a solution as affirmative action. We cannot expect businesses to solve the problems of racism and sexism society-wide, but we can expect them to work toward solutions for how the problem operates within their organizations. By their very operations, for example, businesses must hire people, assign them to work tasks, occasionally promote them or fire them, and pay them for their work. They can either make these decisions in a discriminatory fashion (overtly or covertly), or they can undertake efforts to stop discrimination in these decisions.

Why should they bother? At present, they must take action because governments pressure or require them to do so, because of the threat of lawsuits, and because of the possibility of adverse publicity. But they may also wish to do so because it may in fact be a more efficient use of human resources, because it may reduce pressures on governments to regulate them, and because it may even be the right thing to do. At least in the case of corporations, the board of directors, as I described in Chapter 8, could play a leading role in pressuring management into formulating affirmative action plans and nondiscriminatory practices that are most suitable for their operations. Such a commitment within a business and at its highest level is more likely to produce substantial results than is a grudging conformity to minimal governmental regulations.

One further observation about our future as a society should serve to spur business concern over discrimination in employment. It is projected that by the year 2040 perhaps as many as 44 percent of working age adults and 53 percent of children will be minority members (African Americans, Hispanics, Asian Americans, Native Americans). In order for our businesses to remain competitive and profitable in an increasingly global economy, it will become more and more necessary to increase worker productivity by addressing issues of diversity in the workplace and by expanding employment opportunities for our nation's minorities. To fail to do this would jeopardize our economic future.[49]

Chapter 11

Consumers

The business-oriented society not only has transformed us into employees, it has also re-made us into consumers. In this chapter I discuss how the meaning of our lives has been shaped by our having become consumers, and I discuss the unique problems we now encounter as consumers in a business-oriented industrial society. I also consider how governments and private- and business-related entities have operated to create the modern consumer movement.

Consumer as Lifestyle and Identity:
"Here a Consumer, There a Consumer, Everywhere a . . ."

The commercial market is a keystone feature of our society today. This is in striking contrast to social conditions encountered by our ancestors. We can better understand our business-oriented society today if we try to imagine the nonconsumer lifestyle of our ancestors.

Imagine for a moment a society in which there are no stores or markets from which to purchase goods and services. If you were in such a society, what would you do to obtain such basic necessities as clothing, food, and lodging? Let's consider clothing first. Behind your closet door or in your dresser are many items of clothing that have been purchased in a marketplace. If markets did not exist, how would you obtain these clothes?

Can you imagine personally gathering from plants or animals all the fibers you would need to weave your own fabric? Can you imagine making clothing from this fabric for yourself and your family? In view of the substantial time and effort that would be required, how likely is it that you would possess more than one or two garments (and what need would you have for a closet or dresser)?

Let's also consider food and housing. If there were no grocery stores, restaurants, or other markets for food, how would you eat? Can you imagine finding or raising your own food each day? Can you imagine preparing meals from this food with nothing but tools and utensils that you made, and can you imagine preparing the food on an open fire or hearth?

Can you imagine making a shelter and all its internal furnishings entirely out of materials you found "as is" in nature or that you shaped yourself by hand with homemade tools?

Who would you "be," living under such conditions? What would your personal identity and your outlook on life be? If we took away our housing market so we were entirely on our own to find or construct our shelter, if our clothing and food markets disappeared so we were entirely on our own to find and prepare our clothing and food, indeed if all the markets of our business-oriented society ceased to exist, so we could not purchase canned or frozen foods, candy and pastry, refrigerators, stoves, microwave ovens, ready-made clothing, shoes, soap, toothpaste, toilet paper, toilets, books, newspapers, televisions, automobiles, gasoline, and so forth, what would our standard of living be and who would we be as a people?

On reflections such as these, it becomes evident that markets and the products and services they provide play a central role in shaping, organizing, and giving meaning to our lives today. Neither you nor I created these markets; rather they are mysterious "gifts" of the business-oriented society. These markets cloth us, feed us, amuse us, and care for us. And in this process of providing for us, they motivate us and give meaning and order to the world around us. Indeed, in this process they work themselves into our very inner being to structure our consciousness and our identity. It would not be an exaggeration to say that markets have made possible and motivate so much of our contemporary daily behavior that they have made us over into their own image: they have made us into "consumer people." Our "being" as human beings is now so intertwined with markets that in a very real sense we, as consumers, are the markets that keep the business-oriented society humming along. Take away the many cherished goods and services that we are accustomed to purchasing, and not only would our daily lives become dramatically impoverished but our identities also would become greatly changed.

Here are some more examples of how important the products and services made possible by markets are to us as consumer people. I don't know about you, but if I lost my car and could never again own and operate another, a large and significant part of my personal identity would be lost. It would be a loss for me on the order of that of losing a parent, a spouse, or a child; it would constitute a dramatic and devastating change in my daily round of life and in my sense of "who I am," in the meaning of my life and in my feeling of social potency.

Do you feel this way about your car? Probably you do to some degree if you own a car. But if you don't, consider again how dependent you are today on markets for clothing: how would you feel if you lost all of your clothes, every stitch, and had no market from which to purchase more? Standing now naked before the world, would this affect how you live, your daily routine, and your relations with others? Would it affect how you feel about yourself as a person or how you feel about your social status and social potency? Or what if suddenly there were no longer markets from which to purchase food? Would this affect how you lived or how you viewed the world around you or your personal identity? Suppose you went home tonight and found no food at all in your house and there were no markets from which to purchase more. Under such circumstances, what would you do? How would you go on living?

Questions such as these are unsettling precisely because our society has made us all into consumers—that is, it has made us into social creatures who must purchase goods and services from markets to survive and to maintain a meaningful existence. From the perspective of our market-dominated lives, it is incomprehensible to us how our ancestors could have lived without markets from which to purchase goods and services (likewise, no doubt, it would be just as incomprehensible to them to try to understand how we could live as consumer people, so wholly dependent on markets to provide for our needs).

Consider too how we become socialized to be consumers. It is sometimes so endearing and often so frustrating to try to teach a small child how to be a consumer person. Given a coin or paper money, children are quite likely to put it into their mouth or simply to toss it away as though it were useless (which, outside of a consumer society, it is). Money means nothing to them, and they must be taught to value it for its market use.

Children also have no natural sense of proper consumer person decorum when inside a shop or store. They may run around touching everything in sight, they may tear open merchandise boxes, play with goods, perhaps pocket things they want, and howl if parents attempt to separate them from goods the parents do not think they can afford or consider inappropriate.

It takes several years and a lot of work for parents to train children to exhibit proper consumer person behavior. But this is an important parental responsibility, because the making of us into consumer people is a transformation that is critical to the viability of markets and to the ultimate success of our business-oriented society. Such is the nature of life in the business-oriented society.

Consumer Problems

From cradle, with the purchase of obstetrical services for our delivery, to grave, with the purchase of burial services, we are consumers.[1] And we are consumers every day along the way, as we pay our housing and utility bills, drive our automobiles, buy food from supermarkets, pay for diversionary events, stop at fast food places, buy gifts for others (birthdays, weddings, graduations, Christmas, etc.), pay for college expenses, and so on. Because being a consumer has become so critical to the daily round of our lives today and to our personal identities, it is only natural that we should be concerned over anything that may threaten our welfare as consumers. And, with the maturing of our business-oriented society and the corollary transformation of us into consumer people who are dependent on these markets, it is only natural that we should seek to establish and enforce some fundamental human rights for ourselves as consumers and that we should seek to exert some control over markets for our own welfare.

Let the Buyer Beware

Most of our ancestors for 40,000 years had little or no experience with markets and hence were not consumer people. Under the circumstances in which they lived, the potential abuse of consumers naturally drew little or none of the concern that we feel today. Indeed, at least from the era of the Roman Empire the motto of *caveat emptor* (let the buyer beware) characterized the legal view of the consumer in the marketplace. The assumption underlying this motto was that the buyer and seller had equal power and knowledge in each market transaction. Therefore, any average buyer in face-to-face negotiations with any average seller should be able to judge the quality of a good or service and dicker knowledgeably over what would constitute a fair price. Under these circumstances there certainly was no reason to offer legal protection to someone to safeguard them from their own stupid mistakes about either the quality or price of a good or service.

As long as our lifestyles were minimally dependent on markets and as long as markets and businesses were small, our knowledge and social power as individual consumers were on an order closer to that held by business owner/operators. Under such circumstances we could directly confront owner/operators over issues of fairness of price, quality of goods, adequacy of warranty, product misrepresentations and so on, and we could expect to have our concerns attended to by the businessperson, provided that the businessperson did not fold up tent and steal away into the night. This situation still exists today in our relations with small businesses; the successful small businessperson knows only too well that the survival of his or her business depends directly on showing respect for customers, looking out for customer welfare, and satisfying customers.

Buyers Lose Control in Market Exchanges

By contrast, in today's complex business-oriented society we are increasingly dependent on products and services that we don't understand and that are delivered to us by large impersonal businesses. As a consequence, we consumers lose control over many aspects of markets and products. Our increasingly disadvantaged position can result in all sorts of abuses of us.

For example, typically the mass markets of large businesses become highly concentrated, and the corresponding merchandising efforts become highly bureaucratic and impersonal. Under these circumstances, considerable social distance exists between the consumer on the one hand and the owners and senior managers of large businesses on the other. If you as a consumer have a complaint over price, quality, product design, safety, or what have you, you may voice it to a low-level local manager who you probably have never seen before and who doesn't know or care about you as a person. Perhaps you will get some satisfaction from voicing your complaint, or perhaps you will choose, as many people do, simply to save your breath and get on with your life instead.

Potential consumer control over product design and quality provides a good example of an area in which our power in market transactions has become greatly diminished. One of the central features of mass market merchandising is the requirement that everyone wants the same thing. Because mass-produced products are typically designed in bureaucracies in which consumers have no direct input and these products are typically sold in highly concentrated, oligopolistic markets, there is often a lack of exact fit between the features that mass-produced objects offer and what you actually desire. Under these circumstances poor design, poor quality, lack of easy user-servicing features, inadequate warranty, and vastly overpriced service extension contracts are just some of the frustrations we all find ourselves resigned to if we are not to do without the mass-produced products altogether. Perhaps nowhere has this problem been more egregiously evident than in the automobile industry in the 1960s and 1970s. It was only the introduction of foreign competition in the U.S. market that forced U.S. automakers to become somewhat more consumer oriented.

Another example of the relative powerlessness of consumers in a mass market society concerns pricing. Through the market concentration that mass marketing entails, through price leadership, and through the bureaucratization of sales, we consumers lose direct influence over pricing. To demonstrate this to yourself, try haggling over the price of any of the scores of products you buy on a weekly basis (e.g., milk, gasoline, a hamburger at a fast food establishment) and see how much influence you personally have over their price.

Consumer Knowledge and Advertising

Yet another important factor that contributes to our powerlessness as consumers lies in the lack of a reasonable means for us to become knowledgeable about the quality and safety of the products and services that complex technology and mass production makes available to us. The safety of the products and services we purchase is a particularly significant issue, with about 29,000 deaths and 33 million injuries per year related to the use of consumer products. These annual figures do not include an additional 50,000 deaths from automobile accidents,[2] or an estimated 100,000 deaths and 400,000 deaths, respectively, resulting from long-term alcohol and tobacco use.[3]

Because of their increasing complexity, few of us can hope to become knowledgeable about the likely safety or quality of most of the products and services that we use every day. Can you, for example, tell which is a safe food additive, which is a safe insulation for your home, which is a superior design for an air-conditioner, which is a less flammable material for your clothing, which foods in your supermarket are contaminated with pesticides, what exactly went into the last hotdog you ate, whether the premium gasoline you buy is actually premium and not simply a mislabeled regular with a higher price, or so on?

When products on the market were little different from what we could make at home, we could all make these judgments. Now we simply buy goods and services with the hope that the businesspersons selling them will have our personal safety and welfare at heart. We personally do not control whether they do or do not.

Advertising is our major source of information about products and services, but it does very little to help us to become knowledgeable consumers. Rather it serves other purposes. One major function of advertising is to create name recognition for a product or service. Because we are ignorant as consumers, we quite reasonably rely on our common sense assumption that a product or service that is "known" is likely to be of better quality or value than an equivalent product or service that is "unknown." After all, why would we risk our money and the health of our family on something of unknown quality and safety? One of the central purposes of advertising is to work to give us the feeling that a product is known.

Advertising is also designed to emphasize name brands as status symbols. Unlike our ancestors, we as consumer people draw our status symbols from our market purchases. As we seek to elevate our social standing and our feelings of self-worth, we may be more inclined to buy a particular name brand product or service over a cheaper but identical competitor simply because it has been heavily advertised as being of the sort that is desired by persons of discriminating social status.

Of course some advertising also amounts to gross deception. We are often confronted with product and service claims that are exaggerated or that are merely intended to attract consumers to a merchandiser who will then use a variety of high pressure sales techniques to induce consumers to purchase different and more expensive products or services than they intended, and so on.

Not only are we confronted with hundreds of advertisements each day in newspapers, magazines, television, radio, and billboards, but advertisers also now play a significant role in determining the content of media programming (such as in television, in magazines, and on radio). As a consequence, advertising has become one of the most important socializing agents in our society (our other major sources of socialization are family and school; advertising is now arguably far more powerful than the church in its influence on our daily lives). The values that advertising promotes foster a market orientation by depicting consumption as an end in itself and as a measure of social status and human value. Whether it is hawking overpriced designer jeans and underwear, prescription drugs, credit cards, or any one of tens of thousands of other products and services, advertising's messages to us are, "be a consumer," "spend it now," "live for today," "your worth is measured by the name brands you buy."

A related issue of interest is advertisers' use of sexual themes to sell their products. The emphasis on sexual themes in advertising is intended primarily to gain viewer attention and to heighten the likelihood of name recognition of a product or service. It is very possible, however, that the vast contemporary sexual transformation of the content of advertising and of the content of media programming that advertisers subsidize (again as exemplified by television programs and in magazines) has worked societywide to promote values conducive to sexual promiscuity, to a view of women and adolescent girls as principally being sex objects, and to a belief that our sense of self-esteem is tied not only to our ability to purchase status-bearing goods and services, but also to our ability to be sexually desirable and sexually virile.

Advertising is very much big business, supporting many major advertising firms as well as the mass media. By the mid-1990s, advertising in the United States amounted to $128.6 billion dollars per year.[4] This is about $500 per person, or $2,000 for a family of four, per year. Major drug companies are estimated to spend much more on advertising their new drugs than on all costs of research and development of these drugs.[5] Who pays for advertising? Who pays for its pervasive presence in our everyday lives? Who pays for its control of the mass media? Who pays for its influence on human values and behavior? You and I as consumers pay in higher prices for the goods and services we purchase. If all advertising were to disappear overnight, our cost of living would be greatly reduced and our standard of living elevated. However, there would be dramatic repercussions for the mass media, which would lose their major source of funding in our business-oriented society.

Consumer Response

If we are going to live in a bureaucratic, impersonal, mass market society in which we personally and individually have no reasonable means of controlling product quality, safety, or price, it is only natural that we would seek to create some social mechanisms to protect our welfare. Not surprisingly, organized responses to potential abuses of consumer welfare have grown in size in tandem with the growth of big businesses throughout the twentieth century. Social responses to consumer concerns have taken three forms: governmental efforts to define consumer rights and to ensure consumer welfare, private consumer activist movements, and business initiatives. I shall describe each in turn.

Government Protection

Among the earliest historical records that set out governmental regulations for businesses are those found in King Hammurabi's code of roughly 1,750 B.C. This code included provisions for the protection of consumers, some of which might seem to us today to be quite extreme (for example, brick masons who did shoddy work were to be put to death). It is not at all surprising that consumers would expect political processes to control or to end abuses perpetrated against them. Indeed, political leaders who would stand by insensitively while forces other than themselves abuse their people could well expect soon to be looking down to find their own heads on platters. In what follows I shall describe the actions that governments have taken in response to the growth of consumer pressures in the United States. First I shall consider three waves of major federal legislation. Then I shall look at Presidential action and action by special federal agencies (the FTC, the CPSC, the NHTSA, the FDA, and the USDA).

Legislation

As shown in Chapter 7, we saw in the United States in the late 1800s a considerable outcry among small businesspersons and farmers over railroad price discrimination practices. The governmental response was the passage of the Interstate Commerce Act of 1887, creating the first major federal agency for regulating businesses for the protection of consumers (in this case small business buyers of services) against discrimination in price and service. With the continuing development of monopolistic practices, federal consumer protection against unfair pricing (and later unfair advertising) was further expanded over the ensuing thirty years to cover other industries through the antitrust legislation of the Sherman Antitrust Act in 1890, the Federal Trade Commission Act of 1914, and the Clayton Act of 1914. However, this body of legislation has been very ineffective in safeguarding us from monopolistic pricing practices in our markets.

Public concern also arose near the beginning of the twentieth century over the safety of foods and drugs in our country. By this time prepackaged foods and medications had become an important part of everyday life, so concerns over their safety and purity would quite naturally be expected to become a social issue. Indeed, reports on the meat packing industry at that time accused it of selling diseased and contaminated products, of the mislabeling of products, and of using unsafe additives to preserve foods or to enhance their visual appeal. At the same time the patent medicine industry was reported to be lacing over-the-counter medications with opium, heroin, and alcohol; of mislabeling products; and of making promises of effectiveness that were without scientific basis. The ensuing public reaction created the impetus for the passage of the Pure Food and Drug Act of 1906 and the Meat Inspection Act of 1907. These two acts were initially rather toothless and flimsy as safeguards of consumer health, but a few enforcement teeth were later added.

Together with the antitrust and interstate commerce acts, the foregoing body of legislation, coming in the late 1800s and early 1900s, constituted the first wave of consumer protection action initiated by our federal government. It came in response to the growing importance of big businesses as providers of goods and services in the marketplace. To get a perspective on it, on the growth of our business-oriented society, and on the relatively recent evolution of consumer-people and of a consumer lifestyle, it is useful to note that this initial body of consumer legislation occurred so recently as to be within the lifetime of a few living Americans, and certainly within the lifetime of either our grandparents or our greatgrandparents.

The Great Depression brought not only the ending of any pretense of the viability of a *laissez-faire* economy (see Chapter 6), but it also brought a second wave of federal actions designed to protect consumers from big business and mass market abuse. Consumer concerns were addressed, for example, through the creation of the Federal Power Commission in 1930 to regulate abuses in interstate power transmission, the Federal Communications Commission in 1934 to regulate abuses in interstate communications services, the Securities and Exchange Commission in 1934 to regulate abuses in the stock market, the Banking Act of 1933 to regulate abuses in banking and to create the Federal Deposit Insurance Commission (FDIC), the Civil Aeronautics Board of 1938 to regulate interstate air transportation, and in the creation of other commissions that dealt partly with consumer concerns.

Then too, the 1938 Federal Food, Drug and Cosmetics Act strengthened the regulatory powers of the Federal Drug Administration by requiring, for the first time, that all drugs be tested for safety (though not for their effectiveness) before being introduced to the market (no pretesting requirements were set at this time for cosmetics, however). Another important piece of legislation was the 1938 Wheeler-Lea Amendment to the 1914 Federal Trade Commission Act, which gave the Federal Trade Commission responsibility for protecting consumers from unfair or deceptive advertising and related sales practices.

The maturing of our industrial economy resulted in the largest wave yet of legislation in the 1960s and 1970s designed to protect consumers. This more recent outpouring of federal concern for the well being of consumer-people has occurred within the lifetime of almost all of us, or within the lifetime of the parents of those of us born in the 1980s and 1990s. Here is but a sampling of this wide body of legislation:

- Hazardous Substances Labeling Act (1960), requiring warning, storage, and safe usage labels on toxic household chemicals
- Kefauver-Harris Drug Amendments (1962), requiring that new drugs be proven to be effective before being marketed, and requiring that labels indicate the generic name of a drug
- Cigarette Labeling Act (1965), requiring cigarette packages to carry a safety warning label
- Child Safety Act (1966), banning the sale of children's toys that contain hazardous chemicals
- Fair Packaging and Labeling Act (Truth-in-Packaging Act, 1966), setting requirements for labels on packaged products to list the net weight of the contents and, under certain conditions, to list the ingredients themselves in order of their decreasing contribution to the product
- National Traffic and Motor Vehicle Act (1966), setting safety standards for motor vehicles
- Wholesome Meat Act (1967), requiring states to inspect meats (but not poultry) that are processed and sold within state borders

- Flammable Fabrics Act Amendments (1967), an update to the 1953 Flammable Fabrics Act that strengthens its requirements for children's clothing
- Wholesome Poultry Products Act (1968), requiring federal inspection of poultry sold within states if state requirements are less stringent than federal standards
- Radiation Control for Health and Safety Act (1968), requiring minimal standards of safety for electronic products and setting recall procedures if these products are found unsafe
- Consumer Credit Protection Act (Truth-in-Lending Act, 1968), requiring lenders to disclose all finance charges in terms of dollars and annual percentage rates
- Child Protection and Toy Safety Act (1969), putting to an end interstate commerce in toys with known mechanical, electric, or thermal hazards
- Poison Prevention Packaging Act (1970), requiring minimal standards for making packages containing hazardous substances child proof
- Fair Credit Reporting Act (1971), requiring credit bureaus to disclose credit reports to consumers and to correct inaccurate information
- Consumer Product Safety Act (1972), creating the Consumer Product Safety Commission to set consumer product safety standards and to aid consumers in judging the relative safety of products
- Toxic Substances Control Act (1973), requiring testing of the safety of all new chemical substances prior to their introduction to the market
- Real Estate Settlements Act (1974), requiring disclosures of all costs to buyers of real estate
- Equal Credit Opportunity Act (1974), requiring that women should not be discriminated against in applications for credit
- Magnuson-Moss Warranty Act (1975), specifying the types of product warranties that may be issued and requiring that they be easy to read and to understand

This body of legislation sits atop a large body of state laws and regulations that are concerned with protecting consumers. Looking at the items on the list, it is rather disheartening to think that businesses could be so irresponsible that they would have to be forced by political means to treat consumers fairly and to show concern for consumer welfare in the ways indicated by each of the pieces of legislation. Such, however, has been the case, is predictable from a *laissez-faire* market model, and has become just one more reason for political restraints to be placed on business autonomy. Do you think, in lieu of governmental intervention, that you as an individual consumer could alter business behavior on each of the items on this list? How? By not using credit, automobiles, electronic products, mass produced drugs, cosmetics, foods, and so forth? By designing and producing your own products? By complaining to your local vendor? As an individual, there is really very little you can do.

Presidential Action
Presidents also became active in the consumer movement in the 1960s. President Kennedy, for example, unilaterally declared the existence of an unwritten consumer bill of rights in the United States that consists of four fundamental rights that we have as consumers: the rights to choose, to be informed, to safety, and to be heard. President Johnson appointed a consumer advisor to the White House. President Nixon, not to be outdone, created the

National Business Council for Consumer Affairs, which consisted of high-level business-persons who considered consumer issues and advised government and businesses about better consumer-oriented practices.

The deregulatory movement intervened at this point. In order to avoid the creation of a federal consumer protection agency, President Ford appointed a consumer affairs representative to each executive department and agency to serve as resource persons in federal policy formation. President Carter went a step further by appointing several persons who were consumer activists to head up key regulatory agencies. The Reagan administration, however, cut back considerably on enforcement of regulations related to consumer protection. The Bush administration was inconsistent in its approach to consumer issues, but the Clinton administration has shown a more aggressive posture, particularly through the FDA.

What will the future hold for governmental involvement in consumer issues? I am not a gambling man, but I would bet all of my assets that a new surge in governmental involvement in consumer issues will come within the next two decades unless the business community itself becomes more aggressive in addressing these issues.

The Federal Trade Commission

In addition to legislation and Presidential action, a number of federal agencies play significant roles in consumer protection. The Federal Trade Commission (FTC) is one such agency. It was created in 1914 as a part of the antitrust movement to monitor methods of competition in interstate commerce and to issue cease-and-desist orders when these methods were judged unfair. Its mission was broadened in the 1930s to include all "unfair or deceptive acts or practices in commerce." Consumer protection is a major function of this agency, and unfair or deceptive advertising is a special focus of its efforts as it has increasingly insisted that companies prove their advertising claims. The FTC also has responsibility for regulating packaging and labeling requirements for products, and for consumer credit disclosure and reporting requirements.

The five commissioners who head up the FTC are nominated by the President and confirmed by the Senate for seven-year terms. Though they then operate independent of Presidential control, the politics involved in the appointment and confirmation process, coupled with the very substantial influence of the business community on Congress, have made the FTC highly sensitive to political concerns. For these reasons it should not be surprising that, with the exception of the decade of the 1970s (when a public furor resulted in the appointment and confirmation of a more active chairman of the FTC commission), the FTC has not been especially aggressive in its efforts to protect consumer interests.

The Consumer Product Safety Commission

As noted earlier, consumer product safety is a significant issue, with about 33 million people being injured each year by consumer products and 29,000 being killed. In response to growing pressures from consumers, the Consumer Product Safety Commission (CPSC) was created in 1972 to provide regulatory oversight for several major consumer-related safety laws involving the design, construction, contents, performance, and labeling of over 10,000 products, the banning of unsafe products, and the initiation and monitoring of product recalls.

Politics intrude again in the nomination and confirmation process of the five CPSC commissioners, who each serve seven-year terms. In addition, the legislative mandate for the CPSC holds that almost all of its efforts are to be directed toward getting industries to engage in voluntary standard-setting for product safety. Furthermore, political pressures from the business community on Congress and on the President have worked against the effectiveness of the CPSC, especially during the deregulatory movement. Nonetheless, by the mid-1980s the CPSC had issued over thirty mandatory regulations,[6] and in a two-year period from 1990 to 1992 it successfully negotiated the recall of over ninety-eight million products.[7]

The National Highway Traffic Safety Administration

The National Highway Traffic Safety Administration (NHTSA) was created in 1966 to set motor vehicle standards, fuel economy standards, regulations on other issues that are believed to affect auto safety (such as speed limits), and to order automobile recalls for defects. This agency has played a substantial role in automobile redesign in the United States, including the installation of seat belts, padded dashboards, and air bags.

The FDA and the USDA

The Food and Drug Administration (FDA), located in the Department of Health and Human Services, sets standards for safety, effectiveness, purity, and labeling of drugs, foods, food additives, cosmetics, and some medical devices and radiation. The Delaney Clause on food additives (a part of the 1958 Food, Drug, and Cosmetic Act) holds that the FDA cannot approve any food additive shown to produce cancer in humans or laboratory animals. In addition, the FDA operates an inspection system for food processing plants and related marketing operations. Headed by a commissioner who is appointed by the Secretary of Health and Human Services, the FDA is generally regarded to be one of the more aggressive of federal agencies, particularly in monitoring and controlling the introduction of new drugs. The U.S. Department of Agriculture (USDA) sets standards and conducts inspections of meat, poultry, and egg products and of their labelling, though it has been severely criticized for its lax policing efforts.

Consumer Action

Consumer Activist Groups

Just as employees formed their own private political groups (unions) to force businesses to stop abusing them, so private consumer activist groups have been formed as a political means to try to stop business abuses of consumers. By the late 1800s, impure, mislabeled, or hazardous products had become a problem of sufficient scope that Consumer Leagues began to form, first in New York City in 1891 and then elsewhere throughout the country. These local groups joined together to form a National Consumer League to publicize problems with consumer products.

Today there are over 100 consumer activist groups at the national level and over 600 at the state and local level.[8] The largest, the Consumer Federation of America (chartered in 1967), encompasses over 200 smaller groups representing over 30 million Americans.[9] Its functions are to lobby Congress on consumer-related legislation and to testify at congressional and regulatory agency hearings on consumer issues.

Receiving more headlines, however, have been the efforts of Nadar's Raiders and the Public Citizen, which was created by Ralph Nadar in 1971. Nadar initially gained public attention for his attacks on the safety of the Chevrolet Corvair,[10] but the Public Citizen has been active in publishing reports on the safety of prescription drugs, of food color dyes, and of many other products and services. The Public Citizen also assists citizens in bringing lawsuits against companies and in lobbying for consumer legislation.

Also well known is the Consumers Union, which was created in 1936 and is best known for its publication, *Consumer Reports. Consumer Reports* regularly conducts research and reviews the quality and safety of many consumer products.

Consumer Lawsuits

Ours is the most litigious nation in the world. With far more lawyers per capita than any other industrialized country, consumers in the United States have ample assistance in seeking legal redress (and ample urging to do so). Current legal interpretation relying on strict liability places a substantial onus on businesses for consumer injuries. Under this interpretation, manufacturers are legally accountable for all injuries to consumers arising from defects or unsafe features of their products, regardless of whether negligence can be proven to have occurred on the part of the manufacturer. The result of this interpretation has been an increased number of successful settlements and awards, some of which have involved substantial sums of money.[11] This, in turn, has caused liability insurance rates to skyrocket for businesses and has placed pressure on profits and prices.

Business Action

Persons who run small businesses know that a response to an angry customer who is confronting them must be immediate and effective if repeat business and a good community reputation is to be maintained. Prudence and self-respect are the only limitations on the self-effacement and concessions that a small businessperson may need to endure under such circumstances. Not all small businesses are destined to survive long lives, however, and the abuses of consumers perpetuated by floundering and fly-by-night establishments can be considerable before their demise. Large businesses, by contrast, have no natural communication pathway between consumers on the one hand, and owners or senior managers on the other. Consequently, consumers may not easily protest the abuses they endure. In this final section I shall describe two efforts by businesses to control abuses of consumers: efforts by the better business bureaus and by corporate consumer affairs offices.

Small Businesses and Better Business Bureaus

A better business bureau (BBB) is an association of local businesspersons who seek to promote business interests and good business practices in a community. One of the major activities of a BBB is to keep files that document consumer complaints about businesses in the area when these complaints are brought to the attention of the BBB. Consumers are able to call in to inquire about these files before making purchases of goods and services from a local business. In this way consumers can become more informed about questionable businesses in their area. The BBB also typically will work as a consumer advocate in an effort to ensure that a local business responds fairly to a consumer complaint. One vehicle they often provide for this purpose is an arbitration board to hear and rule on consumer complaints.

The Council of Better Business Bureaus (CBBB) was created in 1970 as a national umbrella organization for all local BBBs. In addition, CBBB's National Advertising Division responds to complaints about the accuracy of national advertising through investigations and the issuance of requests to offending businesses to modify or withdraw inaccurate advertising.

The formation of BBBs has been a very positive step on the part of local business communities. However, they are often understaffed and frequently cover very large geographic areas (for example, there is only one for all of the state of Maryland, a state with over five million people). As a consequence, a frequent complaint is that consumers have a very difficult time reaching BBB staff by telephone. Limited staff and dependence on businesses for funding may also affect the quality of record keeping in the tracking of consumer complaints against local businesses.

Large Corporations and Corporate Consumer Affairs Offices
Public pressures will continue to grow on businesses, particularly large businesses, to become more active in ensuring consumer welfare. If businesses fail to respond on their own to these pressures, additional government involvement and increasingly costly lawsuits can be expected. Likewise, recent experience has shown that market share may continue to be lost to those foreign producers who are more consumer oriented. (As noted earlier, this is what happened in the case of the automobile industry in the United States.)

One response to growing consumer pressure by corporate businesses has been the creation of consumer affairs offices to provide a means of focusing more of management's attention on consumer issues. Consumer affairs offices handle consumer complaints, monitor current and proposed consumer-related legislation, operate special consumer programs, and advise managers on consumer concerns. The Society of Consumer Affairs Professionals in Business has been organized to foster and support people who head these consumer affairs offices. Such offices are, of course, a positive business step in addressing the consumer movement.

However, as I have suggested before (see Chapter 8), corporations should go further than this by including in their management system a review process for judging the responsiveness of the corporation to consumer welfare. Management goals and periodic internal assessments of progress toward these goals, with suitable accountability implications, should be an ongoing topic for corporate board consideration and evaluation.

Full consumer information disclosure should be one of the important goals in this process. The business is in the best position to know its own products and services and to share this information with consumers. At a minimum, reports that summarize research on the safety of a company's products and services should be made public, perhaps through the public affairs office. Measures of quality (e.g., durability, purity, reliability), preferably using industry standards, should also be reported.

Such an exercise would, palpably, make for better informed consumers. But the more significant effect it would have is to make consumer issues into a more central concern in management decision making. This effort would be a positive step toward the creation of what has popularly come to be called a total quality management system.[12]

Conclusion

Let's face it, we consumer people are the most ignorant humans who have walked the earth. We are far more ignorant than the most primitive and savage of our food gathering and hunting ancestors.[13] In contrast to us, our ancestors knew how to make for themselves every item and service required by them in their society: their homes, their clothes, their food sources, their tools, their health care services, and their diversionary events. Ironically as society has become more technologically advanced, a process has occurred to render us humans progressively less self-sufficient than any people who lived before us. If we were shorn of the products and services that the markets of our business-oriented society make available to us, we would quickly die. Our primitive ancestors, who would have, and did have, no trouble living without markets, would surely pity (or despise) us for how helpless we have become.

We consumers are wholly dependent for our housing, food, clothing, health care, and amusements on technologies that we do not understand. Helpless as individuals to know the quality, safety, or fairness of price of goods and services made available to us by businesses, it is not surprising that we have banded together in the form of a consumer movement. This too is the nature of life in a business-oriented society.

C h a p t e r *12*

Businesses and Our Environment

Of increasing public concern in industrialized societies are the problems of pollution, resource depletion, and environmental destruction. Businesses today are central forces in the creation of these problems. However, as I shall discuss in this chapter, businesses cannot resolve these problems alone. Rather, solutions will necessitate the development of social control mechanisms at a global level.

Pollution and Environmental Destruction

All life forms pollute their environment. This fact derives from the nature of life itself. Each living thing absorbs the nutrients it needs from its environment and then excretes back into that environment wastes from its own metabolic processes. The buildup of these wastes inside its own tissues would be toxic to the life form. But it would also be toxic to the life form for these wastes to accumulate in its immediate environment. In this latter case the life form would be confronted by a situation of environmental pollution of its own making.

Just as the metabolic processes of any living organism pollute its environment, so too do the economic processes of societies. Through economic processes related to production and consumption humans possess the means to contaminate and destroy their environments on a concerted and grand scale. This phenomenon was seen in a more limited scale among our food gathering and hunting ancestors in their trash heaps, in the smoke from their campfires, and in their contamination of local water supplies. It was seen on a much larger scale in the farming practices of agricultural societies, including the exposure of soil to erosion through slash-and-burn and plowing techniques and through the use of fertilizers and irrigation. Environmental destruction, particularly the destruction of forests and wildlife and the overfarming of land, are believed to have been major factors in the decline and collapse of a number of ancient agricultural civilizations, such as were found in the Indus Valley, in Mesopotamia, and in Greece. Environmental pollution and destruction, in short, can become society killers.

Though every known society pollutes and destroys some parts of its environment, two things are significant about the scope of environmental pollution and destruction carried out by the business-oriented societies of today. First, industrialization brings into existence production processes and consumption items that make possible the pollution and destruction of our environment on a truly extraordinary scale. Second, as the most powerful forces in business-oriented societies, businesses and business markets themselves include no internal social mechanisms to limit the amounts of pollution and environmental destruction that they create. Indeed, market mechanisms in a commercial system driven by a *laissez-faire* ideology work directly to promote pollution and environmental destruction in order to achieve the market virtue of efficiency.

Pollution, Environmental Destruction, and the Efficient Market

Show me a person who is extremely efficient in all things that he or she does, and I'll show you someone who is viewed as inhuman and as uncaring by others and who will be ostracized by almost everyone. Show me an organization that dedicates itself first and foremost to a goal of efficiency, and I'll show you an organization that will experience very high rates of staff turnover and that cannot hope to survive without significant human relations reform.

Social order relies on a wide range of human emotional attachments, most of which do not make for efficient goal-oriented behavior. Included among these emotional attachments are a strong sense of traditional duties, obligations, and privileges; loyalty to family, to in-groups, and to community; and a sense of piety, honor, courtesy, and decency. Throughout history, efficiency has been little valued. Indeed it often has been reviled precisely because it dehumanizes us by threatening so many of the emotional attachments that are necessary for us to sustain social life.

Nonetheless, prevailing market model views on businesses and on business markets hold efficiency to be a great virtue in human economic affairs. Allegiance to this view is often expressed with such zeal as to be suggestive of a cult, one which we might call the cult of efficiency. And while our businesses and markets are not, never were, and can never be singularly efficient, they may be pressed to become more so by those mesmerized enough by this cult to try to put efficiency into practice. I sometimes wonder if devotees of efficiency would not do handsprings with joy if all humans were replace by efficient robots that conformed fully to the principles and predictions of the market model (on the other hand, handsprings are probably not an efficient way to exhibit joy, and joy may not itself be an efficient emotion in a marketplace).

In the name of efficiency, businesses may engage in and justify substantial abuse of employees and the environment with the goal of producing the most goods and services possible at the least costs. I have discussed many of the problems this situation poses for employees in an earlier chapter. Employees, however, have the annoying (and from the point of view of followers of the cult of efficiency, possibly immoral and destructive) habit of complaining about the working conditions that efficiency demands. Worse still, they may form unions as political pressure groups in an effort to reform business practices in directions that are less abusive of employees and that are simultaneously more inefficient. Environments, on the other hand, lack any means of organized response to abuse. There simply is nothing within the market model to keep businesses from polluting and destroying vast parts of our environment. Pollution and environmental destruction are problems that lie outside the bounds of *laissez-faire* market dynamics to resolve. Indeed, in typical market model vernacular, they constitute externalities—they are production costs not covered by businesses, but rather they are left to the external public to pay for. What could be more efficient from a business point of view than letting someone else pay for cleaning up and repairing the damage that businesses cause to our environments through their production processes or through the use of the consumer goods that businesses produce?

How significant have the problems of environmental pollution and environmental destruction become in our business-oriented society today? If you have the stomach for it, read on.

Pollution and Environmental Destruction in the Business-Oriented Society

The wonders of mass production and mass markets have given us a standard of living unparalleled in history, but they also have made possible unparalleled mass pollution and mass destruction of our environment. Consider the following:

- By some estimates, our business-oriented society has killed over 80 percent of our forests and 85 percent of our wildlife.[1]
- Our business-oriented society produces between five and six billion metric tons of solid waste each year in order to provide us with the lifestyle we enjoy today.[2] (That is between 20 and 25 metric tons per U.S. citizen, or not quite a half a metric ton per person per week. Has your half metric ton of solid wastes been produced yet this week?)
- Excluding agricultural and mining wastes, disposal costs of wastes are now roughly $8 billion annually and growing, making waste third only to education and highways in service costs.[3]
- Each year our business-oriented society produces sixty billion metal cans, most of which end up in our dumps.[4]
- The standard of living of our business-oriented society requires us to toss about 200 million metric tons of wastes every day into the air as airborne particulate matter and as gases. (That is a bit less than a ton per U.S. citizen per day. Has your metric ton of pollution been tossed into the air yet today?) Major sources of this pollution are automobiles, municipal incinerators, utility companies, and manufacturing industrial plants.[5]
- As a result of air pollution, about half of Canada and much of the Northeastern United States now experience high levels of nitric and sulfuric acid rains, causing approximately $5 billion in damage and contributing to as many as 50,000 fatal illnesses annually.[6]
- Of the roughly thirty to forty-five million tons of toxic pollutants created by industry in the United States each year (which is more than 250 pounds of toxic pollutants per U.S. citizen, or about two-thirds pound per person per day), the EPA estimates that only about 10 percent are disposed of in a safe way.[7]
- The U.S. Environmental Protection Agency has identified roughly 30,000 hazardous waste dumps that pollute surrounding water.[8]

- Each day chemical and petroleum industries in the United States produce 2.5 million pounds of pesticidal and herbicidal poisons and 0.7 million tons of dangerous waste products, all of which end up in our environment.[9]
- The National Cancer Institute estimates that between 60 and 90 percent of all cancers arise from substances we humans have made.[10]

A number of environmental problems in our business-oriented industrial society are receiving increased media attention. Among these are the thinning of the world stratospheric ozone layer, the world greenhouse effect, acid rain, hazardous agricultural practices (soil erosion, fertilizers, insecticides/herbicides), and problems in the disposal of trash and nuclear wastes. A brief review of each topic would be useful for highlighting how extensive and multifaceted the impacts of an industrial economy are on our environment.

The Ozone Hole

The stratospheric ozone layer that encompasses our earth absorbs radiation from the sun (particularly ultraviolet radiation) that would otherwise be harmful to plants and animals. (Some of the effects include disruption of photosynthesis in plants, skin cancers, cataracts, and suppression of the human immune system.) Recent evidence shows that the earth's ozone layer is being destroyed, and a leading cause of its destruction is the emission of chlorofluorocarbons (CFCs) into the environment during industrial production processes and when certain consumer products are used. CFCs were invented in 1930 as a cooling agent and have found many other uses since. They have been widely used in the production of foam plastic, as a coolant in refrigerators and air-conditioners, as a solvent for cleaning metal and electronic parts, and as a propellant in aerosol cans. The United States is a major producer of CFCs, and about a third of all CFCs in the world are used in the United States.[11]

Greenhouse Effect

Another environmental concern centers on a pattern of global warming known as the greenhouse effect. Certain gases emitted by industrial processes and by consumer products build up in the global stratosphere where they trap heat and cause global temperatures to rise. Roughly half of the problem derives from carbon dioxide, which is released through the burning of fossil fuel (oil, coal, gasoline) by industries and through the use of certain consumer products (such as automobiles). CFCs, nitrous oxides, methane, and ozone emissions are also implicated. Agricultural practices (including deforestation and the use of fertilizers), auto exhaust, emissions from trash landfills, and a variety of other industry-related practices are involved. Continued global warming will likely have the effects of melting polar ice caps and glaciers, raising sea levels, flooding coastal and other low-lying land areas, turning the Midwest into a desert, and shifting tropical climates to include areas further north and south of the equator. While substitutes for CFCs to reduce the threat to the ozone layer are now available, the problem of global warming is more intractable largely because of the heavy dependence of industries on the burning of fossil fuels for energy.

Acid Rain

Acid rain is caused by certain gases emitted by production processes and certain consumer products. Foremost is the release of sulfur and nitrogen oxides through the burning of fossil fuels (with the burning of coal causing the greatest problems). When mixed with water vapor, these gases cause acid rains, which kill plants and marine life.

Hazardous Agricultural Practices

Agricultural practices carried out by increasingly larger agri-businesses pose substantial threats to our environment. Soil erosion resulting from plowing, irrigation, and wind and rain erosion has resulted in a dramatic decline in available topsoil in U.S. agricultural areas during the twentieth century. The resulting runoff clogs waterways, kills marine life, and turns previously productive areas into deserts. When fertilizers, insecticides, and herbicides are carried to local water bodies by rain and wind, the result is algae blooms, heavy metal contamination, increasingly "dead" water systems (i.e., water systems that are greatly deficient in marine life), and contaminated ground water supplies.

Trash Disposal

Trash disposal has also become an increasingly difficult problem. Trash dumps leak toxic contaminants into local ground water, may take thousands of years to decompose, give off methane gas, and are near capacity in many parts of the country. A convenience society based on throw-away product containers and short-lived disposable products, is a major source of the problem. Also of significant concern is the disposal of industrial wastes, especially hazardous wastes. The dumping of wastes at sea contaminates our major water bodies and seafood (and results in debris washing up on our shores). Incineration gives off toxic gases and particulate matter (such as dioxin, DDT, lead, mercury, and arsenic) and leave mounds of hazardous ash for disposal. If we don't want these wastes stored close to populated areas or water bodies, we must look at greatly increased shipping expenses to move them to isolated areas.

Nuclear Wastes

Nuclear wastes pose an even more difficult problem. The United States produces about 2,000 tons of nuclear-contaminated heavy metal waste per year[12] (which is only a mere ounce for every four Americans). But disposal is a major problem because radioactive-contaminated materials are highly hazardous and require millions of years to become inert. Currently these wastes are being buried, but shipping and containment costs (and risks) are considerable.

Consumer Products

Although production wastes are major sources of pollution, the products marketed to us also pose major problems. Examples include the automobile, which is a major source of air, noise, and water pollution (in the form of oil in the waterways); refrigerators and air-conditioners, which all eventually leak CFCs; plastics in the form of polyvinyl chlorides (PVCs) and styrofoam; asbestos products; insecticides, herbicides (which contain toxic heavy metals), and fertilizers; and products containing polychlorinated biphenyl (PCBs). Our very homes and lawns have become chemical warehouses and dump sites. And most of us as consumers are too ill-informed to know what hazards are posed by the products we use.

If our business-oriented industrial society had already reached its peak of pollution and environmental destruction and we were now systematically reducing the scope of these problems, we could all rest much easier in our beds tonight. Unfortunately, environmental problems continue to grow larger and larger at an alarming rate. To get a better understanding of this situation, let's consider how pollution and environmental destruction impact on our common environmental heritage and what we have tried to do about this situation.

Safeguarding Our Commons

Common resources are public resources that anyone can use. Air and water are the two primary examples of resources held in common by us all. This is to say that we all own them in common or collectively, and no one person is permitted to lay claim of private ownership over them. In contrast to private property, these resources are public or common property.

Now consider this. Suppose you owned some private property adjacent to a common river. It would only be natural for you to draw off as much water as you needed from the river to, say, water your crops or use in a factory that is situated on your land. You have as much right to the water of the common river as anyone else, don't you? Furthermore, what simpler means of disposing of your wastes is there than to toss them all into the river?[13] Or maybe you could burn some of your wastes and let the wind blow the resulting gases and particulate matter away to wherever (maybe over the rainbow). Suppose everybody did this? What would the quality of the river water, underground water, and air become? It would be like America has become in the twentieth century.

Water

The dumping of raw sewage and other wastes into rivers historically has been a major contributor to epidemics of typhoid, yellow fever, cholera, and dysentery as well as for most fish kills. By the late 1800s (which is within the lifetime of our grandparents or great-grandparents and during the early phase of industrialization in the United States), the situation was already getting so bad in many major water bodies that something had to be done. Congress responded by enacting the Rivers and Harbors Act of 1890 (and amendments to it known as the Refuse Act of 1899) to regulate obstructions to water navigation and to bar private individuals from throwing their refuse into rivers without federal permit. Unfortunately, little or no enforcement of the provisions of the legislation occurred until 1970.

Most serious efforts to stop water pollution began only within the lifetime of most of us (or of our parents). The Water Pollution Control Act of 1948, for example, permitted the federal government to investigate and conduct research on water pollution problems, but left to the states primary responsibility for pollution control. Amendments to this Act in 1956 provided grants for the construction of municipal water treatment plants.

In 1965 the Water Quality Act provided somewhat stronger federal enforcement powers over polluters, and in 1966 the Clean Water Restoration Act sought not only better control over sources of oil discharges into water but also sought to facilitate the setting of regional standards for water pollution. In 1970 the Water Quality Improvement Act set up regulations for sewage and waste discharges from ships and from mines. Then in 1972, new amendments to the Water Pollution Control Act set in motion limits to be set on individual sources of pollution and greatly increased funding for municipal waste treatment plants. (Further amendments to this Act in 1977 strengthened its standards.) In 1974 the Safe Drinking Water Act set regulations on drinking water quality (including on underground water supplies), and the 1987 Clean Water Act amendments added more funding for sewage treatment plants and for waterway cleanup. The Comprehensive Environmental Response, Compensation, and Liability Act of 1980 (and amendments in 1986) set up a superfund and procedures for cleaning up hazardous waste sites, including water systems. Financing for this fund is by corporate taxes and a special tax on chemical and oil producers.

The results of these regulatory efforts have been mixed. Some clean-up of our lakes and rivers has occurred, and about 90 percent of industrial polluters of water now meet federal standards,[14] but many bodies of water remain "dead" or nearly so (i.e., greatly deficient in marine life). Furthermore, chemical pollution continues to constitute a major threat to our water supplies. The disturbing thing is that, once toxic pollutants get into our underground water supplies, there is little we can do to get them back out. Meanwhile, the total amount of our uncontaminated underground water supply is dwindling rapidly.

Air

The first efforts to control air pollution occurred through laws passed by cities in the late 1800s (such as by Chicago and Cincinnati in 1881). Next, states took up the issue of air quality during the twentieth century, particularly in connection with auto exhaust. The federal government became involved only in 1955 with the passage of the Air Pollution Control Act, which authorized federal research on the issue.

The Clean Air Act of 1963 gave some enforcement powers to the federal government, and the 1965 Motor Vehicle Air Pollution Control Act set in motion a process for establishing auto pollution control standards. These standards were finalized in the Air Quality Act of 1967, which also authorized federal oversight of the efforts by states to set air quality standards and implementation plans. Subsequent Clean Air Amendments of 1970, 1977, and 1990 expanded federal powers in setting and enforcing these air quality standards.

The Clean Air Act Amendments of 1990, for example, set pollution standards for power plants that would reduce allowable pollution output to significantly lower levels. An interesting feature of this legislation is that the plants that produce less pollution than allowed by the standards may sell their unused allowable pollution allotment to plants that produce more pollution than allowed. In other words, a market has been created for pollution production allowances. Other provisions set stricter standards on ozone-depleting chemicals and on the release of nearly 200 toxic chemicals.

In some respects the regulatory efforts undertaken over the past three decades related to air quality have been successful, particularly in reducing airborne particulate matter, sulfur dioxide, nitrogen dioxide, and lead.[15] The greatest success can be attributed to the use of pollution control devices and unleaded gasoline in our automobiles However, air quality remains a serious problem in major urban areas, with a fifth of U.S. counties being out of compliance with federal guidelines.[16] Acid rain continues to be a major threat to wilderness areas, and limited efforts have been made to restrict greenhouse gas emissions.

The Environmental Protection Agency

By the late 1960s the increasing concern over our environment and the number of laws already passed on this issue resulted in pressure to create a new federal agency to consolidate federal pollution control efforts. The National Environmental Policy Act of 1969 created the Council on Environmental Quality to recommend national policies on the environment in annual reports to the President and to oversee environmental impact statements for federally assisted projects. In the following year, 1970, President Nixon, with congressional consent (Reorganization Plan No. 3), created the Environmental Protection Agency (EPA).

The legal charge of the EPA, with expansion over the ensuing years, includes: setting up regulatory procedures for enforcing the Clean Air, Clean Water and Safe Drinking Water Acts; monitoring solid waste management in accordance with the Resource Conservation and Recovery Act; setting and enforcing pesticide regulations in accordance with the Federal Insecticide, Fungicide and Rodenticide Act; setting and enforcing noise pollution regulations in accordance with the Noise Control Act; setting and enforcing toxic substance regulations in accordance with the Toxic Substances Control Act; setting and enforcing regulations to protect marine life from the dumping of toxic waste, as required by the Marine Protection, Research and Sanctuaries Act; overseeing toxic waste site cleanup pursuant to the Comprehensive Environmental Response, Compensation and Liability Act; and selected issues related to other environmental concerns such as for radiation contamination, food contamination, and so forth.

The EPA has been a controversial, highly political, and not especially effective vehicle for controlling environmental pollution. This was especially true during the Reagan administration's contribution to the deregulatory movement, when Anne Gorsuch Burford was named to head up the EPA (but was later forced to resign under controversy). During this time the EPA budget was slashed and Rita Lavelle was put in charge of the Superfund cleanup programs (but later sentenced to six months in jail for lying under oath about cleanup efforts). The ineffectiveness of the EPA is illustrated too by the observation that, as of 1990, twenty years after it was created, the EPA had issued regulatory standards on only seven of the hundreds of toxic chemicals used in manufacturing in the United States.[17]

Nonetheless, the costs imposed on businesses by federal regulations on pollution have been considerable. For example, by one estimate, pollution control and abatement efforts in the U.S. cost a total of more than $100 billion in just the four-year period from 1980 to 1983. The total cost in 1983 alone, $62 billion, represented roughly 2.6 percent of our GNP, or about $300 per person in the United States. The additional costs to car owners of auto-related pollution control regulations in 1983 alone was estimated at approximately $11 billion.[18] All of these costs, of course, are passed along to you and me as consumers and necessarily reduce our standard of living, so we find ourselves able to buy less than before with our money.

In summary, businesses have no incentives on their own to do anything about the wholesale pollution of our environment, governmental efforts to force businesses to behave more responsibly have been lackluster, and meanwhile our environment continues to deteriorate in ways that may be irrevocable. Is this too a cost (perhaps our final cost) of living in the business-oriented society?

Resource Depletion

Having identified several major issues related to environmental pollution in the business-oriented society, I turn your attention here to the topic of resource depletion. Industrialized economies require massive amounts of resources from our environment to produce the goods and services available to us today. Energy sources (coal, oil, gas) and a large assortment of metals, minerals, and other raw materials are needed. Logically a time will come, however, when these resources will become depleted.

Here is a simple way to begin thinking about resource depletion. Suppose you had ten large, mature trees in your back yard. The first year you cut down one tree for firewood, which met your energy needs for the year. The next year you cut down another for firewood, and the year after that you cut down yet another, and so on. In your tenth year you cut down the last of the fine old trees. Now what will you do? You of course planted one new tree during each year that you were cutting down one of the big old ones. So in your eleventh year you now have ten immature trees. Even after you cut them all down you don't have enough firewood, so you knock down your woodshed and picket fence as well for firewood in your eleventh year. But what are you going to do next year?

A parallel to this simple illustration can be found in the history of deforestation worldwide. The slash-and-burn clearing of forests is a farming practice that is quite common and quite old in human history. However, truly large-scale deforestation is much more modern. The process of clearing trees from land for the purposes of farming and to use the wood in construction and as a fuel has resulted in the decimation of much of the forests of Europe over the last few centuries. As wood, a previously cheap, renewable, natural resource, became more scarce, some European countries, such as England, turned in the 16th and 17th centuries to burning coal. Coal is a more expensive, nonrenewable resource that creates significantly more air pollution. Coal, however, has played a key role in fueling industrialization and continues to be a principal source of energy in our society. It is believed that coal is sufficiently plentiful in nature to last us several hundred years before it too is gone.

The settlers "timbered" their way across our continent, turning woodlands into fields and pastures for cash crops and livestock, and destroying most of our native forests in the process. Even now, the wholesale destruction of the rain forests of South America is underway largely to serve the needs of cattle ranchers who desire cheap grazing land to raise the beef that is sold on buns in fast food industries in the United States.[19] It may be that "only God can make a tree," but such trifles as trees do not stand in the way of the commercial interests of a business-oriented society.

The destruction of the earth's forests is just one example of resource depletion in the business-oriented society. All of the other material resources that we derive from nature to feed our commercial production processes are finite and are being depleted. Here is a simple way to conceptualize what is happening. Suppose all of the copper (or aluminum or oil or "what have you") that existed in the world were put into a big bucket, and each year we took out as much as we needed to maintain our current industrialized standard of living. Eventually we are going to reach the bottom of the bucket. Even if we try to recycle as much as we can, some, and probably most, will be lost to recycling, and we will still reach the bottom of the bucket. When the resources that are needed to maintain our industrial lifestyle are used up or are no longer easily accessible, what will we do? What will our lifestyles become? What will our children and grandchildren do? What will their lifestyles be?

Thoughts such as these led a group of intellectuals to use computer simulations and mathematical models to project how much longer we might have before we run out of many of the important metals, fuels, and minerals that we need in an industrialized society. Their findings were published in 1972 as the report *The Limits to Growth.*[20]

Based on estimates available at that time of all existing major world resources, and under the assumption of no future growth in demand for these resources, these researchers predicted in 1972 that by 1993 we would have used up the entire known world's supply of gold, mercury, silver, tin, and zinc. By contrast, assuming an exponential growth in demand, an assumption they favored, they predicted that by 1993 we would also have run out of copper, lead, natural gas, and petroleum and would be near to exhausting our world supplies for aluminum and tungsten.

In fact, we have not run out of any of these natural resources (though our government has taken copper out of our pennies because of the decreasing relative value of the penny in comparison to the value of copper). Obviously the estimates that were used were wrong, particularly about the amounts of resources that exist in the world. However, as these authors pointed out, even if actual amounts of these resources were five times larger than believed at the time of their estimates, at an exponential rate of usage we still would run out of fifteen of the most important resources we need for our industrialized society within twenty-nine to ninety-six years. The point is, returning to my simple bucket analogy, eventually we will run out, and if not in our own lifetimes (though this is quite likely for some resources), than certainly within the lifetimes of our children and grandchildren.

Industry in the United States is estimated to require $140 billion in new metals each year. Only roughly 10 percent of these metals are currently imported.[21] But just as we are now dependent on world oil supplies, we will witness a growing dependence of our economy on the resources of the Third World as we use up our own natural supply of metals. Our usage of world resources is already substantial. With less than 5 percent of the world population, it is estimated that we nonetheless use between 14 to 63 percent of the world's production of a number of the major resources used in industry (such as manganese, coal, tungsten, tin, silver, zinc, copper, molybdenum, nickel, aluminum, petroleum, and natural gas).[22]

What do you think is likely to happen as we come closer to exhausting the available supply of these resources? Certainly recycling will gain increasing importance. In addition, prices are going to increase, and our standard of living necessarily will decline. Then too, what do you think will be our military stance toward other countries that have the largest remaining reserves of these resources? (Our recent involvement in the Gulf War to preserve our interests in Middle East oil might be an example.) As "underdeveloped" countries try to industrialize and in the process create a new, even larger source of demand on these remaining resources, what impact do you think this will have on known world resources and on our international relations? I don't like speculating on these issues, do you? But these issues will inevitably command more and more of our attention. (I do, in fact, speculate on these issues in Chapter 14.)

What Can Business, Government, and Science Do?

Businesses, as I noted before, did not invent environmental pollution and resource depletion, nor are they solely responsible for them today. Nonetheless, they are a central source of these problems and, therefore, must become central players in attempts to address them.

In this section I examine the relative roles of science, technology, business, and government in posing solutions to the environmental problems of the business-oriented society.

Will Science and Technology Save Us?

Perhaps new technologies and scientific breakthroughs will find substitutes for depleted resources and find ways to decontaminate our environment. Scientists, after all, are often regarded as being extremely smart, and often they do things that appear to be miraculous. Surely science and technology can save us from whatever environmental problems our businesses and our business-oriented life-styles are creating for us, our children, and our grandchildren.

One can take either a psychological or a sociological view of science. From a psychological perspective, science is a way of thinking in which conceptual frameworks are created that contain as many empirically confirmable referents as is possible. Our task as scientists then is to confirm with our observation whatever claims we may draw from our conceptual framework.

From a sociological perspective, however, science is a social phenomenon—it is a means for organizing behaviors, thoughts, and emotions according to the standards (the scripts) of a scientific community. As is true for any social phenomenon, science is interwoven with other sectors of society in ways that frequently serve their mutual needs. But, as I point out in Chapter 1, the most powerful sectors of society are more likely to have their needs served at the expense of the other sectors than vice versa. Furthermore, the means by which relations among social sectors arise and by which needs are defined and met are, of course, political in nature. As is true for any social phenomenon, then, science is driven by political pressures.

In our society, as I have taken pains throughout this book to detail, the most powerful social sector is that of businesses. And the needs of businesses are those that shape the politics of society, the nature of its social phenomena, and their interrelations. Science, then, though not created by businesses, nonetheless has developed in a fashion that largely serves the needs of businesses in a business-oriented society.

Under such circumstances, can we reasonably look to science to save us from the abuses created by businesses and our business orientation? Hardly. Rather, science has been the devoted servant of businesses in the exploitation, destruction, and pollution of our environment. And scientists have little reason to do otherwise. Outside of the health sciences, rarely does one find in science the view that scientists are supposed to be saviors of humankind (though sometimes a sociologist or an economist may conceive of himself or herself as having such a calling).

Unless forced to do so by governments, businesses have no particular reason to hire scientists specifically for the purposes of developing pollution-control systems or for designing ways to clean up production-related environmental pollution. Pollution, after all, is conceived by businesses to be an externality, so it is natural to take the attitude that the government should worry about it, not businesses.

Not only do scientists lack any particular intrinsic motivation to try to save us, or any political pressure to do so, but scientific and technological advances often carry their own untoward effects. Scientific and technological advances, after all, have brought us mustard gas, nerve gas, mind incapacitating drugs (e.g., LSD), napalm, guided missiles, and, perhaps "best" of all, the nuclear bomb. Where would warfare be today if not for science? Science and technology have also brought us ozone-eating chlorofluorocarbons, groundwater contaminating carcinogenic chemicals, forest- and lake-killing acid rains, and even silicon-leaking breast implants. Surely we can conclude from these examples that science and technology possess no divine guidance to work single-mindedly for our welfare.

Science, rather, is best conceived of as a social tool with powers often considerably greater than those of a crystal ball or talisman, but far short of those of a benevolent, attentive, and paternal god. As a social tool it may be used, or may not be used, as the political forces of our time dictate. It neither offers guarantee of successful results nor warrantee against unexpected and undesirable outcomes. What is lacking today is political pressure to put science to work on problems of pollution and environmental restoration. I comment further on this issue in a later section.

What Can Businesses Do?

A good many of the problems of environmental pollution, environmental destruction, and resource depletion are intertwined with business operations, so we should expect a socially responsible business to do something about them. With small businesses there is no mechanism internal to the businesses to monitor and self-correct business actions on these issues. Consequently the small businessperson is dependent on his or her insight and intrinsic motivation, if any, to determine ways that his or her business may adversely impact the environment and to determine strategies for reducing these impacts. Because this is expecting too much of small businesspersons, there is no alternative but for governments to provide regulatory oversight.

A point made in Chapter 8 about corporate businesses, however, is that they do have the internal organizational apparatus to provide their own oversight and initiative if they choose to do so. Assuming that environmental pollution/destruction becomes a part of the scorecard on which senior management is judged by independent corporate boards, as described in Chapter 8, then we could expect a far more serious and aggressive review of environmental issues to occur within corporations. Additional steps that a corporation might take include appointing an appropriate environmentalist to the corporate board, creating a vice-president for environmental issues, conducting regular environmental audits detailing the effects of their business on the physical environment, including environmental impact assessments in all research and development efforts, marketing services to consumers for the safe disposal or recycling of their products, and finding markets for their production wastes.[23] An incentive system may be necessary because the efforts to create environmentally sound production systems and product designs may make a company's products uncompetitive with those of companies that do not undertake a comparable effort. Incentives might take the form of a reduction or elimination of corporate taxes on environmentally conscious companies.

None of the measures identified here are satisfactory or sufficient in themselves, however, because environmental problems by their nature cut across the borders of nations. Therefore, a worldwide response is needed. This is most easily seen when resource depletion is examined. Businesses have no particular reason to do anything about resource depletion until the increasing scarcity of a resource drives up the costs of production to the point at which it is no longer profitable to continue production. If a substitute can be easily found or invented, fine. If not, the reasonable business decision is simply to switch to producing some other more profitable product or service.

Likewise, as businesses in different countries, and governments on their behalf, vie for remaining world resources, military confrontation becomes more likely. Then too, countries that require stringent ecological standards for their businesses can very well expect to lose world market share, to lose industry and jobs, and to experience a decline in standard of living relative to other countries that do not set equivalent standards. Furthermore, even if the most rigorous environmental standards on earth are enforced within a country, what will stop toxic pollutants from coming across its borders by water or air from other countries that have not set these standards.[24] (One should consider here, too, the global problems of ozone depletion and global warming.)

In short, though responsible businesses could do a good deal on their own about environmental problems, and though federal incentives may facilitate such actions, the nature of these problems cry out for international standards, monitoring, and enforcement. A step in this direction is indicated by the signing of two international agreements (the 1985 Vienna Convention on the Protection of the Ozone Layer and the 1987 Montreal Protocol) to try to eliminate the use of chlorofluorocarbons (CFCs) by the year 2000. In 1987 the international Brundtland Conference was sponsored by the United Nations to discuss how economic growth (i.e., jobs, income, and standards of living) can be promoted worldwide while nonetheless establishing proper safeguards for the environment. It has become increasingly obvious that efforts devoted to economic growth worldwide carry a cost in terms of an environmental capital that may not be replaceable, and that it is important to marshal wisely for the good of generations to come.

In Europe, where countries are so close as to have many "commons" (water and air), a green political movement has developed over the course of the past two decades. In the 1990s this movement has resulted in efforts by the European Union (EU) to create a unified European Environmental Agency. Many environmental regulations have been issued by the EU to member countries, but adequate oversight and enforcement mechanisms have been lacking. In 1993 a voluntary Eco-Management and Audit Scheme was devised to promote environmental goals, management, and evaluating systems among European-based corporate operations.

Additional international conferences in 1989 and in the early 1990s focused on ozone depletion and on the greenhouse effect. The Bush administration, while supportive of efforts to eliminate CFCs, balked at proposals to limit carbon dioxide emissions if this effort adversely affected U.S. economic growth. In the 170-country Earth Summit that was held in Rio de Janeiro in 1992, an international treaty was signed on global warming. Bush was successful in having targets and timetables removed from this treaty that would limit carbon dioxide and other greenhouse emissions.

It is evident that a worldwide effort is evolving, pushed principally by business-oriented societies, to design and agree on a common set of standards to set limits on the environmental pollution that is to be permitted either by production processes or from the use and disposal of consumer products. To be successful, I believe, a global social mechanism is needed that will monitor and enforce these standards and that will impose fines on nations where random checks show violations of these standards. These fines, paid by nations, could be used to create a world fund for programs for pollution control, pollution containment, and pollution cleanup.

The world monitoring and enforcement mechanism that I am envisioning could leave it to nations to design and implement their own internal mechanisms for meeting agreed-upon world standards. With national standards conforming to world standards, my own preference would be for nations then to let their businesses have as much freedom of action as possible in deciding how to meet national standards, while heavily fining those that do not (and using these fines to pay the world fines). The merit of this whole system is that it would produce a level playing field, so all companies within the same industry would encounter pretty much the same production costs related to safeguarding our environment no matter where they set up shop. As a consequence, a competitive edge could not be gained by any company by failing to protect our environment.

Could such a system be corrupted and rendered ineffective? I have every confidence in human ingenuity and deviance that we will be successful in corrupting such a system. Be that as it may, what alternative do we have?

Won't we all take a cut in our standard of living by adding environmental protection and cleanup costs to production? Yes, but maybe we can feel good again about the world we are handing to our children and grandchildren.

For resource depletion I suggest that we create a corollary world program that draws up an agreed-upon list of endangered metals, minerals, and fuels that the world will run out of within fifty or so years. Then a special tax could be imposed on the use of these materials, with the revenues going into a world fund to be used for finding or inventing suitable substitutes or for improving recycling programs. If all users of these materials are taxed, then again a level playing field will be created for distributing these costs so that no company gains a marketing advantage. Then too, as these funds are used to finance scientific research and technological development, a political mechanism will have been created to push scientists to save us, if our salvation is possible.

Vice President Al Gore proposed a similar global political effort in his book, *Earth in the Balance.*[25] Just as the Marshall Plan sought to create political stability and economic recovery in war-ravaged Europe, Gore proposes that we need the equivalent of a new Global Marshall Plan that would essentially involve a set of international agreements to set and meet common environmental standards. His plan, however, proposed no central social mechanisms for monitoring and enforcing the standards that are determined. I do not see how we can avoid such a mechanism.

In summary, the environmental problems created by the rise of industrial economies require global solutions. World political responses are now in the process of evolving in an attempt to address these problems. In the next chapter I examine business activities more closely in the world context

C h a p t e r 13

Businesses in International Perspective

International Exploitation and Business-Oriented Society

Our business-oriented society is built on a pattern of international relations that has been highly exploitative of people around the world. Intersocietal exploitation, however, is certainly not a recent invention in the history of human affairs.

Hunting and gathering societies appear to have had minimal recourse to warfare, plunder, enslavement, and domination of peoples from other societies. However, intersocietal exploitation was quite common in agricultural societies. Indeed, the history of agricultural peoples shows them to have endured a seemingly endless succession of wars intended for plunder and empire building. The great civilizations of the past, those of the Mediterranean, India, China, and South and Central America, arose as empires of intersocietal exploitation involving plunder, enslavement, vassalage, and tribute.

Business-oriented societies, therefore, are not the inventors of intersocietal exploitation, but rather have built on and expanded in novel ways the exploitative practices of antiquity. Chapter 5 describes the rise of the business-oriented societies through the colonial and mercantile practices that carried the dominant European powers of the time around the globe in search of riches and trade routes. Much of the world (both the Old World of Africa and Asia and the New World of North and South America) fell conquest to these European colonizers. The amount of suffering inflicted on peoples from diverse cultures around the world as a result of these mercantile and colonial efforts staggers the imagination, while Europeans enjoyed from it such pleasantries as tea and coffee sweetened with sugar; chocolate cake; a good smoke; light, pretty cotton and silk clothing; spices to enhance the taste of their food; fine beaver fur hats; gold and silver trinkets; and many other sundries and amusements to enhance their civilized lifestyles.

271

Manifest Destiny

Our own U.S. society, born of mercantile and colonial practices, followed what it eventually proclaimed as its "manifest destiny" of intersocietal exploitation. First the English-American foreparents of our society seized the east coast of the North American continent from the Native American societies that occupied it. They then purchased European-recognized legal rights to much of our Midwest from France and proceeded to seize these lands from the Native American societies that resided on them.

After the United States was formed as an European-recognized political and legal entity, other European colonies contiguous to the United States were not spared from expansionism. Our attempts to seize Canada to the north were foiled both in our Revolutionary War and in the War of 1812. Mexico to the southwest of the United States, subsequent to winning its freedom from Spain, was not so fortunate. After many years of U.S. immigration and settlement in the northeastern sector of Mexico, immigrants from the United States staged a revolution to create Texas out of a piece of Mexico. Then, following on a flow of U.S. immigrants into Mexican territory further west and following other U.S. provocations, the United States declared war with Mexico. After crushing the Mexican military forces, the United States forced Mexico to sign the Treaty of Guadalupe Hidalgo in 1848 giving over to the victor all of northern Mexico (what we now call the Southwest United States). Suddenly, Mexicans in formerly northern Mexico became aliens in their own land.

Ironically, to this day we actively guard against Mexican wetbacks who would dare to sneak into old Northern Mexico. The term *wetback* comes from the act of swimming across the Rio Grande, which separates much of the present-day United States from present-day Mexico.

United States diplomacy, enunciated in the Monroe Doctrine, has made South and Central America into our own quasi-colonial backyard. Many of the banana republics that we have helped to create and maintain in our hemisphere provide us with a bountiful supply of cheap agricultural products to elevate our standard of living to a grand level, while the bulk of the people of these countries live at subsistence levels and under conditions of few or no human rights. Their suffering has been our gain, and their suffering continues as a support to keep our economy strong and our lifestyle high.

Developing Global Economic Interests

Our own industrialization, coupled with the abundant resources available on the lands that we had seized and put together in forming the present-day United States, have made us into a major economic power. But so, too, did our role in World Wars I and II, as we became in these worldwide conflagrations a major war profiteer in the export of war-related materials. Then the decimation of the European economic base, especially during the massive bombing of World War II, left the United States not only as the only intact industrial power to export goods to meet world demand, but also provided the United States with a great many opportunities to make industrial investments in post-war Europe. The result was a great acceleration of what has been called the "American invasion," a period of time from the late 1800s to the present when U.S. companies and U.S. investors came to control larger and larger portions of the economies of many European countries.

In short, we emerged from World War II as the most powerful economy in the world, with economic relations (including investments and trade) that encompassed the globe and made much of the industrial and resource exporting world dependent on our economy. Because we were isolated from Europe, Africa, and Asia by two oceans and did not possess a ruling nobility concerned with enhancing their international prestige through political empire building, we lacked two of the primary sources of motivation for political seizure and rule over people not contiguous to our land borders. Rather, our principal motivations in world affairs have been largely economic.

Not possessing a particularly apt political structure for the active promotion of mercantile policies (such as a monarchy provides), our international relations have been driven in large part by the many diverse, and occasionally conflicting, interests of particular businesses in our industrial economy. The multinational corporation is particularly important in this regard.

The Multinational Corporation

Corporations, of course, are chartered by legal authorities (such as nations or states) to possess certain legal rights, including the right to own property and the right to enter into legally binding contracts. Thus corporations have a home base in the legal jurisdiction that confers on them their legal rights as corporations. Industrial corporations, however, have the potential to produce goods in such mass quantities that they quite naturally seek to find or to create correspondingly large mass markets through sales efforts made beyond the legal jurisdiction of their home base. This dual effort of mass production and mass marketing creates economies of scale that can greatly facilitate the competitiveness and profitability of a corporation.

In the United States, for example, business interests wishing to incorporate often choose as their home base of legal jurisdiction a state such as Delaware or New Jersey that sets minimal restrictions on corporations. The products they peddle, however, typically reach national markets.

These national markets lend to us as a people a cohesiveness and homogeneity of life interests that is far more comprehensive and profound than anything resulting from current actions by our federal government (or our churches). Thus increasingly throughout this century we have been pulled ever closer together as a common people in possession of a common identity because of the effects of these large corporations on our economy (e.g., we almost all eat the same commercially prepared foods; wear the same in-fashion, off-the-rack clothing; watch the same top box office movies and television shows; read the same newspapers, magazines, and top-seller books; drive the same types of cars; shop at the same national chain stores; revere the same commercial icons, such as McDonalds; and so on).

In the pursuit of a mass national market, it is natural for corporations to seek to reduce their distribution costs whenever possible by setting up production plants at several locations in the United States. Such an organization of business operations might be called a multistate corporation; the multinational corporation is just a variation on this basic model.

Pressures to Go International

A number of pressures operate to drive large businesses into international markets. First, as noted here, the mass production capacities of industrial corporations only become profitable when combined with mass markets, and this fact motivates industrial corporations to seek new markets wherever in the world they can be found or created. A multinational sales effort, then, is one distinguishing feature of a business that is being transformed into a multinational corporation.

Costs and Political Pressures

Costs involved in transporting goods to another country and in paying import tariffs may be substantial, however. Then too the effects of a large number of imports on the economies of countries in which sales are to be made may be so adverse as to make such sales politically unwelcome, possibly moving the political authorities of these countries to set severe import restrictions. Consequently, in the process of creating a worldwide sales effort, there is a natural evolution of pressures placed on corporations to set up on-site production plants in the countries or regions of the world in which sales are to occur. This step toward the development of a worldwide network of production facilities is often deemed to be the most important factor in deciding to say of a corporation that it is truly multinational.[1]

Raw Materials

A third pressure operating to drive corporations into international markets is the need for raw materials. Mining, agricultural, and other resource-gathering ventures often must be undertaken by large corporations on a worldwide basis in order to feed their ever-churning mass production systems. U.S. corporations, for example, have gone worldwide in search of oil, fruit, and beef, to name a few products needed to keep our industries and markets perking along and to keep our standard of living high.

Labor Costs

A fourth pressure operating to drive corporations into international markets is the search for cheap labor. Why pay American workers the wage they would need to maintain a "decent" lifestyle by American standards if one can pay persons living in almost absolute squalor in the Third World next to nothing for doing the same work? The great savings in labor costs translates into a fat profit for the corporation and into lower prices in the sale of goods in international markets. Although the lost jobs and lost wages of American workers decreases market demand at home (unemployed people are not buying automobiles, electric products, and so on), everyone else at home (other than the workers who lost their jobs) enjoys an elevated standard of living because products are priced cheaper. Even the Third World workers may enjoy a slightly elevated standard of living, so long as they remain healthy enough to work.

Restrictive Home-Base Regulations

A fifth pressure driving corporations into international markets are restrictive regulations placed on them by their home base governments concerning how they treat employees, communities, and the environment. The many federal regulatory efforts described in earlier chapters in this book, for example, may make it difficult for corporations to operate their businesses in the United States, so why should they bother? By moving production plants abroad, business managers may be able to work foreign employees for long hours under dangerous conditions at low pay, pollute the environment with impunity, and pretty much have their way with local communities. Then the business may be able to ship its goods back to its home country at lower costs and bigger profits. Is this a description of *laissez-faire* business paradise, or what?

Lucrative Inducements

A sixth pressure driving corporations into international markets is that the political leadership of many countries may be very eager for corporations to set up production processes in their countries as a means to simulate their economy, create jobs for their people, and possibly enrich their personal bank accounts. This eagerness may result in them offering a number of lucrative inducements to businesses to relocate or expand operations in their country.

Other Reasons

There are yet other reasons for businesses to go international: to expand conglomerate holdings by the purchase of foreign companies, to find markets with little competition and, therefore, more potential for profits than is provided by the market in one's home country, to keep in step with competitors who have already made a move on international markets, to establish operations close to major corporate buyers of one's products and services who have already set up foreign plants, and so on. All of these factors have combined to make the contemporary era one that we may call the age of the multinational corporation and to make multinational corporations important players in international relations and in international exploitation. A survey of top business leaders in U.S. international companies conducted by the U.S. Department of Commerce found that the principal reasons given for international expansion were the desires to increase markets and to avoid transportation and tariff costs in shipping products.[2]

American Investment Abroad

Probably the first corporation to reach multinational status was Singer in 1867, when it built production facilities in several countries to manufacture sewing machines. International corporations thereafter multiplied in number as a result of several inventions: the invention of rapid means of transportation to move goods from country to country (such as by railroads and steamships), the invention of rapid means of communication to make possible bureaucratic corporate control over production and sales efforts as they are carried out on an international scale (i.e., by telegraphs, radios, and telephones) and developments in worldwide currency standards to facilitate commercial transactions (e.g., the gold standard, the dollar standard, or the floating of currencies in an international currency market).

As a result of the American invasion of investments in Europe, approximately 80 percent of U.S. multinational corporate capital that is invested outside of the United States is now invested in production and commercial processes in Western Europe; about 10 percent is invested in the newly industrializing countries of Brazil, Taiwan, Korea, and Singapore; and about 5 percent each is invested in the OPEC countries and in the other developing countries around the world.[3] There are roughly 300 major multinational corporations in the world today, with industrial giants such as IBM having about half of its sales in foreign markets. By the early 1980s, U.S. multinational corporations collectively held about $500 billion in assets, accounted for more than $200 billion in foreign investments, and contributed roughly one-third of the gross world product.[4] The dependence of the U.S. economy on exports is considerable, with more than 16 percent of U.S. manufacturing jobs directly depending on exports and roughly 40 percent of U.S. agricultural products being exported.[5] By the mid-1980s, exports and imports amounted to nearly one-fourth of the total U.S. GNP.[6]

Problems Posed by Multinational Corporations

Political Problems

One problem posed by multinational corporations is that, as they become more worldly, their allegiance to the national interests of their home country necessarily becomes less. If, for example, great profits can be had by an American-based multinational corporation by producing a product in Brazil for sale in Japan, why should the corporation care "a jot" what is in the best national interest of the American people regarding either country? Or if a multinational can profit from sales to a dictator or political demigod bent on denying human rights (as several companies did in sales to, and production efforts on behalf of, Adolph Hitler's regime prior to World War II), why not?

Furthermore, as these large corporations exert influence over U.S. political affairs, our national interests may themselves become increasingly defined as those that help our multinational corporations to promote and develop their production and distribution systems worldwide. Hence, it has become in our national interests to create and maintain a military presence worldwide and to engage in a number of small-scale wars that have worked principally to further the interests of our multinational corporations (and through them our economy and standard of living).

Multinational corporations in the United States are not in direct control of foreign policy, however, and at times they have found themselves instead becoming tools of the foreign policy set by our political leaders. This was seen, for example, in the trading sanctions that have on occasion been imposed by political leaders in the United States on certain socialist and Third World countries, but which have worked considerably to the detriment of U.S. businesses. A recent example was Reagan's embargo on high technology equipment sales for use in construction of the Soviet gas pipeline.

Then too multinational corporations may be subjected to intense political pressure from the host countries in which they set up their production or sales operations, so that they may become simultaneously squeezed by the political demands of both the host and home base countries. For example, when Reagan ordered U.S. companies not to sell high technology products to the Soviet Union, Dressler's French subsidiary was ordered by the

French government to proceed with such sales. Dressler, a U.S. based multinational corporation, was stuck in the middle.

Finally, multinational corporations face the ever present risk of having their property expropriated or confiscated in revolutions that may occur in host countries. For example in its 1959–1960 revolution, Cuba nationalized $1.5 billion in U.S. business assets.

Other Problems for Multinational Corporations

Multinational corporations face many other types of problems in setting up sales, investment, and production operations abroad. One major problem concerns the differences in cultural practices between host and home base countries. Because of these differences, products, production systems, financial arrangements, management systems, sales strategies, and many other facets of business that work well in the home country may not work at all, or may work badly, in the host country. For example, cultures frequently vary in how time is treated as a social commodity, with U.S. culture tending to be more clock oriented and clock-time efficient than other cultures. As a result, people in host countries are often seen by Americans as lazy, inefficient, or irresponsible, a situation which poses a considerable management problem in designing business operations that return a profit. Likewise other cultures may be more family oriented, kinship loyal, group oriented, sexist, authoritarian, oriented to nonverbal communication, or to basing their business decisions on friendships rather than on economic considerations. These proclivities, too, pose major management problems for American multinational corporations.

The only realistic solution to problems posed by cultural differences is for the multinational corporation to be fully prepared to adjust business practices, sometimes radically, to fit within host country conventions. This is a solution business leaders from the United States have been notoriously slow to pursue, with the result of lost world market opportunities. In some cases, however, U.S. laws bar their participation in local customs. An example is the barring of bribery by the Foreign Corrupt Practices Act (to be discussed later).

Management Difficulties

A second related problem facing multinational corporations is the difficulty involved in establishing an effective management team in the host country facilities. U.S. managers often experience severe culture shock when relocated to a host country, with the result that their effectiveness as managers is seriously degraded. On the other hand, it may be exceedingly difficult to find qualified local personnel in the host country to hire onto the management team.

Legal Differences

A third problem derives from differences in the legal and domestic policing environments between host and home countries. These differences may pose a great threat to the safety of corporate investments and personnel. In addition, multinational corporations may find that a lack of a uniform international legal system poses special problems. For example, U.S. antitrust laws bar our multinational corporations from forming cartels to monopolize international markets. The legal systems of other countries are not so restricting, with the result that international cartels in oil, in electronic products, and in other goods and services are able to gain hold of large world market shares. Then too, the governments of other countries are not only far more likely than ours to own outright major domestic industries, but also are more likely to subsidize certain of their industries heavily, with the result again that their businesses in these industries may be able to underbid ours in international competition.

Currency Fluctuations

A fourth problem concerns currency fluctuations. Rapid fluctuations in the value of host country currencies relative to that of home country currency may seriously erode profitability—or may greatly enhance it. Multinational business, therefore, may become as much a matter of financial management relative to currency fluctuation as it is a matter of producing and selling goods.

Problems for the Host Country

Multinational corporations may bring many benefits to a host country. For example, they may reduce local unemployment, bring in new investment capital, create a favorable balance of trade (to the degree that they export the goods they produce rather than simply sell them in the local market), elevate the national standard of living, and bring in new technology and skills that could benefit other sectors of the local economy.

On the other hand, multinational corporations may pose many problems for the host country. They may create considerable unrest among local workers if intense competition occurs for the limited jobs they provide and if rising expectations for an improved standard of living are unmet. They may displace large numbers of workers from jobs in other necessary industries in the country (e.g., agriculture) and may hire away all available local talent so that there are fewer talented people available for other important social functions.

Multinational corporations may also soak up all available local capital, leaving too little for other important economic and social purposes. They may deplete local natural resources and engage in extensive pollution of the environment. Furthermore, they may form a local monopoly in the sale of their products and may buy up other local firms so that they gain a stranglehold on the local economy; through their controls on pricing they may then become a major inflationary force in the host country. They may also simply produce goods for host country consumption, resulting in a decrease in the balance of trade for the host country and sending resulting profits back to the corporate headquarters of the home country (in effect they may soak up whatever wealth may be found in the host country and ship it back to the home country).

Multinational corporations also may not permit enough local control over their operations (for example by failure to hire locals into local senior management positions) or they may not train locals in advanced skills that would enhance the local economy as such persons move on into positions in other businesses elsewhere in the economy. They may ignore or seriously violate local customs, causing adverse reactions from local people and possible political and religious unrest. And, as noted earlier, they may intrude on local politics (such as ITT's role in the overthrow of President Allende of Chile) or they may become an instrument of U.S. foreign policy to bludgeon the host country to do the bidding of the United States.

"When in Rome": The Problem of International Corruption

As noted in Chapters 2 and 3 and described throughout this book, businesses are intricately intertwined with the other sectors of the society in which they operate. Consequently, the propriety of business practices is defined against the backdrop of the interests and conventions of these other sectors, and businesses have social responsibilities for the welfare of these other sectors whenever their practices impinge on them. The complexity of any one society, such as ours, is considerable, and the determination of what constitutes the social responsibilities of businesses in our society is, therefore, made equally complex as a result. But now imagine making these determinations in a multinational context, in which the characteristics and social conventions of the various sectors of societies vary enormously one from another. How are multinational businesses to know what are the socially responsible policies to pursue under such circumstances?

A good example of this problem is that of the hullabaloo over foreign business bribes. As a foundation for discussing this issue, let's consider how bribes work in everyday life.

Bribery and extortion play important roles in all sectors of our society. For example, we learn the etiquette of bribery early in our lives as our parents bribe us to do their bidding by offering us some special favor. We also learn as children how to extort such favors through promises of being good or through threats of being bad if the favors are not forthcoming.

Bribery and extortion also operate in other family relations, as for example when we deliberately seek to placate or win the affections of a current or potential spouse, of a parent, or of an influential or possibly wealthy relative through gift giving and special attention. These relations are equally subject to extortion. That we can find such relations in families makes it not surprising that we can find them as well in businesses.

For example, anyone who operates a small business knows that giving out small promotional gifts to customers or to potential customers can be a good way to build a customer/client base. Pencils, pens, balloons, calendars, refrigerator magnets, and other doodads may all serve this purpose. Larger businesses may also give out such gifts and in addition offer cents-off coupons or rebates to stimulate customer purchases. For example, automobile companies have on occasion offered potential customers a cash rebate of as much as $1,000 for purchase of one of their new cars. These incentives are a means of gaining attention and good will and of influencing purchasing decisions. They are also examples of business bribery in its most mundane and elemental form.

Such practices occur on a grander scale between businesses, as suppliers wine and dine buyers and shower them with gifts in the hopes of making a sale. Good personal relations with buyers supplemented by lots of gift giving and rebate arrangements may go a long way toward facilitating deals worth thousands or even millions of dollars. In our society, this is all just good business practice, and the company that does the most of it may stand the best chance of beating out competitors for a sale.

Carried into the political sector, these business practices may take such forms as PAC contributions and honoraria payments to political candidates and to other politically influential persons. The intent clearly is to influence political policy and votes, but only rarely do such practices result in the raising of ethical or legal charges of misconduct (and even then, rarer still is it for anyone to be punished for these practices).

Our moral sensibilities are not offended by the fact that recipients expect these favors or by the fact that these favors are offered by businesses purely to influence a recipient. Our moral sensibilities are offended, if at all, only when these favors cause what we conceive to be a dereliction of public duty by the recipient or of a violation of our political principles. More particularly, we are offended if public officials, who in a democracy such as ours are expected to make decisions based solely on the public good, in fact make these decisions based solely or principally on who gives them the most favors. We are also offended if candidates for public office in a democracy such as ours are elected based not on the general public will, but rather on the gifts and contributions they receive from special interests (and our outrage is even greater if these special interests represent other countries).

Consider now the situation of international business bribery of government officials. Historically it has been a tradition for the rulers of agricultural societies to increase their income through the sale of the governmental offices that they controlled; this was their noble and accepted right as rulers. Purchasers of these public offices expected to use them as a highly lucrative source of lifetime income through the sale of their official services. Thus justice, in practice, very often was accorded to the highest briber, and officials at every level expected a gratuity or commission to be paid them for the performance of their duties.

Even when these practices were officially deemed improper, they were usually unofficially condoned and accepted. Conventions such as these continue to be widespread and very visible in the agricultural societies of developing countries today and are often found in more than vestige form in industrial democracies.

Now consider the situation of U.S. multinational corporate businesspersons who confront these practices in other countries. These businesspersons are well accustomed to our versions of these practices in the forms of gift giving to public officials, showing public officials a good time in country club outings, parties, ski weekends, yachting cruises, call girl/boy services, the making of honoraria payments for speeches and other services, the payment of PAC money, and so on. But what prepares the U.S. businessperson for widespread demands for favors (i.e., extortion) by public officials at all levels in return even for the simplest public approvals, clearances, or processing of paperwork?

The amount of money to be paid out and the number of officials to be paid may be so great that corporations may find it necessary to hire a local agent to handle all of these arrangements, usually on the basis of a hefty percentage commission. Often the local government officials themselves require the corporation to hire a local agent, and the agent is typically a crony, and possibly a relative, of the governmental official.

Local political aspirants may also seek deals with U.S. corporations in which, in return for corporate funding of their campaign efforts, the aspirant may promise to support corporate interests if the aspirant is successful in gaining political control. This is just the obverse situation of that in which existing political officials demand cash in return for their efforts on behalf of corporate ventures.

The growth of multinational corporations as a worldwide presence throughout the twentieth century, in conjunction with the previously described political practices, quite naturally has fostered a considerable amount of bribery by U.S. corporations, some of which spilled over into their dealings with public officials within the United States. By the early 1970s political pressure mounted in the United States for something to be done about this situation.

In the investigations surrounding the Watergate incident, it was discovered that over 300 U.S. corporations had made illegal contributions to U.S. political candidates, and more than 400 major U.S. corporations had made questionable payments (i.e., bribes) to foreign officials in an effort to foster their goals of economic expansion and sales worldwide.[7] These revelations not only brought an immediate public outcry and tarnished the United States international image, but also contributed to a serious eroding of public trust in American businesses.

The response to illegal contributions to Nixon's campaign and to other election improprieties took form in the body of campaign reform legislation of the 1970s (which ironically stimulated the use of corporate PACs as circuitous vehicles for corporations to make campaign contributions to candidates for federal elections). The response to the charges of widespread international bribery was the Foreign Corrupt Practices Act of 1977.

The Foreign Corrupt Practices Act was a poorly drafted, hastily constructed piece of legislation that outlawed most forms of corporate payments to foreign officials, to agents for distribution to foreign officials, or to foreign election campaigns. The legislation also set accounting requirements for U.S. corporations in an effort to ensure an adequate paper trail for documenting compliance.

Unfortunately, the language of the legislation indicates that lawmakers did not know precisely how to set up such an accounting system, largely because at a more fundamental level they did not know precisely how to define what constituted corrupt business practices as distinguished from conventional or good business practices. This fundamental confusion has left corporate lawyers and accountants unsure of how to conform to the accounting requirements of the law.

The problems posed for U.S. businesses by this legislation throw into sharp relief how, on the one hand, each society may evolve over time so that all of its social sectors, including businesses, work out common conventions for what constitutes acceptable, conventional, or responsible behavior and how, on the other hand, these conventions may themselves differ from society to society. How then are U.S. businesses to act when confronted with different conventions for bribery than are found at home in the United States?

"When in Rome," as the saying goes, "do as the Romans do." This is a lesson U.S. multinational corporations have had to learn in their dealings with governments and with cultures of other countries as they have sought to expand their markets worldwide. Many cultures operate under conditions in which the conventions for the bribery of public officials permit more widespread, intensive, and open bribery than is the case in our society. To compete in these environments, many U.S. multinational corporations had bowed to such local conventions by practicing bribery on a scale that they would not likely consider undertaking in the United States. Now, however, the Foreign Corrupt Practices Act was ordering them to refrain from such acts of bribery even in cultures in which these practices are a conventional part of the local political economy and quite possibly a necessity for business survival.

What should U.S. businesses do in response to this law? Of course we expect them to obey this law as we do all laws, but very little federal enforcement of this law has occurred or is likely to occur for the foreseeable future. A unilateral restriction placed on our businesses in the international market is unwise in any case. Here, as in the cases of pollution, environmental destruction and resource depletion, social mechanisms are needed at an international level to define and enforce standards for bribery and thereby to create a level playing field for competing companies around the world.

Bilateral and multilateral trade agreements that stipulate these standards are a positive step, such as those which were formulated in 1976 by the Organization for Economic Development and Cooperation. Some enforcement teeth, however, are needed to make these agreements binding. As the industrialized countries that serve as the home bases for the world's multinational corporations work out suitable agreements and enforcement policies, bribery should become better controlled as an international business practice. And from the basis of such agreements and policies, it should not be hard for home countries to apply concerted pressure on host countries to control or reduce extortionist practices by their public officials.

Trade Protectionism

How many of us are willing to sit back in our chairs and laugh as our major industries are threatened with bankruptcy and our economy comes to be increasingly controlled by foreign interests? None of us, of course, and herein lies the roots of popular support for national protection of our industries. The other impetus for national protection of our industries comes, of course, from these endangered industries themselves, as affected business and union leaders alike lobby Congress for assistance.

In steel, automobiles, wheat, dairy products, beef, clothing and shoes, electronics, and many other products, our U.S. businesses have found themselves not only unable to compete in the world market, but also losing out their home market as well to foreign competitors. As a consequence, U.S. industrial jobs were being threatened or lost either through domestic plant closings or through cost-cutting downsizings. This process was occurring throughout the 1970s and 1980s in many major cities in the United States, especially in the Midwest, and is now called deindustrialization. A number of U.S. companies simply moved their manufacturing operations to other countries to take advantage of lower production-related costs (such as for employee compensation, union work rule restrictions, and government regulations). In this way they could continue to be competitive in the world and United States domestic markets.

The Postindustrial Society and Deindustrialization

Some theorists have suggested that the deindustrialization process is a potentially positive one for United States society. Dirty industries would be given up; cleaner, higher-paying, less work-intensive industries, especially those that are service oriented, would remain. This vision, for example, is represented in Daniel Bell's[8] concept of the postindustrial society. However, it is now clear that the industries that are being lost in the United States are not only dirty industries such as steel, but clean, high tech industries as well, such as in electronics (radios, televisions, camcorders, VCRs, computer components, etc.). Furthermore, international competition in service industries also has become keen, with Japan, for example, having become one of the world's major bankers and financiers. In short, U.S. deindustrialization threatens jobs of all sorts, and with them the U.S. standard of living. Without question, the primary losers, of course, are those who are structurally unemployed or forced into lower paying jobs as a result of this industrial dislocation process. Community tax bases are also hit hard, resulting in deteriorating public services. Capital investors too are hit by the process of U.S. deindustrialization.

Why Have We Lost Market Competitiveness?

Why have U.S. industries lost market competitiveness? Certainly the first and largest problem has been a lack of managerial insight, toughness, and willingness to innovate in the face of a changing international economic environment. We have by far the best paid managers in the world. But the Olympian-size compensation packages our managers have obtained for themselves best reflect their ability to manage their own incomes rather than their ability to manage the fortunes of the companies they direct. Rather than working creatively with labor to give all employees a stake in increasing productivity and product quality, many of our managers simply caved in to union wage and benefit demands for years, passing along increased labor costs to consumers through increased product costs, and leaving products made in the United States less and less competitive in the domestic world market. Rather than planning for the future with increased investment in robotics and other product and production capacity updates, many of our managers focused on the short-term returns obtainable from financial manipulations and used this to justify their own pay bonuses. Then too, rather than focusing on product innovation and product quality, our managers counted on advertising and oligopolistic market control to keep prices high and U.S. consumers captive. The earlier hegemony of U.S. industries in the world markets throughout the early to mid part of the twentieth century made many of our managers jaded, short sighted, and self-indulgent. Now that their mismanagement has crippled our industries, they want government trade protection (and give themselves another bonus when they get it).

A second and certainly critical factor in the decline of U.S. dominance in domestic and world markets has simply been the rebuilding of war-ravaged Europe and Japan. This rebuilding process (with U.S. support and aid) was inevitable and has meant that Europe and Japan have been able to absorb larger and larger shares of the world markets that previously went by default to the United States. Even more than this, however, is the fact that their recent rebuilding efforts have meant that they have newer, more state-of-the-art manufacturing plants than we do and that they possess a renewed spirit of determination that carries them into making sacrifices that our more jaded management and union leaders have been unwilling to make. Putting these advantages together means that they are able to make products of higher quality and of lower price than we are able to do and, consequently, they are increasingly able to outsell us in world markets and in the U.S. domestic market as well.

A third factor in the decline of U.S. dominance in domestic and world markets is that some of the foreign competitors of U.S. companies have less adversarial and more cooperative arrangements with their governments. Although the U.S. government provides price supports, financial aid, and bailouts to a number of businesses (as described in an earlier chapter), many other industrialized or industrializing nations are far more aggressive in providing these and other government subsidies. Japan's government support of its steel, automobile, and computer industries provide examples. In some cases other governments also have assisted at a national level in promoting interbusiness cooperation and development. Again Japan provides a leading example through its Ministry of International Trade and Industry. Staunch protectionist policies of other countries (including import tariffs, import quotas, and buy domestic practices and laws) also play a major role in reducing U.S. penetration in world markets. Japan again is a good example, as it has import restrictions on more than twenty-five major products[9] and is well known for the informal tradition among its corporations of buying from only Japanese suppliers. Government price supports too have made it possible for companies to dump their goods on the world market at prices below their production costs. As foreign competitors are run out of business as a result, these companies may move increasingly into a position of world monopoly so that they can raise prices and profits accordingly. Once again, this charge has been leveled at Japanese steel and automobile makers.

A fourth factor involves collusive practices among firms in other countries that are otherwise barred in the U.S. (e.g., the use of merchant banks). Japan once again is an outstanding case example. Its industrial groups ("zaibatsu") are cooperative arrangements among firms that provide low financing and a flow of technological information and assistance for entering foreign markets. Then too merchant banks have major holdings in industrial firms and provide the capital commitment and technical expertise needed to execute plans for long-term product development and market penetration.

Yet another factor has been the high cost of capital in the United States, resulting from giant government and consumer debt (see my discussion in Chapter 14). Other countries have enjoyed cheaper domestic costs for capital, and this has made possible more investments in newer production processes.

Many other factors are involved in the decline of U.S. corporate dominance in domestic and world markets. Ironically, many of the same factors that propelled the initial industrialization of the United States, including protectionist trade policies, cheap labor, government subsidies, and limited government regulation, now are at work to give advantage to our newer world competitors.

Industrial Placement by Comparative Advantages

Economists of the market model school like to argue that industries in the international arena either are, or should be, subject to a simple shake-down process based on the comparative advantages that each country offers for each type of industry in a worldwide trading environment. In an ideal market model world, in which industries were free of political manipulation or of political aid and protection (a world humans have never experienced), the mere natural advantages that each country possessed would determine in which countries industries could operate most efficiently. Consider these examples: climatic difference determine which country can most efficiently grow and sell bananas, coffee, or wheat; geographical location determines which countries might best fish the seas; and the natural distribution of resources determine which countries might best market coal, oil, aluminum, molybdenum, or so on and, correspondingly, where major industries using these resources might best be located. Then too, natural labor conditions and cultural variations might determine which countries might possess the cheapest labor or be best suited for plantation-style production, for factory production, or for services such as banking, or so on.

Adherents to this economic model, therefore, shrug aside concerns over loss of our industries. They assert that we will all be better off with the loss of these industries as production of the industrial goods that are involved will naturally gravitate to those counties where comparative advantages make them most efficient. As countries begin to specialize in trade for which they are most naturally suited, the world will, therefore, make most efficient use of its resources, and the price of products will come down to their lowest possible point.

Shortcomings in the Comparative Advantages Model

Unfortunately, even assuming the ideal of a situation in which political influences on markets cease to operate, this model of comparative advantages nonetheless breaks down in the face of the range and complexity of the comparative advantages that must be considered in order to decide that an industry has truly found its natural home country. The case might be most easily made for oil production, but it is less easy to draw for most other manufacturing industries requiring extensive capital outlay, such as for steel or automobiles or computer production. Furthermore, a production system that is most efficiently distributed worldwide may not be in our best interest as a country, as high technology industries and industries critical to our national defense and to our ability to feed ourselves may go elsewhere, leaving us in the United States with low paying, low technology jobs, a lowered standard of living, and at risk of foreign military takeover. There is no formula for determining that a domestic industry is necessary for our national interests, and so these determinations are always political in nature (as is evident in efforts to enforce the U.S. National Security Law that bars companies from selling U.S. technology to foreign interests when this would threaten U.S. national security).

Forces for Mercantilism

Reduced restrictions on international trade and on industrial development can create great impetus for innovation in the development of new and cheaper goods, and this has frequently been a goal in business-oriented societies. But it is a goal that is always tempered by national interests, so that free trade and national interests in market protection lie ever in a shifting balance. In this respect, mercantilism remains a vital principal in the business-oriented society.

United States mercantilistic efforts have, of course, been directed toward protecting and promoting our industries. Automobiles, steel, textiles, bicycles, motorcycles, watches, sugar, sheet glass, and many other products have all been extended market protection by U.S. governments. One form of protection is a price support system to pay domestic producers more than existing world market prices. This has been a standard practice in the United States since the Great Depression for many types of agricultural goods.

Another form of protection is an import tariff placed on products coming into our country from foreign companies to force the price of these products up to levels typical of those of U.S. domestic producers. Yet another form of protection is an import quota or informal agreement barring foreign producers from shipping into the United States more than a specified number of designated products. This keeps their market share down in the United States so producers in this country can control the rest of the market. We place substantial tariffs, for example, on textiles, apparel and footwear, dairy products, vegetables, fruit juices and other beverages, tobacco, ceramic and glass products, and many others.[10]

Yet other forms of protection exist, including restrictions on trade permits, financial and employment restrictions on multinational corporations, buy-domestic restrictions, the relaxing of regulations on endangered domestic companies, the bail out of dying companies, and others. The United States is not the only country playing the protection game, or even the most aggressive at this game. By one estimate, nearly half (48 percent) of all world trade in 1980 was subjected to some form of protectionism.[11]

The Costs of Trade Protection

Are you wondering who pays for all of this protection? If so, you must have skipped the earlier chapters of this book. You and I pay, of course. We always pay for any business or governmental action through higher prices on goods and services, through higher taxes, or both. All of the price supports and tariffs undertaken for protectionist purposes are passed along to us as hidden taxes, which elevate the prices of the goods that we buy. Likewise, as import quotas and trade restrictions keep lower priced goods out of our country, you and I pay more in order to buy the higher priced domestic versions of these goods. This translates, at least for the short term, into a reduced standard of living for us all, as our dollars buy fewer goods than otherwise.

The costs to consumers of protectionist policies are considerable, adding an estimated $0.7 billion to what we pay for shoes, $4.5 billion for cars, $1.2 billion for meat, $7.2 billion for the steel that is present in so many consumer goods, $18.4 billion for textiles and apparels, and $3 billion for sugar. By one estimate the total cost to consumers in 1980 of protectionism was $58 billion, or approximately $255 per consumer.[12]

Protectionism also backfires as a strategy when it serves to goad other countries into reciprocating, so that our economy is slowed down by lost sales abroad. The whole process by which countries impose protectionist plans in response to those of other countries can easily escalate to the point of a trade war in which everyone gets hurt. Clearly, when pushed to its extreme, protectionism is no more viable as an economic policy than is completely free international trade. The practical course between these two extremes is continually subject to political renegotiation. The situation we face in the world market is much like a highly disorganized, primitive international economic war that is fought with figurative moats, walled fortresses, and friendly gestures of Trojan horses. We may not be shooting missiles at each other, but the stakes are nonetheless high. This international struggle is a fundamental part of life in a business-oriented society.

The Politics of Free Trade, GATT, and NAFTA

The most fundamental problem with protectionist policies in the United States is that, although they may at best shield our domestic companies from international competitors in our own domestic market, they do nothing to address the problem of decreased international market share for U.S. domestic firms. The U.S. global economic hegemony thus remains threatened. The alternative to protectionism is free trade, and a number of political initiatives have been undertaken in the name of free trade in an effort to protect and promote U.S. interests.

We often hear U.S. economic elites claim that international competition is being conducted in unfair ways. The argument frequently is heard that we allow for the free (or, more accurately, relatively free) import of goods into the United States from other countries, but these countries in turn place significant barriers on the import of our goods into their markets. If free trade practices could in fact be implemented internationally, it is argued, we would have a fair chance to compete in the world market and might be able to stop the economic hemorrhaging of our industries.

Free trade and free markets are central concepts in the market model. The freeing of markets from restrictions on sellers and buyers, or more generally on products, services, labor, and capital, is believed to result in the most efficient production systems, the lowest consumer prices and the highest collective standard of living possible. This argument, of course, is wholly hypothetical because, as I have noted repeatedly in this book, no observable markets are free of restrictions on buyers and sellers. For example, in every known society, ethnicity, age, gender, race, and national origin affect market access and related privileges. So too do prevailing socioeconomic structures, such as those of class, estate, or party. Then again, businesses, governments, workers, and consumers have all attempted, with some success, to control markets in the business-oriented society. At the international level, military power also plays a critical role in shaping trade arrangements and trade privileges.

In the real world, the rhetoric of free trade typically issues from those who believe themselves to be in a strong position to gain advantage by altering selected existing trade protectionist practices. Those who believe they may lose are understandable less desirous of free trade.

Free Trade as Market Control

In contrast to the classical approach to economics, an institutional or historical approach regards the control of markets as a central feature of economic phenomena. Profits increase for individuals, firms, or nations directly with the increasing level of control that they are able to exert over their markets. This principle underlies, for example, the widespread development of market concentration throughout the U.S. economy (e.g., monopolies and oligopolies) and the formation of worker unions for the control of labor pools.

Because trade practices throughout history have naturally followed vested interests and have never been free, it can only be by a substantial effort to control the natural order that market participants could be forced to operate as the free agents that the market model poses them to be. The assumption is that free markets or free trade represent the natural order of affairs and are made less free by restraints placed on them by vested interests, particularly by governments. In reality, however, vested interest restrictions on market practices are the natural order so far as we can observe historically. Any effort to remove such restrictions would have to involve substantial control over the market to make it match the economic ideal of being free.

In short, when viewed outside the realm of abstract economic theory, calls for free trade are merely a part of the political rhetoric of vested interests in search for the means to better control markets to their own advantage. For example, England was the leading proponent of worldwide free trade when it was the leading industrial and military power in the world and stood to gain much by the removal of international trade barriers to its products. Likewise, the United States as the world's largest industrial power has become as well the world's leading champion of free trade in the twentieth century.

The Need for Free Trade Agreements

From the perspective of market control, U.S. trade protectionism, as traditionally exercised in the forms of tariffs and import barriers, have been unsuccessful because they have not in fact provided a means to control the most important market elements that threaten U.S. interests. These uncontrolled elements are the trade practices of foreign firms and foreign governments which threaten U.S. economic hegemony in the world market. Consistent with this line of reasoning it follows that in its efforts to maintain a highly profitable economic hegemony worldwide, the United States must act to force open the markets of other countries to U.S. imports. It can attempt to do this by seeking bilateral or worldwide free trade agreements and by seeking to develop international enforcement mechanisms that will control foreign commercial ventures in ways consistent with these agreements. Free trade then becomes a means for exerting control over international trading practices.

GATT

One way the United States has attempted to obtain such agreements is through negotiations of the General Agreement on Tariffs and Trade (GATT), which dates back to 1947 and is periodically renegotiated. The most recent GATT agreement among 117 countries removes a number of protective tariffs and other import barriers and makes the World Trade Organization (WTO) the judicial system for hearing and ruling on complaints of agreement violation. The GATT seeks to provide a more stable and uniform trading environment in which disruptive trade wars and costly internal industrial supports can be minimized. Because the United States already has fewer import restrictions than most other countries, the reduction on trading restraints should be of considerable advantage to U.S. interests. In particular, the United States stands to gain substantially from the reduction of trade barriers for industries in which it currently has world leadership, such as in pharmaceuticals, medical equipment, grain production, and a number of service industries.[13]

Trading Blocs

Another international free trade movement has been the formation of trading blocs. Perhaps the most important example has been the formation of the European Union (EU, previously called the European Economic Community or the European Community). This union was undertaken primarily for the political purpose of reducing the likelihood of another European war by tying the economies of Western European countries more closely together. The removal of trade barriers among these countries creates opportunities for the emergence of European industrial firms with far greater economies of scale for serving an Europe-wide market and for competing with giant competitors worldwide. Furthermore, if this new trading bloc works to exclude imports through informal "Buy EU Only" agreements, the United States could find its European market reduced. For example, in 1990 62 percent of all EU trade was internal.[14] Thus this trading bloc has the potential of circumventing some of the opportunities GATT otherwise makes available to U.S. exporters.

Indications of closer ties among Asian countries pose the prospect for a similar threat to U.S. exports to Asian markets. Partly in response to those developments, the United States signed a Free Trade Agreement (FTA) with Canada to significantly reduce trade barriers between the two countries and thereby foster a larger unified market. This brings us to NAFTA.

NAFTA

The NAFTA is a five-volume, 2,000 plus-page legal document that sets out in detail a prescription for market control on trade and investments, all in the name of freeing the economic markets in North America. Side agreements on the environment, on labor policy enforcement, and on import surges are designed to add supplemental controls for additional market-related issues of political concern. Snap-back provisions and strict rules of origin add yet additional vehicles for safeguarding vested interests. Specifically excluded is the freeing of labor markets, other than the permission for company support staff to cross borders for limited purposes.

The agreement creates a trading bloc that is slightly larger than the EU in population and combined GNP. For vested interests in Mexico, it provides a means for locking in and sanctioning the ruling party's economic agenda and attracting increased foreign investment. For vested interests in the United States, it bolsters a new political and economic environment in Mexico that is believed to be favorable to U.S. interests, and it facilitates U.S. deindustrializing plant relocations and capital investments into a nearby country, Mexico, where profits may prove very attractive.

As the United States has deindustrialized, selected manufacturing operations have either faced a severe profit squeeze, gone bankrupt, or shifted to overseas locations to take advantage of reduced costs. Mexico provides a convenient location for manufacturing relocation because of its proximity to the United States, its low wages, and its lax regulatory enforcement efforts. Such relocations present the potential for reducing manufacturing costs to a level that makes U.S.-owned firms much more competitive in the world market. NAFTA not only facilitates the movement of the U.S. capital needed to accomplish this end, but its free import provisions also give Mexican-based U.S. firms a competitive advantage in exporting goods back into the United States. By contrast, competitors elsewhere in the world will continue to face U.S. tariffs and other U.S. import barriers. In summary, this free trade agreement has decided advantages to the United States in the control of world markets.

It would be easy to overdraw the potential advantages of NAFTA. As a vehicle for the United States to exercise control over world trade, NAFTA may be like a horse-drawn carriage with three broken wheels. Mexico still lacks the social and economic infrastructure to make it an efficient "engine" for U.S. profits. It has also become increasingly unstable politically, so that one must be concerned about the long-term support of its political elites for policies that are in the U.S. interest. Its political stability is particularly of concern given the massive structural unemployment that its trade liberalizing policies are producing, especially in its agricultural sector and in several other industries. In addition, Mexico's policing and judicial systems are corrupt and unreliable as a means for protecting U.S. capital interests. Then too its transportation and communication systems are deficient and create delays and extra costs. Also, the Mexican labor pool that U.S. firms can draw on requires extensive training and has evidenced very high turnover rates and associated costs.[15] All of these circumstances make major capital investment in Mexican manufacturing operations quite risky.

Transforming the World's Cultures to Suit Business-Oriented Needs

The problems of multinational business practices, of international business bribery, of trade wars, and of protectionism, represent just a few of the many cultural conflicts that arise as a business-oriented society such as ours expands its economic interests and holdings worldwide. Our business interests and conventions, forged in the caldron of our unique cultural context, conflict at many points with those of other cultures, and particularly so with cultures in the Third World. Our business interests and conventions fit best in cultural milieus that possess stable democracies, where churches hold little power, where family life and communities are splintered, where most people are business employees and consumer-people, and where prevailing practices of class stratification, racism, and sexism favor a small group of economically elite, white, Anglo-Saxon males. In short, our business interests and conventions work best in societies that are most like ours, and these societies are found especially in the countries of northwestern Europe. Is it any surprise, then, that roughly four-fifths of U.S. foreign business investments are in those countries?

Emerging, and in some cases fully emerged, business-oriented industrial societies in the Far East (including Japan, Taiwan, South Korea, Hong Kong, Singapore, and Malaysia) have also provided an increasingly good fit for our business interests and conventions. But what about countries in the Third World (and some of those previously in the Second World of the communist orbit)? The physical resources of these countries, their cheap labor pools, their lax regulations, and their potential market for U.S. products all present a natural allure for businesses. But their political, legal, and religious traditions often don't conform to, and possibly even are intolerant of, our business-oriented conventions. Furthermore, their people often are not motivated by a work ethic and are more oriented to kinship obligations than market relations. Then too their stratification systems, coupled with their primarily agricultural economic base, leave much of their populations in conditions of poverty that provide little market demand and that are appalling to our refined sensibilities.

These are the societies that we are most likely to exploit; in these societies we are most likely to bribe public officials; to use our economic and military clout to manipulate the political elite to act in our national interests; to exploit workers of all ages, including the young, through dangerous working conditions, long hours, and low pay and benefits; to pollute and destroy the local environment; to extract, exploit, and exhaust available resources; to dump our unsafe products that are either illegal or unwanted in our society; and to soak up existing wealth for shipment back to our society. This exploitation, carried out worldwide, elevates our national wealth and our standard living. But how do we justify it morally?

The "White Man's Burden"

Consider the case of the earlier European colonial powers that engaged in extensive patterns of exploitation in their worldwide business ventures. A justification for their exploitation took the form of an ideology which, on occasion, was referred to as the white man's burden. In this ideology the pious, civilized colonizers saw their actions toward heathen, primitive peoples as serving a number of greater goods. For example, they brought these peoples to the true religion (Christianity) and thereby aided in their spiritual salvation; they imposed a civilizing influence on the bestial character of these people; they gave these people jobs and a means of support whereas before they often lived in primitive squalor; and they brought medical assistance and other forms of aid. In the view of this ideology, these peoples were regarded as wholly ignorant, savage, and childlike ("bush bunnies" really) and unfit for self-rule.

The European colonizers, far from seeing themselves first and foremost as being murderous exploiters, saw themselves rather as having taken on an onerous burden—the white man's burden—to manage the affairs of the peoples of the world (often of brown or yellow skin) for the good of these people. Of course many examples of benefits accruing to a number of colonized societies can readily be described (improved sanitation and health care, shipments of food during times of famine, aid in developing farming techniques, etc.) and may have occurred at the same time that there was much exploitation through enslavement and enserfment of the indigenous peoples and through the destruction of their major social structures (political, religious, and kinship) in the pursuit of economic gain. Eventually, of course, most of these colonies either successfully revolted or were granted independent rule.

The white man's burden was a convenient ideology for justifying what the European colonizers were doing to peoples around the world, and in some respects this ideology may have motivated them in fact to undertake actions for the welfare of these peoples. In modern-day form this ideology is still with us today, often encapsulated in the thinking and arguments involving development and modernization.

Modernization and Development

Modernization theory has its roots in the cold war effort to assert the superiority of capitalistic principles as a world economic model over those of socialism.[16] It holds that we can distinguish between societies that are developed or modernized (namely business-oriented, industrial societies) and those that are undeveloped, underdeveloped, primitive, traditional, premodern, or modernizing (i.e., the nonbusiness-oriented societies that we modernized societies often exploit). The very terms themselves (such as modernized or developed) indicate the moral judgment that is being passed (ours is the better social form—theirs is not). To be as good as us, they must become like us, by giving up their old traditional allegiances to kin, church, and community and adopting instead our social conventions that emphasize individualism. They should seek to transform their social structures to look more like ours in education, government, law enforcement, family, fertility pattern, religion, and economy. With foreign aid (gifts, loans, and investments), foreign technology, and a restructuring of their social order, they can take off as an industrializing country and thereby gain the standard of living that we enjoy.

The question then becomes to what degree we should help these societies to give up their old social order and to become like us? This question, of course, is especially pressing in those cases where pursuit of our economic interests already places us in extensive interaction with these societies and their social conventions get in the way of our economic interests.

The new "white man's burden" is the burden of the modern business-oriented industrial societies to create civilized social order in the Third World countries so as to better make them fit social conventions amenable to our business-oriented interests. Given the great diversity of the cultures of the world, this is no small task. And, although this new ideology glosses over and justifies a great deal of the exploitation that we carry out in these countries, it may also motivate us to do some things that promote the welfare of these countries: we give them an independent vote in the United Nations (while keeping for ourselves veto power), we set up worldwide charitable organizations to aid them in the form of food or health supplies, we provide foreign aid for the development of agricultural techniques, we aid in the development of their infrastructure, and, when our economic interests dictate it, we may protect them from foreign invasion.

Obstacles to Modernization

Ultimately, however, efforts to industrialize or modernize Third World countries run into several major obstacles. First, such efforts may threaten powerful interests in the existing religious, governmental, and kinship systems. In some cases, such as Iran, these interests are powerful enough to resist modernization. Second, foreign aid not infrequently becomes pocketed by these powerful interests, rather than serving the purposes for which it was intended. Third, our cultural naivety has occasionally lead us to provide technical support that is inappropriate for existing social and economic conditions. Fourth, education, often regarded as a critical force in efforts to modernize societies, is, as I have shown earlier, a product of industrialization and not a cause of it (see my comments also in Chapter 14).

Fifth, and perhaps most significant, is that the market model that underlies modernization theory assumes that countries are able to compete independently in world markets, as though the world were one large level playing field. But, as a contrasting point of view known as *dependency* theory[17] points out, this simply is not so. The history of the relations among nations is one of dominance and exploitation by a few rich, powerful countries (the so-called developed countries) over the many poor countries (the so-called undeveloped or underdeveloped countries). The economic relations that have arisen are largely to the advantage of the rich countries and make the poor countries commercially (and to some degree politically) dependent on the rich countries. The result is a form of neocolonialism in which rich countries control poor countries through economic ties, but do not govern them politically (as happened, for example under the earlier colonial practices of England in its control of India or the American colonies).

Under modern relations of neocolonialism, poor countries are frequently crippled by large foreign debt[18] and are too small and weak to control or dominate market relations in comparison to the control and dominance exerted by multinational corporations or political interests in rich countries. Indeed, as I noted in Chapter 6, a number of large U.S. companies that do business worldwide have gross revenues equal to or greater than the entire GNP of most poor countries in the world.

The world market arrangements that develop often reduce the economies of poor countries to a focus on the export of only one or a few resources to rich countries (such as of fruit, sugar, coffee, or beef) or to service as a supplier of cheap labor. Under these circumstances their inhabitants have suffered in the past and will continue to do so well into the foreseeable future. These countries are like milk cows for rich countries. We live well at their expense.

These economic relations become an exceedingly difficult barrier for poor countries to overcome even if they commit themselves to doing so. That it can be done by some countries is illustrated by the successes of Singapore, Hong Kong, South Korea, and a handful of other countries. That it is difficult to do is illustrated by the vast majority of countries that have not succeeded.

To summarize, the business-oriented industrial society in the United States has become increasingly multinational in its economic interests (much as we were at the time of the founding of this nation and before our long period of isolation). Multinational corporations are the principal social vehicles through which the expansion of our economic interests has occurred. In the process of this expansion, we are being forced to confront social and moral contradictions between the practices and conventions of societies worldwide. Our response typically has been to press for our conventions to supersede those of peoples in other societies, even if this would require fundamental alterations in the social structures of these other cultures. Ideologically this process has been viewed in a framework similar to that encompassed by the earlier view on the white man's burden; it carries the burden of changing the social conventions of underdeveloped societies into those more in keeping with the needs of modernized business-orientated societies. This process is one our society is actively engaged in today as we seek markets worldwide, and it is to be expected from the maturation of a business-oriented industrial society. Furthermore, the appearance of a spin-off ideology both to justify what we are doing and hopefully to motivate us at times to do something for the welfare of the societies we exploit is consistent with prior precedence for mercantile and colonial business-oriented societies.

The Role of Multinational Corporations

What role should the multinational corporation play in this process? As I described in Chapter 3, all businesses have social responsibilities to promote the welfare of the various sectors of their social environment while pursuing their profits. But multinational corporations sit in several, often conflicting social environments simultaneously, and actions undertaken to serve the welfare considerations of one social environment may result in disadvantages in view of the welfare considerations in another.

This situation would best be addressed by having decision making decentralized, with as many decisions being made at the local level within countries as is possible. It also would be wise to make use of a local managerial team consisting of persons indigenous to a culture so that maximal sensitivity to local cultural conventions can be achieved.

As described in Chapter 8, a social mechanism is needed to monitor and pressure management into being responsible, and I have recommended that boards play a more active role as such a mechanism. For the multinational corporate board, efficient oversight of the level of responsibility entailed in managerial efforts in many countries would suggest the need to expand the board to include directors indigenous to each country where there are major corporate operations or holdings. These additional directors would be best able to evaluate the responsibility of senior management efforts in their home countries.

With decentralized decision making, with senior managers native to a host country, and with native board members providing major policy oversight, multinational corporations are more likely to behave morally within the context of each of the cultures in which they operate. Without such steps, multinational corporations leave themselves open to increased intervention and control by governments around the world because governments are the only other major social vehicle that societies have for pressuring businesses to become more responsible.

Continued efforts to create governmental structures at the world level are needed to provide a political forum in which global principles can be developed to guide, monitor, and sanction commercial practices worldwide. As multinational corporations free themselves more and more from having a cultural and political identity with a home country, they become increasingly more likely to embrace the notion of a world government that can create a global economic pax most conducive to worldwide commerce.

C h a p t e r 14

The Future of Business-Oriented Societies

It is traditional to conclude a book such as this one with a chapter that speculates about the future. I feel very reluctant to include such a chapter, however, for the simple reason that I have found myself to be wholly inept at predicting the future.

If you feel as much impatience as I do with efforts to predict the future, you should probably skip this final chapter. If, on the other hand, you feel stimulated when thinking about the possible lines of development that the future might hold, read on.

In this final chapter I first present a summary of the nature of our life in a business-oriented society and of business social responsibilities. Then I discuss several future possible developments for business-oriented societies related to resource depletion, pollution, and nationalism. Finally, I discuss other topics that did not fit elsewhere in this book but are often discussed in a business context. These topics include national productivity, job security, education, and our federal debt.

Life in a Business-Oriented Society and the Social Responsibilities of Businesses

Suppose it is true that you and I are but actors performing a diversity of roles on the multiple stages that constitute our society. If you and I are but actors, the unwritten scripts that motivate us and that give order, purpose, and meaning to our lives take their current form largely in response to the presence and needs of businesses in our society (as I have attempted to show throughout this book). Because business scripts have evolved to the point at which they now so interweave with and so dominate the other scripts of our society, the result is a society that is business oriented in form. As a consequence, our personal lives, too, have become business oriented.

Both in their form and in their function, the multiple sectors of society now work to support businesses. I have described how this situation has evolved historically and how it is reflected in our current governments, religions, schooling, communities, family structures, work life, and life-style. We have reformulated our family, community, friendship, and love relations to better fit the script needs of businesses in our society. We have created schools and subject ourselves to them, and we now willingly tolerate a bureaucratic way of life that is so central to modern corporations, mass production systems, and mass markets. We have created a democratic government that better serves business interests, and our international relations and military efforts now hinge on the needs of our businesses. From cradle to grave our lives, our thoughts, and our emotions are now organized by social scripts that reflect the dominant position of businesses in our society. This is the nature of life in a business-oriented society. None of our ancestors of more than a few generations before us experienced such a life.

I have argued that we are so mesmerized by the flow of goods and services provided to us by industrialized business-oriented societies that we now behave as though we are the fervent followers of a large secular religious cult. This cult of the business-oriented society demands our obedience, our devotion, and our disciplined efforts to create and perpetuate the type of societal stage plays that are so pleasing to business interests and to a commercial way of life that businesses foster. The dogmas of this secular religion, which are the ideologies of our time, define meaning and measure human value in business terms. All other ways of living, as represented by our ancestors, appear to us now to be primitive and to be lacking in morality.

In the formation of the business-oriented society, we have become individualized, free, and self-centered. Our lifestyles have become driven by business interests from birth, to family and community life, to schooling, to work life, and to our graves. Unlike our ancestors, the status symbols that we value and seek, that engender our feelings of self-esteem, and that serve to signify society's social hierarchy and social order are those that represent not our personal prowess or piety, but rather our purchasing power (e.g., a new car, designer clothes, name brands). We have become consumer people tied together by market dynamics. And we have become micro-business laborers and worker prostitutes. Our human rights and welfare now hinge centrally on business prerogatives, as do the quality and safety of our physical environment and of our futures.

If the business world now plays for us the role of a deity, we would nonetheless like for it to behave less capriciously and less harmfully. Thus we have put our governments to work in efforts to promote business growth and to reduce business down cycles. Through military-industrial spending our governments work to protect business interests and business properties. Through welfare-industrial spending our governments additionally work to alleviate forms of human misery that are fostered in a business-oriented society, but that may threaten social order if left unaddressed. Our governments have also come to serve as counterweights to limit the abuse of employees and consumers by businesses and to control and clean up environmental contamination resulting from business production systems and from our business-oriented lifestyle. Our governments and businesses too work hand in hand to promote business interests worldwide.

A society cannot remain viable, however, if a significant degree of harmony is not developed among all of society's major scripts. If business actions threaten the very existence of its commercial partners (e.g., suppliers, buyers, employees, consumers) or other sectors of society (e.g., families, communities, governments, the physical environment), then society ceases to be sustainable. Thus all major players in society have responsibilities to act in ways that ensure that the entire collective play of society can go on. Herein lies the necessity for businesses to act in socially responsible ways.

I have argued that governments played central roles in fostering socially responsible behaviors among businesses, and I have argued that governments cannot be wholly successful in this endeavor. Rather, it is essential that businesses themselves work more conscientiously toward defining and carrying out their responsibilities to other social sectors in the business-oriented society. Toward this end I have described the various social responsibilities that businesses have in contemporary society, and, when appropriate, I have suggested specific courses of action that businesses may take to better fulfill these responsibilities.

Are we better off living in a business-oriented society? In terms of our material standard of living and our health, yes we are. Are businesses an evil force? I have argued that the very meaning of right and wrong, or of good and evil, is shaped by the social forces of our time. Businesses have become the central social force in contemporary society and the linchpin that holds social order itself together. Under these circumstances, we not only regard businesses to be an important component of society, but even more so, we regard them to be necessary and beneficial. Indeed, we now hold that the presence of free enterprise in our society is a feature that makes us better than other nations or other peoples who do not have a business-oriented life. Thus we view businesses today predominantly as forces of good; and such they are, so long as they hold society together in a sustainable form. As is true with any great force, however, they have a dark side, which is expressed through irresponsible behaviors that are harmful to other sectors of society. A better business-oriented society can only be obtained and sustained into the future by efforts by businesses to become socially responsible. What, then, is the future of our business-oriented society?

The Future of Business-Oriented Societies

Many great civilizations have collapsed and disappeared into the mists of time. The extraordinary civilizations of the pharaohs, the Babylonians, the Indus Valley, the Phoenicians, the Greek city states, Rome, and the Mayan and Incan peoples are but a few examples. It is doubtful that many of our ancestors in these civilizations believed that their civilization could come to an end, but it did. Most of these civilizations, however, did not simply disappear without trace. Rather, they were radically altered to a form involving a significantly lowered standard of living, loss of pre-existing political and economic structures and possible control by foreigners. Could such a thing happen to our business-oriented society? Of course it could, and it probably will.

In this section I shall consider three major factors that present natural limits on the lifespan of business-oriented societies. These factors are resource depletion, environmental pollution, and nationalistic movements.

A Society without Oil and Other Major Resources

Consider the following. Can you imagine an industrialized society without oil? Quite possibly within our lifetime, but certainly within the lifetime of our children, such a thing won't have to be imagined; it will be a reality.

Oil is an inexpensive fuel that derives from the decaying bodies of dinosaurs and other ancient life forms (which, according to your views on the theory of evolution, you may regard as your ancestors). But in a mere century we have burned up oil reserves that took hundreds of millions of years to accumulate. Our industrial society and our standard of living have been built from these reserves, and I am sure that you, like me, can say that we have had a very good time consuming these resources. But what becomes of our economy and standard of living when these reserves are gone? You guessed it, our economy and standard of living will become significantly eroded and possibly will collapse.

The collapse, if it comes, is unlikely to be precipitous. Two related events are likely to occur to create substantial modifications in our economy before oil reserves run out. One is the effect that dwindling oil reserves will have on the prices of industrial goods. Less oil, of course, will mean higher oil prices, and this will translate into higher production and transportation costs for the wide assortment of goods that we consume in our current lifestyle. As these prices rise, fewer and fewer goods will be in the reach of our pocketbooks. As a consequence, the bulk of Americans will experience an increasingly eroded standard of living. In this way both the economic and lifestyle repercussions of a depleting oil reserve should be felt relatively gradually.

Second, as we run out of oil those countries with the strongest militaries, ourselves in particular, quite reasonably will be tempted to manipulate world affairs, especially through military intervention, to assure themselves of first claim to all oil resources that remain. The industrialized countries have done this throughout much of this century in our involvements in the political affairs of the Middle East. Most recently we all agreed to go to war with Iraq, for example, to safeguard our interests in the oil reserves in that region. Today the industrialized countries are sparring with the political systems in the underdeveloped societies in that region; tomorrow we will be sparring with each other over these dwindling resources.

World wars are, therefore, highly likely in response to the dwindling of resources needed for industrial processes. And these wars are most likely to be resolved, if at all, by the creation of world empires, with the winning industrial society (or coalition of societies) in control. But these empires are themselves likely to be very unstable due to the forces of nationalism to be discussed below. Furthermore, the duration of these wars could be quite long (assuming we avoid using nuclear weapons, a not altogether plausible assumption). The costs of waging these wars will lower our standard of living and move the military into a more central role as an organizational force in our societies. We can expect the business-oriented society, therefore, to become transformed increasingly into a military-oriented society.

Even if we substitute other fossil fuels for existing oil reserves (such as shale oil, gas, or coal), eventually (perhaps over one or more centuries, depending on the substitute) we will run out of these cheap energy sources as well. Furthermore, the process of shifting to these other energy sources will create a very "bumpy ride" for our economy and our standard of living until we eventually run out of these resources.

This scenario is rather bleak, but it is made likely not only by our dwindling energy reserves but also by our dwindling reserves for all sorts of metals, minerals, and other materials that we need to keep our industrial standard of living as high as it is at present. If an energy crisis is averted somehow, we will still be faced with many dozens of crises related to the dwindling supply of a great many types of important raw materials for our industrial economy. There simply are too many snares awaiting us for even the most optimistic of us to believe that we won't be caught in a situation of resource depletion that will translate into severe alterations to our economy and to our way of life.

Pollution

Pollution poses additional threats to the future of our business-oriented societies. Perhaps most significant is the contamination of water supplies. Many Americans are already using commercially marketed, bottled water because of concerns over contamination of their local water supplies. This strategy may not be a reasonable one, given the lack of quality control mechanisms to ensure that commercially marketed, bottled water is any safer than local water. Many localities too are already running out of areas for the safe disposal of their trash; the problem is particularly serious for the disposal of toxic wastes (including nuclear wastes). In many congested areas, air pollution alerts have become fairly routine. During these alerts people are urged not to breathe the air outside their homes if at all possible. What will we do when the air and water available to us no longer sustain life?

The growing problems of pollution will result in increased costs for purifying our foods, water, and air. As a result, prices on goods and services will rise and our standard of living will decline. Furthermore, as we move to control industrial pollution, economic dislocations will result. One trend already evident from this development is for the most polluting of our industries to move abroad where, at least for the present, local political authorities permit freer reign to businesses to pollute the environment.

Then too, where will we ship our trash, and at what cost? If we don't want to pollute our own environment with our trash and our industrial wastes, we will encounter increased costs and a corresponding decreased standard of living as more expensive trash and pollution control procedures are put into place. The alternative is to send our dirty industries and trash abroad. If other countries don't agree to this arrangement, then we face the additional costs of applying military coercion to gain their compliance. This strategy also would likely increase the military-orientation of our country.

To summarize, when considering both resource depletion and pollution, the final stages in the life span of a business-oriented industrial society are likely to contribute to the emergence of a military-orientation and to a reduced standard of living.

Nationalism

A third major factor that I wish to consider is the effect of nationalism on the future of business-oriented societies. Nationalism is a major type of social movement that frequently works at cross-purposes to business-oriented interests. Therefore, it is useful, at least in this final chapter, to consider some of its parameters.

Far more fundamental than our allegiance to political structures, to religious structures, or to economic structures is our allegiance to our kin, however variably we may define the boundaries of that concept. At the level of a food gathering and hunting band, the persons who are one's kin are easy to identify. In complex agricultural and industrial societies, however, the boundaries on kinship can become much more abstract. In such societies people tend to define an abstract, all-encompassing cultural kinship group that contains persons who share with them a common language, common cultural conventions, and possibly common physiological features as well (such as skin color, hair color and texture, and size and shape of facial features). It is our ability to identify such cultural kinship groups that is at the heart of nationalistic movements.

A cultural kinship group conceived of in this way constitutes what we often refer to as ethnicity. And what we refer to as nationalism is the allegiance that we express toward such an all-encompassing cultural kinship group through our efforts to create a political apparatus to marshal public affairs in a manner consistent with what we conceive to be the interests of this group. Nationalism, then, is a form of political movement among a group of people based on their perceived ties to a common cultural kinship destiny.

The motivating forces of businesses in a business-oriented society operate at a kilter to those of nationalism. Whereas nationalism expresses the common political interests of a single cultural kinship group, whether these interests be economic or otherwise, business interests are at once more encompassing of diverse groups of people and more limited in intended goals to those of a pecuniary nature.

For example, when business interests in an emerging business-oriented society serve as pressures toward nation building, they do so through the formation of a political organization designed principally to protect and foster commercial interests. In its development, the emerging business-oriented society serves to break down kinship, cultural and other noncommercially based national separations through the formation of common markets. As I described in earlier chapters, it is through such markets that common identities are fostered among otherwise unrelated people. As a result, this process may create the foundation for a new, more broadly based kinship and for a related nationalistic movement that subsumes peoples previously separated into different cultural groups.

However, history has shown that a business-orientation has seldom succeeded in extinguishing pre-existing cultural identifications and related nationalistic forces as influences in shaping world events. For example, we have seen the priority that nationalism has as a motivating force in human affairs in the rise of nationalistic movements around the world in opposition to the mercantilist and colonial policies of preceding business-oriented societies. Our earlier mercantilist and colonial business-oriented societies destroyed most of the world's few remaining hunting and gathering societies and forced many existing agricultural societies into patterns of economic and social relations most suitable for trade with the business-oriented societies. Under these circumstances, nationalism in these underdeveloped societies became a logical response of people confronted with a far different social environment than they previously had known. Political unification as a national kinship group that emphasized their cultural commonality, therefore, became their best hope for escape from direct domination by the colonial and mercantilist outsiders. We saw these nationalistic movements in Africa, in Asia, and elsewhere, wherever the commercial interests of mercantile and colonial societies took them.

When nation building is little more than the formation of an empire by political elites or occurs as a result of fiat by major world powers (such as in the formation during the twentieth century of several of the countries in Eastern Europe, in Africa, and in the Middle East), then such political entities can be quite unstable if they house different ethnic groups (i.e., groups of people with different languages, cultural conventions, or physiological features). We see this phenomenon worldwide. For example, the business-orientation of Canada has not overcome the rather sharp differences between its English and French sectors, and an active French separatist movement persists. As another example, the business-oriented society of the United Kingdom continues to be a very unstable alliance of diverse, reasonably well-defined ethnic groups, with very strong separatist pressures continuing to operate, for example, in Ireland, and to some degree in Wales.

Russia too, through conquest and empire building, created the now defunct Soviet Union out of the many diverse ethnic groups of Eastern Europe. As we have all seen, the collapse of the Soviet Union has unleashed a veritable bloodbath in ethnic conflict and ethnic nationalistic movements. Then too, much of business-oriented Western Europe has for some time been trying to create an "European Union" as a common market equivalent in size of population served and economic power to that of the United States. Its efforts at each turn have been hampered by nationalistic concerns of the participating countries.

The nationalism of the business-oriented society of the United States operates in a unified fashion only to the degree that we have in fact been a melting pot, with our diverse ethnic immigrant groups taking on a common language (English) and common social conventions (mostly English). However, racism has kept some minorities, particularly African Americans, from "melting" fully into the American "pot," with the consequence of the emergence of a black nationalist movement in the United States that is likely to gain greater force in shaping the future of this country if current patterns of discrimination do not change.

Nationalism, then, clearly limits the hold that a business orientation has on a society and produces a militancy that always threatens to create social disorder at home and internationally. Nationalism has played major roles in pushing the world into the two great wars of the twentieth century, and there is every reason to believe that it can and probably will do so again. If the elite of a business-oriented society ever dreamed of a worldwide economic empire run for their benefit (that is, a worldwide system of so-called capitalistic imperialism), nationalism makes this dream forever unreachable.

Assorted Issues in Our Business-Oriented Society

In this section I discuss four contemporary issues of importance to us in our business-oriented society: (1) national productivity, (2) job security and recent corporate downsizing, (3) education, and (4) government debt.

National Productivity

National productivity is a topic of great interest in business-oriented industrial societies (though it is certainly not of similar interest in other types of societies). Let's consider the topic in broader terms than is usual.

In order to determine whether the national productivity of a society is declining, rising, or staying the same, and before one can discuss what significance this has for the society, it is necessary first to specify what products are valued by a society. If no society valued underarm sprays, computers, automobiles, and frozen TV dinners, but instead all valued human fecundity, then Ethiopia would be among the most productive societies on Earth. By contrast, our business-oriented society would be judged to have fallen precariously in its national productivity. Consider another example: if acts of religious devotion were valued highly, then Iran might be judged as among the most productive of societies, while our own national productivity rate would be regarded internationally as scandalous.

No one can be surprised that economists prefer to define productivity from a commercial point of view. For them, productivity concerns the production of goods and services for sale in a market. In other words, they see productivity in business-oriented terms.[1]

The measurement of economic productivity, however, is a complex affair that involves indicators of outputs relative to inputs over a given period of time. The more outputs (goods and services) that occur within the time frame relative to existing inputs, the more productive the system is. Likewise if outputs remain constant over the time frame while inputs decrease, the system in more productive. Unfortunately, there is no one way to specify and measure all of the inputs and outputs in a production system. Indeed, there are a great many ways to make these specifications. Consequently, the assessment of productivity rates is much like an art form, with the perspective of the artist who makes the assessment playing a major role in what number is eventually estimated as the productivity rate. Under such circumstances, we are wise to take productivity rate estimates with more than a grain of salt.

Our national productivity, of course, sets limits on our standard of living. Societies that are highly productive in producing things that they value have high standards of living in these same terms. If our national productivity is rising relative to our population base, our national standard of living is rising. And likewise if our national productivity is falling relative to our population base, our national standard of living is falling.

Looking at these issues historically, we can easily see that industrialized societies are far more productive of marketplace goods and services than are agricultural societies. The difference is not one of degree but is more on the order of a giant chasm between economic potentials. This means that our material standard of living is far, far better than that found in agricultural societies.

The major factors contributing to the vast increase of our productivity of market goods as an emerging industrial society, as noted in Chapter 5, were the use of inanimate energy sources (such as oil), the use of machines, the creation and use of new production technologies (such as the assembly line), and the freeing up of social order and the entrepreneurial spirit from monolithic domination and subjugation by governments and churches. As a result of these factors, we now produce colossal amounts of food (with fewer than five percent of our labor force committed to agricultural production), and we fill our shopping malls to their ceilings with material goodies.

Another way to look at the vastly increased national productivity of industrial societies is to consider the effects that industrialization has had on our labor markets. The industrialization of farming (especially with crop rotation and the use of fertilizers, but also later with mechanization) has forced many laborers out of farm jobs, which had previously been a type of work with very low productivity. Instead, laborers were forced into jobs in factories and elsewhere in the economy where productivity was greater. This shift in itself played a major role in boosting estimates of American national productivity to the extraordinary heights of the twentieth century, heights that are equaled only by the other major industrial countries of the world.

Now let's consider the concerns raised over estimates that show a decline in the rate of growth of U.S. national productivity. In the light of the colossal economic productivity that we have attained relative to agricultural societies and the great difficulty in making precise productivity estimates, contemporary estimates of declines in the rate of growth in our productivity are obviously minuscule by comparison. Indeed, they could well be within the bounds of the measurement errors that arise in obtaining these estimates. Even if real, the decline in our standard of living, or in the growth in our standard of living, if any, would have modest implications for us at best in comparison to the economic standards of living available to peoples in agricultural societies. In short, concerns over declines in the rate of growth of U.S. national productivity are hardly on an order worth working oneself into a lather over.

Often our national productivity rate or growth in productivity rate is compared to those of other industrialized countries to suggest that theirs are better than ours. This comparison usually is limited to selected industries to simplify the computation of the estimates.

Again, however, comparing all industrial societies as a group to agricultural societies as a group makes it easy to see how far apart the two groups are and, relatively, how close the industrialized societies are to each other. There really is no particular reason to believe that any industrialized society is going to get a big jump in productivity over other industrialized societies at this point in history because we all have similar occupational, religious, and government structures, we are all workaholics, we all purchase needed raw resources at similar prices often from the same suppliers, we all have highly developed infrastructures, we all share an increasingly world market for capital, we all have similar technologies (or are quite willing to steal them or to sell them to each other), we all have substantial market penetration into each other's economies and are increasingly interdependent on each other in our production processes, and we all place considerable governmental restrictions on our industries to control business abuses.

Much of the difference in estimates of growth in national productivity among industrialized countries over the last few decades has simply been a matter of the World War II ravaged industrialized countries finally catching up with the United States. It is a reasonable assumption that as we all mature as industrial societies, we are likely to reach the same limitations (and opportunities) on further growth in productivity. Under these circumstances, I cannot get excited over talk about whether the Japanese or Germans or "whoever" are getting ahead of us in productivity growth.

In reality, we do have many "drags" on our productivity, including piratical and inept management, often modest capital investment in updating our technology of production, suffocating governmental regulations, and many more. As we begin to feel a crimp in our lifestyle, which I argued will happen as a result of resource depletion and pollution, we will attack some of these problems with more vigor.

Job Security and Corporate Downsizing

Most of human experience has been lived out in the context of food gathering and hunting societies. In these societies job security was not a concern because nobody had jobs (or would likely to have wanted them if they could have been made to understand what we mean by jobs). For most of our ancestors in agricultural societies, job security also was not at issue, because most were slaves or serfs. Although the commercial sector in agricultural societies did make jobs available to a limited number of persons, it was not until the maturing of the business-oriented society that jobs have taken on central importance in our round of daily life and in the quality of life that is possible for our families and communities. It is in this latter context, then, that job security has become a critical issue.

The business-oriented society has set us free to support ourselves and our families by being laborers in a labor market. As laborers we have become an input to the national productivity equation, as businesses draw on us as needed to exploit commercial opportunities. As these commercial opportunities change, labor needs change. Thus our role as laborers is one that has been constructed for us by business interests. We are jerked around from employment, to unemployment, to reemployment, and our lives, our families, and our communities are altered "willy nilly," sometimes disastrously so, as changing business interests dictate.

Because none of us knows with certainty how business interests will change in our lifetimes, we do not know how best to position ourselves as individual laborers so as to be continuously employed and to make the best provisions for our families and communities. Whereas in the past our food gathering and hunting ancestors relied on the band as a whole to provide for their welfare in lean times and whereas noblesse oblige provided an unwritten pact of lifelong support for our serf ancestors in agricultural societies, in the business-oriented society the interests of business leaders become the central factors in determining job security of laborers and of the individual, family, and community welfare that job security represents. It is in this context that I wish to talk about the recent phenomenon of downsizing by large corporations.

Downsizing (which is one form of corporate restructuring) is an euphemism for mass firing of employees. By firing lots of workers, a company reduces its costs. If over the short term the output of goods and services remains essentially the same or is only slightly diminished, a sizeable short-term gain in corporate productivity is achieved.

Many large businesses followed a corporate strategy of downsizing during the 1980s and 1990s. Here from the early 1990s are some examples of companies that downsized (included also are the number of jobs lost and the salary of the company CEO): AT&T (123,000 jobs lost; CEO Robert Allen had an annual salary of $3.4 million when he downsized the company); IBM (122,000 jobs lost; CEO Louis Gerstner, salary of $2.6 million); General Motors (99,400 jobs; former CEO Robert Stempel, salary of $1 million); Boeing (61,000 jobs; CEO Frank Shrontz, salary of $1.4 million); Sears, Roebuck (50,000 jobs; former CEO Edward Brennan, salary of $3.0 million); Digital Equipment (29,800 jobs; CEO Robert Palmer, salary of $0.9 million); McDonnell Douglas (21,000 jobs; former CEO John McDonnell, salary of more than $0.5 million); Delta Air Lines (18,800 jobs; CEO Ronald Allen, salary of $.5 million); GTE Corp (18,400 jobs; CEO Charles Lee, salary of $2 million); Nynex (17,400 jobs; former CEO William Ferguson, salary of $0.8 million); Phillip Morris (14,000 jobs; former CEO Michael Miles, salary of $1 million); and Chemical/Chase Manhattan (12,000 jobs; CEO Walter Shipley, salary of $2.5 million). In all, over a half million laborers (568 thousand) were to lose their jobs in these downsizings, with their families and communities suffering the economic consequences. Meanwhile, just twelve men, the CEOs of these companies, were able to go to their banks and investment brokers with $19.6 million in annual salaries and a far larger amount in stock options and bonuses. Just one person, former CEO of Scott Paper, Albert Dunlap, is reported to have walked away with over $100 million in total compensation after firing 11,000 people at Scott in 1994 and then merging Scott with Kimberly-Clark.[2]

Why didn't the more than one-half million employees who lost their jobs in these downsizings work as hard for their companies as did the twelve CEOs so that they, as was true of the CEOs, could have kept their jobs and gotten big bonuses? We have no evidence that these employees were not working faithfully at the jobs they were instructed to do by management. Rather, in most of these cases of downsizing the companies had for a number of years been so mismanaged and so short-term focused that they had failed to adjust to long-term changes in consumer demand, international competition, new technologies, and government regulation. As a consequence, they found themselves faced with a productivity problem, as indicated by severely constrained or falling profits. The quickest short-term fix to this productivity problem was to return free laborers to the free labor market (i.e., to fire their employees in droves).

Generally the stock market has reacted to the prospect of productivity growth resulting from mass firings by posting large gains in share values, and short-term investors have walked away from the companies with hefty profits as a result. Top managers too usually reward themselves with hefty pay raises for their courage in firing thousands of company employees. At least these two groups of people (short-term investors and top managers), have profited handsomely over the short term from downsizing. Indeed as a business strategy for raking in large profits for short-term investors and senior managers, downsizing is much less effort than having to go to all of the trouble of actually having to produce and sell goods and services in a market.

A reduction of a work force is certainly not a new phenomenon in human history. In agricultural societies slaves have been executed, starved, or freed when they were no longer needed. The freeing of the serfs in the middle ages was also a work force restructuring that made a more mobile labor force readily at hand for commercial use by the emerging business interests of the time. In industrial societies we see cycles of booms and busts when, as in the latter case, large numbers of workers lose employment or become underemployed. The potential release of large numbers of employees serves as a safety value to protect business interests, and our ideological commitments lead us all to believe that this action is quite appropriate.

Therefore, in the larger historical context, we can see that downsizing is hardly new, nor can we expect it to cease to recur in business-oriented societies. A number of mismanaged and floundering companies turned to downsizing in the 1980s and 1990s, but we have also seen other highly profitable companies do the same in a sort of monkey-see-monkey-do pattern of imitation.

Monkey-see-monkey-do is one of the most important ways in which any actor is able to determine appropriate behaviors on the stage plays of social life. Corporate managers are no different in this regard. In the corporate environment, it has become fashionable among corporate leaders, even for those in corporations that are highly profitable, to use downsizing as a strategy for protecting and inflating stock values (and, perhaps not inconsequentially, for increasing top management compensation). The fashion in contemporary corporate ideology holds that a manager is not tough and competent unless he or she repositions a company for the future by downsizing (mass firings), even if mass firings are not in fact needed.

Over the past few decades, efforts to increase corporate and national productivity have resulted in an increased flow of cash into the pockets of stock holders and senior corporate managers. Unfortunately, these efforts have not otherwise proven beneficial to the current generation of American workers, who take it on the chin in downsizings and other corporate restructurings. Indeed, trends over the past three decades, but especially in the early 1990s, have not shown increased national productivity to result in increased wages for nonmanagement workers. Rather, real worker wages have been falling. Data from the U.S. Bureau of Labor show that, as the productivity of nonfarm labor in the private sector of the United States rose 25 percent between 1973 and 1995, real hourly wages for workers fell by 12 percent in this same period of time.[3]

In the more recent cases of downsizing, not only are wages lost to workers during their subsequent job searches (and of course these wages are lost to their families and communities as well), but many of the new jobs that workers are able to find pay them less than the one they lost, or provide them with fewer benefits. In the early 1970s, for example, most people who lost their employment were able to find jobs paying as well or better than the jobs they had lost; by the mid-1990s, however, only about 35 percent could still do so.[4]

Ironically, too, the ballooning profit margins of the downsized companies and the rapid rise in their stock prices have not translated into higher salaries for those nonmanagement job holders who remain employed in the companies after downsizing. Again, senior management and stockholders have been the persons who have gained over the short run in the manipulation of productivity rates that downsizing represents. This phenomenon is consistent with the current trend in which the rich are getting richer and U.S. laborers more dispossessed. For example, one estimate indicates that 97 percent of the average gain in the United States in household income between 1979 and 1994 went to the richest 20 percent of households.[5]

As downsizing has become such a popular financial strategy for top management in the 1980s and 1990s, one can expect as a result an increasingly cynical American work force that is lacking in loyalty to their companies. The long-term effects of downsizing on productivity, quality of goods and services, and the health of the economy as a whole needs further analysis. In downsizing, a reduced work force must take on more work responsibilities under conditions of exceedingly low morale. As a result, one can expect significant problems over the long term in efforts to maintain productivity and the quality of goods and services. Furthermore, the loss of wages by the many thousands of downsized family "breadwinners" serves to reduce overall market demand, to increase the burden on government welfare programs, and to increase human suffering and resultant social discord. Also, if senior employees (i.e., top management) appear to be acting only out of their immediate self-interest, we can expect other workers up and down the organizational lines to act otherwise. None of this bodes well either for the quality of life for our children and grandchildren in our business-oriented society or for the ability of companies to pull employees together to create the team effort that is needed to compete in the emerging global economy.

Education

Our ancestors were minimally educated when they industrialized this nation. In 1880, when industrialization was just underway in this country, less than 3 percent of our nations's 17-year-olds were receiving a high school diploma.[6] With so few educated people entering our economy, it is hard to believe that our nineteenth century ancestors were able to create the most powerful industrial economy in the world. Surely it was only dumb luck that could have accounted for their accomplishments, bowed down as almost all were under the weight of their lack of schooling. With nearly 90 percent of our nation's 17-year-olds now receiving high school diplomas, and with nearly 60 percent of our eighteen- to twenty-one-year-olds pursuing college degrees today, we could surely industrialize this nation from scratch in a tenth the time taken by our ancestors.

Education is almost always the proposed answer for every problem. Education is supposed to make us do our civic duties, to vote intelligently, and to elect competent political leaders. Education is supposed to make us drive automobiles more safely, eat more healthy foods, avoid being cheated by flim-flam artists or by price fixing corporations, buy safer products and use them safely, use condoms, and listen to classical music rather than to rap. And yes, education is now supposed to help us beat the Japanese and Germans in world market competition.

Among the more important social functions of schools is to provide day care to keep our children off the streets. This is a need of no small consequence to us all. Equally important is the role of schools as a mechanism for socializing our children. Through schooling children become increasingly more oriented to accommodating the dictates of impersonal, bureaucratic organizations more so than those of the family (they also, as a coincidental side effect, become more oriented to the dictates of a same-age, peer group and hence to the fads and fashions of a generation). Schools, in short, work to transform people into organizational people capable and willing to follow orders and to perform activities at the whims of impersonal directives from on high regardless of the stress this places on themselves, on their friendships, on their families, or on their communities. For these purposes, schools are very successful and useful in a business-oriented society. But this educational process could certainly never produce entrepreneurs or innovative leaders, if that is what we want to stimulate our economy and political processes.

Why then do some people believe that schooling is getting the Japanese or Germans ahead of us in the world markets? Why do they think that more schooling (longer school days and longer school years) or more demanding schooling (more and more severe requirements for students to perform on bureaucratic demand) will make us more innovative and entrepreneurially aggressive? Because education is always the answer, regardless of the problem.

Think about it. How long do you think it should take a person to learn how to read? My daughter was reading simple books in first grade. At that time she lacked only the development of a complex vocabulary to be able to read adult-level books. But how long should it take to expand one's vocabulary to adult conventions? Should it take as much as a month to learn to read phonetically and another two years to master a reasonably substantial vocabulary? Surely the whole educational process could be mastered by virtually all persons, even at a snail's pace, within six years. Likewise how long should it take to learn how to add and subtract and to multiply and divide? Cannot these concepts be mastered in a matter of months? Why then do we require of our youth twelve years of schooling to learn these things?

And what of history, biology, geography, social studies, physical sciences, and so forth? Don't we rapidly (and mercifully) forget most of what we learn of these subjects from our schooling? Isn't memory a repository mostly for information that is useful to us or of recollections that are uniquely important to us, such as of our first kiss or of our parents "blowing a gasket" over some dumb thing we did (such as the time we wrecked the family car)? How then is schooling going to fill our memories up with whatever it is that is going to be required to beat the Japanese or Germans in world markets?

Think about this too, if you're employed: most of what you do at work you learned on the job, didn't you? This is true for all of us and for all jobs (including lawyers, doctors, college professors, corporate CEOs, janitors, trash collectors, and fast food preparers). Very little of schooling beyond learning how to take orders from impersonal superiors and how to read, write, and do arithmetic directly translates into something most of us do at our work place. How then is schooling going to improve our job performances and through these improvements beat the Japanese and Germans?

It has become commonplace to hear that job opportunities are changing and that these changes require improved education if people are to qualify for jobs and if we are to beat our world competitors and meet the challenges of a new age economy. But what does this all mean? The largest numbers of new jobs expected in our "new age" economy will be in the service sector, primarily in food services and in clerical jobs. Do we really need an expanded schooling effort to prepare our children for the challenges of these jobs?

Mass schooling does not create technological innovations or new industries. Research, investments and entrepreneurs do this. Furthermore, schooling has always been a social luxury. In the business-oriented society, the wealthiest of all societies, we have created the luxury that allows us to support the most extensive of schooling systems. It is the business-oriented industrial society that has made mass schooling possible, and not vice versa.

If there are skills employers believe their employees or prospective employees should have but don't, those employers should set up schooling programs to train and educate their work force. Why should we expect the government to bear the cost of providing this input into a business's productivity equation? There is much contemporary talk about the need to privatize government services. Why not let businesses privatize the otherwise government-supported schooling programs that they think their employees need? I'll bet that, if businesses had to pay for it, we would suddenly discover that we need a whole lot less education in our industrial economy than we previously thought.

Viewed either as a training program for the job market (to beat the Japanese and Germans or for any other market-related reason) or as a training program in civic preparedness for life in a democratic society, mass education is a "boondoggle." But it nonetheless serves other useful functions and is occasionally fun for participants and could be made more so. If we are not beating the Japanese and Germans in world markets or are falling behind them in the capacity to do so, the blame must rest squarely on the shoulders of businesses and businesspersons, especially corporate managers. If our business-oriented society should fall behind others in international competition, it will do so because of a lack of entrepreneurial spirit and quality among our business leadership, not because of a lack of quality in our schools or of educational credentials among the masses.

Government Debt

If each one of us over the age of 19 would sit down and write out a check for $25,000 to Uncle Sam, we could retire our national debt.[7] Calculated on average, that is what you owe for the services and favors our federal government has rendered on your behalf to the many sectors of our business-oriented society over the past few decades that were in excess of what could be paid for from incoming tax revenues.

In some respects the problems posed by federal government debt ($4.6 trillion in 1994[8]) are rather easy to understand. Think about it this way. Suppose you wanted to show everyone a good time and make everyone think you were a really great person. You might run out and buy gifts for everyone and set up a number of amusements for them (such as parties, pleasure trips, etc.), charging everything as you went along to your credit cards. You might reason that, because you have many years of wage earning ahead of you, you can always pay off these charges at some future time.

Unfortunately, the next year and every year thereafter, everyone expects you to give them the same or better gifts and amusements. So you must run your unpaid credit charge balance ever higher to maintain their good will and your good reputation. As an individual, you would rather quickly reach the limits that credit lenders would be willing to extend to you, and you would soon be in big trouble. Should you die, your estate would be liquidated to repay all lenders and your children would be left without inheritance, but at least they would not be liable for your debt.

Government debt differs from this description in a few details. Through the miracles of modern pork barrel politics, favors are freely handed out in all directions to make as many voters and special interest groups happy and to glorify the reputations of as many legislators as is possible. In a further effort to keep voters happy and to provide a continuing Keynesian stimulus to our economy, taxes are kept lower than expenditures. The result is mounting federal debt. Because the reputation of the federal government is good, lenders have been willing to continue to fund this mounting debt. But they must be induced to do so by being paid an attractive interest rate relative to interest rates on other prevailing investment possibilities. Thus it is quite costly to increase the federal debt through borrowing. Furthermore, the federal debt consumes more and more of society's available capital, so capital investments elsewhere are increasingly constrained.

Over time, a pattern of expanding debt creates a situation in which interest payments on existing debt consume a greater and greater percentage of annual federal budget expenses (by 1990 this percentage had grown to 14.7 percent of annual federal budget outlays as compared to 7.3 percent in 1970 and 8.9 percent in 1980[9]). Furthermore, unlike your personal debt, which, as was described earlier does not have to be paid by your children and grandchildren on your death, the federal debt that is increasing on your behalf will have to be paid off by your children and grandchildren. At least part of the grand lifestyle that you and I are living today is not just a gift of the business-oriented society and of our own hard work. Rather, it is a gift we are giving ourselves on government credit, while sending the bill to our children. This situation is difficult to justify morally.

Another problem with our current giant debt is that we are no longer in a position to apply a Keynesian solution of increased government spending during recessions. Reagan applied a Keynesian solution of decreased taxes and increased defense spending in response to the recession of the early 1980s, and we saw during his administration alone the creation of a public debt greater in amount than that accumulated under all prior presidential administrations put together.[10] Our children and grandchildren will be paying for Reagan's Keynesian solution for many years to come. In the recession of the early 1990s, we found ourselves already too far in debt to permit contemplation of another Keynesian solution.

It is in the interest of businesses and the business-oriented society as a whole to put the financial house of government back into order. But to do this means painful cuts in programs, increases in taxes, and the creation of a budget surplus. These moves could stagger our economy, already held aloft on a bubble of borrowed money, and could mean a dramatically reduced standard of living. Who among us is willing to pay this price? Which political leader would have the temerity to push for such budget reductions and tax increases? Who among us would vote for such a person? So far as I can see, only catastrophe will galvanize us to action in attempting to reform our federal spending habits. Because our large debt and profligate spending habits have severely decreased our ability to apply another Keynesian solution to business downturns, that catastrophe may not be far in the future.

An Upbeat Ending

I apologize for speculating about the future, given (as I said at the outset) that I have no talent for such an endeavor. I also apologize for being such a "gloomy Gus" in these speculations. In an effort to make amends, I wish to end this chapter on an upbeat note. To do this I will not point to a single negative facet of the business-oriented society, but instead shall emphasize its considerable strengths.

The business-oriented society has freed us from the bonds of patriarchal, royal, and church dictates and provided us with many luxuries. It has made us the best-fed and best-housed people with the best health care systems (and, yes, best schools) in history. We are an inventive, restless people conditioned by our business-oriented society to a champion's level in the skills required to adjust to change. In short, the business-oriented society provides us with better living conditions and better prospects for the future than has been known by any of our ancestors. Whatever the future holds, we are better prepared to deal with it and to make the most of it than any other group of people in history.

Notes

Chapter 1

1. Some examples of books on the role of businesses in society derived from nonsociological perspectives include: Gerald F. Cavanagh, *American Business Values*, 3rd ed. (Englewood Cliffs, N.J.: Prentice-Hall, 1990); Donna J. Wood, *Business and Society* (Glenview, Ill.: Scott Foresman, 1990); James E. Post, William C. Frederick, Anne T. Lawrence, and James Weber, *Business and Society: Corporate Strategy, Public Policy, Ethics*, 8th ed. (New York: McGraw-Hill, 1996); Fred Luthans and Richard M. Hodgetts, *Social Issues in Business: Strategic and Public Policy Perspectives*, 6th ed. (New York: Macmillan, 1989); Grover Starling, *The Changing Environment of Business: A Managerial Approach*, 4th ed. (Cincinnati, Ohio: South-Western Publishing, 1996); Frederick A. Sturdivant and Heidi Vernon-Wortzel, *Business and Society: A Managerial Approach*, 4th ed. (Homewood, Ill.: Irwin, 1990); Rogene A. Buchholz, *Business Environment and Public Policy: Implications for Management and Strategy Formation*, 3rd ed. (Englewood Cliffs, N.J.: Prentice-Hall, 1989); George A. Steiner and John F. Steiner, *Business, Government, and Society: A Managerial Perspective*, 7th ed. (New York: McGraw-Hill, 1994); and Murray L. Weidenbaum, *Business, Government, and the Public*, 4th ed. (Englewood Cliffs, N.J.: Prentice-Hall, 1990).

2. This book you are reading must ultimately find its home somewhere in the developing body of ideas on economic sociology. In truth, however, I did not write this book as a dialog with this body of ideas. I wrote it because I believe sociological insight is lacking in the literature on business and society represented by the list of books in endnote 1. For this reason this book follows in organization (especially in Part III) the major topics found in a typical business and society text. For this reason too, this book focuses throughout on the issue of the social responsibilities of businesses and on practical recommendations for actions that businesses can take to become more responsible. Most of the interest in economic sociology as a subdiscipline in sociology dates back only ten to twenty years, despite early pioneering work at the beginning of the twentieth century by Max Weber (*The Protestant Ethic and the Spirit of Capitalism, Economy and Society* and *General Economic History*) and Emile Durkheim (*The Division of Labor in Society*) and a few efforts since by Neil Smelser and Talcott Parsons (*Economy and Society*) and by Smelser (*The Sociology of Everyday Life* and *Readings on Economic Sociology*). More recent seminal works that have led to a renewed interest in economic sociology include Harrison White ("Where Do Markets Come From?," *American Journal of Sociology*, 1981, 87:514–547), Mark Granovetter ("Economic Action and Social Structure: the Problem of Embeddedness," *American Journal of Sociology*, 1985, 91:481–510), and Amitai Etzioni (*The Moral Dimension: Towards a New Economics* [New York: The Free Press, 1988]). An excellent review of this developing body of literature can be found in Neil Smelser and Richard Swedberg, *The Handbook of Economic Sociology* (Princeton, N.J.: Princeton University Press, 1994). A central argument in economic sociology that is

shared in this book is that economic phenomena (such as businesses and markets) are socially constructed and, therefore, must be understood in the larger context of the social structure and social processes of society as a whole.

3. C. Wright Mills, *The Sociological Imagination* (New York: Oxford University Press, 1959).

4. Useful summaries of interpretive, structural–functional, and conflict perspectives in sociology can be found in George Ritzer, *Sociological Theory,* 2nd ed. (New York: Alfred A. Knopf, 1988) and Randall Collins, *Four Sociological Traditions,* Rev. Ed. (New York: Oxford University Press, 1994).

5. It is for this reason that Max Weber recommended the construction of "ideal types" or that Herbert Blummer recommended the use of "sensitizing concepts" in efforts to portray and understand social phenomena.

6. I draw here from the "dramaturgical perspective" of Irving Goffman. See his *Presentation of Self in Everyday Life* (Garden City, N.Y.: Anchor, 1959).

7. Here I am drawing from W. I. Thomas' famous theorem: Situations we define as real become real in their consequences. See W. I. Thomas, *The Unadjusted Girl* (Boston: Little, Brown, 1923), p. 42.

8. It is not necessary at this point to restrict our attention to only activities that are motivated by a desire to maximize profits. Though a profit motivation is a critical feature in defining businesses, the maximization of profits is not. The assertion that businesses should maximize their profits is a peculiar one that I examine in some detail in later chapters.

9. It is not necessary at this point to limit the definition of business further by specifying a pricing mechanism for the marketplace, either in terms of supply and demand factors or in terms of price setting by trusts, guilds, governments, or churches. I comment on the significance of these distinctions in later chapters.

Chapter 2

1. See, for example, R. Edward Freeman, *Strategic Management: A Stakeholder Approach* (Boston: Ballinger, 1984).

2. A useful review of techniques of stakeholder analysis appears in Donna J. Wood, *Business and Society* (Glenview, Ill.: Scott Foresman, 1990), pp. 90–103.

3. With my own modifications to fit the sociological approach I have taken, I have drawn these three models from George A. Steiner and John F. Steiner, *Business, Government, and Society: A Managerial Perspective,* 4th ed. (New York: Random House, 1985), pp. 7–14. See also similar models in Lee E. Preston and James E. Post, *Private Management and Public Policy: The Principle of Public Responsibility* (Englewood Cliffs, N.J.: Prentice-Hall, 1975), pp. 14–28.

4. Two well-known books that present sociological perspectives on religion are: Milton J. Yinger, *The Scientific Study of Religion* (New York: Macmillan, 1970) and Robert N. Bellah, *Beyond Belief: Essays on Religion in a Post-Traditional World* (New York: Harper & Row, 1970). More recent textbooks surveying the sociology of religion include Ronald L. Johnstone, *Religion in Society: A Sociology of Religion,* 3rd ed. (Englewood Cliffs, N.J.: Prentice-Hall, 1988); Keith A. Roberts, *Religion in Sociological Perspective,* 2nd ed. (Belmont, Calif.:

Wadsworth, 1990). I will be discussing how religions are related to businesses further in Chapter 5.

5. I use the term *cult* here in a general sense to refer to any unusual or nontraditional religious movement. Many sociologists prefer to restrict the use of this term to short-lived, small, counter-cultural religious groups.

6. Research on cargo cults is summarized in Peter Worsley, *The Trumpet Shall Sound: A Study of "Cargo" Cults in Melanesia,* 2nd ed. (New York: Schocken Books, 1968) and in Vittorio Lanternari, *The Religions of the Oppressed* (New York: Knopf, 1963).

7. It will become obvious in the portrayal to follow that by focusing on our ritualistic sacrifices in education I am presenting a limited and rather negative perspective on the otherwise multiple functions of schooling in our society. I use other perspectives on schooling in Chapters 5 and 14. Excellent reviews of the purposes of schooling in society can be found in the following sources: Randall Collins, *The Credential Society: An Historical Sociology of Education and Stratification* (New York: Academic Press, 1979); Samuel Bowles and Herbert Gintis, *Schooling in Capitalist America* (New York: Basic Books, 1976); John Boli, Francisco O. Ramirez, and John W. Meyer, "Explaining the Origins

and Expansion of Mass Education," *Comparative Education Review,* 1985, 29:145–170.

8. Because children in industrial societies have no economic value as productive members of family units or communities, schooling gives children something to do to occupy their time. Schooling also gives them opportunities to socialize with their peers and to form peer groups, which might be fun for them to do. Although schooling has multiple functions, I am focusing on only a few functions in this exercise.

9. Of course a great many children fail to be fully converted and confirmed into this belief system. Like the "unsaved" or "backsliders" of any religion, they do not control their behavior, thoughts, and emotions into patterns as I have described. Rather they may become dropouts or may perform poorly in schooling by exhibiting what school authorities consider to be behavioral, emotional, or attitudinal problems.

10. I shall discuss the workworld in considerably more detail in Chapters 9 and 10. Some useful books reviewing the workworld from a sociological perspective include Curt Tausky, *Work, Organization and Power: Introduction to Industrial Sociology* (Itasca, Ill.: Peacock Publishers, 1983) and Ramona L. Ford, *Work, Organization, and Power: Introduction to Industrial Sociology* (Boston: Allyn and Bacon, 1988).

11. Researchers tend to focus on industrialization as a factor in urban growth. However, a larger historical pattern of business-related forces has been at work. Thus, while the mass production systems and mass markets of industrialization have created industrial jobs and city lifestyles that have "pulled" people into urban areas, other business-related factors have "pushed" people away from rural areas. Examples of these commercially related "push" factors are the English enclosure movement and a number of agricultural advances that greatly expanded crop production. These "push" factors, undertaken by large landowners, left many farm laborers without the means to support themselves. Hence they were pushed toward cities in search of a livelihood.

12. Again, industrial businesses are not alone in accounting for the breakup of extended family structures. A larger pattern of business-related forces operating over several centuries pushed people out of their agricultural lifestyles and family structures. See endnote 11.

Chapter 3

1. Milton Friedman, "The Social Responsibility of Business is to Increase its Profits," *New York Times Magazine,* September 13, 1970.

2. Research and Policy Committee of the Committee for Economic Development, *Social Responsibilities in Business Corporations* (New York: Committee for Economic Development, June 1971), p. 28.

3. Frank W. Abrams, "Management's Responsibilities in a Complex World," *Harvard Business Review,* May 1951, pp. 29–30, 31, quoted in William C. Frederick, Keith Davis, and James E. Post, *Business and Society: Corporate Strategy, Public Policy, Ethics,* 6th ed. (New York: McGraw-Hill, 1988), p. 30.

4. Research and Policy Committee of the Committee for Economic Development, p. 16.

5. Robert Ford and Frank McLaughlin, "Perceptions of Socially Responsible Activities and Attitudes: A Comparison of Business School Deans and Corporate Chief Executives," *Academy of Management Journal,* September 1984, pp. 670–671.

6. Business Roundtable, *Statement on Corporate Responsibility* (New York: The Business Roundtable, October 1981), p. 12.

7. Some of the ideas I present in this brief history parallel those developed by Clarence C. Walton in his article, "The Three Eras of American Business," in Clarence C. Walton, ed., *Business and Social Progress* (New York: Praeger, 1970), pp. 122–36.

8. Matthew Josephson, *The Robber Barons* (New York: Harcourt Brace, 1934).

9. Similar arguments were developed almost a century ago by Thorstein Veblen, a sociologist who was writing about big businesses at the time that they were coming into prominence. See Thorstein Veblen, *The Theory of Business Enterprise* (New York: Scribner, 1904), pp. 16–23.

10. John Kenneth Galbraith, *American Capitalism* (Boston: Houghton Mifflin, 1952).

11. This point is highlighted in Michael Useem, *The Inner Circle: Large Corporations and the Rise of Business Political Activity in the U.S. and U.K.* (New York: Oxford University Press, 1984), pp. 76–115.

Chapter 4

1. Of course our food gathering and hunting ancestors lived in prehistoric times: that is, they lived before the invention of writing and its use in the preparation of written documents that might have described their lifestyles. Thus we must speculate a good deal about them based on limited archaeological findings and on studies of contemporary food gathering and hunting societies. I have found the following sources useful in preparing this discussion of food gathering and hunting societies: Marshall Sahlins, *Stone Age Economics* (Chicago: Aldine–Atherton, 1972); Stephen K. Sanderson, *Macrosociology: An Introduction to Human Societies*, 2nd ed. (New York: HarperCollins, 1991); Gerhard Lenski, Jean Lenski, and Patrick Nolan, *Human Societies: An Introduction to Macrosociology*, 6th ed. (New York: McGraw-Hill, 1991); and Gerhard Lenski, *Power and Privilege: A Theory of Social Stratification* (New York: McGraw-Hill, 1966).

2. Sahlins argues that the lifestyle of food gatherers and hunters was affluent and typically required little exertion because they desired little or no durable goods and usually found enough to eat in easy reach. Furthermore, if food supplies did become scarce during their continual migrations, they could maintain their affluence by such population control measures as infanticide, abortion, senilicide, and selective prohibitions against sexual intercourse (Sahlins, p. 34; see also Lenski, Lenski, and Nolan, p. 99; and Lenski, p. 104).

3. Though sharing was the norm within the band, cheaters who did not always share as they were expected to were not unheard of, particularly during times of famine (see Sahlins, pp. 125–126 and 203–204). As a norm, sharing also typically carried the expectation in the band that receivers would reciprocate by sharing whatever they found at some future time. Violations of the norm of sharing resulted in considerable public ridicule or worse.

4. Sahlins (pp. 185–275) provides a much more refined classification of the nature of exchanges between food gatherers and hunters than I can or need to develop here, including gradations from altruistic giving to reciprocal giving and to stealing, and including normative variations based on kinship, the existence of a surplus, and differences in the types of good to be traded.

5. I have included horticultural and pastoral societies under the term agricultural societies despite the differences these societies have from each other and from societies based on more advanced agricultural techniques. I shall describe these differences whenever they are important in this book, but in general the features that are common to all agricultural societies and that are most critical for business development are those I wish to emphasize. In preparing this discussion of agricultural societies, I have found the sources cited in endnote 1 useful, as well as the following: Jean-Philippe Levy, trans. by John G. Biram, *The Economic Life of the Ancient World* (Chicago: University of Chicago Press, 1967 [originally published in 1964]); Shepard B. Clough and Richard T. Rapp, *European Economic History: The Economic Development of Western Civilization*, 3rd ed. (New York: McGraw-Hill, 1975); John Gledhill, Barbara Bender, and Mogens Trolle Larsen (eds.), *State and Society: The Emergence and Development of Social Hierarchy and Political Centralization* (Boston: Unwin Hyman, 1988).

6. Certain types of ants probably operated pastoral and horticultural societies based on aphid herding and fungus growing long before humans developed comparable practices. But among ants these activities appear to be genetically determined rather than deriving from intellectual accomplishments, so ants do not have as much reason as we do to boast about themselves on this score.

7. Sahlins (pp. 41–99) points out by contrast that primitive horticultural societies did not involve particularly hard work and instead involved much leisure because only a minimal amount of food to satisfy hunger was typically grown and no effort usually was made to create a surplus of goods.

8. Actually, it remains an open question why our food gathering and hunting ancestors shifted to the use of agricultural techniques. Food scarcities resulting from climatic changes, population increases, or the overhunting of big game animals may have played roles. Furthermore, it also remains an open question why, having shifted to agricultural techniques, our ancestors bothered to create a surplus of food rather than just enough for daily needs. No doubt the rising influence of political and religious leaders had a role in directing economic efforts toward the creation of a surplus (for discussions of these issues see Sahlins, pp. 130–148; Lenski, Lenski, and Nolan, pp. 120–122, 151–155, 162; Sanderson, pp. 81–84).

9. There are a few specialized roles frequently found among food gatherers and hunters, such as the role of shaman or group leader. These specialized roles,

however, are expected to be performed only on a part-time basis (see Lenski, p. 100).

10. With minor spelling change, I borrow the term and concept of a "leisured class" from the famous American sociologist, Thorstein Veblen, *The Theory of the Leisure Class* (Boston: Houghton Mifflin Company, 1973 [originally 1899]).

11. Levy, p. 23.

12. Levy, pp. 28–29; Clough and Rapp, pp. 31–33.

13. As I will note in the next chapter, the fully developed business-oriented society occurs when the problem of extreme labor intensity in food production is solved. This frees the masses from farm work and instead makes them wage laborers who are oriented toward and dominated by markets. In this way business markets come to pervade all aspects of the lives of people in business-oriented societies.

14. Ancient Egypt, for example, is well-known for having been operated by the pharaohs much as though it were a gigantic proprietary venture (see Levy, pp. 7–9, 40–43).

15. Lenski, Lenski, and Nolan, p. 160. See also Morgens Trolle Larsen, "Introduction: Literacy and Social Complexity," in Gledhill, Bender, and Larsen, pp. 175–191; and John Baines, "Literacy, Social Organization, and the Archaeological Record: The Case of Early Egypt," in Gledhill, Bender, and Larsen, pp. 192–214.

16. Major corporate business leaders in the United States, for example, argue that profit maximization necessarily takes a back seat in their corporation to the more fundamental goal of the survival of their businesses as ongoing concerns, a goal which requires attention to and maintenance of good relations with their social environment (see Alfred C. Neil, *Business Power and Public Policies* (New York: Prager, 1981), pp. 84–91, 98). You can probably confirm from your experience that business survival and its corollary of good public relations take priority over profit maximization in the successful small businesses with which you are acquainted.

17. I realize that this view of evil will be seen as too "squishy" by some philosophers who prefer to conceive of evil as an absolute ideal rather than as an empirical, social construction. In Chapter 8 I describe in more detail the sociological perspective I am taking on morality and set out at that point specific suggestions for improving the moral performance of businesses.

Chapter 5

1. Two examples of books on this subject by sociologists are by Immanuel Wallerstein, *Historical Capitalism* (London: Verso, 1983) and Peter L. Berger, *The Capitalist Revolution* (New York: Basic Books, 1986). Wallerstein clearly prefers the term capitalism and focuses his discussions on capital formation and its role in social relations. Berger, by contrast, places himself more in the movement of thought represented by the term modernization (see Berger, pp. 27–28).

2. I found the following sources helpful in preparing this chapter: Shepard B. Clough and Richard T. Rapp, *European Economic History: The Economic Development of Western Civilization,* 3rd ed. (New York: McGraw-Hill, 1975); R. R. Palmer and Joel Colton, *A History of the Modern World,* 6th ed. (New York: Alfred A. Knopf, 1984).

3. Palmer and Colton, p. 21.

4. Clough and Rapp, p. 69.

5. Clough and Rapp, pp. 78–79, and Palmer and Colton, pp. 32–33.

6. Clough and Rapp, pp. 91–92, and Palmer and Colton, pp. 31–32.

7. Because mercantilism generally involved a collusion between political leaders and businesspersons based on their reciprocal interests, the actual principles and practices of mercantilism varied somewhat from country to country depending on variations in the unique character of these interests. Mercantilism, therefore, is not a uniform social phenomenon (see Clough and Rapp, pp. 203–229, and Palmer and Colton, pp. 116–118).

8. See Michel Beaud, *A History of Capitalism: 1500–1980,* translated by Tom Dickman and Anny Lefebvre (New York: Monthly Review Press, 1983 [originally 1981]), pp. 43–47.

9. Beaud argues that merchants supported the mercantilist policies of the rising monarchial nation-states both as a means to provide a counterforce to foreign competition and as a means to increase their profits through expansion and monopolization of international trade routes. But when these merchants felt they were wealthy enough to dominate the world markets on their own, they shifted political positions, opposing mercantilism and favoring instead economic liberalism and democracy. See Beaud, pp. 33–42, 74.

10. On this point see Gerhard Lenski, *Power and Privilege: A Theory of Social Stratification* (New York: McGraw-Hill, 1966), p. 106.

11. Clough and Rapp, pp. 70–72.

12. Clough and Rapp, pp. 56–59.

13. Clough and Rapp, pp. 57–58.

14. Clough and Rapp, pp. 59–60.

15. Palmer and Colton, pp. 35–36, 49.

16. The French Edict of Nantes in 1598, for example, provided for religious tolerance and plurality, as did the English Toleration Act of 1689. The United States, of course, was founded on the principle of a secular government with religious tolerance and plurality.

17. The downside to Calvanism is the proscription that held that one should not squander one's wealth on high living but instead should invest and marshall it as if it were a gift from God. Therefore life as a Calvinist may not be much fun for those of us who like to spend money. However this restriction on spending does foster private capital accumulation and investment. And pockets of private capital were critical to the development of industrial businesses. The sociologist Max Weber is well known for highlighting the significance of Protestantism to business interests in his book *The Protestant Ethic and the Spirit of Capitalism,* translated by Talcott Parsons (New York: Charles Scribner's Sons, 1958 [originally 1905]).

18. France and Italy are apparent exceptions to this rule, but in both cases we have seen a history of successful efforts by political leaders of these two countries to contain the influence that the Roman Catholic Church has on internal matters. Political leaders in France, for example, exerted considerable political control for many centuries over the Roman Catholic ecclesiastics in France. French political leaders also engaged in much intrigue in opposition to the Hapsburg Holy Roman Empire that encircled most of its land borders. One way they did this was by providing considerable support to the Reformation leaders against the Hapsburgs. Furthermore, Roman Catholic Church property was seized and religious tolerance was proclaimed in the French Revolution.

Italy, on the other hand, had a long history of politically independent city-states, many of which were controlled by wealthy merchants. In the national unification of Italy in the 1800s, a secular, parliamentary monarchy was created, and the Roman Catholic Church lost political authority over the previous Papal states of Italy and eventually over the city of Rome itself. This left the Church in political control only over the small patch of land known as the Vatican. Despite the political maneuvering that removed the Roman Catholic Church as a significant political force, the citizens of France and Italy have remained predominantly Catholic. The fact that there are such exceptions as France and Italy shows that Protestantism among the masses is not itself a necessary correlate of industrialization. The more important issue is the political control that the church is able to exert over society.

19. Palmer and Colton, p. 41.

20. Clough and Rapp, p. 106.

21. Palmer and Colton, p. 40.

22. The angst of emerging individualism is evidenced in the development of the body of thought known as the existential movement. Key figures include Pascal (1623–1662), Kierkegaard (1813–1855), Dostoevski (1821–1881), Nietzsche (1844–1900), and Sartre (1905–1980).

23. The allusion here, of course, is to Erich Fromm's book, *Escape From Freedom* (New York: Holt, Rhinehart and Winston, 1941).

24. As a society we now have, in short, a situation of organic solidarity. See Emile Durkheim's *The Division of Labor in Society,* translated by George Simpson (New York: The Free Press, 1933 [originally 1893]).

25. See a review of this issue by Alfred C. Neil, *Business Power and Public Policies* (New York: Prager, 1981), pp. 50–51, 122–125.

26. See Neil, pp. 132–133, 135.

27. This problem is variably described as the consumer's "lack of full information" or as the consumer's "imperfect" or "incomplete" information. A useful discussion of this issue appears in M. A. Utton, *The Economics of Regulating Industry* (New York: Basil Blackwell Inc., 1986), pp. 9–11, 37–75.

28. See, for example, the discussion of product differentiation as a barrier to competition by Neil, pp. 131–132.

29. I shall not consider human happiness or life satisfaction in this review because these are subjective characteristics that all too often appear to be unrelated to social conditions. We don't know if other species experience such subjective states, but it is remarkable how often humans can be found to be happy or satisfied under the most extreme conditions of privation or unhappy and dissatisfied when in the lap of luxury.

30. Adam Smith's most important work is his book *An Inquiry into the Nature and Causes of the*

Wealth of Nations (New York: The Modern Library, 1965 [originally published in 1776]).

31. Source: Bureau of the Census, *Statistical Abstract of the United States: 1995,* 115th ed. (Washington, D.C.: Government Printing Office, 1995, Table 1373).

32. Source: *Statistical Abstract of the United States: 1995,* Table 1363.

33. Source: *Statistical Abstract of the United States: 1995,* Table 1363.

34. A short, highly readable presentation of Marx's key arguments is found in his pamphlet with Frederick Engels: *The Communist Manifesto,* translated by Frederick Engels (New York: International Publishers, 1948 [originally published 1848]. I have also found useful the discussion of his ideas by John McMurtry, *The Structure of Marx's World-View* (Princeton, N.J.:

Princeton University Press, 1978). Also useful as a reference in the analyses of modern capitalism is Robert L. Heilbroner, *The Nature and Logic of Capitalism* (New York: W. W. Norton & Company, 1985).

35. See however the contrary argument by Wallerstein (pp. 100–102) who suggests that when looking worldwide one finds the majority of the world population to have been impoverished by the worldwide commercial ventures of capitalistic societies.

36. See, for example, the analyses by Wallerstein (pp. 54–56) and Heilbroner (pp. 101–106).

37. See the useful analyses on freedom in capitalism by Berger (pp. 72–114) and Heilbroner (pp. 125–129).

38. See particularly Wallerstein, who is well-known for his view of capitalism as an international exploitative process. A comparable perspective can be found in Beaud.

Chapter 6

1. Drawn from a description in Grover Starling, *The Changing Environment of Business: A Managerial Approach,* 3rd ed. (Boston: PWS-Kent Publishing Company, 1988), p. 41.

2. These 1983 figures are derived from Bureau of the Census, *Statistical Abstract of the United States, 1986,* 106th ed. (Washington, D.C.: U.S. Government Printing Office, 1985), Tables 907 and 881.

3. See, for example, the discussion by Shepard B. Clough and Richard T. Rapp, *European Economic History: The Economic Development of Western Civilization,* 3rd ed. (New York: McGraw-Hill, 1975), pp. 348–350. An excellent discussion of how competition and state intervention affected the growth of corporations is found in Neil Fligstein, *The Transformation of Corporate Control* (Cambridge, Mass.: Harvard University Press, 1990).

4. These 1991 figures are from Bureau of the Census, *Statistical Abstract of the United States, 1995,* 115th ed. (Washington, D.C.: U.S. Government Printing Office, 1995), Table 847.

5. These 1991 figures are from *Statistical Abstract of the United States, 1995,* Table 848.

6. This 1993 figure is computed from *Statistical Abstract of the United States, 1995,* Tables 884 and 1373.

7. This 1992 figure is from *Statistical Abstract of the United States, 1995,* Table 882.

8. Drawn from summaries in Marshall B. Clinard and Peter C. Yeager, *Corporate Crime* (New York:

The Free Press, 1980), p. 33, and David R. Simon and D. Stanley Eitzen, *Elite Deviance,* 2nd ed. (Boston: Allyn and Bacon, Inc., 1986), p. 74.

9. Figures drawn from Alfred C. Neal, *Business Power and Public Policy* (New York: Praeger, 1981), pp. 126, 157.

10. Drawn from a summary in Simon and Eitzen, p. 10.

11. These 1991 figures on gross state products are from *Statistical Abstract of the United States, 1995,* Table 703.

12. These 1993 figures on state revenues are from *Statistical Abstract of the United States, 1995,* Table 488.

13. See, for example, the discussion in Robert L. Heilbroner, *The Economic Transformation of America* (New York: Harcourt Brace Jovanovich, Inc., 1977), pp. 80–82.

14. The decreasing power exerted by owners in the control of modern corporations was the subject of the classic work by Adolf A. Berle and Gardiner C. Means, *The Modern Corporation and Private Property* (New York: Macmillan, 1932). Their study found that 44 percent of the 200 largest corporations in 1930 were controlled by management. In these management-controlled corporations, no owner owned more than 5 percent of the corporation's stock, and therefore no owner was believed to be in a position to have much say over corporate business decisions. An update to this study found that 84.5 percent of the 200 largest corporations

were under management control in 1963, see Robert J. Larner, *Management Control and the Large Corporation* (New York: Dunellen, 1971).

15. Business interests were central to the American Revolution. Heilbroner (p. 17), for example, points out that six of the people who signed our Declaration of Independence had direct involvement in the iron industry.

16. See Heilbroner, pp. 17–18.

17. See Heilbroner, pp. 19, 23, 62.

18. See Heilbroner, pp. 30–36, and Neal, pp. 16–17. Heilbroner (p. 62) notes that the Homestead Act of 1862 resulted in government land grants to railroad builders which handed over to them as much as 10 percent of the area of the states through which they constructed their lines. This was certainly a very nice subsidy, but it was not enough: The Immigration Act of 1864 was passed to allow railroads (and other industries on the West and East coasts) to bring Chinese and Europeans into the United States under temporary contract to provide a labor pool of men willing to work long hours in hazardous working conditions at very low pay in order to build the railroads across the West.

19. The provision of systems for the administration of justice and for protection from foreign powers were, of course, recognized by Adam Smith as fundamental governmental duties in an otherwise free market society. See Adam Smith, *The Wealth of Nations* (New York: The Modern Library, 1965 [originally 1776]), p. 651.

20. It is the human brutality glossed over by the elegant abstractions of the *laissez-faire* model, a model which so many economists contemplate with great affection from the comfort of their arm chairs, that accounts for why economics has come to be known as the "dismal science."

21. Bureau of the Census, *Historical Statistics of the United States, Colonial Times to 1970*, Bicentennial Edition (Washington, D.C.: U.S. Government Printing Office, 1975), Tables Series Y 457–465 and Y 567–589.

22. *Historical Statistics of the United States, Colonial Times to 1970*, Table Y 457–465.

23. This 1995 figure is from *Statistical Abstract of the United States, 1995*, Table 522.

24. This 1992 figure is from *Statistical Abstract of the United States, 1995*, Table 475. The 1950 figure is from *Historical Statistics of the United States, Colonial Times to 1970*, Tables Series A 9–22 and Y 533–566.

25. The 1992 figure is from *Statistical Abstract of the United States, 1995*, Tables 475 and 1373. The 1950 figure is from *Historical Statistics of the United States,*

Colonial Times to 1970, Tables Series F 1–5 and Y 533–566.

26. These 1992 figures on GNPs are from *Statistical Abstract of the United States, 1995*, Table 1373.

27. The 1992 figure is from *Statistical Abstract of the United States, 1995*, Table 507. The 1950 figure is from *Historical Statistics of the United States, Colonial Times to 1970*, Table Series Y 272–289.

28. These 1990 figures on metropolitan populations are from *Statistical Abstract of the United States, 1995*, Table 43.

29. These 1990 figures on populations are from *Statistical Abstract of the United States, 1995*, Table 1361.

30. The 1992 figure on employees was computed from *Statistical Abstract of the United States, 1995*, Tables 884 and 885.

31. This 1994 figure is from *Statistical Abstract of the United States, 1995*, Table 633.

32. These 1993 figures are from *Statistical Abstract of the United States, 1995*, Tables 699, 1373, 707.

33. I have found the following sources helpful in preparing this section: Shepard B. Clough and Richard T. Rapp, *European Economic History: The Economic Development of Western Civilization*, 3rd ed. (New York: McGraw-Hill, 1975), pp. 380–463; R. R. Palmer and Joel Colton, *A History of the Modern World*, 6th ed. (New York: Alfred A. Knopf, 1984), pp. 660–695, 761–772; John Kenneth Galbraith, *Economics in Perspective: A Critical History* (Boston: Houghton Mifflin, 1987), pp. 193–265; Alfred C. Neil, *Business Power and Public Policy* (New York: Praeger, 1981), pp. 12–26; Robert L. Heilbroner, *The Economic Transformation of America* (New York: Harcourt Brace Jovanovich, Inc., 1977).

34. Toward the end of his four-year term, and with re-election chances dwindling, Hoover did begin some programs to aid farmers and to put people back to work in public projects (including the construction of what is now called Hoover Dam). In 1932 he also went along with Congress in creating the Reconstruction Finance Corporation, designed to lend public money to troubled businesses, and to the passing of the Home Loan Bank Act, designed specifically to help failing banks. His efforts to protect U.S. businesses by the signing of the Smoot-Hawley Tariff Act in 1930, however, may have contributed to the intensification and prolongation of the depression. On this point, see Heilbroner, pp. 181–182.

35. John Maynard Keynes, *The General Theory of Employment, Interest, and Money* (New York: Harcourt Brace, 1936).

36. Computed from *Historical Statistics of the United States, Colonial Times to 1970,* Tables Series F 1–5 and Y 57–465.

37. Computed from *Historical Statistics of the United States, Colonial Times to 1970,* Tables Series F 1–5 and Y 457–465 and from *Statistical Abstract of the United States, 1995,* Tables 517, 699, 1373.

38. All figures are from 1992. See *Statistical Abstract of the United States, 1995,* Tables 548, 584, 585.

39. A good summary of corrupt practices in the military-industrial complex can be found in Simon and Eitzen, pp. 130–146.

40. Keynes, p. 129.

41. These 1992 figures are from *Statistical Abstract of the United States, 1995,* Tables 475 and 585.

42. This 1994 figure is from *Statistical Abstract of the United States, 1995,* Table 981.

43. A usefully detailed account of the Chrysler bailout can be found in Murray L. Weidenbaum, *Business, Government, and the Public,* 3rd ed. (Englewood Cliffs, N.J.: Prentice-Hall, 1986), pp. 330–341.

44. A federalization of the credit markets for capital has occurred in the United States. As of 1983, for example, 56 percent of all credit funds were borrowed under federal auspices. This point is made in Weidenbaum, p. 10.

45. See Frances Fox Piven and Richard A. Cloward, *Regulating the Poor: The Functions of Public Welfare* (New York: Pantheon Books, 1971).

46. Variations on this model appear in William C. Frederick, Keith Davis, and James E. Post, *Business and Society: Corporate Strategy, Public Policy, Ethics,* 6th ed. (New York: McGraw-Hill, 1988), p. 130; Grover Starling, *The Changing Environment of Businesses: A Managerial Approach,* 3rd ed. (Boston: PWS-Kent Publishing Company, 1988), p. 29; Peter L. Berger, *The Capitalist Revolution* (New York: Basic Books, 1986), pp. 21–22.

47. The sociologist Daniel Bell argued several decades ago that the two great ideologies of capitalism and communism had become exhausted and were no longer useful as models for describing social order or for motivating reformations of social order. See Daniel Bell, *The End of Ideology: On the Exhaustion of Political Ideas in the Fifties,* rev. ed. (New York: Collier, 1962).

48. The prediction of this movement has been called the "convergence hypothesis." See William Form, "Comparative Industrial Sociology and the Convergence Hypothesis" in eds. Alex Inkeles, James Cole-

man, and Ralph H. Turner, *Annual Review of Sociology,* vol. 5 (Palo Alto, Calif.: Annual Reviews, 1979).

49. See, for example, the discussion by Berger, pp. 181–185.

50. Economic pluralism has little impact on the property rights of the owners of the giant corporations that dominate our economy because, as mere shareholders, these owners of U.S. corporate assets already possess very little control over the corporations they "own." The constraints of economic pluralism on property rights are most immediately felt when they are applied on proprietary and partnership businesses and on the average homeowner. In short, economic pluralism does not allow anyone to be an absolute monarch (king or queen) of their own home or business. But, on the other hand, few political monarchs in history ever possessed absolute control over their domain.

51. Board of Governors of the Federal Reserve System (study directors: Dorothy S. Projector and Gertrude S. Weiss), *Survey of Financial Characteristics of Consumers* (Washington, D.C.: Federal Reserve System, 1966). See also reanalyses and new summaries of these data in Executive Office of the President, Office of Management and Budget, *Social Indicators, 1973* (Washington, D.C.: U.S. Government Printing Office, 1973), Chart 5/15; Frank Ackerman and Andrew Zimbalist, "Capitalism and Inequality in the United States," in eds. Richard C. Edwards, Michael Reich, and Thomas E. Weisskopf, *The Capitalist System,* 3rd ed. (Englewood Cliffs, N.J.: Prentice-Hall, 1986), pp. 217–227. These estimates are consistent with others that have been obtained in the United States between the years of 1922 and 1972, when estimates of all U.S. wealth held by the top 1 percent of wealthholders ranged from 20.1 percent to 36.3 percent. For these estimates, see Bureau of the Census, *Statistical Abstract of the United States, 1985,* 105th ed. (Washington, D.C.: U.S. Government Printing Office, 1985), Table 774. A more recent estimate by the Joint Economic Committee of Congress in 1986 places the total wealth of the top 1 percent of wealthholders at 41.8 percent of all U.S. wealth, and the bottom 90 percent of wealthholders at a mere 28.2 percent of U.S. wealth. A table of these results is presented in D. Stanley Eitzen and Maxine Baca Zinn, *In Conflict and Order: Understanding Society,* 5th ed. (Boston: Allyn and Bacon, 1991), Table 10–1, p. 226.

52. Figures reported in Ackerman and Zimbalist, p. 220, Table 6–D.

53. Figures from U.S. Bureau of Census, *Statistical Abstract of the United States, 1982–1983,* 103rd ed. (Washington, D.C.: U.S. Government Printing Office), Table 742.

54. Real Horatio Alger success stories are rare indeed. For example, one study of 303 top industrial business leaders in the 1870s, a period when industrial development was intensifying in the United States, found that 90 percent came from what were considered middle class backgrounds. See Heilbroner, p. 71.

55. The now classic study on occupational mobility in the United States is by Peter M. Blau and Otis Dudley Duncan, *The American Occupational Structure* (New York: Wiley, 1967).

56. One great difficulty to be encountered in efforts to control governments in the United States lies in the large number of governments. For example, there are currently more than 86,000 units of government at the local level in the United States; 1992 figure drawn from *Statistical Abstract of the United States, 1995,* Tables 471.

57. C. Wright Mills, *The Power Elite* (New York: Oxford University Press, 1956).

58. This 1992 figure is from *Statistical Abstract of the United States, 1995,* Table 548.

59. G. William Domhoff, *Who Rules America?* (Englewood Cliffs, N.J.: Prentice-Hall, 1967).

60. See also G. William Domhoff, *The Higher Circles* (New York: Random House, 1970); *The Powers that Be: Processes of Ruling Class Domination in America* (New York: Vintage Books, 1978); *Who Rules America Now?* (Englewood Cliffs: Prentice-Hall, 1983).

61. Though millionaires constitute a minute fraction of our population, they have dominated the White House: Seven of our ten Presidents over the past sixty-five years were millionaires.

62. For example, as of 1985, 76.8 percent of the U.S. House of Representatives and 91 percent of the U.S. Senate came from business, banking, or law backgrounds. Source: *Statistical Abstract of the United States, 1986,* Table 423.

63. One study found that, at any given time between 1897 and 1973, the proportion of federal cabinet heads coming from the business sector ranged from a low of 60 percent upward to virtually 100 percent (see Simon and Eitzen, p. 13).

64. Michael Useem, *The Inner Circle: Large Corporations and the Rise of Business Political Activity in the U.S. and U.K.* (New York: Oxford University Press, 1984).

65. There is yet another way big businesses may influence politics that is worthy of note. When large corporations have facilities in many local political jurisdictions, which is a typical situation, politicians representing each jurisdiction have a vested interest in the corporation as a contributor to local employment and to local economic vitality. This gives big businesses ample political representation in the U.S. Congress as well as in the many governments to be found at the state and local level.

66. We see such conspiratorial failures, for example, in organizations that are specifically designed to operate secretly, such as the FBI or CIA. These organizations are well-known for bungling their operations, violating their missions, and leaking information. Likewise the secret plans of military operations are frequently leaked and typically bungled on implementation. Even organized crime fails to operate secretly, relying instead on buying people off, on intimidation, on murder, or on people looking the other way, winking, shrugging at their actions, or not wanting to get involved.

67. The fertility rate in the United States as of 1992 was 2.0 children per woman. See Population Reference Bureau, *1992 World Population Data Sheet* (Washington, D.C.: Population Reference Bureau, 1992).

68. The famous sociologist, Ferdinand Tonnies, referred to this process as the movement of community relations from a state of Gemeinschaft to Gesellschaft.

69. Figures on official poverty thresholds are from *Statistical Abstract of the United States, 1995,* Table 746. Note that, at a minimum wage of $4.25, in 1993 a worker would earn $170 for a 40-hour week, or $8,840 for a 52-week work year, which would put him or her just above the official poverty line for a single person but below the poverty line if he or she had a dependent.

70. These 1993 figures are from *Statistical Abstract of the United States, 1995,* Table 754.

71. These 1993 figures are from *Statistical Abstract of the United States, 1995,* Table 747.

72. These 1972 figures were computed from U.S. Bureau of Census, Current Population Reports, Series P60–185, *Poverty in the United States: 1992* (Washington, D.C.: U.S. Government Printing Office, 1993), Tables 6, 15. Recall again that, at minimum wage, a worker does not earn enough to lift his or her family out of poverty.

73. A similar argument can be found in Andrew W. Dobelstein, *Politics, Economics and Public Welfare,* 2nd ed. (Englewood Cliffs: Prentice-Hall, 1980), pp. 105–106.

Looking at the nearly eleven million AFDC recipients in 1980, Dobelstein notes that 69 percent were children. Of the remaining 3.4 million who were adults, 97 percent were women providing care to children in their homes and only 3 percent were adult males. Again, the prospects of a workfare program lifting AFDC recipients out of poverty are highly unrealistic.

74. This 1993 figure is from *Statistical Abstract of the United States, 1995,* Table 744.

75. These 1993 figures are from *Statistical Abstract of the United States, 1995,* Table 648.

76. These 1993 figures are from *Statistical Abstract of the United States, 1995,* Table 609.

77. This 1992 figure was computed from *Statistical Abstract of the United States, 1995,* Table 589.

78. This estimate was computed from *Statistical Abstract of the United States, 1995,* Tables 726, 733.

79. The federal record of handouts for the nonpoor is substantial. For 1988, federal preferential tax treatment (not counting preferential treatment for capital gains) amounted to a federal subsidy to the nonpoor of more than $150 billion, including for home ownership, public bond ownership, retirement pension plans other than Social Security (i.e., employer plans, IRAs, Keoghs), and a number of investment credits and special depreciation plans for businesses. Source: *Statistical Abstract of the United States, 1991,* Table 513. In addition, federal loans and loan guarantees made to businesses are substantial and typically are accompanied by highly favorable rates and terms. In 1983, for example, the federal government estimated its business

loans and business loan guarantees to amount to $96.2 billion. An additional $114.2 billion was committed to the Federal Home Loan Bank system and to the Federal National Mortgage Association, which help not only individual homeowners and savings account holders (both of whom, of course, are nonpoor) but also financial institutions and the home building industry (figures cited in Weidenbaum, pp. 315–316, 320). A more recent estimate based on government figures for total tax breaks given principally to the nonpoor in the United States puts the figure at $200 billion for 1990. Considering not only these tax breaks but also all other public support programs offered to both poor and nonpoor, total federal welfare costs are estimated at about $1 trillion. Again, it is the nonpoor who benefit most from these programs and tax breaks. For example, U.S. households with under $10,000 in income averaged $5,690 in such public support benefits in 1991, and households with over $100,000 in income averaged $9,280 in benefits. In addition, it is estimated that half of all federal public support benefits in 1991 went to households with over $30,000 in income, while a quarter went to households with over $50,000 in income. These figures, along with analyses and description, are presented in Neil Howe and Phillip Longman, "The Next New Deal," *The Atlantic Monthly,* April 1992, pp. 88–99. See also Steven Waldman, "Benefits 'R' Us: Stop the Griping; Most of Us Get Our Share of the Government Dole," *Newsweek,* August 10, 1992, pp. 56–58.

80. This 1992 figure is from *Statistical Abstract of the United States, 1995,* Table 403.

Chapter 7

1. For examples, see Ayn Rand, *Capitalism: The Unknown Ideal* (New York: Signet Books, 1967) or *The Virtue of Selfishness: A New Concept of Egoism* (New York: Signet Books, 1964).

2. See for example Friedrich von Hayek, *The Road to Serfdom* (Chicago: University of Chicago Press, 1944).

3. See Milton Friedman and Rose Friedman, *Free to Choose* (New York: Avon Books, 1979).

4. Contemporary distrust of governments remains strong in the United States. A review of public opinion polls, for example, indicates that people in the United States are more fearful of the power of governments than of the power of businesses. See Seymour

Martin Lipset and William Schneider, *The Confidence Gap: Business, Labor, and Government in the Public Mind* (New York: The Free Press, 1983), p. 289. These findings are confirmed again in 1994. See U.S. Bureau of the Census, *Statistical Abstract of the United States, 1995,* 115th ed. (Washington D.C.: U.S. Government Printing Office, 1995), Table 457.

5. Much of the social order in the early history of this nation centered on farms and farm labor. Commercial enterprises were, by today's standards, quite small. It is interesting to note, nonetheless, that a great deal of concentration in commerce did exist at that time. By one estimate, as of 1760 most of the banking, mining, and commerce in the thirteen colonies was controlled

by fewer than 500 men. Not surprisingly, leading men of commerce and industry, as well as major plantation holders, played central roles in the creation of the new constitutional government. They did so with a clear objective of protecting their property and business interests. See the discussion in Michael Parenti, *Democracy for the Few,* 5th ed. (New York: St. Martins Press, 1988), pp. 54–57.

6. See Robert L. Heilbroner, *The Economic Transformation of America* (New York: Harcourt Brace Jovanovich, Inc., 1977), p. 115. An excellent historical review of the antitrust movement and its impact on corporate business strategy is found in Neil Fligstein, *The Transformation of Corporate Control* (Cambridge, Mass.: Harvard University Press, 1990).

7. See Matthew Josephson, *The Robber Barons: The Great American Capitalists, 1861–1901* (New York: Harcourt, Brace, 1934).

8. Heilbroner, pp. 109–115.

9. State governments occasionally scored successes during this time frame in efforts to apply regulatory controls over businesses. For example, in 1873 the Illinois state legislature passed a law giving the state authority to set the rates charged to farmers by grain elevator owners. The constitutionality of this law was upheld by the U.S. Supreme Court in its 1877 Munn *v.* Illinois ruling.

10. The courts did not show initial enthusiasm for enforcement of antitrust regulations. For example, five years after the Sherman Antitrust Act, the U.S. Supreme Court ruled that even though a single company (American Sugar Refining) had grown through combination to control 98 percent of the U.S. market, this did not in itself prove intent to restrain trade. In the ensuing decades, of course, the courts have changed their views on antitrust several times, often in unpredictable and contradictory ways.

11. The outcry arose largely in response to Upton Sinclair's book, *The Jungle*, which was published in 1906 and revealed the unsanitary conditions of the slaughter and meat packing industry.

12. Figure cited in Rogene A. Buchholz, *Business Environment and Public Policy: Implications for Management and Strategy Formation,* 3rd ed. (Englewood Cliffs, N.J.: Prentice-Hall, 1989), p. 37.

13. Figure obtained by telephone interview from the Finding Aids Unit of the Office of the Federal Register.

14. Figures drawn from William C. Frederick, Keith Davis, and James E. Post, *Business and Society: Corporate Strategy, Public Policy, Ethics,* 6th ed. (New York: McGraw-Hill, 1988), p. 170. One of my favorite

tidbits about the growth of regulation concerns the regulation of hamburger, which is currently subjected to 41,000 federal and state regulations, 200 laws, and 111,000 court decisions. This regulatory effort, I am sure, puts all of our minds at ease when we sit down to consume a burger. Figures reported in John L. Hysom and William J. Bolce, *Business and Its Environment* (New York: West Publishing Company, 1983), p. 319.

15. Cited in Hysom and Bolce, p. 319.

16. Cited in George A. Steiner and John F. Steiner, *Business, Government, and Society: A Managerial Perspective,* 4th ed. (New York: Random House, 1985), p. 179.

17. Figures from this study are cited in Hysom and Bolce, pp. 308–310.

18. Internal GM report described in Allyn Douglas Strickland, *Government Regulation and Business* (Boston: Houghton Mifflin Company, 1980), pp. 9–10.

19. Reported in Frederick, Davis, and Post, p. 190.

20. Reported in Steiner and Steiner, p. 540.

21. "Environmentalism Prompts Backlash," *The Capital,* Thursday, May 14, 1992, p. A2.

22. U.S. Office of the Vice President, *Creating a Government that Works Better and Costs Less: Report of the National Performance Review* (Washington D.C.: U.S. Government Printing Office, September 10, 1993), p. 32.

23. Reported in Buchholz, p. 189.

24. Reported in Grover Starling, *The Changing Environment of Business,* 3rd ed. (Boston: PWS-Kent Publishing Company, 1988), p. 312.

25. See for example the discussion of this point by Michael A. Utton, *The Economics of Regulating Industry* (New York: Basil Blackwell Inc., 1986), pp. 22–23.

26. The great difficulty that the scientific community has in estimating the costs of regulations on U.S. industry is, in my view, indicative of the futility of cost-benefit analysis as a strategy for rational decision making in designing regulatory systems.

27. On this issue see the discussion by Lester C. Thurow, *The Zero Sum Solution: Building a World-Class American Economy* (New York: Simon and Schuster, 1985), pp. 27–35.

28. An excellent review of the relations between the regulatory agencies and OMB during this period can be found in Barry D. Friedman, *Regulation in the Reagan-Bush Era: The Eruption of Presidential Influence* (Pittsburgh: University of Pittsburgh Press, 1995).

29. The usefulness of this strategy as a step toward deregulation is questionable. In 1981 the U.S.

Supreme Court ruled that it is improper for OSHA (and by logical extension for certain other agencies) to conduct cost-benefit analyses given that the legislation that created OSHA prespecifies that fostering worker health is a benefit to be sought regardless of costs (except when it is economically unachievable). Furthermore, the realistic needs for regulation, coupled with the unrealistic time and resource demands required to conduct cost-benefit analyses, led OMB to exempt many agencies from doing these analyses. See, for example, the discussion by Steiner and Steiner, pp. 183–184.

30. Thomas, of course, has since been made a Supreme Court Justice by President Bush. Ironically, he won confirmation despite allegations that he himself had engaged in sexual harassment. In a case before the high court in 1993, he voted in favor of legal standards that make it substantially more difficult for women or African Americans to win job discrimination suits.

31. An overview of literature on the effects of airline deregulation is presented in Murray L. Weidenbaum, *Business, Government, and the Public,* 3rd ed. (Englewood Cliffs, N.J.: Prentice-Hall, 1986), pp. 181–184. A similar pattern of price wars, bankruptcies, and employee wage and benefit losses occurred in the trucking industry subsequent to its deregulation in 1980. Growing market concentration is also evident. In a deregulated environment the top six railroads increased their share of the national market from 56 to 90 percent. The six top airlines increased their market share from 75 to 85 percent, and the ten top truckers increased their market share from 38 to 58 percent. See Archie B. Carroll, *Business and Society: Ethics and Stakeholder Management,* 3rd ed. (Cincinnati: South-Western College Publishing, 1996), p. 250.

32. *Federal Election Commission Record,* March 1986, vol. 12, p. 7.

33. Cited in Michael Useem, *The Inner Circle: Large Corporations and the Rise of Business Political Activity in the U.S. and U.K.* (New York: Oxford University Press, 1984), p. 134.

34. U.S. Bureau of the Census, *Statistical Abstract of the United States, 1995,* Tables 465, 469.

35. Drawn from Carroll, p. 376.

36. See Dan Clawson, Alan Neustadtl, and Denise Scott, *Money Talks: Corporate PACs and Political Influence* (New York: Basic Books, 1992).

37. Clawson, Neustadtl, and Scott, pp. 155–190.

38. Clawson, Neustadtl, and Scott, pp. 15–16.

39. U.S. Bureau of the Census, *Statistical Abstract of the United States, 1995,* Table 465.

40. The other side of the story is that legislators may essentially compel corporations to form PACs to contribute to their campaigns by denying corporate access to them and a hearing of corporate concerns until such payments are made. See Clawson, Neustadtl, and Scott, pp. 59–62.

41. Washington-based trade associations spend $2 billion annually and are surpassed only by government and by tourism as the largest industry in the Washington area. Figure reported in Hysom and Bolce, p. 319.

42. In 1987 the 435 members of the U.S. House split $6.7 million in "honoraria" fees, and the 100 U.S. Senators split $3.1 million (an average of $31,000 per Senator). Top "honoraria" receivers in 1987 were Robert Dole ($106,000) and Representative Dan Rostenkowski ($245,000). Among the largest "honoraria" payers were the Tobacco Institute and several of the biggest corporations in the defense industry. See Marshall B. Clinard, *Corporate Corruption: The Abuse of Power* (New York: Praeger, 1990), p. 7. Since 1991, members of Congress are no longer permitted to keep these honoraria as personal income, but may (presumably) increase their potential voter support by donating them to charities. See Clawson, Neustadtl, and Scott, p. 77.

Chapter 8

1. The exceptions to the rule were the traditional relations that existed between the nobility or church (or occasionally the military) on the one hand and the peasantry, slaves, and tenant farmers on the other. These exploitative, profit-making relations were usually accepted by our ancestors as quite proper.

2. A number of good sources describe the range of corruption in the business sector. See in particular Marshall B. Clinard and Peter C. Yeager, *Corporate Crime* (New York: The Free Press, 1980); M. David Erman and Richard J. Lundman, *Corporate Deviance* (New York: Holt, Rinehart and Winston, 1982); David R. Simon and D. Stanley Eitzen, *Elite Deviance,* 2nd ed. (Boston:

Allyn and Bacon, Inc., 1986); Michael Clarke, *Business Crime: Its Nature and Control* (New York: St. Martin's Press, 1990); Marshall B. Clinard, *Corporate Corruption: The Abuse of Power* (New York: Praeger, 1990).

3. See Clinard and Yeager, pp. 110–132.

4. Irwin Ross, "How Lawless Are Big Corporations?" *Fortune,* December 1, 1980, pp. 56–64.

5. "Corporate Crime: The Untold Story," *U.S. News & World Report,* September 6, 1982, pp. 25–29.

6. This 1993 figure is computed from Bureau of the Census, *Statistical Abstract of the United States:1995,* 115th ed. (Washington, D.C.: Government Printing Office, 1995), Tables 884, 1373.

7. These figures are cited in William C. Frederick, Keith Davis, and James E. Post, *Business and Society: Corporate Strategy, Public Policy, Ethics,* 6th ed. (New York: McGraw-Hill, 1988), p. 65.

8. Cited in Ian Robertson, *Sociology,* 3rd ed. (New York: Worth Publishers, Inc., 1987), p. 204.

9. Figures are cited in George A. Steiner and John F. Steiner, *Business, Government, and Society: A Managerial Perspective,* 4th ed. (New York: Random House, 1985), pp. 336–337.

10. Drawn from a description in Clinard, p. 12.

11. Drawn from a description in Clinard, p. 55.

12. Described in Clinard, p. 165.

13. "Big Brother May Be Watching You Work," *The Daily Reflector* [Greenville, NC], May 25, 1997, pp. D8, D7.

14. "Sears, Ford Respond to Consumer Complaints," *The Capital,* June 23, 1992, p. A3.

15. Figures cited in Paul Blumberg, *The Predatory Society: Deception in the American Marketplace* (New York: Oxford University Press, 1989), pp. 65–66. See also Simon and Eitzen, p. 80.

16. Blumberg, p. 16.

17. Blumberg, pp. 30–31.

18. Blumberg, pp. 53, 71–72.

19. General Acounting Office, *Gasoline Marketing: Consumers Have Limited Assurance That Octane Readings Are Accurate.* (Washington, D.C.: U.S. Government Printing Office, 1990).

20. Drawn from summaries in Simon and Eitzen, p. 122; and Clinard and Yeager, p. 11.

21. Figures reported in Grover Starling, *The Changing Environment of Business,* 3rd ed. (Boston: PWS-Kent Publishing Company, 1988), p. 283.

22. Drawn from summaries in Simon and Eitzen, pp. 5, 8; Clinard and Yeager, pp. 9–10; and Clinard, pp. 114–115.

23. Cited in Simon and Eitzen, p. 38.

24. Drawn from a description in Clinard, pp. 70–71.

25. "Bid-Rigging Dairies Keep Bidding For School Contracts," *The Capital* [Annapolis, MD], November 17, 1992, p. A3.

26. Drawn from a summary in Simon and Eitzen, p. 6.

27. "Corporate Crime: The Untold Story," p. 26.

28. Clinard and Yeager, pp. 81–83.

29. Drawn from summaries in Clinard, pp. 41–43 and Robertson, p. 204.

30. "Airlines Settle Price-Fix Lawsuit," *The Capital* [Annapolis, MD], June 23, 1992, p. A2.

31. "Corporate Crime: The Untold Story," p. 25.

32. Cited in Simon and Eitzen, pp. 4, 91, and Clinard and Yeager, pp. 6–7.

33. Drawn from a summary in Clinard and Yeager, p. 7.

34. "State Farm Settles Bias Case," *The Capital* [Annapolis, MD], April 29, 1992, p. A3.

35. Described in Clinard, pp. 121–126, and Simon and Eitzen, pp. 4, 130–133.

36. Drawn from summaries in Clinard, pp. 129–131, and Murray L. Weidenbaum, *Business, Government and the Public,* 3rd ed. (Englewood Cliffs, N.J.: Prentice-Hall, 1986), p.453.

37. See Stephen Taub, "Trading by Insiders is Alive and Well," *Financial World,* vol. 160, no. 24, November 26, 1991, pp. 12–13.

38. Figures drawn from a summary in D. Stanley Eitzen and Maxine Baca Zinn, *Social Problems,* 6th ed. (Boston: Allyn and Bacon, 1994), pp. 352–353.

39. Figures drawn from *General Social Surveys, 1972–1993: Cumulative Codebook* (Chicago: National Opinion Research Center, University of Chicago, 1993), pp. 265, 715.

40. Figures are drawn from Robertson, pp. 233–234.

41. This 1992 figure is from Bureau of the Census, *Statistical Abstract of the United States:1995,* Table 111.

42. Some issues related to family and sexuality are seen as immoral by some and as moral by others. For example, half of all marriages in the United States now end in divorce, almost three million Americans simply live together rather than marrying, and about 10 percent of the population is homosexual. (Estimate on living together reported in "Domestic Bliss," *Newsweek,* March 13, 1992, pp. 62–63; estimates on sexual abuse are reported in "Rush to Judgment," *Newsweek,* April 19, 1992, pp. 54–60; all other estimates are drawn from Robertson, pp. 351, 361, 367–368).

43. Both figures are reported in Robertson, pp. 419–420.

44. "The Sins of the Father," *Newsweek,* June 1, 1992, p. 60.

45. Drawn from a summary in Simon and Eitzen, p. 3.

46. Simon and Eitzen, p. 4.

47. Simon and Eitzen, p. 3.

48. Simon and Eitzen, pp. 187–188.

49. "Detroit Police Chief Quits After Convictions," *The Capital* [Annapolis, MD], May 9, 1992, p. A2.

50. "It's Not Just New York," *Newsweek,* March 9, 1992, p. 26.

51. "Health Costs: 10 Percent For Fraud?," *The Capital* [Annapolis, MD], May 7, 1992, pp. A1, A16.

52. A Department of Health and Human Services study indicates that 82 percent of physicians are offered inducements by drug companies to prescribe their drugs. These inducements include gifts, vacation junkets, and cash payments for what amounts to bogus research projects. (Drawn from a summary in Jack Anderson, "Money Flows as Drug Firms Woo Doctors," *The Capital,* May 23, 1992, A10; see also a description of these practices in Clinard, pp. 58–60).

53. "At United Way, Charity Began at Home," *Newsweek,* March 9, 1992, p. 56.

54. "Charity, Foundation Heads Average $155,000," *The Capital* [Annapolis, MD], September 9, 1992, p. A8.

55. These 1991 figures are from U.S. Department of Justice, *Crime in the United States 1991: Uniform Crime Reports* (Washington D.C.: U.S. Government Printing Office, 1992), p. 4.

56. Figures are cited in William C. Frederick, Keith Davis, and James E. Post, *Business and Society: Corporate Strategy, Public Policy, Ethics,* 6th ed. (New York: McGraw-Hill, 1988), pp. 322–323.

57. In 1984 the IRS estimated that taxpayers failed to report as much as $200 billion in taxable income (reported in Robertson, p. 208).

58. This 1991 figure is from U.S. Department of Justice, *Crime in the United States 1991: Uniform Crime Reports,* p. 4.

59. These 1993 figures are from Bureau of the Census, *Statistical Abstract of the United States:1995,* Table 322.

60. Figures are reported in Gerald F. Cavanagh, *American Business Values,* 3rd ed. (Englewood Cliffs, N.J.: Prentice-Hall, 1990), p. 178.

61. Useful reviews of sociological theories on deviance can be found in Marshall B. Clinard and Robert F. Meier, *Sociology of Deviant Behavior,* 7th ed. (New York: Holt, Rinehart and Winston, 1989); Jack D. Douglas, The *Sociology of Deviance* (Boston: Allyn and Bacon, Inc., 1983); Nanette J. Davis and C. Stasz, *Social Control of Deviance* (New York: McGraw-Hill, 1990).

62. See particularly Emile Durkheim, *The Division of Labor in Society* (New York: The Free Press, 1964 [originally 1893]); *The Rules of Sociological Method* (New York: The Free Press, 1964 [originally 1895]); *Suicide: A Study in Sociology* (Glencoe, Ill.: The Free Press, 1951 [originally 1897]).

63. In this connection it should be pointed out that deviance as an expression of the urge to create may occasionally be viewed in retrospect as having served as a positive force for social improvement, even though at the time it is regarded as a destructive or evil force. Thus the great prophets, including Jesus, Mohammed, and Buddha, were regarded negatively by many persons during their own time, yet were seen as agents for constructive social change by a great many people in ensuing generations. Likewise, whether one regards the American "founding fathers" (Jefferson, Washington, and others) as rabble rousing traitors or as "moral beacons" for "inalienable human rights" depends on one's vantage point. Regardless of one's perspective, however, their acts of creative deviance have clearly had long-term impacts in changing our social order and in providing new "moral" directives for our behavior.

64. Potential deviance, of course, is also held in check by the "socialization" process by which we internalize social scripts as an individual-centered, psychological conscience that then provides us with guides for our behavior, thoughts, and feelings. The relative efficacy of individual conscience in contrast to social control mechanisms in providing checks on deviance is a subject that has not yet been adequately researched, and no doubt their relative influences on human behavior vary from situation to situation.

65. Of course a social environment of such complexity and lack of social control as we live in is an anomic one. The fractured state of most of our social institutions today (family, community, church, government) leaves us, in contrast to our ancestors in prebusiness-oriented societies, with a much greater level of uncertainty over critical moral questions: what is right and wrong, what is the meaning of our life, and what should we do with our life? We are increasingly individuated and left on our own to find purpose and direction for our life. Today, businesses, markets, and industrial order provide the most significant framework within which we may find motives and meanings for our existence.

66. There have been, of course, some minor shareholder efforts to pressure corporations into socially responsible behavior. The New York–based Interfaith Center on Corporate Responsibility (ICCR) provides research and advice for church investors who wish their investments to be made in responsible corporations and who wish to know how best to vote on shareholder resolutions. The Investor Responsibility Research Center (IRRC) serves a similar function for universities and foundations. The shift from investments in irresponsible corporations to responsible ones by subscribers to these centers probably has little impact on corporations. Nonetheless, the attendant negative publicity may have some effect on corporate policy.

On the other hand, shareholder-initiated resolutions to foster increased social responsibility generally are voted down by very large margins, since management controls both the voting process and most of the votes through proxy. The desire to avoid adverse publicity, however, may cause management to accede to shareholder demands in some cases. This occurred, for example, in the 1970 *Campaign GM* resolution for the addition of public policy representation on the board of directors of GM. Management control of proxy votes ensured that the resolution was overwhelmingly voted down, but management otherwise subsequently acceded to it informally.

67. Figures are from Jeremy Bacon, *Corporate Boards and Corporate Governance* (New York: The Conference Board, 1993), p. 23.

68. Bacon, p. 23.

69. Management control over the board often involves keeping board members in the dark about upcoming meetings by providing little or no information ahead of time. For example, one study of large industrial corporations found that only 6 percent of corporations supplied board directors with an agenda before board meetings and only 17 to 21 percent sent out manufacturing or sales data to board members before meetings. Cited in Rogene A. Buchholz, *Business Environment and Public Policy: Implications for Management and Strategy Formation,* 2nd ed. (Englewood Cliffs, N.J.: Prentice-Hall, 1986), p. 241.

70. Figures on compensation are averaged across 592 corporations in 1986 and are cited in Frederick, Davis, and Post, p. 248.

71. Prestige plays a major role in deciding whom to select for new board members. As one corporate businessperson put it: board members are like "orna-ments on the corporate Christmas tree." See Myles Z. Mace, *Directors: Myth and Reality,* rev. ed. (Boston: Harvard Business School Press, 1986), pp. 89, 90. The boards of top U.S. corporations typically also serve as a bastion for white "good old boys." Only 45 percent even have a woman as a member, and only 25 percent have a minority member (see Frederick, Davis, and Post, p. 248). In addition, boards serve as a place for the interests of powerful people in society to coalesce. See Michael Useem, *The Inner Circle: Large Corporations and the Rise of Business Political Activity in the U.S. and U.K.* (New York: Oxford University Press, 1984).

72. Estimate reported in Frederick, Davis, and Post, p. 254.

73. Estimate reported in Frederick, Davis, and Post, p. 248. The proportion of board directors who are managers of the company that the board oversees has been declining as a result of public pressure. See Bacon, p. 6.

74. See a useful discussion of board mission statements in Ada Demb and F.-Friedrich Neubauer, *The Corporate Board: Confronting the Paradoxes* (New York: Oxford University Press, 1992), pp. 153–157.

75. Drawn from Louis Briotta, Jr. and A. A. Sommer, Jr., *The Essential Guide to Effective Corporate Board Committees* (Englewood Cliffs, N.J.: Prentice-Hall, 1987), pp. 49–58.

76. Briotta and Sommer, p. 97–108.

77. Demb and Neubauer, p. 153.

78. See Briotta and Sommer, p. 63.

79. Demb and Neubauer, p. 153.

80. Bacon, p. 14.

81. From a cross-cultural perspective, an especially useful discussion of the diverse social areas for expanded board oversight appears in Demb and Neubauer, pp. 14–69.

82. Responsible managerial action, of course, may include contesting regulations or laws when deemed appropriate.

83. Many board directors do not believe that they are overcompensated. See Mace, pp. 101–104. Because they typically come from high-income brackets, they have an inflated view of what their time is worth. This perspective carries over rather nicely in their willingness to give out giant compensation packages to CEOs.

84. "How to Pay the CEO Right," *Fortune,* April 6, 1992, pp. 61–69.

85. See, for example, Frances J. Aguilar, *Scanning the Business Environment* (New York: MacMillan,

1967); Ralph Estes, *Corporate Social Accounting* (New York: Wiley, 1976); John J. Corson and George A. Steiner, *Measuring Business Social Performance: The Corporate Audit* (New York: Committee for Economic Development, 1974); George A. Steiner, *Strategic Planning: What Every Manager Should Know* (New York: The Free Press, 1979).

86. The central importance of senior management's commitment to ethical behavior is underscored in a study by Marshall B. Clinard, *Corporate Ethics and Crime* (Beverly Hills, Calif.: Sage Publications, 1983), especially pp. 53–58, 71–83, and 132–133.

87. For example, a study of 1,443 managers in 1982 indicated that the behavior of their superiors was the most influential factor determining whether they themselves would engage in unethical behavior. By contrast, the mere existence of formal company policies barring unethical behavior was ranked as much less influential. See Barry Z. Posner and Warren H. Schmidt, "Values and the American Manager: An Update," *California Management Review,* Spring, 1984, pp. 202–216.

88. Emile Durkheim, one of the founders of sociology, was himself widely criticized for his view of ethics as a social phenomenon. See his *The Division of Labor in Society* (New York: The Free Press, 1964 [originally 1893]); *Sociology and Philosophy,* translated by D. F. Pocock (New York: The Free Press, 1953 [originally 1924]; and *Moral Education: A Study in the Theory and Application of the Sociology of Education,* translated by Everett K. Wilson and Herman Schnurer (New York: The Free Press, 1961 [originally 1925]).

89. The most popular contemporary justice-oriented approach derives from work by John Rawls. See his *A Theory of Justice* (Cambridge, Mass.: Harvard University Press, 1971). My own moral reasoning, as illustrated in this book, falls generally into the domain of ends-oriented frameworks (which is not unusual for sociologists and indeed for most social scientists). For example, I argue that businesses should behave more responsibly for the desirable end of the good of society as a whole and of its constituent sectors. On the morality of means for achieving this end and of the distribution of costs and benefits, I am relatively, though obviously not entirely, mute. The strengths and weaknesses of the line of moral reasoning I present throughout this book certainly must be judged by my readers.

Chapter 9

1. Slavery and many elements of serfdom continued to be practiced throughout the early rise of business-oriented societies but have fallen out of fashion in industrial societies. Women, however, have been bound by a domestic form of slavery that is only now in the process of breaking up, with more and more women escaping from husbandly economic domination to become free as wage-laborers in the labor market of a business-oriented society.

2. Estimates drawn from Gerhard Lenski, Jean Lenski, and Patrick Nolan, *Human Societies: An Introduction to Macrosociology,* 6th ed. (New York: McGraw-Hill, Inc., 1991), pp. 189, 323; Gerhard Lenski, *Power and Privilege: A Theory of Social Stratification* (New York: McGraw-Hill, 1966), pp. 266–268, 309.

3. Our ancestors were not always so stoic and lamb-like about their disadvantaged position in society. Peasant efforts to evade obligations and taxes, peasant crimes against the nobility, and peasant uprisings occurred with some frequency, though such actions typically involved few peasants and usually had little effect on prevailing social order and social inequality. See Lenski, pp. 266–276.

4. These 1993 figures are from the Bureau of the Census, *Statistical Abstract of the United States, 1995,* 115th ed. (Washington, D.C.: U.S. Government Printing Office, 1995), Table 733.

5. See for example, David W. Ewing, *Freedom Inside the Organization: Bringing Civil Liberties to the Workplace* (New York: E. P. Dutton, 1977).

6. Henry Ford is reported to have created a "sociology" department at Ford Motors for the purpose of going to the homes and neighborhoods of employees to ensure that they were living in a fashion that Ford considered moral. He also created a department to spy on his employees at work so as to confirm their moral character and company loyalty. See John D. Dahlinger, *The Secret Life of Henry Ford* (New York: Bobb-Merrill Company Inc., 1978), pp. 150–151.

7. Figure cited in John L. Hysom and William J. Bolce, *Business and Its Environment* (New York: West Publishing Company, 1983), p. 187.

8. See for example David R. Simon and D. Stanley Eitzen, *Elite Deviance,* 2nd ed. (Boston: Allyn and Bacon, 1986), pp. 61–62.

9. Bureau of the Census, *Statistical Abstract of the United States, 1995,* Table 697.

10. These 1993 figures are from Bureau of the Census, *Statistical Abstract of the United States, 1995,* Table 688.

11. Cited in Rogene A. Buchholz, *Business Environment and Public Policy: Implications for Management and Strategy Formation,* 2nd ed. (Englewood Cliffs, N.J.: Prentice-Hall, 1986), p. 344.

12. Cited in Buchholz, p. 358.

13. Reported in Bob Port and John Solomon, "OSHA Short on Inspections, Analysis Shows," *The Daily Reflector* [Greenville, NC], September 5, 1995, p. A2.

14. Figures reported in George A. Steiner and John F. Steiner, *Business, Government, and Society: A Managerial Perspective,* 7th ed. (New York: McGraw-Hill, 1994), p. 295.

15. Reported in Port and Soloman, p. A2.

16. Cited in Murray L. Weidenbaum, *Business, Government, and the Public,* 3rd ed. (Englewood Cliffs, N.J.: Prentice-Hall, 1986), p. 161.

17. For examples, see the discussions in Weidenbaum, pp. 157–161, and Buchholz, pp. 366–367.

18. Reported in Michel Beaud, *A History of Capitalism: 1500–1980,* translated by Tom Dickman and Anny Lefebvre (New York: Monthly Review Press, 1983 [originally 1981]), pp. 156–157.

19. See Frederick Winslow Taylor, *Scientific Management* (New York: Harper & Brothers, 1947). See also Daniel Nelson, *Frederick W. Taylor and the Rise of Scientific Management* (Madison: University of Wisconsin Press, 1980).

20. Important early works in the human relations movement include: Elton Mayo, *The Human Problems of an Industrial Civilization* (New York: Macmillan, 1933); F. J. Roethlisberger and William J. Dickson, *Management and the Worker* (Cambridge, Mass.: Harvard University Press, 1939); F. J. Roethlisberger, *Management and Morale* (Cambridge, Mass.: Harvard University Press, 1941); Frederick Herzberg, *Work and the Nature of Man* (New York: Harcourt Brace Jovanovich, 1966). Other classic works in the sociological tradition touching on one or more aspects of issues in human relations are Reinhard Bendix, *Work and Authority in Industry* (New York: John Wiley and Sons, 1956); Robert Blauner, *Alienation and Freedom* (Chicago: University of Chicago, 1964); and Rosabeth Moss Kanter, *Men and Women of the Corporation* (New York: Basic Books, 1977). Yet other works on related topics include: David A. Whitsett and Lyle Yorks, "Looking Back at Topeka: General Foods and the Quality-of-Work-Life Experiment" *California Management Review,* Summer, 1983, 25(4): 93–109 and William Ouchi, *Theory Z: How American Businesses Can Meet the Japanese Challenge* (Reading, Mass.: Addison-Wesley Publishing Co., 1981).

Chapter 10

1. Two especially penetrating analyses of the role of education in upward mobility are Samuel Bowles and Herbert Gintis, *Schooling in Capitalist America* (New York: Basic Books, 1976); Christopher Jencks, Susan Bartlett, Mary Corcoran, James Crouse, David Eaglesfield, Gregory Jackson, Kent McClelland, Peter Mueser, Michael Olneck, Joseph Schwartz, Sherry Ward, and Jill Williams, *Who Gets Ahead? The Determinants of Economic Success in America* (New York: Basic Books, 1979).

2. If you already had heard the riddle and therefore were not surprised by the solution, consider your views on the following question: "Is it more important in our society for a male to have a good job and pay than it is for a female?" Think about it for a moment. If you answer "yes," regardless of how you justify your view, aren't you reinforcing the sexist distribution of opportunities for who gets ahead in our society? In short, aren't you yourself sexist? If you are a woman, won't you be limiting your own opportunities in life if you hold this view? Furthermore, regardless of your gender, won't holding this view adversely affect the opportunities you make available to women around you, including your daughters, your wife (if your are male), and any women who work under your supervision? Again, this illustrates the insidious way in which sexism can operate in our society through our own attitudes and actions, regardless of whether we are aware of our participation in this process.

3. Infanticide is estimated to have resulted in the death of between 15 and 50 percent of newborns in food

gathering and hunting societies; in a number of horticultural societies perhaps as many as 30 percent of newborn females died from infanticide. Infanticide, especially against females, was also widespread in agricultural societies. A 19th century report on China suggested that in some districts perhaps as many as one-fourth of the female infants were killed. Signs were reported to have been posted by some ponds that read, "Girls may not be drowned here." The concern embodied in these signs apparently had little to do with the propriety of killing female babies, but rather with the possibility of defiling or contaminating the water supply. Cited in Gerhard Lenski, Jean Lenski, and Patrick Nolan, *Human Societies: An Introduction to Macrosociology,* 6th ed. (New York: McGraw-Hill, 1991), pp. 99, 144, 179–180.

4. The rape of women by men is treated in our society almost as though it were a victimless crime, or as if it were no crime at all. Research indicates, for example, that between 20 and 50 percent of rapes are never reported, only between 14 and 17 percent of rapists in reported incidents are even brought to trial, and a mere 3 percent serve any jail time for their actions. Figures reported in Nijole V. Benokraitis and Joe R. Feagin, *Modern Sexism: Blatant, Subtle, and Covert Discrimination* (Englewood Cliffs, N.J.: Prentice-Hall, 1986), p. 50.

5. For example, 95 percent of sexually abused children in the United States are girls, one in five emergency room visits by women is the result of battering, and between a fourth to a third of all murders of women are by husbands or "boyfriends." Altogether between one to two million women in the United States are the victim of beatings in their own homes each year. (At the upper estimate, this represents a figure roughly equivalent to the entire combined population of people in two large United States cities such as Detroit and Dallas being beaten each year.) Could you imagine that this same magnitude of violent crimes could occur against men in our society without causing such an uproar that our political system would be forced to take strong anticrime measures to jail the persons who commit these crimes? Figures are cited in Benokraitis and Feagin, pp. 9, 48.

6. The movement to establish the equality of the legal rights of women compared to men in the United States has floundered badly. For example, the proposed Equal Rights Amendment to the U.S. Constitution was worded as follows, "Equality of rights under the law shall not be denied or abridged by the United States or any state on account of sex. The Congress shall have the power to enforce, by appropriate legislation, the provi-

sions of this article." Does this proposed amendment to ensure the equality of rights under law sound scary? Apparently it does for a great many people because it failed to be ratified by the number of states necessary for it to be added to the U.S. Constitution.

7. Drawn from the U.S. Bureau of Labor statistics as summarized in William C. Frederick, Keith Davis, and James E. Post, *Business and Society: Corporate Strategy, Public Policy, Ethics,* 6th ed. (New York: McGraw-Hill, 1988), p. 308.

8. Jobs in the United States tend themselves to possess a gender, with male jobs paying much more than female jobs. This is seen not only for doctors (84 percent male) in contrast to nurses (96 percent female), but also for many rank and file jobs. For example the "female jobs" of secretary (99.2 percent female), receptionist (97.5 percent female), typist (96.6 percent female), keypunch operator (94.5 percent female), and bank teller (92.0 percent female) all pay between 47 and 79 percent of what the following "male jobs" pay: fire fighter (99.5 percent male), plumber (99.2 percent male), auto mechanic (99.1 percent male), surveyors (98.5 percent male), and truck driver (97.9 percent male). Drawn from 1982 U.S. Department of Labor figures summarized in Murray L. Weidenbaum, *Business, Government and the Public,* 3rd ed. (Englewood Cliffs, N.J.: Prentice-Hall, 1986), p. 143.

9. Another drawback for women is that they are still expected to do the bulk of household chores in addition to their paid jobs. Women, for example, do an average of thirty hours of household chores per week versus 4 hours by men. Cited in Ian Robertson, *Sociology,* 3rd ed. (New York: Worth Publishers, Inc., 1987), p. 330.

10. Figures are from U.S. Bureau of the Census, *Current Population Reports,* Series P–60, No. 184. (Washington D.C.: U.S. Government Printing Office, 1993).

11. Cited in Grover Starling, *The Changing Environment of Business,* 3rd ed. (Boston: PWS-Kent Publishing Company, 1988), p. 584.

12. Figures reported in Benokraitis and Feagin, p. 55.

13. Figures are from "Educational Attainment in the United States: March 1991 and 1990." In *Current Population Reports,* Series p–20, No. 462 (Washington D.C.: U.S. Government Printing Office, 1992).

14. Figure reported in Robertson, p. 313.

15. Reported in "GAO Report: Academy Aims For Fairness: But Women and Minorities Lag Academically, While Facing Higher Offence-Conviction Rates,"

The Capital, [Annapolis, MD], May 22, 1992, pp. A1, A12.

16. Figures reported in John L. Hysom and William J. Bolce, *Business and Its Environment* (New York: West Publishing Company, 1983), p. 228.

17. Figure reported in Hysom and Bolce, p. 229.

18. Except for figures for the U.S. Supreme Court and for the U.S. Congress, all other figures are reported in Robertson, p. 329.

19. Estimates drawn from "Sexual Harassment: The Inside Story," *Working Women,* June 1992, p. 48.

20. The Civil War was fought over the issue of whether states, individually or collectively, have a right to withdraw from the United States. The outcome of the war demonstrated, at least at that time, that states did not have such a right. The first bloodshed of the war occurred soon after the seceding states in the Confederacy declared their independence in early 1861. Northern congressional Republicans responded by passing the Confiscation Acts of 1861 and 1862 to punish seceding states by freeing their slaves. These legislative acts directly threatened the economies of the states in the Confederacy, which depended heavily on slave labor. Under much pressure from Northern Republicans and in an effort to hasten the end of the war, Lincoln subsequently issued the Emancipation Proclamation (in two parts— the first part on September 22, 1862 and the second on January 1, 1863). This proclamation threatened to free all slaves in any part of a Confederate state where the citizenry continued to rebel; slaves in non-Confederate states (and in those areas of Confederate states then occupied by Norther troops) were not to be freed by this proclamation. Shortly after the war, slavery was abolished nationwide with the passage of the Thirteenth Amendment to the U.S. Constitution. See discussions in Richard T. Schaefer, *Racial and Ethnic Groups* (Boston: Little, Brown and Company, 1979), p. 167; John E. Farley, *Majority–Minority Relations,* 3rd ed. (Englewood Cliffs, N.J.: Prentice-Hall, 1995), pp. 125–126; and Mary Beth Norton, David M. Katzman, Paul D. Escott, Howard P. Chudacoff, Thomas G. Paterson, and William M. Tuttle, Jr., *A People & A Nation: A History of the United States,* 3rd ed. (Boston: Houghton Mifflin Company, 1990), pp. 416–420.

21. In 1913 as our nation celebrated the 50th anniversary of the Emancipation Proclamation, 79 African Americans were lynched (beaten and hung) and President Woodrow Wilson (a President known for his intellect and liberality) signed an executive order that required the racial segregation of all cafeterias and restrooms in federal office buildings. Drawn from a summary in Schaefer, p. 174.

22. Figures reported in James E. Blackwell, *The Black Community: Diversity and Unity,* 3rd ed. (New York: HarperCollins, 1991), pp. 78–81.

23. Looking at a different estimate of income discrepancies, per capita income of African Americans in 1988 was 60 percent of per capita income of European Americans. Figures reported in Blackwell, pp. 69–75.

24. A review and commentary on this body of research is in Claude M. Steele, "Race and the Schooling of Black Americans," *The Atlantic Monthly,* April 1992, pp. 68–78.

25. Figures are for 1987 and are computed from Table 2.8 of Blackwell, pp. 76–77.

26. See Blackwell, p. 229.

27. A useful review of findings on racial discrimination in the criminal justice system can be found in Farley, pp. 316–334.

28. Figures from Blackwell, p. 457.

29. Figure from a study by The Sentencing Project, "Study: 1 in 3 Young Black Men Serving Time," *The Daily Reflector* [Greenville, NC], October 5, 1995, p. A4.

30. Figure reported in Blackwell, p. 434.

31. Figures from George A. Steiner and John F. Steiner, *Business, Government, and Society: A Managerial Perspective,* 4th ed. (New York: Random House, 1985), p. 533.

32. Figure reported in Blackwell, pp. 400–403.

33. All of our Presidents from the founding of this country to the present were northern European white (mostly English, with some German and a few Irish).

34. Figures from a 1986 Gallup Poll, reported in D. Stanley Eitzen and Maxine Baca Zinn, *In Conflict and Order: Understanding Society,* 6th ed. (Boston: Allyn and Bacon, 1993).

35. These distinctions derive from Robert Merton, "Discrimination and the American Creed." In *Sociological Ambivalence and Other Essays* (New York: Free Press, 1976), pp. 189–216.

36. Even as of 1960, there were twenty-nine states in the United States that barred interracial marriage by law. It wasn't until 1967 that the U.S. Supreme Court struck down these laws. As of 1987, 1.5 percent of all marriages in the United States were interracial. See Blackwell, pp. 116–188.

37. African Americans are half as likely to hold a seat in the U.S. House of Representatives, but their seats

would be even fewer if not for court-ordered gerrymandering of voting districts in order to increase the political voice of African Americans. However, in the 1990s the U.S. Supreme Court has ruled increasingly against the use of gerrymandering for this purpose. The predictable result will be fewer African Americans holding seats in the U.S. Congress.

38. Reported in Steiner and Steiner, p. 533.

39. Figures from Blackwell, p. 57.

40. Figures from Blackwell, p. 57.

41. The most salient feature of race relations between African Americans and European Americans in the United States is, of course, the unusual social distance that exists between them in social life. See, for example, the discussion by Charles V. Willie, *The Caste and Class Controversy* (Bayside, New York: General hall, 1979). A particularly poignant recent discussion of this issue is by Andrew Hacker, *Two Nations: Black and White, Separate, Hostile, Unequal,* 2nd ed. (New York: Ballantine Books, 1995).

42. Even after several decades of desegregation laws and court-imposed busing plans, roughly a third of African American children today still attend schools that are more than 90 percent African American; European American children attend schools that are mostly European American. Figures reported in Robertson, p. 388.

43. Indeed, very little effort has been made to enforce these laws. By contrast, the federal government has done much to increase housing segregation. The Federal Housing Administration, created in 1934, established policies early on to dissuade residential integration and worked with lenders to ensure that minority loan applications for housing purchases in European American areas were denied. Then too, its policies of fostering home loan funds for middle class European Americans has played a major role in promoting and making possible the white flight from the cities (see the discussion by Blackwell, pp. 278–281, 291–293). That racial bias in home loans continues unabated is shown in a Federal Reserve Board study of 1990 mortgage loans. This study found that low-income whites in 1990 were still more likely to be approved for home loans than were high-income blacks (reported in "Mortgage Loan Biases," *The Capital* [Annapolis, MD], July 5, 1992, p. B5).

44. See the discussions in Willie; Reynolds Farley, *Blacks and Whites: Narrowing the Gap?* (Cambridge, Mass.: Harvard University Press, 1984).

45. See the discussion in Frederick, Davis, and Post, p. 307.

46. Although he did not end affirmative action, President Reagan did drop the informal requirement under the OFCCP for goals and timetables to be set on the pursuit of affirmative action. He and President Bush also ordered the Justice Department to argue against affirmative action preferences in cases before the U.S. Supreme Court.

47. Figures reported in Weidenbaum, p. 134.

48. The U.S. Supreme Court, of course, is a political force that serves as easily to deny civil rights to certain groups of Americans as to protect their rights. For examples, in its 1874 decision in Minor *v.* Happerset, the high court ruled that the "equal protection under the law" clause of the Fourteenth Amendment did not apply to women. In its 1896 Plessy *v.* Ferguson decision, the Court put its stamp of approval on the racial segregation of African Americans from European Americans in public facilities and public services. In effect, it upheld a system of apartheid in the United States. If you think the U.S. Supreme Court is a reliable social vehicle for protecting the rights of all people in the United States, guess again.

49. I borrow this argument from John Farley, pp. 260–261.

Chapter 11

1. Our ancestors were so primitive as to be born without cost, outside of the hospital and obstetrical market. We consumer-people are far more sophisticated, making our fetuses into products that are delivered to us in health care markets for a fee. Our ancestors also had no access to the luxurious and costly mortuary market available to us today. Instead they were so unrefined as to have their bodies buried unprotected in dirt, covered with rocks, burned, or left at no cost in caves.

2. Consumer Product Safety Commission and National Highway Traffic Safety Administration figures reported in George A. Steiner and John F. Steiner, *Business, Government, and Society: A Managerial Perspective,* 7th ed. (New York: McGraw-Hill, 1994), p. 496.

3. Figures reported in Steiner and Steiner, p. 512.

4. This 1992 figure is from *International Marketing Data and Statistics, 1995,* 19th ed. (London: Euromontor, 1995), Table 1302, p. 386.

5. See Heidi Vernon-Wortzel, *Business and Society: A Managerial Approach,* 5th ed. (Boston: Irwin, 1994), p. 404.

6. Figures reported in George A. Steiner and John F. Steiner, *Business, Government, and Society: A Managerial Perspective,* 4th ed. (New York: Random House, 1985), p. 450.

7. Figure reported in Vernon-Wortzel, p. 454.

8. Figures reported in Steiner and Steiner, 1985, p. 445.

9. Figures drawn from Steiner and Steiner, 1994, p. 446.

10. Ralph Nadar, *Unsafe At Any Speed: The Designed-in Dangers of the American Automobile* (New York: Grossman, 1972).

11. By one estimate, there was an increase of 758 percent in product liability suits taken to federal courts between 1975 and 1985. Figure reported in Vernon-Wortzel, p. 194.

12. See for example D. Ciampa, *Total Quality* (Reading, Mass.: Addison-Wesley, 1992).

13. I borrow this argument from Paul Blumberg, *The Predatory Society: Deception in the American Marketplace* (New York: Oxford Press, 1989).

Chapter 12

1. Estimates reported in Gerald F. Cavanagh, *American Business Values,* 3rd ed. (Englewood Cliffs, N.J.: Prentice-Hall, 1990), p. 110.

2. Estimates reported in Rogene A. Buchholz, *Business Environment and Public Policy: Implications for Management and Strategy Formulation,* 2nd ed. (Englewood Cliffs, N.J.: Prentice-Hall, 1986), p. 435.

3. Estimate reported in Fred Luthans, Richard M. Hodgetts, and Kenneth R. Thompson, *Social Issues in Business: Strategic and Public Policy Perspectives,* 5th ed. (New York: Macmillan Publishing Company, 1987), p. 409.

4. Estimate reported in Luthans, Hodgetts, and Thompson, p. 425.

5. Estimate reported in Buchholz, p. 416.

6. Drawn from a description in George A. Steiner and John F. Steiner, *Business, Government, and Society: A Managerial Perspective,* 4th ed. (New York: Random House, 1985), pp. 170–175.

7. Estimates reported in John L. Hysom and William J. Bolce, *Business and Its Environment* (New York: West Publishing Company, 1983), p. 423.

8. Estimate reported in John L. Macionis, *Sociology* (Englewood Cliffs, N.J.: Prentice-Hall, 1995), p. 599.

9. Estimates reported in William C. Frederick, Keith Davis, and James E. Post, *Business and Society: Corporate Strategy, Public Policy, Ethics,* 6th ed. (New York: McGraw-Hill, 1988), p.583. The classic study on the effects of pesticides on wildlife appears in Rachel Carson, *Silent Spring* (Boston: Houghton Miflin, 1962). See also Philip M. Boffey, "20 Years After 'Silent Spring': Still a Troubled Landscape." In *New York Times,* May 25, 1982, pp. c–1, c–7; "Silent Spring Revisited?" *Newsweek,* July 14, 1986, pp. 72–73.

10. Reported in Cavanagh, p. 16.

11. Figure reported in Alfred A. Marcus, *Business and Society: Ethics, Government and the World Economy* (Homewood, Ill.: Irwin, 1993), p. 447.

12. Estimates reported in Marcus, p. 441.

13. To give just one example, in 1974 the Reserve Mining Company was found to be dumping into Lake Superior 67,000 tons of asbestos fiber–containing wastes *every day.* Drinking water supplies 55 miles away were found to be contaminated by these fibers. (Drawn from a description in Steiner and Steiner, p. 382.)

14. Figures reported in Grover Starling, *The Changing Environment of Business,* 3rd ed. (Boston: PWS-Kent Publishing Company, 1988), p. 286.

15. See, for example, the report by the Council on Environmental Quality, *Environmental Quality,* 15th Annual Report, 1984.

16. Figure reported in Starling, p. 286.

17. Cited in Dan Clawson, Alan Neustadtl, and Denise Scott, *Money Talks: Corporate PACs and Political Influence* (New York: Basic Books, 1992), p.3.

18. Figures drawn from "Pollution Abatement and Control Expenditures, 1980–83." In *Survey of Current Businesses,* (U.S. Department of Commerce, Washington D.C.) March 1985, pp. 18–22.

19. The impact of beef production on our environment is presented in detail by Jeremy Rifkin, *Beyond Beef: The Rise and Fall of the Cattle Culture* (New York: Plume, 1992).

20. Donella H. Meadows, Dennis L. Meadows, Jorgen Randers, and William W. Behrens, III, *The Limits to Growth* (New York: Universe Books, 1972).

21. Estimates reported in Hysom and Bolce, p. 411.

22. Meadows, Meadows, Randers, and Behrens, pp. 56–60.

23. A useful overview of steps corporations can take to control pollution is presented in Marcus, pp. 413, 453–459.

24. For example, four of five U.S. companies that set up operations just over the border in Mexico admit having done so because of Mexico's relatively weak environmental laws. Roughly 1,000 American plants now produce hazardous wastes in Mexico, including PCBs, which foul local water supplies. (Source: "A House of Cards," *Newsweek*, June 1, 1992, p. 30). Over one period in the early 1990s, nearly fifty babies were born, miscarried, or aborted without brains in the Mateos/ Brownsville border area of Mexico and Texas. All businesses in the area have denied responsibility.

25. Al Gore, *Earth in the Balance: Ecology and the Human Spirit* (New York: Plume, 1993).

Chapter 13

1. Additional steps are also common in the development of a multinational corporation. One is for the local operations of a multinational corporation in a host country to become increasingly placed in the managerial hands of professionals indigenous to the host country. Frequently there is considerable pressure from the government of the host country for this to be done to ensure the loyalty and sensitivity of the local corporate operations to host country national interests. In addition, pressures may be placed on the corporation to create opportunities for local ownership of its host country operations. The most developed of multinational corporations, therefore, possess not only multinational production and sales capacities, but also multinational management and ownership.

2. U.S. Department of Commerce, *The Multinational Corporation: Studies On U.S. Foreign Investment,* vol. 2 (Washington, D.C.: U.S. Government Printing Office, 1973), p. 6.

3. Figures reported in John L. Hysom and William J. Bolce, *Business and Its Environment* (New York: West Publishing Company, 1983), p. 374.

4. Figures reported in George A. Steiner and John F. Steiner, *Business, Government, and Society: A Managerial Perspective,* 4th ed. (New York: Random House, 1985), p. 588. Another estimate indicates that just 600 major multinational corporations in the world account for half of the world gross product. See Michael Kidron and Ronald Segal, *The New State of the World Atlas* (New York: Simon and Schuster, 1991).

5. Figures reported in Steiner and Steiner, p. 603.

6. Figure reported in Grover Starling, *The Changing Environment of Business,* 3rd ed. (Boston: PWS-Kent Publishing Company, 1988), p. 322.

7. Figures reported in Marshall B. Clinard, *Corporate Corruption: The Abuse of Power* (New York: Praeger, 1990), pp. 121–126, 129–131.

8. Daniel Bell, *The Coming of Postindustrial Society* (New York: Basic Books, 1973).

9. See the discussion by Murray L. Weidenbaum, *Business, Government, and the Public,* 3rd ed. (Englewood Cliffs, N.J.: Prentice-Hall, 1986), pp. 287–289.

10. See a summary in Weidenbaum, p. 300.

11. Estimate reported in Steiner and Steiner, p. 603.

12. Estimates presented in Weidenbaum, p. 285, and Starling, p. 335.

13. See Rich Thomas, "The ABCs of the GATT Pact." In *Newsweek,* December 27, 1993, p. 36.

14. Figures from Sidney Weintraub, "North American Free Trade and the European Situation Compared." In *International Migration Review,* (New York: Center for Migration Studies), vol. 26, no. 2 (Summer), 1992, pp. 506–524.

15. See Laurence Hecht and Peter Morici, "Managing Risks in Mexico." *Harvard Business Review,* vol. 7, no. 4 (July–August), 1993, pp. 32–40.

16. See for example two books by Walt W. Rostow, *The Stages of Economic Growth: A Non-Communist Manifesto* (New York: Cambridge University Press, 1960); and *The World Economy: History and Prospect* (Austin: University of Texas Press, 1978). See also P. T. Bauer, *Equality, the Third World, and Economic Delusion* (Cambridge, Mass.: Harvard University Press,

1981); Peter L. Berger, *The Capitalist Revolution: Fifty Propositions About Prosperity, Equality and Liberty* (New York: Basic Books, 1986).

17. See Andre Gunder Frank, *On Capitalist Underdevelopment,* (Bombay: Oxford University Press, 1975). See also related works by Wallerstein describing a capitalist world economy: Immanuel Wallerstein, *The Modern World-System: Capitalist Agriculture and the Origins of the European World-Economy in the Six-* *teenth Century* (New York: Academic Press, 1974); *The Capitalist World-Economy* (New York: Cambridge University Press, 1979); *The Politics of the World Economy: The States, the Movements, and the Civilizations* (New York: Cambridge University Press, 1984).

18. Poor country debt to rich countries is estimated to be more than $1 trillion. Figure from World Bank, *World Development Report 1993* (New York: Oxford University Press, 1993).

Chapter 14

1. This economic definition, of course, means that housewives, househusbands, and unemployed old people are unproductive, because they provide no goods or services for the market.

2. Figures on job loss and CEO salaries are from Allan Sloan, "The Hit Men," *Newsweek,* February 26, 1996, pp. 44–48; "The Downsizing of America," *The New York Times,* March 3, 1996, p. 26.

3. Figures reported in Simon Head, "The New, Ruthless Economy," *The New York Review,* February 29, 1996, pp. 47–52, 47.

4. Drawn from "The Downsizing of America," pp. 1, 26.

5. Figures reported in "The Downsizing of America," p. 26.

6. Education figures in this paragraph are drawn from Table 17.2 of Stephen K. Sanderson, *Macrosociology: An Introduction to Human Societies,* 2nd ed. (New York: HarperCollins, 1991), p. 409.

7. This 1991 estimate is computed from Bureau of the Census, *Statistical Abstract of the United States, 1995,* 115th ed. (Washington, D.C.: U.S. Government Printing Office, 1995), Tables 14 and 517.

8. Gross federal debt in 1994. Drawn from *Statistical Abstract of the United States, 1995,* Table 517.

9. Figures drawn from *Statistical Abstract of the United States, 1995,* Tables 520 and 521.

10. Total gross federal debt when Reagan took office was $909 billion. During his eight years in office, $1,692 billion was added to that amount, so that when he left office he left the country holding a cumulative $2,601 billion debt. By 1994 gross federal debt had reached $4,644 billion. One does have to wonder where the "buck stops" in federal financial accountability. Figures drawn from *Statistical Abstract of the United States, 1995,* Table 517.

Index